Burghardt, Belton, Lane, Luce & McVey

Eurodollar Futures and Options

CONTROLLING
MONEY MARKET
RISK

An Institutional Investor Publication

IRWIN
Professional Publishing®
Chicago • London • Singapore

Library of Congress Cataloging-in-Publication Data

Eurodollar futures and options : controlling money market risk / Burghardt . . . [et al].
   p.   cm. —(An Institutional investor publication)
  Includes index.
  ISBN 1-55738-159-3
  1. Euro-dollar market. 2. Futures market. 3. Option (Finance)
I. Burghardt, Galen. II. Series.
HG3897.E92 1991
332.4′5—dc20   91-10423
                                                 CIP

Printed in the United States of America

ISBN 1-55738-159-3

8 9 0

Contents

Preface

This volume on Eurodollar futures and options is the second book produced by Discount Corporation of New York Futures. The first, *The Treasury Bond Basis,* was published in 1989 and is already in its second printing. We hope to bring out a revised edition at the end of 1991.

Our purpose in writing this book has been to draw together the many forces that bear on the trading of Eurodollar futures and options. Only a few people at very big, international banks have the privilege or opportunity to see exactly how the bank deposit market relates to the interest-rate swap market, how the swap market relates to the market for caps and floors, and how all of these markets relate to the market for exchange-traded futures and options. This book is intended to provide a comprehensive guide to the relationships between these markets for people who otherwise would see only part of the picture.

Those of you who are familiar with Discount Futures as a brokerage firm will know that this has been a central mission of ours since our inception in 1979. In the early 1980's, we provided our clients with a "Blue Book" of hedging and trading examples involving futures on Treasury bills, certificates of deposits, and Eurodollars. Those examples provided a framework of understanding for many years of trading in Eurodollar futures. We now know that those examples were incomplete in their analysis of cash and futures relationships because they did not take cash flow considerations into account. As trading margins have been compressed by competition, we find that it has become necessary to examine more closely the details of each and every transaction. We believe the present text does this and represents the state-of-the-art in the analysis of short-term futures markets.

I have no doubt that we will bring out a revised edition some years from now drawing attention to the even finer distinctions that will have to be made then. For the moment, however, this text represents as fine an education as one can have in this important area.

Over the years, both staff and customers have contributed to our understanding of these markets. While we cannot mention them all, we do want to thank them all for their help over the years. For the present, however, I would like to acknowledge people who have made specific contributions to this text. From the Research Department of Discount Futures, Susan Kirshner shared authorship with Rick McVey on our first research note on hedging interest rate caps. Vir Doshi (who assisted in the preparation of the original "Blue Books") pulled together data for charts and tables. Marilyn Torraco prepared all of the exhibits and helped keep the project together during the final days of revisions and proofing. Alan Becker programmed much of *The Short End* software that we use to analyze various relationships in the book. Cathy Prible pulled together the materials for Appendix A on international bank deposit futures and managed the staggering flow of information that this project generated. Other members of Discount Futures outside of the Research Department who have helped us with their comments on early drafts and with trading and hedging examples include Patrick Ingram, Bill Killam, Rupert Sturges, and Jim Theorell.

We also appreciate the help we received from people outside of Discount Futures. These include Rick Kilcollin, Todd Petzel, Steve Youngren, and Richard McDonald of the Chicago Mercantile

Exchange. Rick and Steve were both present at the creation of the Eurodollar futures contract and helped us keep our history straight. Kirt Rasmussen of First City Houston, Anne Cordes of Continental Illinois, and Andrew Royce and Steve Sinacore of The Morgan Bank were also generous with their time and patience in answering our questions.

Five people are listed as authors of this text, and you will note that they are not listed alphabetically. There is a reason. The principal author is Galen Burghardt, who, single-handedly at times, pulled together our differing thoughts and put them into clear and eloquent language. Without Galen, this text would not have been written. Beyond Galen's name, the rest of us are listed alphabetically, although it is a happy accident that Terry Belton is the next most important contributor to this effort. Indeed, Terry's gift is his capacity to analyze complex problems clearly and to give concrete substance to issues that the rest of us could describe only imperfectly. Rick McVey and I are the only authors who have traded deposit instruments—Rick at Ameritrust and I at the World Bank. Rick's experience, however, is both more recent and more relevant. Rick McVey and Geoffrey Luce analyze the Eurodollar futures and options markets daily from the floor of the Chicago Mercantile Exchange. Their advice and insight is sought by some of the most sophisticated traders in the world. Geoffrey also helped design *The Short End* software and reports.

Morton Lane
President
Discount Corporation of New York Futures
Chicago
December 1990

Introduction

The high stakes and exciting life of futures trading have thoroughly captured the public's imagination. This world has been portrayed on stage, in films, and in books. By now, *Serious Money*, *Trading Places*, and *Burden of Proof* are well entrenched in our popular culture. The futures industry has come of age.

To see why, consider the Eurodollar pit.

The Chicago Mercantile Exchange (CME) rings the opening bell for Eurodollar futures trading at 7:20 a.m. every weekday morning. Even before the bell rings, the pit is jammed with hundreds of traders, brokers, clerks, and price reporters. There is no elbow room, and everyone is jostling for position.

The pit itself is ringed by several hundred more traders, brokers, and clerks who are linked by direct telephone lines to nearly every major bank in the world. Some of these telephone lines have been active for more than an hour before the open. Traders are following the progress of trading in London. Brokers are talking with their clients about what has happened overnight in the Asian and European markets. Adrenaline is pumping; everyone is on edge.

What is all the excitement about?

From the time the opening bell rings at 7:20 a.m. to the close of trading at 2:00 p.m., the crowd in and around the Eurodollar pit will be the center of the entire world's short-term interest rate trading. The volume of business will be staggering, and the stakes will be high. During the day, Eurodollar futures with a risk exposure equivalent to that of $100 billion to $300 billion of three-month bank deposits will change hands in this arena.

The success of the CME's Eurodollar pit has not been lost on the rest of the world. Other cities have followed the CME's example in one or both of two ways—one by copying the CME's Euro-dollar contract, the other by extending the concept to rates on bank deposits in other currencies. Eurodollar futures are traded in London, Singapore, and Tokyo as well as in Chicago. Further, there are short Sterling, Euromark, Euroyen, and PIBOR (Paris Interbank Offered Rate) futures listed for trading in London, Paris, Singapore, and Tokyo. And these offshoots are proving successful. Most of the growth in the world's short-term money market futures trading is taking place outside of the U.S.

Serious Money

Bank balance sheets are huge, but the tolerances in banking are tight. Banks operate on extremely thin profit margins, so one doesn't have to add many basis points to a bank's bottom line to be a hero.

With this in mind, consider the position of the seven largest banks in the U.S. At the end of 1989, the total value of their consolidated assets was about $675 billion. During the same year, their total operating income amounted to less than $4.5 billion—a mere 65/100 of a percentage point of their on-balance-sheet assets. In other words, total operating income was only 65 basis points of their total assets. This is not a large number.

Against this backdrop, we see that a single basis point increase in the return on these banks' assets would increase their income by $67.5 million. A 10-basis-point increase in return on assets would increase their net operating income by 15 percent.

The role of a basis point looms larger still if we consider the positions that banks keep off their balances sheets. The constellation of interest rate derivatives—including swaps, caps, swaptions, forward rate agreements (FRAs), futures, and options—are not treated as conventional assets or liabilities and are, for a variety of reasons, kept off balance sheet. Even so, they represent a source of very real exposure to interest rate risk and have become very big business.

For example, these seven banks had roughly $1 trillion of various swaps outstanding at the end of 1989. If we make the comparatively safe assumption that the average life of these swaps is around three years, a one-basis-point change in swaps yields translates into a gain or loss of between $200 million and $300 million.

This is what we mean by serious money.

Where Do Eurodollar Futures Fit In?

The Eurodollar market, which is now the world's focal point for dollar-denominated, short-term interest rate trading, barely existed in the 1960s. Today, partly as a result of the demand for dollar-denominated trade outside of the U.S. and partly because of restrictive bank regulations within the U.S., the total value of Eurodollar deposits outstanding has grown to more than $3 trillion. To this, one can add huge stocks of interest-rate derivatives. The International Swap Dealers Association found that by the end of 1989, there were nearly $2 trillion outstanding of various interest rate swaps and over-the-counter options such as caps and floors. Most of these are tied in one way or another to a Eurodollar interest rate. At the CME, the portfolio equivalent value of Eurodollar futures and options outstanding (open interest) by the end of 1989 was around $1.25 trillion.

Taken together, the Eurodollar cash market and its derivatives constitute a huge fraction of the banking system's assets and liabilities. Eurodollar futures represent a big chunk of this exposure.

Who Uses the Eurodollar Futures Market?

Eurodollar futures (and options on Eurodollar futures) are, for the most part, a tool for financial professionals.

In the world of professionals, banks are extraordinarily big users of Eurodollar futures. Banks find these contracts exceptionally appealing for gap management and for hedging swaps and caps. A big reason for this appeal is the offset of longs and shorts that is available in the futures market but not in the forward deposit market.

To casual students of futures markets, this may seem a small thing. But to a bank, the offset of longs and shorts in the futures market is a big plus. Banks find it prudent to limit their exposure to any one trading partner. For banks that want to manage their interest rate exposure actively in the forward deposit market, these limits quickly become a problem because a purchase and sale of forward deposits, even if done with the same bank, leaves both a long position and a short position on the books. But the purchase and sale of Eurodollar futures offset each other. As a result, banks can manage interest rate exposure to their hearts' content without bloating their balance sheets or using up credit lines with their bank trading partners.

Evidence of the importance of Eurodollar futures to the banking industry can be found on the trading floor of nearly every bank of substance in the U.S. and abroad. A bank that does not have access to futures and options finds that it must turn to other banks for managing the cost of funds or hedging positions in swaps and caps. Banks that buy these services from other banks soon find that they cannot compete in the same markets. While this may be a satisfactory arrangement for small banks with niche markets outside of the world's money centers (including regional money centers), it simply will not do for a bank that wants to compete with other banks. As a result, we find a Eurodollar desk on the trading floor of almost any bank we visit.

Organization of this Book

In preparing this book, we divided the material into two parts—subjects that we consider absolutely fundamental and subjects that we consider advanced applications. The first part of the book is devoted to things that we believe you simply cannot do without if you want to use Eurodollar futures and options effectively as professional traders or interest rate risk managers. The second part of the book provides a picture of how rich and subtle the world of Eurodollar futures and options can be.

Market Fundamentals

Where Did Eurodollars and Eurodollar Futures Come From?

The financial futures business is still quite young, and many of the people who use the markets are young too. For those of you who are new to these markets, Chapter 1 provides a brief but useful look back at the history of the Eurodollar market and the emergence and growth of interest rate derivatives such as swaps and Eurodollar futures.

Basic Building Blocks

In Chapter 2 we give you the tools you need to understand the working relationships between the Eurodollar time deposit market on the one hand and the Eurodollar futures market on the other. We also lay out the relationships between futures and key over-the-counter derivative products such as swaps and forward rate agreements (FRAs).

Interest Rate Swaps

Chapter 3 shows how interest rate swaps are structured and how closely strips of Eurodollar futures resemble swaps. We show how the two are priced and how to reckon the sensitivity of swap and strip prices to changes in money market rates. Chapter 4 focuses on the specific question of how to hedge a swap book with Eurodollar futures. In this chapter, we find that properly constructed hedges must allow for changes in the slope and shape of the yield curve, and we show how to make these allowances. We also take a look at the problem of trading strips of Eurodollars against Treasury notes.

Interest Rate Caps, Floors, and Collars

Chapters 5 and 6 are given over to problems of pricing and hedging interest rate caps, floors, and collars, which are over-the-counter interest rate options. We show in Chapter 5 that caps strongly resemble strips of put options on Eurodollar futures. We also examine the ways in which they are different. In Chapter 6, we show how exchange-traded Eurodollar options can be used to hedge even longer-dated interest rate caps and floors.

Advanced Applications

For those with the strength to carry on, Chapters 7 through 10 offer advanced material.

Practical Considerations

Futures markets require that the losers pay the winners every day. This marking-to-market feature of futures markets has important implications for the pricing of longer-dated Eurodollar futures. In particular, Eurodollar futures prices should be lower than their "fair values" would suggest. In short-dated futures, this bias is barely noticeable. In futures with three or four years to expiration, the bias can be ten basis points or more. Swap hedgers often rely on longer-dated Eurodollar futures. Now that the CME carries these longer-dated futures, swap hedgers should pay particular attention to the material in Chapter 7.

Options on Swaps

Options on swaps, including "swaptions" and cancelable swaps, were a natural outgrowth of the caps market. Chapter 8 explains how these options work, how they are priced, and how to estimate and hedge against the risk exposure in these longer-dated options.

SLICs, BICs, and GICs

Many options are not traded explicitly. Instead, they are embedded or built into more complex financial instruments. Chapter 9 explores the options built into guaranteed investment contracts (GICs), bank investment contracts (BICs), and savings and loan investment contracts (SLICs). These are offered widely by insurance companies, banks, and savings and loan associations, and are popular investment vehicles among pension funds and 401(k) plans. The open deposit and withdrawal windows that many of these arrangements provide the investor represent valuable call options (for example, the right to deposit money at a known rate if market rates fall) and put options (for example, the right to withdraw money without penalty if market rates rise). This chapter explains how basic GICs work and shows how to approach the problem of hedging the interest rate risk in these embedded interest rate options.

Hedging the Price Risk in ARMs

Adjustable-rate mortgages (ARMs) make up a large share of the mortgage market. Although the rates on these mortgages are adjustable, most ARMs contain a complex bundle of options. These include limits on the amount the rate can rise or fall, either from year to year or over the ARM's life. Other ARMs are tied to indexes that respond only slowly to changes in market interest rates. Either way, ARM prices are influenced heavily by the value of these embedded put and call options. Moreover, even though ARMs seem to be hard to hedge, Eurodollar futures and options may have been the best of the available hedging vehicles.

Appendixes

International Bank Deposit Futures

Much of the growth in short-term interest rate futures trading has taken place in non-dollar bank deposit contracts. These include futures on three-month Sterling, Euromarks, Euroyen, and PIBOR (Paris Interbank Offered Rate). This appendix provides contract specifications and descriptions of these markets as well as information about Eurodollar futures traded outside of the U.S.

Basic Arbitrage Transactions

The business of keeping futures prices in line with deposit market rates is handled in most circumstances by the ebb and flow of banks seeking to borrow at the lowest possible cost or to invest at the highest possible rate of return. The backstop for these efforts are pure arbitrage transactions that banks can do to profit from large mispricings in Eurodollar futures. This appendix describes the mechanics of constructing riskless positions to profit from selling overpriced futures or buying underpriced futures.

The Short End

This appendix describes the tools that Discount Corporation of New York Futures uses to compare private short-term interest rates across markets. These include The Short End report, which is compiled every morning before the opening of futures trading in Chicago and The Short End software that can be used to compare markets throughout the course of the trading day.

ISDA Standard Swap Documentation

The International Swap Dealers Association (ISDA) is the home grown regulatory organization for swaps trading. Among their varied accomplishments is the standardization of contract terms. This appendix provides up-to-date examples of the ISDA's standard contract terms and related documents.

CHAPTER 1

Emergence of the Eurodollar Market

The Eurodollar market is perhaps the largest and most liquid of the world's short-term dollar markets. At the same time, swaps based on the London Interbank Offered Rate (LIBOR) and Eurodollar futures, together with their option counterparts, are without question the most actively traded and liquid money market derivatives.

Our purpose in this chapter is to provide a thumbnail history of where these markets came from and how they got to be as big as they are.[1]

---

1. This chapter touches only on the high points in the emergence of the Eurodollar and Eurodollar futures markets. You can find fascinating and more complete discussions of the histories of these markets and changes in the world of banking in *Instruments of the Money Market*, Federal Reserve Bank of Richmond, 1986, and in Marcia Stigum's *The Money Market*, Dow Jones-Irwin, 1983 (or any more recent edition).

The Revolution in Finance

The last two decades have been wild ones for financial markets in general and for commercial banking in particular. Interest rates fluctuated over ranges that had not been seen in the U.S. since the turn of the century. The stresses and strains created by the collision of regulation, inflation, and economic turmoil led to a breathtaking pace of innovation.

The result was a complete reworking of the world of banking and finance. By the middle of the 1980s, the awful picture was clear. Banks knew that they could no longer simply accept deposits at low regulated rates and extend business and personal loans at higher rates. Money instead had become a traded commodity, in the form of both cash and interest-rate futures.

Of course, the rocket scientists of the financial world did everything they could to fan the flames of revolution. The intellectual offsprings of Markowitz, Modigliani and Miller produced a great outpouring of new ideas that led to the trading of options on exchanges, the stripping of Treasury bonds into their individual parts, and the worldwide integration of money markets.

During this time, every conventional instrument of finance was reduced to its components, and the challenge in the new world of banking was to learn how to buy and sell those parts in a way that would continue to make money.

The Futures Revolution

A key part of this revolution was the introduction of financial futures in Chicago in the 1970s. Although futures had been traded on a wide range of metals and agricultural commodities since the middle of the 19th century in this country and had a history (some of it seamy) reaching back several centuries in other parts of the world, the idea of trading futures contracts on things like foreign currencies and interest rates at first struck people as outrageous.

The idea eventually took hold in the U.S., and spread like wild fire through the rest of the world. Today, there are financial futures exchanges in Hong Kong, London, Montreal, New York, Osaka, Paris, Philadelphia, Singapore, Sidney, Tokyo, and Toronto.

The mainstays of the financial futures world have turned out to be futures on government bonds and short-term bank deposits. For the dollar market, this means futures on U.S. Treasury bonds and notes and futures on three-month Eurodollar time deposits.[2] The focus of this book is on Eurodollar futures and how they fit into the world of finance.

Key Money Market Developments

The Eurodollar market now dominates trading in private short-term money market instruments. This was not always so. For almost two decades, until the early 1980s, certificates of deposit (CDs) issued by U.S. banks played this role.

The seeds of the money market revolution were planted in 1961 when Citibank (then First National City Bank of New York) issued the first CD. This was followed in 1966 with the issuance of the first Eurodollar CD. (See Exhibit 1.1 for a summary of key money market developments.)

The importance of the CD was that it could be traded. Until they came along, bank deposits were a sticky kind of liability or asset (depending on whether you were the bank or the depositor). CDs, however, could be bought and sold just like Treasury bills. As a result, banks and depositors could change the shapes of their respective balance sheets at will. The value that depositors placed on the right to trade CDs was reflected in a lower yield than was paid on conventional term deposits.

CD issuance exploded in the 1970s because of the combined forces of inflation and the ceilings placed on bank deposit rates by the Federal Reserve's Regulation Q. Exhibit 1.2 shows the effect of rising inflation rates on short-term interest rates. The upper limits on the rates banks could pay put banks at a competitive disadvantage in the market for funds.

---

2. Futures on U.S. Treasury bonds and notes are covered in Burghardt, Lane, and Papa, *The Treasury Bond Basis*, Probus, 1989.

Exhibit 1.1

Key Events in the Money Markets

1961 • The first certificate of deposit (CD) is issued by Citibank (then First National City Bank of New York).

1966 • The first Eurodollar CD is issued.

1970 • The Federal Reserve eliminates interest rate ceilings on large CDs with maturities of less than three months.

1972 • The first money market fund is created.

• The Chicago Mercantile Exchange (CME) lists the first financial futures (foreign currencies).

1973 • The Federal Reserve eliminates interest rates ceilings on large CDs with maturities past three months.

1976 • Milton Friedman rings the opening bell for the first money market futures contract, the CME's three-month Treasury bill contract.

1977 • The Chicago Board of Trade (CBOT) lists a 90-day commercial paper contract, which fails.

1978 • Money market fund balances reach $10 billion.

• The CME lists a one-year Treasury bill contract.

1979 • Volcker undertakes his "monetarist experiment," which ushers in a period of extraordinary interest rate volatility and financial turmoil.

• The CBOT lists a 30-day commercial paper contract, which also fails.

(continued)

• DISCOUNT CORPORATION OF NEW YORK FUTURES •

Exhibit 1.1 (continued)

1980 • Bank short-term interest rates reach 20 percent after a 10-percentage-point free fall.

1981 • The CME, the CBOT, and the New York Futures Exchange all list three-month CD futures.

• Citibank arranges the first interest rate swap.

• The CME lists futures on three-month Eurodollar time deposit rates.

1982 • The U.S. CD market is rocked by a series of bank problems including Continental Illinois' withdrawal from the CD market because of its financial woes, and Chases's encounter with Drysdale over defaults in the Treasury repo market.

• The Federal Reserve effectively deregulates bank deposit rates by creating money market deposit accounts, thereby reducing the demand through money market funds for large CDs.

• The London International Financial Futures Exchange (LIFFE) lists Eurodollar futures.

1984 • The Singapore International Monetary Exchange (SIMEX) lists Eurodollar futures that are directly fungible with the CME's Eurodollar contracts through a system of mutual offset.

1985 • The CME lists options on Eurodollar futures.

Exhibit 1.2

Inflation and 3-Month Treasury Bill Yields
(1960 to 1990)

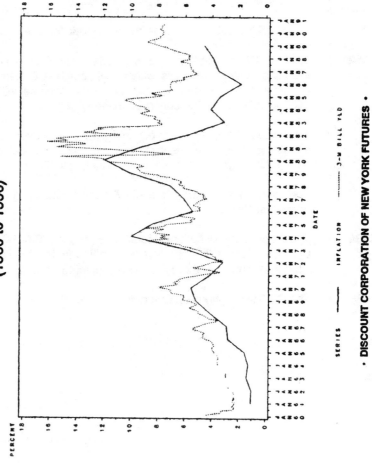

SERIES ——— INFLATION ········· 3-M BILL YLD

• DISCOUNT CORPORATION OF NEW YORK FUTURES •

Large CDs were finally freed from deposit rate regulation, and gave banks a way out. Money market funds became a conduit for placing large CDs in the hands of people who otherwise would have held their liquid assets at banks. Rising inflation throughout the 1970s kept forcing interest rates up, and CDs became a major force in U.S. money markets.

The beginning of the end of the CD market's explosive growth came in 1982. For one thing, the Federal Reserve took a big step in removing regulations from bank deposits by creating money market deposit accounts in December of 1982. These new accounts meant that people could get competitive interest rates directly from banks rather than indirectly through money market funds.

For another, the banks that issued CDs were running into serious financial problems that greatly affected the world's perceptions of banks' credit worthiness. Continental Illinois, for example, faced huge loan losses on its Mexican debt portfolio and had to withdraw from the domestic CD market in the summer of 1982. Chase Manhattan encountered defaults in the Treasury repo market through its dealings with Drysdale. Until these problems surfaced, the CDs of the top ten U.S. banks had been bought and sold as if they were part of a nearly homogeneous, high-quality pool. Continental's and Chase's problems made it clear that not all CDs were the same, and the secondary market for CDs lost much of its liquidity as a result.

The combined effect of the new money market deposit accounts and the credit problems of various large banks was a huge reduction in the demand for CDs.

Whither Eurodollars?

At the same time, the Eurodollar market was moving from strength to strength. As shown in Exhibit 1.3, the Eurodollar market continued to grow even after 1982 when the CD market began to shrink.

The Eurodollar market owes its early success to a variety of forces.

- Eurodollar deposits were always unregulated, and therefore were a competitive source of funds during the years before

Exhibit 1.3

Growth of the Eurodollar Market

Year	Eurodollars Outstanding* ($ Billions)
1973	$ 182
1974	218
1975	267
1976	328
1977	386
1978	481
1979	599
1980	725
1981	847
1982	872
1983	1262
1984	1294
1985	1408
1986	1756
1987	2159
1988	2370
1989	2703

* *End-of-period dollar liabilities of banks outside the U.S. for countries reporting to the Bank for International Settlements*

Source: Bank for International Settlements

the interest rate ceilings on domestic CDs were lifted by the Federal Reserve.

- Eurodollar deposits were a cheaper source of funds to the extent they were free of reserve requirements and deposit insurance assessments.
- The dollar was becoming the currency of choice for a great deal of the world's trade and asset transactions.
- The Soviet Union's international trade dealings required them to hold substantial dollar deposits but they were unwilling to hold them in banks in the U.S.

Reasons for the continued success of the Eurodollar market throughout the 1980s are less clear, but three things stand out.

First, the Eurodollar market escaped the worst of the problems of credit worthiness that had such a depressing effect on the U.S. CD market. Second, money markets were almost completely integrated by the middle of the 1980s so that banks were nearly indifferent about borrowing domestically or borrowing abroad. This point is illustrated clearly in Exhibit 1.4, which shows that the difference between Eurodollar deposit rates and CD rates was nearly constant by the beginning of 1986. The difference between the two rates represented nothing more than the cost of reserve requirements and deposit insurance. Third, interest rate derivatives such as swaps and caps appeared in the early 1980s and proved to be very successful financial instruments.

Events might have played out in any number of ways, but as it happened, the world settled on Eurodollars as the focal point for dollar-based money market instruments. The rest, as they say, is history. Eurodollars left CDs behind starting in 1982 and never looked back.

Eurodollar Futures

The Eurodollar futures contract, which today is the most widely traded money market contract in the world, was the product of considerable experimentation. The key events leading up to the listing of the Eurodollar contract are summarized in Exhibit 1.1. To

Exhibit 1.4

CD Futures Volume versus Eurodollar/CD Futures Rate Spread

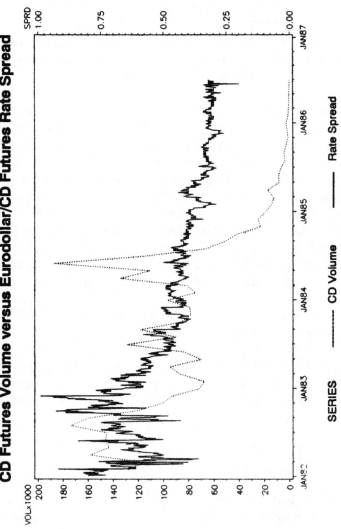

SERIES ----- CD Volume ——— Rate Spread

NOTE: Lead series switches on the first trading day of the contract month.

• DISCOUNT CORPORATION OF NEW YORK FUTURES •

begin, the CME listed futures contracts on foreign currencies in 1972. These were the first financial futures ever traded. Then, in 1976, the CME listed futures on three-month Treasury bills. These were the first money market futures ever traded.

The Treasury bill contract proved successful, and the Chicago exchanges as well as the newly formed New York Futures Exchange (NYFE) began to look elsewhere for new products. As shown in Exhibit 1.5, the events surrounding the financial upheavals of 1973 and 1974 proved just how volatile the spread between private money market instruments and Treasury bills could be. In the face of this much volatility in the private money market credit spread, Treasury bill futures could be a very bad hedge for private short-term liabilities.

From this, the futures exchanges concluded that the world could use a futures contract on private short-term obligations. The first effort was the Chicago Board of Trade's (CBOT) contract on 90-day commercial paper, which was listed in 1977. This contract failed, largely because 90-day commercial paper was not a sufficiently homogeneous commodity. The credit risks behind the individual issuers, especially in light of the problems created by Chrysler's brush with bankruptcy, loomed much too large in people's minds for them to take the contract seriously. The CBOT's second effort, a 30-day commercial paper contract, also failed.

The exchanges turned next to the domestic CD and Eurodollar markets, which had been growing rapidly since 1972. The CME's records show that its Interest Rate Committee was working on the details of both a domestic CD and a Eurodollar contract as early as July 1979, which predates the onset of Volcker's monetary experiment.

By the spring of 1980, the CBOT, the CME and the NYFE had all filed their respective applications. They did not get approval until the next year, and in July 1981, all three CD contracts were listed for trading.

Technically, the NYFE's contract was listed first. Of the three, however, the CME's prevailed and began its short but comparatively active trading life, which is charted in Exhibit 1.6. The race does not always go to the swift!

Exhibit 1.5

The Spread Between
The Three-Month CD and Treasury Bill Rates

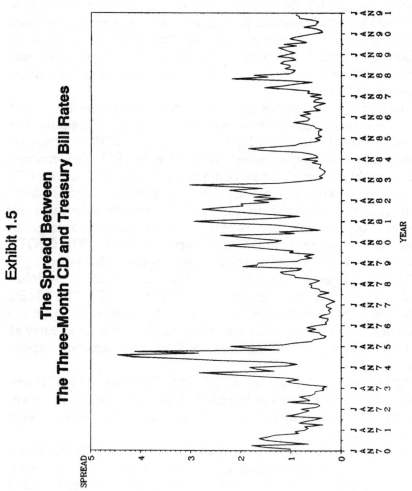

• DISCOUNT CORPORATION OF NEW YORK FUTURES •

Exhibit 1.6

Trading Volume for 3-Month Treasury Bill, Certificate of Deposit and Eurodollar Futures
(Period: December 31, 1976 to December 31, 1989)

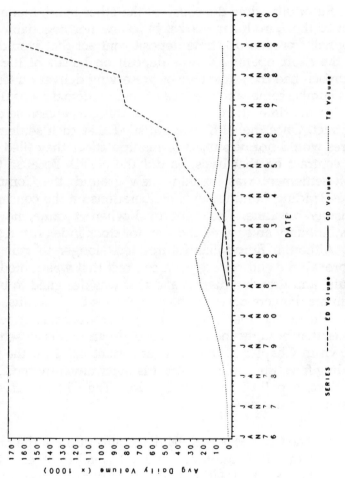

SERIES ----- ED Volume ———— CD Volume ········· TB Volume

• DISCOUNT CORPORATION OF NEW YORK FUTURES •

All three exchanges also had been working on various forms of a Eurodollar contract, which posed interesting design challenges. The biggest of these challenges was answering the question of delivery. Eurodollar CDs were a tradeable commodity, but they represented a comparatively small slice of the Eurodollar market. Even so, the CBOT filed for approval but never listed a contract based on the delivery of Euro CDs.

Eurodollar time deposits, on the other hand, made up a large part of the Eurodollar market but were not negotiable. The CME originally proposed a time deposit contract that would be settled by the short opening a time deposit on behalf of the long. This approach had the advantage of preserving delivery integrity, but it was cumbersome, and the idea of cash settlement was floated.

At the time, there was no such thing as a cash-settled futures contract. Once the CME was satisfied that cash settlement procedures would not be subject to manipulation, they filed a Eurodollar contract on that basis, as did the NYFE. Because the idea of cash settlement was breaking new ground, the Commodity Futures Trading Commission's deliberations on the concept required considerable time. Their approval when it came, however, was revolutionary and paved the way for stock index futures as well.

Although Eurodollar futures took longer to gain regulatory approval, the end result was a contract that was rooted in a large, liquid, and growing market and that was designed to be insulated from the dangers posed by heterogeneous bank credits.

The device that protected the Eurodollar contract from the forces that brought the CD contract down was cash settlement. As shown in Chapter 2, the final settlement price on the last day of trading for a Eurodollar contract is determined by the CME, which conducts a poll of banks in London. The CME's survey has two important features:

- The CME asks each bank its perception of the rate at which banks in London are willing to lend to other prime quality banks. The CME avoids in this question asking a bank the rate at which it is lending to any other particular bank.
- The CME throws out high and low responses, and calculates the final settlement price using the middle quotes.

The effect of the first of these features is that the survey skirts the problem of individual bank credits. The intended effect of the second is to insulate the final settlement price from capricious manipulation. A bank that misrepresents the market outrageously will have no effect on the final outcome. As a result, the banks polled in the CME's survey likely respond truthfully, although it would be naive to suppose that their responses never reflected their positions in the cash and futures markets.

The Death of CD Futures and the Birth of Eurodollar Futures

The big turning point in the lives of these two contracts came in 1982, which was also a watershed for their respective cash markets. The depressing effect on the CD market of deposit deregulation and the financial difficulties of banks such as Continental Illinois and Chase Manhattan were felt as well in the CD futures market. The banks' credit problems also unsettled the market for the CD futures contract by clouding the picture about what would be deliverable.

For some time, the CDs of the top ten banks had been traded almost as if they were a homogeneous commodity. When Continental withdrew from the domestic CD market in 1982 and other banks began to feel the effects of financial stress, the upper tier of the CD market began to lose its homogeneity. Traders became more acutely aware of whose CDs were offered by other traders and how much of any one bank's CDs were on their books.

This concern about credit quality spilled over into the CD futures markets, where traders began to worry about just which bank's CDs they would receive if they took delivery. The price of a futures contract that involves the delivery of an actual commodity is driven by the price of the commodity in the eligible set that is cheapest to deliver. Traders became cautious about trading CD futures because there was so much uncertainty both about what and how cheap the cheapest to deliver might be.

At about the same time, as shown in Exhibit 1.4, the integration of world money markets was stabilizing the spread between

U.S. and Eurodollar CD rates. From the standpoint of futures traders, this stabilization of the spread meant that Eurodollar and CD
futures were becoming nearly perfect financial substitutes for one
another. The only differences came down to issues such as liquidity and deliverable supply. Given the headaches caused by the uncertain quality of deliverable supply for the CD contract, traders
began to favor Eurodollar futures.

The results of these various developments are summarized in
Exhibit 1.6. CD futures trading had peaked by early 1983. By 1984,
Eurodollar futures trading had caught up with and passed trading
in CD futures. By 1985, Eurodollar futures were more actively
traded than three-month Treasury bill futures and have been so
ever since. By 1986, CD futures were dead, although the CME did
not officially bury the contract until 1987.

The Market for Interest Rate Derivatives

Whatever else people say about what futures contracts do, they
are first and foremost arrangements for exchanging money on the
basis of a change in the price or yield of some bond, stock, or
other commodity. In this sense, a futures contract is a financial
derivative of the commodity on which it is based.

In practice, the world of interest rate derivatives encompasses
a vast range of products, many of which had never been traded
before 1980. For example, interest-rate swaps, which we cover in
Chapters 3 and 4, made their debut in the early 1980s. Forward-
rate agreements (FRAs) appeared during these years as well.

These derivatives have proved to be very successful financial
instruments for a number of reasons. Eurodollar futures, for example, allow banks to fine tune the structure of their liabilities on a
regular basis without bloating their balance sheets. Futures can do
this because of the complete offset of longs and shorts. Forward
contracts, on the other hand, are not offsetting. A deposit purchased in the morning and sold in the afternoon leaves the bank
with a long and a short position on the books, even if the transactions were done with the same opposite party. The same trade

done in the futures market would leave the bank with no position, either long or short.

Over-the-counter derivatives have their advantages, of course. Interest rate and currency swaps are very useful financing vehicles that give borrowers and lenders access to markets that otherwise might be closed to them. Swaps, for example, permitted Japanese investors to circumvent restrictions on what assets they could buy. They also permitted borrowers with limited access to long-term debt markets to borrow long term on more favorable terms than otherwise would have been available to them. Their counterparties, in turn, were able to get floating-rate financing on better terms as well, occasionally in the early days of swaps trading at rates below those on Treasury securities.

The recent history of growth in the markets for over-the-counter interest rate derivatives such as swaps, caps, and swaptions is chronicled in Exhibits 1.7 and 1.8. For example, the volume of deals done in U.S. dollar interest-rate swaps grew from $62 billion in the second half of 1985 to $272 billion in the second half of 1989. More than $250 billion worth of caps, floors, and collars (most of which were dollar-based) were transacted in 1989 along with more than $70 billion worth of various swaptions.

The accumulated effect of these transactions on the banking industry's credit and interest rate exposure likely is huge. By the end of 1989, the dollar equivalent value of swaps outstanding amounted to $1.5 trillion dollars. (Exhibit 1.8) The value of caps, floors, and collars outstanding reached $458 billion, and the value of swaptions outstanding reached $80 billion. Most of these swaps, caps, and swaptions are denominated in dollars, and a large chunk of these outstanding positions are off-balance-sheet items for banks that stand between the longs and the shorts.

Exhibit 1.9 shows that trading in Eurodollar futures has grown along with the volume of business done in the swap market. We will show in Chapter 2 that Eurodollar futures appear to be very much a hedger's contract. As a result, open interest in Eurodollar futures reached a portfolio equivalent value of roughly $750 billion by the end of 1989, a full half of the value of all interest-rate swaps outstanding at the same time.

Exhibit 1.7

Off-Balance Sheet Products
Deals Completed during Period
(Notional Principal Amount)

Survey Period	Total Interest Rate Swaps		U.S. Dollar Interest Rate Swaps		Total Currency Swaps		Total Caps, Collars, Floors		Total Swaptions	
	($mm Equiv)	(Percent Change)	($mm)	(Percent Change)	($mm Equiv)	(Percent Change)	($mm Equiv)	(Percent Change)	($mm Equiv)	(Percent Change)
2H85			62,151							
1H86			88,357	42%						
2H86			102,287	16%						
1H87	181,543		138,740	36%	43,536					
2H87	206,315	14%	147,991	7%	42,288	-3%				
1H88	250,502	21%	155,670	5%	60,336	43%				
2H88	317,611	27%	210,578	35%	62,325	3%				
1H89	389,169	23%	272,915	30%	77,639	25%	147,095		39,749	
2H89	444,365	14%	272,312	-.22%	91,970	18%	115,664	-21%	33,016	-17%

Source: ISDA

• DISCOUNT CORPORATION OF NEW YORK FUTURES •

Exhibit 1.8

Off-Balance Sheet Products
Outstanding Notional Principal Amounts
Year End

Survey Period	Total Interest Rate Swaps		Total Currency Swaps		Total Caps, Collars, Floors		Total Swaptions	
	($mm Equiv)	(Percent Change)	($mm Equiv)	(Percent Change)	($mm Equiv)	(Percent Change)	($mm Equiv)	(Percent Change)
1987	682,888		182,807					
1988	1,101,203	48%	316,821	73%	290,708		36,552	
1989	1,502,600	49%	434,849	37%	457,638	57%	79,670	118%

Source: ISDA

• DISCOUNT CORPORATION OF NEW YORK FUTURES •

Exhibit 1.9

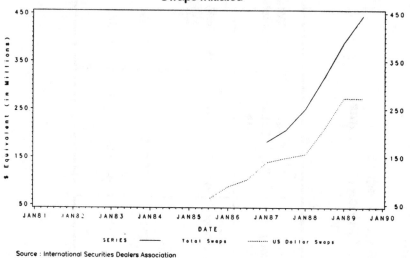

Interest Rate Swap versus Eurodollar Futures Activity
Swaps Initiated

Source : International Securities Dealers Association

Eurodollar Futures Trading Volume

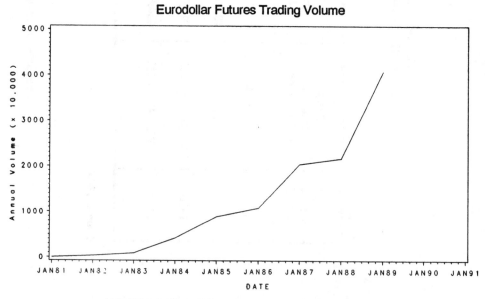

• DISCOUNT CORPORATION OF NEW YORK FUTURES •

Options on Eurodollar futures have kept up their end of the exchange-traded derivatives market as well. By the end of 1989, open interest in Eurodollar options had reached nearly 500,000 contracts, which translates into a notional principal amount of $500 billion, which is only slightly less than the combined outstanding value in all currencies of caps, floors, collars, and swaptions.

Conclusion

The key lesson in these numbers is that derivative products, including futures and swaps, options and caps, are big business and have become an essential part of modern banking. For that matter, they have become an essential part of modern money management and play such a large role in the business of corporate finance that they can no longer be ignored by anyone who seriously wants to compete.

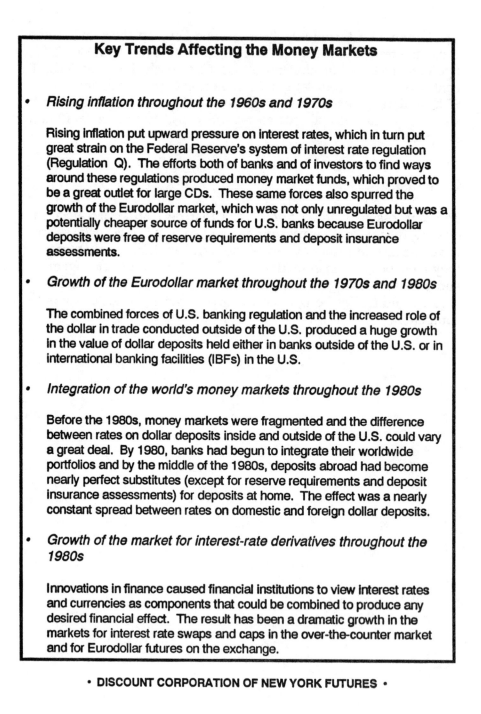

Key Trends Affecting the Money Markets

- *Rising inflation throughout the 1960s and 1970s*

  Rising inflation put upward pressure on interest rates, which in turn put great strain on the Federal Reserve's system of interest rate regulation (Regulation Q). The efforts both of banks and of investors to find ways around these regulations produced money market funds, which proved to be a great outlet for large CDs. These same forces also spurred the growth of the Eurodollar market, which was not only unregulated but was a potentially cheaper source of funds for U.S. banks because Eurodollar deposits were free of reserve requirements and deposit insurance assessments.

- *Growth of the Eurodollar market throughout the 1970s and 1980s*

  The combined forces of U.S. banking regulation and the increased role of the dollar in trade conducted outside of the U.S. produced a huge growth in the value of dollar deposits held either in banks outside of the U.S. or in international banking facilities (IBFs) in the U.S.

- *Integration of the world's money markets throughout the 1980s*

  Before the 1980s, money markets were fragmented and the difference between rates on dollar deposits inside and outside of the U.S. could vary a great deal. By 1980, banks had begun to integrate their worldwide portfolios and by the middle of the 1980s, deposits abroad had become nearly perfect substitutes (except for reserve requirements and deposit insurance assessments) for deposits at home. The effect was a nearly constant spread between rates on domestic and foreign dollar deposits.

- *Growth of the market for interest-rate derivatives throughout the 1980s*

  Innovations in finance caused financial institutions to view interest rates and currencies as components that could be combined to produce any desired financial effect. The result has been a dramatic growth in the markets for interest rate swaps and caps in the over-the-counter market and for Eurodollar futures on the exchange.

CHAPTER 2

Basic Building Blocks

The Eurodollar time deposit market has become the linchpin of the private credit market for dollar-denominated transactions. Maturities in this market extend out as far as 10 years. At the same time, one of the major thrusts of financial innovation has been to separate conventional financial products into their basic components. This is evident, for example, in the creation of many zero-coupon bonds by the stripping of coupons from conventional Treasury bonds. We also find investors breaking up the yield curve into segments. The result is a mix-and-match world in which a borrower or lender can have just about any kind of liability or asset imaginable.

In part because of the extraordinary success of the three-month Eurodollar futures contract, the three-month Eurodollar time deposit has become one of the basic building blocks of the short end of the yield curve.

The purpose of this chapter is to provide what you need to know about the Eurodollar time deposit market and to show how Eurodollar futures fit in. In particular, we will explain what Eurodollar futures are, how they are priced, and how they can be used to hedge the cost of funds. We end the chapter with a brief section on forward rate agreements (FRAs), which some people think of as over-the-counter Eurodollar futures.

The Eurodollar Time Deposit

A Eurodollar time deposit is nothing more than a dollar deposit with a bank or bank branch outside of the U.S. or with an international banking facility (IBF) located in the U.S.. The world's center for Eurodollar trading is London, but there are active Eurodollar markets in other parts of the world as well.

Maturities

Although the standard settlement period for Eurodollar transactions is two days, which means that the money actually changes hands two days after a deal is struck, banks do trade deposits with maturities as short as overnight. Exhibit 2.1 shows that what one finds on Telerate, for example, are three very short-term deposits including overnight (O/N), tomorrow next (T/N), and spot next (S/N). The next basic maturity after these is one week.

Past one week, the standard maturities range from one month to six months in single month increments, then jump to nine months and one year. With the exception of an 18-month deposit, maturities range from one to five years in one-year increments. Past five years, the most common maturities are seven and ten years, which correspond to original issue U.S. Treasury note maturities. Any other maturity can be negotiated.

Quotes

Eurodollar time deposits are add-on as opposed to discount instruments. Consequently, a $1 million Eurodollar transaction requires the initial transfer of $1 million, while a $1 million Treasury bill transaction may require the initial transfer of only $980,000.

Interest rates for Eurodollar deposits are money market yields quoted in percentage points and fractions of percentage points that are powers of 1/2. The finest cut is usually 1/16th, although

Exhibit 2.1*

Money Market Rates

TELERATE SYSTEMS

```
01/22 9:57 EST    NOONAN, ASTLEY & PEARCE — NEW YORK]   01/22 9:51 PG314
    EURO-DOLLAR    |    FED FUNDS    |       FRA'S      |  INT RATE SWAPS |
     09:50 EST     |    9:51 EST     |     9:43 EST     |    9:43 EST     |
                                                        |    ACT/360      |
O/N| 8 1/8 - 8 1/4 | BID      ASK    |1X4  8.29 - 8.34  | MXM  8.63 -8.68 |
T/N| 8 3/16 -8 5/16| 8 1/8    8 3/16 |2X5  8.25 - 8.30  | JXJ  8.72 -8.77 |
S/N| 8 3/16 -8 5/16| LAST     OPEN   |3X6  8.27 - 8.32  | SXS  8.84 -8.89 |
1WK| 8 1/8 - 8 1/4 | 8 3/16   8 3/16 |4X7  8.29 - 8.34  |2MXM  8.79 -8.84 |
                   | TERM FED FUNDS  |5X8  8.30 - 8.35  |1YR   8.60 -8.65 |
1MO| 8 3/16 -8 5/16| 8 1/4  -8 3/8   |6X9  8.32 - 8.37  |18MO  8.64 -8.69 |
2MO| 8 3/16 -8 5/16| 8 1/4  -8 3/8   |9X12 7.93 - 7.98  |   MEDIUM TERM   |
3MO| 8 1/4  -8 3/8 | 8 5/16 -8 7/16  |1X7  8.39 - 8.44  |2 YRS  T + 56 -60|
4MO| 8 1/4  -8 3/8 | 8 9/16 -8 11/16 |2X8  8.37 - 8.42  |3 YRS  T + 63 -68|
5MO| 8 5/16 -8 7/16| 8 3/8  -8 1/2   |3X9  8.39 - 8.44  |4 YRS  T + 74 -78|
6MO| 8 5/16 -8 7/16| 8 3/8  -8 1/2   |4X10 8.41 - 8.46  |5 YRS  T + 81 -85|
9MO| 8 3/8  -8 1/2 | 8 7/16 -8 9/16  |5X11 8.42 - 8.47  |7 YRS  T + 84 -89|
1YR| 8 7/16 -8 9/16| 8 1/2  -8 5/8   |6X12 8.45 - 8.50  |10YRS T + 92 -96 |
[TELEPHONE NUMBER: 212 - 504 - 2900/SEE PG 317 CAPITAL MKTS -SWAP OPTIONS]
```

TELERATE SYSTEMS

```
01/22        9:57 EST     [LASSER MARSHALL INC. - NEW YORK] PAGE 333
         FED FUNDS O/N    |  AGENCY TERM   |    EURODOLLARS       |
           9:50 EST       |   8:59 EST     |     8:59 EST         |
BID  | 8 3/16           |1MO| 8 1/4 - 8 3/8 |1MO; 8 3/16 - 8 5/16 |
ASK  | 8 3/16           |2MO| 8 1/4   8 3/8 |2MO: 8 3/16   8 5/16 |
LAST | 8 3/16           |3MO| 8 5/16  8 7/16|3MO: 8 1/4    8 3/8  |
OPEN | 8 3/16           |4MO| 8 5/16  8 7/16|4MO: 8 1/4    8 3/8  |
HIGH | 8 3/16           |5MO| 8 5/16  8 7/16|5MO: 8 1/4    8 3/8  |
LOW  | 8 3/16           |6MO| 8 3/8   8 1/2 |6MO: 8 5/16   8 7/16 |
     | SHORT DATE EUROS  |   | 8 7/16  8 9/16|9MO  8 3/8    8 1/2  |
O/N :  8 1/8   8 3/16 :  |   | 8 1/2   8 5/8 |1YR; 8 7/16   8 9/16 |
T/N :  8 1/8   8 1/4  :  |   DOMESTIC TERM   |18M: 8 5/8    8 3/4  |
S/N :  8 3/16  8 5/16    :1MO| 8 1/4   8 3/8 |2YR: 8 11/16  8 13/16|
1WK :  8 3/16  8 5/16    :2MO| 8 1/4   8 3/8 |3YR: 8 13/16  9 15/16|
2WK :  8 3/16 - 8 5/16   :3MO| 8 1/4   8 3/8 |4YR: 8 15/16  9 1/16 |
3WK :  8 3/16 - 8 5/16   :6MO| 8 5/16  8 7/16|5YR: 9        9 1/8  |
PPY385-7175 ]            |    385-7141      | [   385-7075    ]  |
```

*   *This page is a transcription of an actual Telerate Systems print-out*

• DISCOUNT CORPORATION OF NEW YORK FUTURES •

quotes in 32nds are not uncommon and quotes in 64ths are not unheard of. For the most part, though, fractional points are quoted in 16ths and multiples of 16ths.

LIBOR and LIBID

In practice, the rate at which a London bank is willing to lend dollars is known as LIBOR, which is an acronym for London Inter-bank Offered Rate. The rate at which a London bank is willing to borrow is referred to by the less well known LIBID, or London Interbank Bid Rate. For example, as shown in Exhibit 2.1, at 9:50 a.m. EST on January 22, 1990, one-month Eurodollars were offered at 8-5/16 (LIBOR) and bid at 8-3/16 (LIBID). That is, the quoting bank was willing to lend dollars for one month to a prime credit at 8-5/16 and to accept anyone's deposit at 8-3/16 for a spread of 1/8.

Interest Rate Calculations

For deposits with maturities less than one year, interest is paid at maturity. For deposits with maturities past one year, interest is paid on each anniversary and at maturity. Interest calculations are based on actual days assuming a 360-day year.

For example, interest on a $1 million deposit with less than a year to maturity would be:

$$\text{Interest} = \$1 \text{ million} \times [\text{Rate} \times (\text{Days}/360)]$$

where Rate is the quoted rate and Days is the number of days to maturity. If this were a three-month deposit, Days typically would be a number around 90 or 91, although short months, weekends, leap years, and holidays will produce numbers both larger and smaller.

Interest on a $1 million time deposit with more than a year to expiration would be calculated in stages. On each anniversary, for example, the interest paid out on a $1 million deposit would be:

$$\text{Interest} = \$1 \text{ million} \times [\text{Rate} \times (365/360)]$$

where 365 is the actual number of days in the year, except for leap years, which have 366. The final interest calculation for any remaining partial year is done just as it would be for a deposit with less than a year to maturity, using the actual number of days remaining in the deposit's life.

Consider the interest calculation for a one-month deposit. Suppose that on January 22 (a Monday), one-month LIBID was 8-3/16. By Eurodollar convention, the deposit settles two days later on January 24. Also by Eurodollar convention, the deposit would mature on February 24, except that the 24th is a Saturday. Faced with a weekend or a holiday, the deposit can settle either on the previous business day (Friday the 23rd) or the next business day (Monday the 26th). For the purposes of this example, we will suppose that the transactors agree on the 26th, which is 33 days after the January 24 settlement. Interest on each $1 million of this one-month deposit is:

$$\text{Interest} = \$1 \text{ million} \times [.081875 \times (33/360)]$$

$$= \$1 \text{ million} \times [.00750521]$$

$$= \$7,505.21$$

Exhibit 2.1 also shows that the rate on an 18-month deposit was bid at 8-5/8ths. The first interest payment would be made on January 24, 1991 (a Thursday) and the amount would be:

$$\text{Interest} = \$1 \text{ million} \times [.08625 \times (365/360)]$$

$$= \$1 \text{ million} \times [.08744792]$$

$$= \$87,447.92$$

The second and last interest payment would be made on July 24, 1991 (a Wednesday). The actual number of days between January 24 and July 24, 1991 is 181, so the interest paid (along with the principal) would be:

$$\text{Interest} = \$1 \text{ million} \times [.08625 \times (181/360)]$$

$$= \$1 \text{ million} \times [.04336458]$$

$$= \$43,364.58$$

The Eurodollar Futures Contract

Eurodollar futures contracts were first listed by the Chicago Mercantile Exchange (a.k.a. CME or Merc) in December 1981. They were followed in 1982 by the London International Financial Futures Exchange (LIFFE), and in 1984 by the Singapore International Monetary Exchange (SIMEX).[1]

Specifications

For the most part, the contracts are the same. As shown in Exhibit 2.2, the nominal contract size is $1 million in all three cases. The underlying rate is three-month LIBOR. Futures prices are quoted as 100 minus the annualized futures interest rate. The basic tick size is .01 (or one basis point). The dollar value of a tick is $25, which accords with the change in the value of a 90-day, $1,000,000 instrument. The delivery months are March, June, September, and December. The last trading day is the second London bank business day before the third Wednesday of the contract month.

A thumbnail summary of how these contracts work is provided in Exhibit 2.3.

Cash Settlement

In all three cases, the contracts are cash settled to a final settlement price that is tied to spot three-month LIBOR, which is the offered side of the Eurodollar time deposit market in London. On the last trading day, for example, the CME conducts two surveys, each covering 12 banks in London selected randomly from a list of no less than 20 banks. The first of these surveys takes place sometime

1. All three of these contracts are based in one way or another on three-month LIBOR. In 1989, the Tokyo International Financial Futures Exchange listed a three-month Eurodollar contract that settles to the offered rate in Tokyo.

Exhibit 2.2

3-Month Eurodollar Futures Contract Specifications

Contract Term	Exchange		
	Chicago Mercantile Exchange (CME)	Singapore International Monetary Exchange (SIMEX)	London International Financial Futures Exchange (LIFFE)
Unit of Trading	$1,000,000	Same as CME	Same as CME
Price Quote	100 - annualized futures interest rate	Same as CME	Same as CME
Tick Size	.01 (1 basis point)	Same as CME	Same as CME
Tick Value	$25	Same as CME	Same as CME
Delivery Months	March, June, September, December	Same as CME	Same as CME
Last Trading Day	Second London Business day before the third Wednesday of the delivery month	Same as CME	Same as CME
Final Settlement Price	100 - spot LIBOR as determined by CME bank survey	Same as CME	100 - spot LIBOR as determined by LIFFE bank survey
Trading Hours	7:20 a.m. to 2:00 p.m. (Chicago time) 7:20 a.m. to 9:30 a.m. for expiring contract on last trading day	7:45 a.m. to 5:20 p.m. (Singapore time)	8:30 a.m. to 4:00 p.m. & 4:25 p.m. to 6:00 p.m. (London time)

Exhibit 2.3

How Eurodollar Futures Work

- Eurodollar futures are cash settled to three-month LIBOR four times a year (March, June, September and December).

- The Eurodollar futures price is equal to 100 less the futures rate (that is, Futures Price = 100 - Futures Rate) where the futures rate is expressed in percentage points.

- The minimum change in the price is one basis point (0.01 percent), and each basis point change is worth $25.

- A decrease of one basis point in the futures rate increases the futures price by one basis point, which produces a $25 gain for the long and a corresponding $25 loss for the short.

- Gains and losses are settled daily. Money is taken from the accounts of those with losses and paid through the clearing house to the accounts of those with gains.

- The Chicago Mercantile Exchange's final settlement rate is determined through two surveys of London banks, one taken during a period selected at random during the hour-and-a-half before the close of trading in the expiring contract and one taken at the close of trading. High and low responses are discarded and the remaining responses are averaged.

  Because these surveys are conducted between 2:00 p.m. and 3:30 p.m. (London time), the CME's three-month Eurodollar contract is not quite a futures contract on three-month LIBOR, which is determined for different purposes by the British Bankers Association at a 10:00 a.m. "fixing." The difference in time, though, is small enough to allow one to think of the Eurodollar futures contract as a three-month LIBOR contract.

• DISCOUNT CORPORATION OF NEW YORK FUTURES •

during the hour-and-a-half just before the close of trading in the expiring contract; the second takes place right at the close (9:30 a.m. in Chicago, 3:30 p.m. in London). In both cases, the banks in the survey are asked to indicate their own perceptions of LIBOR. In particular, the CME asks each bank to quote "its perception of the rate at which three-month Eurodollar Time Deposit funds are currently offered by the market to prime banks." Note that this is a finely worded question that avoids asking any one bank the rate at which it is offering funds to any other bank.

Armed with the results of the two surveys, the CME throws out the two highs and the two lows in each survey. The remaining 16 quotes are used to calculate an average spot LIBOR, which is rounded to the nearest basis point. If the average produced by this procedure is 8.125, the CME rounds the result to 8.13. Any answer less than 8.125 but more than 8.120 is rounded to 8.12.[2] This rounded average is then subtracted from 100 to determine the final settlement price for the expiring contract. Any expiring contracts that remain open at the close of trading are marked to market one last time against the final settlement price.

LIFFE conducts its own survey earlier in the trading day to establish a final settlement price that is used only for settling expiring LIFFE Eurodollar futures. SIMEX, on the other hand, uses the CME's final settlement price so that their futures can be interchanged with the CME's. LIFFE also calculates its final settlement price differently. Given an average LIBOR value of 8.125 percent, LIFFE would subtract this from 100 to get 91.875 and round this result to 91.88 rather than the 91.87 that the CME would get.

Trading Hours and Mutual Offset

Eurodollars, along with foreign currencies, are an actively traded global commodity. Trading begins in the Far East, passes to the Middle East and Europe and then to New York and Chicago. Eurodollar futures trading follows the same pattern. The opening bell

---

2. This may strike many readers as a trivial point, but the difference between the two results is worth $25 per contract. The CME has found over the years that banks with net long or short positions of several thousand contracts at expiration care deeply about such apparently minor matters.

for Eurodollar futures trading on SIMEX rings at 7:45 a.m. in Singapore. Trading continues on SIMEX until 5:20 p.m. in Singapore.

By this time, LIFFE has opened its Eurodollar pit for trading. Eurodollar futures start trading on LIFFE at 8:30 a.m. in London and continue until 4:00 p.m., when the LIFFE pit closes. After 4:00 p.m., Eurodollar trading switches to LIFFE's Automated Pit Trading (APT) system at 4:25 p.m. and continues until 6:00 p.m.

Trading in Chicago starts at 7:20 a.m., which is 1:20 p.m. in London, and continues until 2:00 p.m. in Chicago. Only then, when the sun is firmly set on its journey over the Pacific, is there a lull.

Futures exchanges have grappled for years with the problem of capturing global trading activity. One approach has been to expand trading hours, which most exchanges have done at one time or another.

Another approach to extending trading hours in a contract is mutual offset. The CME and SIMEX designed a system that permits futures contracts traded on SIMEX to be completely interchangeable with contracts traded on the CME. Under mutual offset, the contract specifications are identical except for trading hours. A Eurodollar futures contract traded on the floor of the CME can be transferred through the mutual offset system to SIMEX. Similarly, a contract traded on the floor of SIMEX can be transferred to the CME.

The great virtue of the mutual offset system is its economy in handling open positions. Without mutual offset, a long position established in Chicago could be more or less offset by a short position in Asia or Europe. But the offset would be incomplete because of the mismatch in trading hours. When the time comes to unwind the position, one side of the position disappears first, leaving the trader with several hours of price exposure on the other side. With mutual offset, the long and short positions can be exactly offsetting, leaving the trader with no position at all.

CME and LIFFE

LIFFE's final settlement survey is done a few hours before the CME's. Their final settlement prices are often the same, but the mismatch in timing and the slight variations in their procedures leave room for differences. As a result, the Eurodollar futures contracts traded on the two exchanges are good but not perfect substitutes for one another. The spreads between the two are narrow, and LIFFE's prices provide a good indication of where the opening price at the CME should be. Arbitrageurs are willing to trade one contract against the other with an understanding that there is some residual risk at expiration.

Months Traded

Until 1990, all Eurodollar futures contracts fell into the basic March, June, September, and December quarterly cycle. This is still true for three-month Eurodollar contracts. The exception is the one-month LIBOR contract for which, at this writing, five consecutive months are listed by the CME.

Eurodollar futures are a radical exception to the rule in futures trading. Skim the pages of *The Wall Street Journal* and you will find that trading in most futures contracts is confined to a handful of nearby months. On the other hand, Eurodollar futures at the CME have maturities extending to four years, and all of them are traded to some extent.

Just why this is so will become clear when we discuss interest-rate swaps in chapters 3 and 4. A short explanation, however, is that each contract month in Eurodollars represents a three-month segment of the yield curve. Because these segments can be chained together to create instruments that behave like longer-term assets or liabilities, each contract month has a role to play. This is especially true, of course, when there is considerable action at the short end of the yield curve.

Volume and Open Interest

The growth of trading and open interest in Eurodollar futures at the CME is chronicled in Exhibit 2.4. What began as a contract trading in the shadows of Treasury bill and CD futures has grown to gigantic proportions. At this writing (July 1990), open interest in all contract months combined was just under 750,000 contracts. At $1 million notional amount per contract, this translates into open positions on the books of traders and hedgers that are the equiva-

Exhibit 2.4

Eurodollar Futures Volume and Open Interest

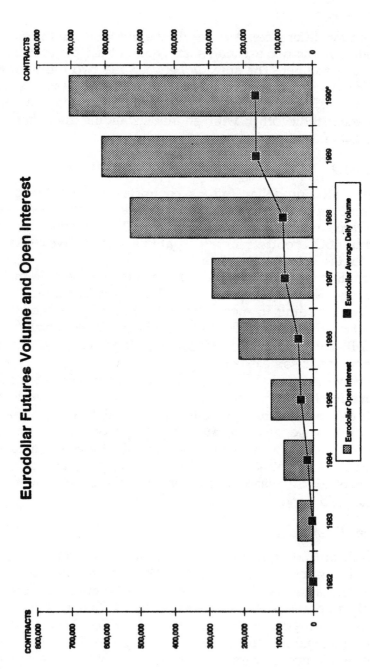

* Volume annualized. Open interest as of October 1990.

· DISCOUNT CORPORATION OF NEW YORK FUTURES ·

lent of nearly $750 billion of three-month deposits. This is big money in anybody's book.

Part of the reason for the success of the contract is illustrated in Exhibit 2.5, which compares the open interest across contract months in Eurodollar and Treasury bond futures. Nearly all of the open interest in bond futures is concentrated in the first two months. In contrast, there is substantial open interest in back-month Eurodollar futures.

Eurodollar futures differ from bond futures in one other key respect. The ratio of daily trading volume to open interest in bond futures is often more than one-to-one. In contrast, the ratio of daily trading volume to open interest in Eurodollar futures is much lower, around one-to-five. Stated differently, the open interest in bonds turns over once a day on average. The open interest in Eurodollars turns over only once a week.

What this suggests is that Eurodollar futures are a hedger's contract, while Treasury bond futures are much more akin to a trader's contract. This fits what we know already about Eurodollar futures. The growth in the contract has been driven by the flexibility it affords in shaping and hedging interest rate exposure at the short end of the yield curve. It is no accident that the market for back-month Eurodollar futures has kept pace with the burgeoning interest-rate swaps market.

Pricing Eurodollar Futures

Because a Eurodollar futures contract settles in cash to a final settlement price equal to 100 minus the value of spot three-month LIBOR at expiration, Eurodollar futures ought to behave much like three-month forward deposits. And they do.

In this section, we lay out the mechanics of pricing a Eurodollar futures contract as if it were a conventional forward contract. From this point of view, the main challenge is figuring out what three-month LIBOR is likely to be on the day the futures contract expires. As we show, this becomes the comparatively simple task of figuring out the rate at which a bank should be willing to lend to a prime bank.

Exhibit 2.5

Bond and Eurodollar Open Interest by Contract
Year End 1989

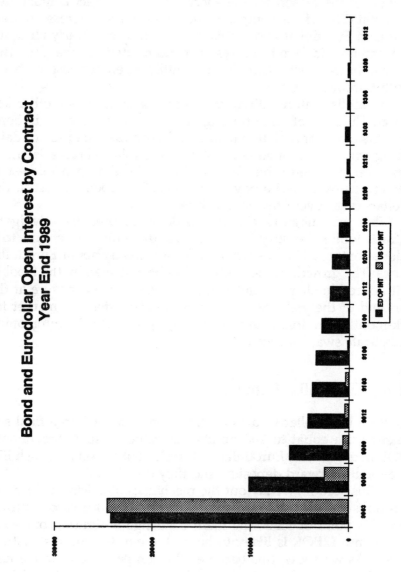

· DISCOUNT CORPORATION OF NEW YORK FUTURES ·

The market's best guess about what a Eurodollar futures price should be, then, is simply 100 minus the current value of the appropriate three-month forward deposit rate.

We buttress this argument with examples that illustrate the kinds of arbitrage transactions banks can do if Eurodollar futures prices are out of line with this guide.

Term and Forward Deposit Rates

As we saw at the outset, one can invest today in Eurodollar time deposits with maturities of five years and longer. Many people, however, face the problem of having to borrow or lend over a period that begins not today but some time in the future. These people do not care about current spot rates on term deposits. They want to know forward deposit rates.

An active market is available to those who want to borrow or lend in the future. For example, the corporate treasurer with accounts receivable is concerned about the rate at which money can be invested, say, one month from now. A construction firm with a well-defined calendar of expenditures may be concerned about the rate at which money can be borrowed at various dates in the future.

There are a number of ways to find forward interest rates, but they all work basically the same way. For example, consider the problem from the perspective of a bank that has been asked to quote a three-month forward deposit rate on a $10 million deposit starting two months from today.

The bank knows that the $10 million is to be received two months from now and is to be paid back with interest five months from now. To set a rate at which it is willing to borrow the money for three months starting two months from now, the bank simply breaks down the five-month period into the two parts shown in Exhibit 2.6. The first is a two-month period running from today to the two-month mark. The second is the three-month period ending with the maturity of the forward deposit.

Having done this, the bank figures that it can lend money for five months at the current five-month spot rate and cover the first two months by borrowing at the current two-month spot rate. If it borrows and lends the correct amounts, the net cash flows (except

Exhibit 2.6

Foward Rate Calculation

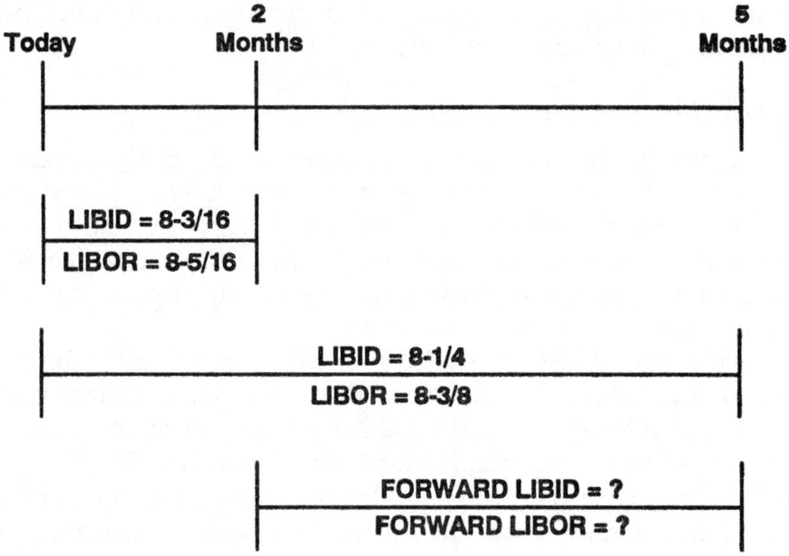

Today	2 Months		5 Months

LIBID = 8-3/16
LIBOR = 8-5/16

LIBID = 8-1/4
LIBOR = 8-3/8

FORWARD LIBID = ?
FORWARD LIBOR = ?

Question:

At what rate will a bank be willing to accept a $10 million three-month deposit starting two months from today?

Answer:

$$\left[\frac{1 + LIBID_5 \ (150/360)}{1 + LIBOR_2 \ (60/360)} - 1\right] \times (360/90) = \text{Three-Month Forward Rate}$$

$$\left[\frac{1 + .0825 \ (150/360)}{1 + .083125 \ (60/360)} - 1\right] \times (360/90)$$

$$\left[\frac{1.034375}{1.013854} - 1\right] \times 4 = 8.10\%$$

• DISCOUNT CORPORATION OF NEW YORK FUTURES •

for the spread between borrowing and lending rates) will be a wash.

Example To make this calculation concrete, suppose that the rates the bank can work with are the term deposit rates shown in Exhibit 2.6. These are:

- two-month spot rates

  LIBID = 8-3/16
  LIBOR = 8-5/16

- five-month spot rates

  LIBID = 8-1/4
  LIBOR = 8-3/8

With these rates, consider how the bank can lock the forward rate on a $10 million deposit.

First, the bank needs to borrow an amount that will equal $10 million in two months. Given LIBOR at 8-5/16, the amount the bank needs today is:

Borrow $= \$10{,}000{,}000 \ / \ [1 + .083125 \times (60/360)]$

$= \$9{,}863{,}351.49$

Two months from now, repaying this loan with interest will be exactly offset by the incoming $10 million deposit. As shown in Exhibit 2.7, this is exactly what happens at the two-month mark.

Next, the bank must lend this money for five months, which it can do safely at a LIBID rate of 8-1/4. At this rate, the amount of money that the bank will have available five months from now is:

Collect $= \$9{,}863{,}351.49 \times [1 + .0825 \ (150/360)]$

$= \$10{,}202{,}404.20$

Exhibit 2.7

Creating a Forward Deposit

If the bank pays 8.10% on a three-month deposit beginning
two months from today, the bank breaks even on a riskless
position.

Today

- Bank borrows $9,863,351.49 for two months at 8-5/16 (two-month LIBOR)

- Bank lends $9,863,351.49 for five months at 8-1/4 (five-month LIBID)

Net Cash Flow = 0

Two Months Later

- Bank repays two-month loan
  ($9,863,351.49 x (1 + .083125(60/360)) = $10,000,000

- Bank accepts $10,000,000 three-month deposit at 8.10 percent

Net Cash Flow = 0

Five Months Later

- Bank liquidates five-month deposit (9,863,351.4 x (1+.0825(150/360)))
  = $10,202,404.20

- Bank pays out on three-month deposit (10,000,000 x (1+ .0810 (90/360)))
  = 10,202,404.20

Net Cash Flow = 0

• DISCOUNT CORPORATION OF NEW YORK FUTURES •

In other words, the bank will be able to pay a total of $202,404.20 interest on a three-month $10 million time deposit starting two months from now. To find out what rate the bank will quote, we simply back out the solution from the conventional interest rate calculation:

$202,404.20 = $10,000,000 × [Rate × (90/360)]

to find

Rate   = ($202,404.20/$10,000,000) × (360/90)

       = 8.1 percent

which might be quoted as 8-3/32 or, if the bank wants to make any money on the transaction, rounded down to 8-1/16.

This exercise shows that a three-month deposit rate two months hence is determined exactly by the two-month and five-month term deposit rates. If the bank can do all three legs of the deal without risk, finding the forward deposit rate is straightforward.

As a practical matter, forward rate calculations are much simpler than this exercise suggests. In practice, the calculation required to find the right forward rate is:

$$[1 + R_5 (150/360)] = [1 + R_2 (60/360)] × [1 + F_{3,2} (90/360)]$$

where R_5 and R_2 are the five-month and two-month term deposit rates and $F_{3,2}$ is the three-month forward rate starting two months from now. Rearranging this expression gives us:

$F_{3,2}$ = {[1 + R_5(150/360)] / [1 + R_2(60/360)] - 1} × (360/90)

Given R_5 = .0825 and R_2 = .083125, we would have found

$F_{3,2}$ = [(1.034375) / (1.013854) - 1] × 4

       = 8.1 percent

Equivalent Deposit Transactions

The forward rates that we have just calculated suggest that a term deposit can be broken down into a number of components. The five-month deposit, for example, can be thought of as a two-month deposit combined with a three-month deposit two months forward. Either combination will produce the same terminal wealth.

Once term deposits have been broken down into their basic parts, we can mix and match the parts in any way that suits us. For example, start with the basic equivalence:

Long five-month deposit =
Long two-month deposit +
Long three-month forward deposit

where the two-month deposit and the three-month forward deposit are the building blocks for the five-month deposit. Rearranging this, we find that:

Long three-month forward deposit =
Long five-month deposit +
Short two-month deposit

This is the combination that allowed the bank to hedge a commitment to borrow for three months beginning two months from the commitment date. The commitment to borrow is the same as a short deposition in the forward deposit. The correct hedge is a long forward deposit or its equivalent. In this case, the equivalent was a short two-month deposit (borrowing for two months) combined with a long five-month deposit (lending the proceeds for five months).

Pricing Futures as Forwards

We must keep in mind that Eurodollar futures settle to the offered side of the market. A Eurodollar futures price is considered "fair" if it is equal to 100 minus the fair value of the appropriate forward LIBOR. In turn, forward LIBOR is considered "fair" if a bank's total borrowing costs are the same from:

- borrowing long term

and

- borrowing short term *and* financing at forward LIBOR.

Put differently, forward LIBOR is fair if:

$$[1+R_L(Days_L/360)] = [1+R_S(Days_S/360)] \times [(1+F(Days_F/360)]$$

where

R_L = spot LIBOR for the long period

R_S = spot LIBOR for the short period

F = forward LIBOR

$Days_L$ = actual number of days in the long period

$Days_S$ = actual number of days in the short period

$Days_F$ = actual number of days covered by the forward
            period

This can be rearranged to look like the forward rate calculation that we made above.[3]

Consider what the fair value of three-month LIBOR should be two months from now if we start with the values of LIBOR shown in Exhibit 2.6. We see that two-month LIBOR is quoted at 8-5/16, while five-month LIBOR is quoted at 8-3/8. From these, we calculate:

---

3. This formula works if the total horizon is less than one year. For periods that extend past one year, allowance must be made for annual compounding. We show how this is done in Chapter 3 when we discuss interest rate swaps and strips of Eurodollar futures.

$$F_{3,2} = \{[1 + .08375 \times (150/360)] / \\ [1 + .083125 \times (60/360)] - 1\} \times 4$$

$$= 8.3 \text{ percent}$$

At this rate, the March 1990 futures price should be:

$$91.70 = 100 - 8.30$$

In Exhibit 2.8, which shows active Eurodollar prices for January 22, which was roughly two months before the expiration of the March 1990 contract, we see that the last trade in the March 1990 contract was done at 91.69. This is just one basis point away from what its fair value should have been given our quotes for spot LIBOR, which were taken at roughly the same time of day.

The High Payoff to Keeping Futures Prices in Line

What keeps the futures price in line with its theoretical value? The answer to this question can be found in the high returns that banks can earn either by buying undervalued futures or by selling overvalued futures.

If the implied Eurodollar futures rate (that is, 100 – futures price) is above fair value, a bank can choose to lend short and buy cheap Eurodollar futures instead of lending long. The result will be a higher rate of return. On the other hand, if the futures rate is below its fair value, a bank can choose to borrow short and sell expensive Eurodollar futures rather than borrow long. The result will be a lower cost of funds. An example of how selling overvalued futures can reduce the cost of borrowing is shown in Exhibit 2.9.

In this example, the bank has a choice between borrowing $10 million for five months at five-month LIBOR of 8-3/8 or borrowing $10 million for two months at two-month LIBOR of 8-5/16, selling 10 Eurodollar futures at 91.90, and refinancing for the remaining three months when the futures settle to spot LIBOR at expiration. Given these values for term LIBOR, which are taken from Exhibit 2.6, the futures price is overvalued by 0.20, or 20 basis points.

Exhibit 2.8*

Treasury Bill and Eurodollar Futures Prices

```
TELERATE SYSTEMS
```

```
01/22      9:56 EST      [  TELERATE FUTURES SERVICE  ]              PAGE 910
```

TREASURY BILLS (90 DAYS) --IMM						EURODOLLARS--IMM					
	LAST	LOW	HIGH	OPEN	CLOSE		LAST	LOW	HIGH	OPEN	CLOSE
MAR 90	9262	9262	9266	9265	9263	MAR 90	9169	9169	9172	72-71	9169
JUN 90	A9276	9276	9279	9276	9274	JUN 90	9165	9165	9168	67-66	9164
SEP 90					9278	SEP 90	9159	9159	9162	9161	9157
DEC 90					9255	DEC 90	9137	9137	9140	9140	9136
MAR 91					9255	MAR 91	9131	9131	9133	9132	9130
JUN 91	B9267				9263	JUN 91	9124	9124	9126	9125	9124
						SEP 91	9121	9121	9124	9123	9121
						DEC 91	9116	9115	9118	9118	9115
						MAR 92	9120	9120	9123	9123	9120
						JUN 92	9116	9116	9119	9119	9116
						SEP 92	9111	9111	9114	9113	9111
						DEC 92	9101	9101	9103	9103	9101
						MAR 93	A9103	9104	9106	05-06	9103
						JUN 93	9099	9099	9100	9100	9098
						SEP 93	B9094				9093

*   *This page is a transcription of an actual Telerate Systems print-out*

• DISCOUNT CORPORATION OF NEW YORK FUTURES •

Exhibit 2.9

Futures Above Fair Value
(Futures trading at 91.90 = 100 - 8.10)

Today

- Bank borrows $10,000,000 for five months at 8-3/8

  OR

- Bank borrows $10,000,000 for two months at <u>LIBOR</u> (8-5/16), and

- Bank sells 10 E$ futures at 91.90 (100 - 8.10)

Two Months Later (if bank borrows two months and sells futures)

<u>Case 1: Futures settle at 91.90 = 100 - 8.10)</u>

- Bank borrows $10,138,541.67 (= $10,000,000 x (1 + .083125 x 2/12)) for three months at 8.10%

<u>Case 2: Futures settle at 91.70 = 100 - 8.30)</u>

- Bank receives $5,000 from short futures

- Bank borrows $10,133,541.67 (= $10,138,541.67 - $5,000) at 8.30%

<u>Case 3: Futures settle at 92.10 = 100 - 7.90</u>

- Bank pays $5,000 on short futures

- Bank borrows $10,143,541.67 (= $10,138,541.67 + $5,000) at 7.90%

(continued)

Exhibit 2.9 (continued)

Five Months Later

If bank borrows for five months:

- Bank repays $10,348,958.33 (= $10,000,000 x (1 + .08375 x 5/12))

- Net interest expense = $348,958.33

If bank borrows for two months and sells futures:

Case 1

- Bank repays $10,343,847.14 (= $10,138,541.67 x (1 + .081 x 3/12))

- Net interest expense = $343,847.14

> Net Saving = $5,111.19

Case 2

- Bank repays $10,343,812.66 (= $10,133,541.67 x (1 + .083 x 3/12))

- Net interest expense = $343,812.66

> Net Saving = $5,145.67

Case 3

- Bank repays $10,343,876.62 (= $10,143,541.67 x (1 + .079 x 3/12))

- Net interest expense = $343,876.62

> Net Saving = $5,081.71

If the bank chooses to borrow term for five months at 8-3/8, the transaction is straightforward. At the end of five months, the bank pays out a total of $10,348,958.33 including $10,000,000 in principal and $348,958.33 in interest.

If the bank chooses instead to borrow term for two months at 8-5/16 and sell the overvalued futures contracts, the transaction can play out in any number of ways, but all with roughly the same financial consequences.

Suppose, for example, that three-month LIBOR at futures expiration turns out to be 8.10 percent. At this rate, the final settlement price for each of the 10 short Eurodollar futures will be 91.90, which is the price at which they were sold. In this case, the short futures position produces neither a gain nor a loss, and the bank is left to refinance a total of $10,138,541.67 [= $10,000,000 × (1 + .083125 (2/12)] at 8.10 percent for the remaining three months. At the end of five months, the bank pays out a total of $10,343,847.14 including $10,000,000 in principal and a total of $343,847.14 in interest. As shown in Exhibit 2.9, the final net interest expense in this case is $5,111.19 less than the interest expense of borrowing for five months at five-month term LIBOR.

Suppose, however, that three-month LIBOR at futures expiration turns out to be 8.30 percent. In this case, futures will settle to a price of 91.70 [= 100 – 8.30] and the short futures position will have produced a gain of $5,000 [= –10 × –20 × $25]. At this point, the bank can use the $5,000 received in variation margin payments on the short futures position to reduce the amount that must be refinanced at the two-month mark. That is, the bank can refinance $10,133,541.67 for three months at 8.30 percent. If it does, the final payment at the five-month mark will be $10,343,812.66, which includes total interest for the five months of $343,812.66. This is $5,145.67 less than the interest expense on the five-month borrowing.

A third possibility is that three-month LIBOR turns out to be 7.90 percent at futures expiration so that futures settle to a price of 92.10. In this case, the short futures position produces a $5,000 loss, which must be included in the refinancing. That is, the bank must finance $10,143,541.67 for three months at 7.90 percent. If it does, the final payment at the five-month mark will be

$10,343,876.62, which includes total interest for the five months of $343,876.62. Here, the net saving from selling expensive futures is $5,081.71.

Three important lessons can be drawn from this example.

The first is that being able to sell expensive futures can reduce a bank's cost of funds. In this example, being able to sell three-month futures at 20 basis points over their fair value reduced the cost of funds from the five-month term borrowing rate 8.375 percent to a net rate of 8.25 percent. The 20-basis-point mispricing of the three-month Eurodollar futures contract was worth 12.5 basis points on a five-month transaction.

The second is the role that variation margin plays in locking the cost of funds. Note that the refinancing in all three cases was done at the prevailing market rate for three-month funds. In this sense, the short futures position did not lock the rate paid on funds. The amount refinanced in each case, however, was different by the amount received or paid in variation margin on the short futures position. The combined effect of adding variation margin to the amount to be refinanced and refinancing the combined amount at the prevailing market rate produces a net final cost of funds that is nearly constant regardless of the cost of three-month money at futures expiration.

The third lesson is that the hedge ratio could use some refining. In this example, the bank chose to sell 10 futures contracts because it was hedging the three-month cost of funds on $10 million. As the results show, the bank is somewhat overhedged. Note that the net cost of funds is lower if three-month LIBOR turns out to be high (and the futures price low) than if three-month LIBOR turns out to be low (and the futures price high).

In this particular case, the bank could not refine its hedge because the borrowing is too small and the horizon too short to matter much. The correct number of futures contracts for this example is only slightly less than 10 contracts, and one must deal in whole numbers of contracts. For longer borrowing or hedging horizons, however, the ratio can be quite a bit different than one contract for each $1 million face value of the transaction. When the correct ratio is very much different than one, getting the hedge ratio right can have a big effect on a hedge's performance. Later in this chapter, in the section on hedging with Eurodollar futures, we show how to calculate correct hedge ratios.

We can return now to the question of what keeps futures prices in line with their theoretical fair values. We argued in the introduction that banks operate on extremely thin profit margins and that a banker does not have to add very many basis points to the bottom line to be a hero. Any time a borrowing can be done at a few basis points below what's available in the cash market, a banker should be interested. If this means selling overvalued futures, the banker should do it. Any time an investment can bring in a few basis points more than what's available in the cash market, a banker should be interested. If this means buying undervalued futures, the banker should do it.

Our experience suggests that bankers are very interested indeed in opportunities to reduce the cost of funds or raise the rate of return on investments. Every day, the world's banks are in and out of the market, sometimes buying funds, sometimes selling funds. Because the amounts of money are so large, and the pressures to maximize net income so intense, mispriced futures represent valuable and low risk opportunities for bankers to improve their bottom lines. As a result, we find that Eurodollar futures prices seldom are more than 10 basis points out of line with their theoretical fair values.

Are Futures Cheap or Dear?

There is a slight imbalance in the way various participants can use Eurodollar futures. Banks can and do arbitrage Eurodollar futures whether they are cheap or expensive. Nonfinancial institutions such as manufacturing corporations do not have the same facility. They can always extend liabilities by shorting financial futures if they are expecting higher interest rates. They also can arbitrage if futures are expensive by shorting Eurodollar futures and borrowing money. When the futures are cheap, however, nonfinancial institutions are at a disadvantage. They cannot arbitrage a price discrepancy by buying futures and lending funds because they are not lending institutions.

Thus, we have two classes of players on one side of the market (banks and nonfinancials) and only one on the other (banks).

As a result, there has been a tendency for futures to be cheap. Banks as a class tend to be long more Eurodollar futures than they are short. Testing this proposition is not easy, but Discount Futures has a unique window on Eurodollar activity. Most of our clients are banks, and, as shown in Exhibit 2.10, the net position of our clients has tended to be long. If we were able to examine the net positions of nonfinancial institutions, we would expect them to be net short.

The only exception we have seen to this persistent bias was in 1989 when the CME added the third and fourth years of contract months. During this period, our clients' net positions were negative. What this suggests to us is that the newly listed deferred contracts may well have been expensive. We explain why we think so in Chapter 7 ("Practical Considerations").

Key Differences between Forwards and Futures

Although Eurodollar futures behave very much like three-month forward deposits, there are some important differences between the two. These are summarized in Exhibit 2.11 and include:

- cash flows
- security deposits
- offsets of longs and shorts
- credit exposure
- settlement dates

The importance of these differences depends a great deal on who you are and what you plan to do with the contracts.

Consider the difference in cash flows. In a forward transaction, money typically changes hands only on the forward date. Gains and losses go unrealized until final settlement. In futures, gains and losses are settled every day in cash.

This daily settlement of gains and losses has important implications both for reckoning hedge ratios (see the next section) and for reckoning the correct price (that is, adjusted fair value) for a Eurodollar futures contract (see Chapter 7).

Exhibit 2.10

Net Open Eurodollar Futures Position of DCNYF Clients

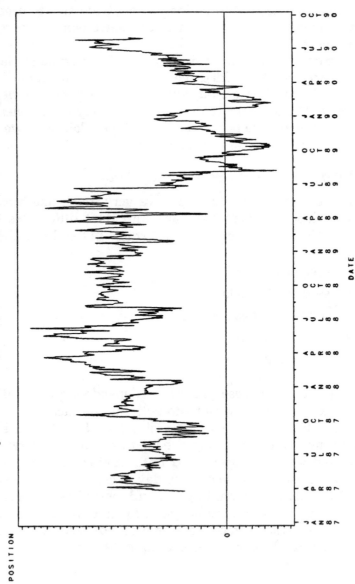

• DISCOUNT CORPORATION OF NEW YORK FUTURES •

Exhibit 2.11

Key Differences Between Forward and Futures Markets

- **Cash flows**

  In forward markets, cash changes hands only on the forward date. In futures markets, gains and losses are settled daily in the form of <u>variation margin</u> payments.

- **Security deposits**

  In forward markets, security deposits are rarely required. In futures markets, security deposits in the form of <u>initial and maintenance margins</u> are standard.

- **Offsets of longs and shorts**

  In forward markets, purchases and sales, even with the same trading partner, remain on the books as open long and short positions. In futures markets, purchases and sales (as long as they are traded through the same broker) offset one another.

- **Credit exposure**

  In forward markets, you face the credit risk of each trading partner. In futures markets, you face the credit risk only of the clearing house and the clearing member.

- **Settlement dates**

  In forward markets, settlement dates can be set to suit the trading partners. In futures markets, expirations are standardized.

The offsets of longs and shorts has important ramifications for bank traders. In a forward market, buys and sells are not offsetting. If Morgan lends to Citibank in the morning and borrows on identical terms from Citibank later in the day, both banks have two open positions with one another—one long and one short. With this arrangement, Morgan does not have to make many adjustments in its rate exposure to fill up even the huge credit lines it may have with Citibank.

But if Morgan traded indirectly with Citibank through the futures market, the positions would offset one another. At the end of the day, their open positions would be zero. Through this arrangement, banks can adjust their exposure all day long without bloating their balance sheets.

Hedging with Eurodollar Futures

Now that we have established that a three-month Eurodollar futures contract should behave like a forward three-month deposit, we can examine the problem of how to fit Eurodollar futures together with Eurodollar time deposits.

To do this, we will show how Eurodollar futures can be used to lock the cost of borrowing at a particular date in the future. This example allows us to explain:

- the mechanics of how variation margin on futures offsets gains and losses on the position to be hedged
- the importance of the daily settlement of gains and losses on futures for reckoning accurate hedge ratios

Locking the Cost of Borrowing

First consider the mechanics of the hedge. Suppose that a borrower wants to lock the cost of funds to be taken down at some point in the future. To do this, the borrower can:

- borrow forward; or
- sell Eurodollar futures.

For example, suppose that a borrower requires $10 million for three months starting two months from now. Suppose further that three-month forward LIBOR for that date is 8.30 percent and that Eurodollar futures are trading at 91.70 [= 100 - 8.30]. The borrower could:

- borrow $10 million forward at 8.30 percent; or
- sell 10 Eurodollar futures contracts at 91.70 and borrow at the prevailing three-month spot rate in two months.

Both methods in this example should produce about the same result.

Borrowing forward clearly provides the necessary $10 million two months from now. At a rate of 8.30 percent, the total interest on the loan at the end of the three-month loan (five months from now) would be:

$$\$207,\!500 \ = \ \$10,\!000,\!000 \times [.083 \times (90/360)]$$

The total amount of money paid out when the loan matures five months from now would be $10,207,500.

Exhibit 2.12 provides a summary of what happens under three different interest rate outcomes if the borrower takes the second approach.

Rates Unchanged

In the first instance, rates are unchanged and the borrower is in exactly the same position as he would have been had he borrowed forward. For example, three-month LIBOR is 8.30 percent, so the final settlement price on the futures is 91.70. There is no gain or loss on the futures position, and the borrower can take down $10 million at the spot rate of 8.30 percent. This case produces the same interest expense as borrowing forward.

Rates Up

In the second instance, rates have risen so that three-month spot LIBOR is 8.50 percent. What effect does this have on the borrower?

Exhibit 2.12

Possible Outcomes with Short Futures

Rates Unchanged (LIBOR = 8.30%)

- Futures settle at 91.70
- Borrower pays or receives no variation margin
- Borrower takes $10,000,000 at 8.30%
- Borrower repays $10,207,500 {=10,000,000 x [1 + .083(90/360)]}

> Interest expense = $207,500

Rates Up (LIBOR = 8.50%)

- Futures settle at 91.50
- Borrower <u>receives</u> $5,000 variation margin
  (= -10 contracts x -20 basis points x $25 per basis point)
- Borrower takes $9,995,000 at 8.50%
- Borrower repays $10,207,394 {= 9,995,000 x [1 + .085(90/360)]}

> Net interest expense = $207,394

Rates Down (LIBOR = 8.10%)

- Futures settle at 91.90
- Borrower <u>pays</u> $5,000 variation margin
  (= -10 contracts x 20 basis points x $25 per basis point)
- Borrower takes $10,005,000 at 8.10%
- Borrower repays $10,207,601 {= 10,005,000 x [1 + .081(90/360)]}

> Net interest expense = $207,601

• DISCOUNT CORPORATION OF NEW YORK FUTURES •

As shown in Exhibit 2.12, the futures settle down 20 ticks at 91.50. As a result, the borrower receives $5,000 in variation margin. This can be combined with a three-month loan for $9,995,000 at the higher spot rate of 8.50 percent. Three months later (five months from today), the borrower repays $10,207,394.

Two things are worth noting about this transaction. First, the borrower got the necessary $10 million at the two-month mark. Second, the *net* interest expense is nearly but not quite the same as it would have been borrowing forward. The fact that the net interest expense is somewhat less is important, and we will explain this point shortly.

Rates Down

In the third instance, rates have fallen to 8.10 percent. In this case, the borrower loses $5,000 on the short futures. To compensate for this, the borrower can take down a loan for $10,005,000 at the lower spot rate of 8.10 percent. The net result is that the borrower still gets the necessary $10 million.

At the end of three months, the borrower must repay $10,207,601. In other words, even though the size of the loan was larger to compensate for the loss on the Eurodollar futures, the final payment is about the same as it would have been if the borrower had taken down $10 million at a fixed forward rate of 8.30 percent.

In this case, however, the net interest expense is somewhat larger.

Refining the Hedge Ratio

What accounts for the slight mismatch in the hedge? The answer is that in Eurodollars, as in comedy, timing is everything.

Suppose we step back from the hedging problem and look at the general problem of locking in the cost of borrowing. The time line shown in Exhibit 2.13 shows that the takedown date is two months away, and that the payback date is five months away.

At the two-month mark, the borrower needs $10 million. If he borrows $10 million at the prevailing three-month spot rate, the total amount paid back at the five-month mark is:

Exhibit 2.13

Locking the Cost of Borrowing

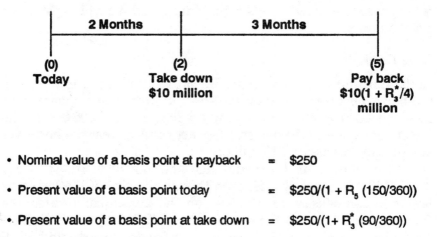

- Nominal value of a basis point at payback   = $250

- Present value of a basis point today   = $250/(1 + R_5 (150/360))$

- Present value of a basis point at take down   = $250/(1 + R_3^* (90/360))$

$$\$10 \; (1 + R^*_3/4) \text{ million}$$

where R^*_3 is the three-month spot LIBOR at takedown.

Our problem is to find the right number of futures contracts to offset the effect of a rise in this rate. How do we do this?

We proceed in two steps.

Nominal value of a basis point The first is to determine what effect a basis point increase in R^*_3 costs the borrower at payback. We call this effect the nominal value of a basis point and in this exercise it is:

$$\$10 \; (.0001/4) \text{ million} = \$250$$

That is, every basis point increase of one in the realized value of three-month LIBOR will increase the interest expense at the maturity of the loan by $250.

Present Value of a Basis Point

The key to calculating accurate hedge ratios for Eurodollar futures is to keep in mind that the gains and losses on the futures contract are settled every day. As a result, if the expected value of forward three-month LIBOR goes up one basis point, its effect will be to increase expected interest costs by $250 *at payback,* five months in the future, but *today* it will produce a $250 gain on a short position in 10 Eurodollar futures contracts. That is, the gain on the hedge comes when the rate changes while the loss is incurred later. The present value of the gain is greater than the present value of the loss. In other words, if the borrower has sold 10 futures contracts to hedge a $10 million borrowing, the borrower has overhedged.

The correct hedge ratio is found by determining the present value of a basis point increase in forward three-month LIBOR. Naturally, the answer depends on how far away the future is. If we do this calculation when there are still five months until payback, the present value of a basis point on the loan would be:

$$\$250 \; / \; [1 + R_5(150/360)]$$

where we use the five-month spot rate for discounting. If we let R_5 = 8.30 percent, the present value of a basis point with five months to payback would be:

$$\$250 \ / \ [1 + .083(150/360)] \ = \ \$241.64$$

If we calculate the present value of a basis point moments before the takedown of the loan, the present value of a basis point would be:

$$\$250 \ / \ [1 + R_3(90/360)]$$

which would be

$$\$250 \ / \ [1 + .083(90/360)] = \$244.92$$

Notice that the present value of a basis point change in the rate rises as time passes. This happens because the effect of discounting gets smaller as the hedge horizon gets shorter.

Getting the Right Ratio

Now we can determine what the hedge ratio should have been in our original exercise. If we were looking at the hedge problem at the beginning of the five-month period, the appropriate hedge ratio would have been:

$$\text{Hedge Ratio} = -\$241.64 \ / \ \$25$$

$$= -9.6656$$

That is, the borrower should sell 9.6656 futures. Later in the game, moments before the takedown, however, the appropriate hedge ratio would be:

$$\text{Hedge Ratio} = -\$244.92 \ / \ \$25$$

$$= -9.7968$$

Here, the borrower must add to the hedge to bring it up to a short position of 9.7968 futures.

To satisfy yourself that this is the right approach, you can re-work the results shown in Exhibit 2.12 using a short Eurodollar futures position of 9.7968 contracts. With this position, if rates rise just before the takedown, the borrower would receive only $4,898.40 instead of $5,000 in variation margin payments. Then he would have to borrow $9,995,101.60 at 8.50 percent. Because this loan is larger, the final payback will be larger. Moreover, the final payback will be within a few dollars of the $10,207,500. The bor-rower must pay if he borrows for five months term at 8.30 percent.

By the same token, the borrower will lose less on the Eurodol-lar futures position if rates fall. So the amount that he must bor-row is less than he needs if the hedge is short the full 10 contracts. Again, the final payback should be very close to the objective.

Extending the Life of a Deposit

The same approach can be taken to finding the appropriate num-ber of Eurodollar futures to use in lengthening or shortening a bank's assets or liabilities. The main complication is the care that must be taken to keep track of interest payments.

Consider the problem of using Eurodollar futures to extend the life of a $10 million two-month deposit to five months. At the end of five months, $10 million invested at the five-month spot rate of R_5 pays $10 \times [1 + R_5(5/12)]$. An alternative to lending or investing for five months would be to lend short term, say for two months, buy three-month Eurodollar futures that expire or mature at the two month, and roll over the deposit including any interest earned into a three-month deposit at whatever three-month de-posit rate prevails at the end of the first two months. If done cor-rectly, the long futures position will make up for any decreases in three-month deposit rates.

The first step in determining the correct number of futures to buy is to determine how sensitive your position is to changes in the new three-month deposit rate. In this example, the total value of your deposit at the end of five months would be:

$$\$10 \text{ million} \times [1 + R_2(60/360)] \times [1 + R^*_3(90/360)]$$

where R^*_3 is the value of three-month *LIBOR* at the end of the first two months and is the spot rate at which the initial deposit plus two months interest can be reinvested for the remaining three months.

From this expression, we find that a one-basis-point change in R^*_3 changes the end-of-period value of the deposit by

$$\$10 \text{ million} \times [1 + R_2(60/360)] \times [.0001/4]$$

or by

$$\$250 \times [1 + R_2(60/360)]$$

The second step in determining the correct number of futures to buy is to convert the end-of-period of effect of a change in the new three-month spot rate into a present value. Because the end of the period is five months away from the initial hedging date, the appropriate present value calculation would be:

$$\$250 \times [1 + R_2(60/360)] / [1 + R_5(150/360)]$$

For example, if R_2 and R_5 were both eight percent, this would be

$$\$250 \times [1 + .08 \times (60/360)] / [1 + .08 \times (150/360)]$$

$$\$250 \times (1.0133 / 1.0333)$$

$$\$250 \times [.9806]$$

$$\$245.15$$

which we can use in the numerator of our hedge calculation.

What goes in the denominator, of course, is the $25 present value of the effect of a one-basis-point change in the new value of three-month LIBOR on the value of a futures contract. The correct hedge ratio is then:

$$\$245.15/\$25 = 9.806$$

That is, if one could do partial futures contracts, one would want to buy 9.806 futures to protect the final value of the deposit against a drop in deposit rates.

This hedge ratio is slightly larger than the correct hedge ratio needed to protect a $10 million forward borrowing against an adverse change in rates. The difference between the two is the accumulation of interest on the deposit over the two-month hedging period. Stated differently, the only difference between the two problems is the amount of money to be hedged.

Tailing

In the futures business, any adjustment to a hedge ratio to account for the fact that the gain on the futures hedge is received today while the loss on the position is not realized until some time in the future is called "tailing."

Tailing is a term that we prefer not to use, largely because it does nothing to cement anyone's understanding of the problem.

Rather, distinguishing between nominal and present values has the virtue of conveying the sense of the problem at hand. If we know that hedging gains and losses are sustained immediately while position losses or gains are deferred, all we need to know to keep our hedge ratios straight is the cost of money between today and the end of the hedge horizon.

Who Really Cares?

A natural reaction to the difference between the back-of-the-envelope hedge that we started with and the correct hedge ratio that we finished with is "Who really cares?" The difference is so small. In the first place, the borrower who wants to lock the cost of funds on a $10 million loan has to sell 10 futures anyway because he has to deal in whole contracts.

The reply to this reaction is that many hedging problems involve much longer horizons and much larger amounts of money. To illustrate, the correct initial hedge for a $100 million three-month loan to be taken down three months from now may be 98 contracts. The correct initial hedge for a $100 million three-month loan to be taken down two years from now would be only 85 contracts—significantly less than 98.

Forward-Rate Agreements (FRAs)

FRAs are described occasionally as over-the-counter Eurodollar futures. In many ways this description is misleading because of the important differences between forward and futures contracts; however, the intuition behind the description is not bad.

An FRA is a clean, straightforward contract that requires cash payments based on the difference between a realized spot rate and an agreed-upon forward rate. Exhibit 2.1 illustrates the quote convention for FRAs. The rates shown next to the 1x4 are the bid and offer for the three-month rate covering the period between one and four months from the quote date. That is, one could buy the 1x4 FRA at 8.34 or sell it at 8.29. Similarly, one could buy the 5x11 FRA, which covers the six-month rate running from June to December, at 8.47, or sell it five basis points lower at 8.42.

How FRAs Work

The mechanics of a FRA are comparatively simple. Consider the $1 million 2x5 FRA illustrated in Exhibit 2.14. The forward rate is set today at 8.30 percent. At the two-month mark, the prevailing value of three-month LIBOR is determined and money is either taken in or paid out depending on whether the spot rate is higher or lower than the agreed-upon forward rate. In general, the size of the payment is calculated as:

$$\text{Payment} = \$1 \text{ million} \times \frac{[(\text{LIBOR} - .083) \, (\text{Days}/360)]}{[1 + \text{LIBOR} \, (\text{Days}/360)]}$$

where LIBOR is the appropriate spot rate prevailing on the payment date two months from the trade date.

Two things about this calculation are worth highlighting. The first is that FRA payments use the same day count convention as the deposit market. This makes sense because FRAs are meant to work in conjunction both with deposits and with other Eurodollar derivatives.

The second is that the payment is discounted at the realized value of spot LIBOR. This is especially interesting because it highlights an important difference in the timing of cash flows for FRAs

Exhibit 2.14

Forward Rate Agreement
$1 Million, 2 x 5 FRA

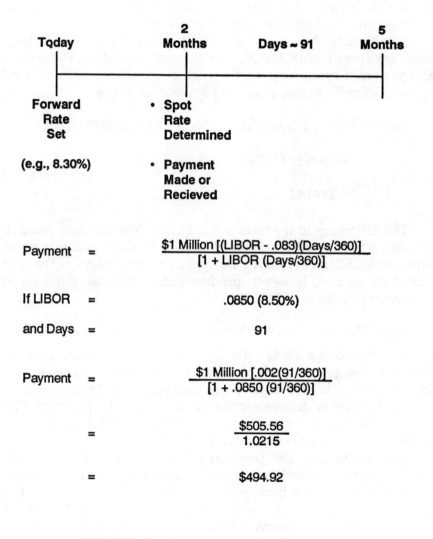

	2 **Months**	**Days ≈ 91**	**5** **Months**
Today			

Forward
Rate
Set

• **Spot**
  Rate
  Determined

(e.g., 8.30%)

• **Payment**
  Made or
  Recieved

Payment = $\dfrac{\$1 \text{ Million } [(LIBOR - .083)(Days/360)]}{[1 + LIBOR \ (Days/360)]}$

If LIBOR = .0850 (8.50%)

and Days = 91

Payment = $\dfrac{\$1 \text{ Million } [.002(91/360)]}{[1 + .0850 \ (91/360)]}$

= $\dfrac{\$505.56}{1.0215}$

= $494.92

• DISCOUNT CORPORATION OF NEW YORK FUTURES •

and deposits. While interest on a deposit is paid at the end of the period, the payment on an FRA is made at the beginning of the period.

The likely reason for settling the FRA at the two-month mark rather than at the five-month mark is convenience. The reason for discounting the FRA payment is to make its present value as close as possible to what it would be if the payment were set equal to the numerator and made at the end of the period.

Exhibit 2.14 shows how an FRA payment is calculated. Suppose that three-month LIBOR two months from the trade date is 8.50 percent. Suppose also that the actual number of days covered by the FRA is 91. In this case, the payment would be:

Payment= $1 million [.002(91/360)] / [1 + .085(91/360)]

$$= \$505.56/1.0215$$

$$= \$494.92$$

The difference in the rates is 0.2 percent. The nominal value of this difference for a $1 million FRA with 91 days in the covered period is $505.56. Discounting this payment for 91 days at the spot rate of 8.5 percent, however, produces an actual cash payment at the two-month mark of $494.92.

Hedging FRAs with Eurodollar Futures

The key to hedging FRAs with Eurodollar futures is the same as the key to hedging the cost of funds. The first step is to determine the present value of a basis point change in the value of three-month LIBOR that determines the value of the FRA payment. The only twist here is that the discounting period for FRA payments is shorter than for most other hedge calculations.

For example, in the problem of hedging the cost of three-month funds two months from the hedge date, we had to discount the nominal value of a basis point over the full five months. But in the case of a 2x5 FRA, the payment already has been discounted over three of those months. Thus, the hedge calculation requires only an additional two months of discounting to get the right answer.

Consider the problem of hedging a $100 million 2x5 FRA at 8.30 percent. As above, the payment at the two-month mark will be:

$$\text{Payment} = \$100 \text{ million} \times \frac{[(\text{LIBOR} - .0830)\ (\text{Days}/360)]}{[1 + \text{LIBOR}\ (\text{Days}/360)]}$$

and so will depend both on the realized value of LIBOR and the number of days in the period covered by the FRA.

The present value of the FRA payment will depend on how many days there are between the hedge date and payment date and on the value of spot LIBOR covering that span. If two-month spot LIBOR is 8-5/16 and there are 60 days between the hedge and the payment date, the present value of the FRA payment would be:

$$\text{Present Value of Payment} = \text{Payment} / [1 + .083125(60/360)]$$

Calculating the hedge ratio is now a straightforward exercise. The upper panel of Exhibit 2.15 shows what the FRA payment will be at three different realized values of three-month LIBOR and for two different day count assumptions. Averaging the present value of the effects of a basis point increase and a basis point decrease on the FRA payment gives us the present values of a basis point shown in the lower panel of the exhibit.

The exhibit shows that with 90 days in the payment period, the present value of a basis point is $2,415.71. At $25 per basis point for a Eurodollar contract, the hedge for a long position in the FRA would be 96.6 [= $2,415.71/$25] long Eurodollar futures.

With 92 days in the payment period, the present value of a basis point is higher ($2,468.28), and the hedge would be 98.7 long Eurodollar futures.

Of course, the hedge ratio will rise over time to reflect the increase in the present value of a basis point as we approach the FRA payment date.

Exhibit 2.15

FRA Cash Flow Calculations
($100 million 2x5 FRA at 8.30 percent)

LIBOR at Settlement	Days = 90		Days = 92	
	Payment	Present Value of Payment	Payment	Present Value of Payment
8.31	2449.12	2415.65	2502.41	2468.22
8.30	0	0	0	0
8.29	-2449.23	-2415.77	-2502.53	-2468.34

Hedge Ratio Calculation

Days	Present Value of an .01	Hedge Ratio	
90	2415.71	96.6	(Long 97 ED Futures)
92	2468.28	98.7	(Long 99 ED Futures)

• DISCOUNT CORPORATION OF NEW YORK FUTURES •

CHAPTER 3

Interest-Rate Swaps and Eurodollar Strips

Interest-rate swaps are similar to bundled strips of Eurodollar futures or forward-rate agreements (FRAs). Like futures and FRAs, swaps are arrangements for exchanging cash payments based on then-current interest rates at various times in the future.

Swaps are used widely to reduce funding costs and to manage interest rate exposure. The first major swap transactions were done during 1980 and 1981 when private short-term interest rates were around 20 percent. At that time, businesses were scrambling for any financing vehicle that would help them reduce interest costs. Some of these early transactions allowed one side or the other to borrow at rates below those on Treasury securities, which is big news any time but was spectacular news at that time. Since then, the swap market has grown to the point where there are roughly one-and-a-half trillion dollars' worth of swaps of all types in all currencies outstanding. The market has even spawned its

69

own trade group, the International Swap Dealers Association (ISDA).[1]

The exchange-traded counterpart to an interest-rate swap is a strip of Eurodollar futures. Although they are not the same, Eurodollar futures can be strung together with proper financial engineering to behave like swaps. Eurodollar futures are much less costly to trade than swaps, and as a result, we find that a strip of Eurodollar futures can do nearly everything a swap can do but with the added flexibility that futures afford over forwards.

The focus of this chapter is on the basic structure of interest-rate swaps and on some of the key features of Eurodollar strips. We will show how Eurodollar futures can be used either to hedge or replace swaps in Chapter 4.

How Swaps Work

An interest-rate swap is an arrangement that requires the two sides of the transaction to make payments to each other based on two different interest rates. The most commonly traded swap requires one side to pay a fixed rate and the other to pay a floating rate. Exhibit 3.1 shows that the two parties can deal directly with each other or through an intermediary.

Perhaps the best way to see how swaps work is to examine the most basic kind of swap.

The Generic "Plain Vanilla" Swap

Although swap conventions permit an almost limitless variety of deals, the mainstay of the swap market is the generic, or plain vanilla, swap. This is a fixed versus floating swap with the floating payment based on either three-month or six-month LIBOR.

The workings of a generic one-year swap are illustrated in Exhibit 3.2. The key features of the generic swap are:

- the floating payment is tied to three-month LIBOR;

---

1. A good source of information covering the mechanics of swaps is the ISDA's *Code of Standard Wording, Assumptions, and Provisions for Swaps*, 1986. See Appendix D for examples of the ISDA's documentation.

Exhibit 3.1
Interest-Rate Swaps

No Intermediary (Brokered Swap)

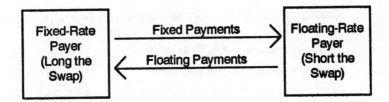

With an Intermediary

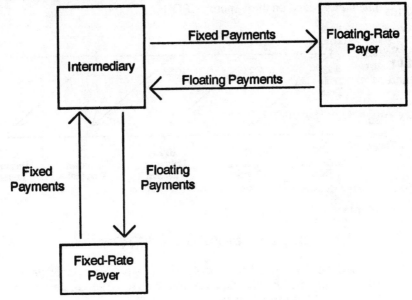

Exhibit 3.2

Plain Vanilla Swap

Basic Terms

- Floating payments tied to three-month LIBOR
- Payments made at three-month intervals
- Floating rate determined three months <u>and</u> two days before each payment date
- Fixed-side day count is 30/360
- Floating-side day count is actual/360
- Index source can be Reuters LIBO page or Telerate page 3750

Swap Example

$1 million, one-year swap done on Monday, April 23, 1990, with quarterly payments based on three-month LIBOR

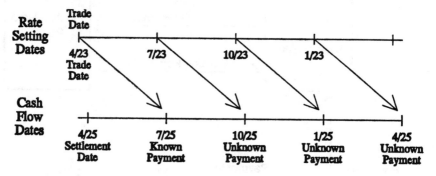

Payments

$1 Million [Fixed Rate (90/360) - LIBOR (Days/360)]

where Days is the actual number of days in the payment period (that is, 91 days from 4/25 to 7/25, 92 days from 7/25 to 10/25, 92 days from 10/25 to 1/25, and 90 days from 1/25 to 4/25)

- the payments are made at three-month intervals;
- the floating rate is determined three months and two days before each payment date (e.g., if the trade date is 4/23, the payment made on 7/25 is determined on 4/23), which means that payments are made in arrears;
- the fixed rate day count is 30/360;
- the floating rate day count is actual/360;
- the payments are netted with the net payment equal to the swap's notional amount (e.g., $50 million) times

[Fixed rate (90/360) − LIBOR (Days/360)]

where the fixed rate often is quoted as a spread over Treasuries (that is, the rate on a Treasury note with a matching maturity), and Days is the actual number of days between payment periods.

The Timing and Size of Cash Payments

The time lines in Exhibit 3.2 summarize the relationship between the swap's trade date and the subsequent cash flows. In this example, the trade was done on April 23. By swap convention, the first payment will be made three months and two days later on July 25. The size of the payment typically is based on the April 23 value of LIBOR. As a result, the size of the first payment is known.

The size of each of the three remaining payments is unknown. For example, the size of the payment made on October 25 will depend on the value of three-month LIBOR observed on July 23.

Calculating the Cash Payments

In this swap, the fixed and floating payments are netted against one another. Not all swaps follow this pattern, but it simplifies our example. The day count conventions shown in Exhibit 3.2 are fairly standard; that is, the fixed-rate payment is based on a 30/360 convention, while the floating-rate payment is based on an actual/360 convention. Each of these conforms to standard practice in their respective markets, bonds in the case of the fixed payment and deposits in the case of the floating payment.

Suppose that the fixed rate is set at eight percent. If the realized value of LIBOR is 8.50 percent, the payment for each $1 million nominal value in the swap would be:

$$\$1 \text{ million } [.08(90/360) - .085(91/360)]$$

$$= -\$1,486.11$$

The negative sign means that the side paying the fixed rate (that is, "paying fixed") would actually receive money from the side paying the floating rate (that is, "paying floating").

Swaps Are Like Strips of FRAs and Eurodollar Futures

The upshot of these basic contract terms is that an interest-rate swap can be reduced to a set of periodic cash flows whose values depend on either a current or future value of three-month LIBOR.

In this sense, except for the first (known) payment, a generic interest rate swap is much like a strip of FRAs or a strip of Eurodollar futures. The chief differences are in the timing and sizes of the amounts paid.

The Varied Ingredients of Interest-Rate Swaps

Although the generic swap plays a major role in the interest-rate swap market, swaps can differ from one another in several key respects including:

- fixed/floating versus floating/floating;
- floating rate index;
- day counts;
- frequency of cash payments;
- exchange of principal.

Fixed/Floating versus Floating/Floating

The most common interest rate swaps are those in which one side's payments are based on a fixed interest rate while the other's are based on a variable rate. The fixed payments may be based on a rate equal to 80 basis points over three-year Treasuries, while the floating payments are tied to three-month LIBOR.

Swaps sometimes entail two floating interest rates rather than one fixed and one floating. These are called "basis" swaps in which one side's payments may be tied to prime while the other side's payments may be tied to LIBOR or a commercial paper rate.

Floating-Rate Indexes

Fixed/floating swaps often are quoted in two parts. The fixed rate on a three-year swap usually is quoted as a fixed spread over the prevailing yield on three-year Treasury notes. The floating rate is then simply tied to either a spot quote or an average value of the appropriate floating-rate index. An extensive list of the more widely used indexes is provided in Exhibit 3.3 together with their respective sources.

Most basis swaps involve two of these indexes.

Day Counts

The business of day counts is complex and resists rational explanation. Even so, convention can be a mighty force, and there are several conventions.

The standard day count conventions used for calculating the periodic payments in a swap are shown in Exhibit 3.4.

For the most part, fixed payments are calculated on a 30/360 basis. If the fixed payments are made quarterly, the relevant interest rate is multiplied by 90/360; if semiannually, by 180/360. Even so, the fixed payments can also be calculated on an actual/360 basis, an actual/365 basis, or on an actual/actual basis. The world of swap trading is quite libertarian in this regard, and whatever consenting swap traders want, they can have.

Variable payments most often are calculated on an actual/360 basis. This is the convention in the LIBOR market and it has carried over to the swap market for swaps based on LIBOR. Treasury

Exhibit 3.3

Floating Rate Indexes

Index	Standard Source*
LIBOR (1,3 and 6 months)	Reuters LIBO Page Telerate page 3750
Prime	Federal Reserve's H.15 Report
Commercial Paper	Federal Reserve's H.15 Report
Federal Funds	Federal Reserve's H.15 Report
Treasury Bills	Federal Reserve's H.15 Report
Banker's Acceptances	Federal Reserve's H.15 Report
Certificates of Deposit	Federal Reserve's H.15 Report
Cost-of-Funds Index (COFI)	San Francisco Federal Home Loan Bank
30-Day Tax Exempt	J.J. Kenny

*   See **Code of Standard Wording, Assumptions and Provisions for Swaps,** ISDA,
     1986, for additional detail on floating-rate indexes used on swaps.

Exhibit 3.4*

Swap Day Count Conventions

Fixed	Floating
30/360	Actual/360
Actual/Actual	Actual/Actual
Actual/360	Actual/365
Actual/365	30/360

* Day counts refer to the assumed number of days in a month and year used in calculating swap net payments. For example, on a quarterly LIBOR swap with a 30/360 fixed-rate day count and an actual/360 floating-rate day count, the payment in a particular quarter equals fixed rate (90/360) - LIBOR (Actual Days in quarter/ 360).

bill payments are calculated on an actual/actual basis, so that swaps tied to bill rates most likely will use an actual/actual day count in their calculation. As with fixed payments, floating payments can be done on any basis the traders want.

Frequency of Cash Payments

Here, too, there is considerable variation in practice, but with most swaps, the fixed and floating payments are tied to the term of the floating rate index. To illustrate, if the floating side is tied to three-month LIBOR, a net payment is calculated and made at three-month intervals. If the floating side is tied to six-month LIBOR, the net payments are made every six months.

There are several possible mismatches, however, depending on the indexes and the traders. The floating payment might be tied to three-month LIBOR, while the net payments are calculated and made every six months. Or, as in the case of many basis swaps, the terms of the two variable rates are different so that the payment frequency will accord with the term of only one of the two.

The payments need not be netted. Instead, the floating payments might be tied to three-month LIBOR and made every three months, while the fixed payments might be made according to U.S. bond convention and paid every six months.

Exchange of Principal

Usually swaps are described as contracts in which there is no exchange of principal; that is, the side making fixed payments has not actually sold a fixed rate note to the other side. Similarly, the side making variable payments has not actually sold a floating-rate note to the other. Rather, the two sides agree to make payments to each other based on different interest rates.

In most cases, but by no means all, swaps are priced at the outset so that no money changes hands.

This does not mean that there is no credit exposure in a swap. Once in place, the net present value of a swap changes with the level of interest rates. The side that pays floating and receives fixed payments loses money if interest rates rise. When this happens, the side that receives floating and pays fixed should have at least some interest in the credit worthiness of the other party. Even without an exchange of principal, the winner faces some chance of a default by the loser.

Although defaults have been rare, some have been spectacular. The Hammersmith default in Great Britain, for example, was prompted by an adverse move in rates that threatened to bankrupt the town council.[2] Since that time, it has been impossible to ignore the credit risk aspects of swaps.

Glitches can develop for other reasons as well. The evaporation of Drexel Burnham Lambert created substantial problems for the swap market that had nothing to do with rate moves. In this case, Drexel was the intermediary in a large number of interest rate swaps. Thus, even though both sides of most of these swap transactions were perfectly creditworthy, their separate transactions were with Drexel, not with each other. The wreckage is still being sorted out at this writing (May 1990).

Variations on the Theme

Beyond the variety of swaps that can be structured with the choices outlined so far, one can find swaps that fit almost any requirement or market convention. As shown in Exhibit 3.5, short-term interest rates can be averaged instead of compounded (e.g., prime versus one-month commercial paper swaps). Swaps can cover different periods (e.g., LLBean, IMM, and forward starting swaps). The size of the swap can decrease over time (i.e., amortizing swaps). The swap can be cancelled by one side or the other (i.e., putable and callable swaps). Or the swap can materialize at some future date (i.e., swaptions).

Pricing Swaps

The key question for those who run swap books is how sensitive swaps are to changes in market yields. This question must be answered correctly before a swap trader can make an accurate as-

---

2. Some have argued that Hammersmith and Fulham's actions did not actually constitute a default in the technical or legal sense of the word. Whether they are right is beyond the scope of this book. The important lesson for swap traders in this episode is that credit risk is a real issue in swaps, irrespective of whether any principal changes hands.

Exhibit 3.5

Swap Variations

Prime

When prime is used as an index for the floating rate, the daily values are averaged. Friday's rate is given a weight of three days.

One-Month Commercial Paper

If the payment dates are more than one month apart, the commercial paper rates are compounded when calculating the floating payment.

LLBean

These are seasonal swaps designed to cover heavy financing periods.

IMM

These are tied directly to Eurodollar futures rates and often have an irregular length starting period between the trade date and the first futures expiration.

Forward Starting

The first rate setting date is after the trade date.

Amortizing

The notional amount falls over the life of the swap according to an agreed upon schedule.

Swap in Arrears

Floating rate set at the end rather than the beginning of the repricing period.

Putable and Callable

One side or the other has the right to cancel the swap at certain times without cost.

Swaption

An option to enter into a swap on preset terms on or before a specified date.

sessment of interest rate exposure or assemble a workable hedging program.

This section shows how to determine the sensitivity of swap prices to changes in yields. For the sake of simplicity, we focus on the price sensitivity of a generic swap. The principles outlined here, however, can be applied to any swap.

Partitioning the Generic Swap

On each payment date, the amount of cash that changes hands with a generic swap is equal to:

Notional Amount [Fixed Rate (90/360) – LIBOR (Days/360)]

If the fixed payment exceeds the floating payment, the side that is long writes a check to the side that is short. If the floating payment exceeds the fixed payment, the side that is short writes a check for the difference to the side that is long.

What makes the swap hard to price is the uncertainty of all but the first of the cash flows. The way out of this difficulty is to treat the swap as if it is:

- a long position in a hypothetical fixed-rate note with periodic coupon payments and a repayment of par (100) at maturity;

combined with

- a short position in a hypothetical floating-rate note with periodic payments tied to an index (LIBOR) and a repayment of par at maturity.

Because the par repayments at maturity are just offsetting, the net cash flows on this combination of hypothetical securities are the same as the net cash flows on the swap.

The advantage breaking the swap into two hypothetical securities is that while we do not know how to price a string of uncertain cash flows without bringing in the heavy artillery needed for handling stochastic processes, we do know how to price fixed rate securities, and we do know how to price floating rate notes. Thus, we turn a messy problem into two simple problems.

The Fixed Rate Note

The price of the hypothetical fixed rate security is calculated just as one would calculate the price of a non-callable, fixed-coupon note that repays par at maturity. If the payments are made semi-annually, the price calculation would be:

$$\sum_{i=1}^{n} [(C/2) / (1 + SY/2)^i] + [100/(1 + SY/2)^n]$$

where C is the annualized value of the fixed payment. Typically, C is set equal to the swap yield *(SY)* on the trade date so that the value of the fixed side of the swap will equal par. The swap yield is expressed on a semiannual bond equivalent basis. The payment number is indicated by *i*, and *n* is the total number of semiannual payments.

For example, if the hypothetical coupon and the swap yield on the trade date are both nine percent, the price of the fixed side of the swap would be:

Note Price = $[(9/2) / (1 + .09/2)] + [(100 + 9/2) / (1 + .09/2)^2]$

$= (4.5) / (1.045) + (104.5) / (1.045)^2$

$= 4.31 + 95.69$

$= 100$

After the swap is up and running, market yields will change, and the price of the fixed side of the swap will change accordingly. For example, if swap yields fall to eight percent immediately after the deal is struck at a nine percent rate, the value of the fixed side of the swap would be:

Note Price = (4.5) / (1.04) + (104.5) / $(1.04)^2$

= 4.33 + 96.62

= 100.95

Allowing for Payment Frequency

If the payment frequency is anything other than semiannual, the calculation would be:

$$\sum_{i=1}^{n'} [(C'/\text{freq}) / (1 + SY'/\text{freq})^i] + [100/(1 + SY'/\text{freq})^{n'}]$$

where C' is the annualized value of the periodic fixed payment (usually set equal to SY' on the trade date). SY' is a modified swap yield geared to the payment frequency, *freq* is the payment frequency, i is the payment number and n' is the total number of payments. For example, in a swap with quarterly fixed payments, *freq* would equal four. In general, the modified swap yield is calculated as:

$$SY' = [(1 + SY/2)^{2/\text{freq}} - 1] \times \text{freq}$$

which is the conversion from a bond equivalent yield to a different frequency. For example, if payments were made quarterly, this conversion would translate a bond equivalent yield into a quarterly compounded yield. The conversion can be reversed to put any swap yield on a bond equivalent basis. So:

$$SY = 2 [(1 + SY' \text{ freq})^{\text{freq}/2} - 1]$$

Such conversions are important because they allow traders to place swaps with different payment frequencies on an equal footing for the purposes of rate comparisons.

Consider a swap with quarterly fixed payments struck at the same time as the nine percent swap with semiannual fixed payments. The modified swap yield would be:

$$SY' = [(1.045)^{2/4} - 1] \times 4$$

$$= [1.02225 - 1] \times 4$$

$$= 0.089$$

Note that the faster compounding associated with the quarterly payment frequency produces a yield measure that is lower than an equivalent swap with semiannual payments. Stated differently, the price of a note paying interest quarterly at 8.90 percent is the same as the price of a note paying interest semiannually at nine percent.

The Floating Rate Note

The price of a floating rate note whose variable payments are equal to its own string of discount rates is one dollar for each dollar of nominal or notional value of the note. Thus, a floating rate note whose variable payments are equal to quarterly LIBOR and whose present value is calculated using quarterly LIBOR will equal par on its trade date and on each successive reset date.

This greatly simplifies the task of pricing the hypothetical floating rate note. At the time a deal is struck, the price of the floating side of the transaction would be 100, or par.

At any time after the deal is struck, the price of the floater is not much harder to calculate. All that needs to be done is to break the floater into:

- the value of its first payment, which is fixed on the trade date and which will be paid on the first payment date;

and

- the value of the floating rate note at the next reset date, which will be 100.

Given this breakdown, the value of the hypothetical floating rate note on any day after a reset date is simply:

(Known Payment + 100) / [1 + R (Days/360)]

where R is the current spot LIBOR rate for the time remaining to the first reset date, and Days is the actual number of days remaining to the first reset date.

For example, if three-month LIBOR on the trade date is nine percent, the value of the first payment on a swap with a notional value of $100 is:

First Payment $= \$100 \times (.09/4)$

$= \$2.25$

if the actual number of days in the payment period is 90. On the trade date, then, the price of the hypothetical floater can be written as:

Floater Price $= (2.25 + 100) / [1 + .09 (90/360)]$

$= (102.25) / (1.0225)$

$= 100.00$

If three-month LIBOR then falls immediately to eight percent, the price of the floater would be:

Floater Price $= (102.25)/(1.02)$

$= 100.25$

As one would expect, the price of the hypothetical floater is less sensitive to a change in its yield than is the price of the hypothetical fixed rate note, whose price increase is 0.96 in response to the same drop of 100 basis points in its yield. The floater, after all, is designed to behave like a three-month money market instrument and exhibits the price risk of a three-month deposit or CD. In contrast, the fixed rate side of the transaction in this example is like a one-year note, which has a duration roughly four times that of the three-month instrument.

As a practical matter, an interest rate swap can be treated as a fixed rate note with a maturity equal to the term of the transaction *less* the maturity of the hypothetical floater. For example, a two-year swap with quarterly payments behaves very much like a 1.75-year fixed rate note. A four-year note with semiannual payments behaves very much like a 3.5-year fixed rate note.

The importance of this observation becomes clear when we tackle the problem of hedging a swap. Further, we will find that there are strong parallels between interest rate swaps and Treasury notes, and that the lessons learned in hedging swaps carry over directly to the problem of hedging Treasuries with Eurodollar futures.

Eurodollar Strips

A Eurodollar strip is widely thought of as a futures position that contains one each of the contracts in a sequence of contract months. For example, a one-year strip might contain one each of the June, September, and December 1991, and the March 1992 contracts. At this writing (May 1990), one can construct Eurodollar strips up to four years long.

The reason people chain Eurodollar futures together is that the value of the strip changes in the same way as the value of a longer-term deposit in response to a change in yields. A standard way to compare Eurodollar strips with conventional term deposits is to calculate what is commonly referred to as a Eurodollar strip rate.

Eurodollar Strip Rates

A Eurodollar strip rate is a measure of the yield on a synthetic longer-term deposit. The conventional calculation of a Eurodollar strip rate is done as:

$$[1+R_0(D_0/360)] \times [1+F_1(D_1/360)] \times \ldots \times [1+F_n(D_n/360)]$$

$$= [1+R(365/360)]^N \times [1+R(D_r/360)]$$

where

R = Eurodollar strip rate stated as an annualized money market yield

R_o = spot LIBOR to first futures expiration

F_1 = lead contract futures rate (= 100 − lead futures price)

F_n = futures rate for the last contract in the strip

D_i = actual number of days in each period, i = 0,...,n

D_r = total number of days in the partial year period of the strip

N = number of whole years in the strip

For example, on the morning of January 22, 1990, two-month LIBOR (which covers the approximate period from January 22 to the expiration of the March Eurodollar contract) was 8-5/16 (= 8.3125 percent). (See Exhibit 3.6) As shown in Exhibit 3.7, the March, June, September, and December futures rates were:

F_M = 8.31 [= 100 - 91.69]
F_J = 8.35 [= 100 - 91.65]
F_S = 8.41 [= 100 - 91.59]
F_D = 8.63 [= 100 - 91.37]

With these data, we can calculate either a one-year strip rate that covers the period from January 22, 1990 to January 21, 1991, or a one-year forward strip rate that begins with the expiration of the March Eurodollar contract. The January to January strip rate is:

R = { [(1 + .083125(56/360)]
    × [1 + .0831(91/360)]

Exhibit 3.6*
Money Market Rates

TELERATE SYSTEMS

```
01/22   9:57 EST      NOONAN, ASTLEY & PEARCE — NEW YORK] 01/22 9:51 PG314
        EURO-DOLLAR    |    FED FUNDS    |      FRA'S        |  INT RATE SWAPS |
        09:50 EST      |    9:51 EST     |    9:43 EST       |    9:43 EST     |
                                                             |      ACT/360    |
O/N | 8 1/8  - 8 1/4 | BID      ASK    | 1X4   8.29 - 8.34 | MXM 8.63 - 8.68 |
T/N | 8 3/16 - 8 5/16| 8 1/8    8 3/16 | 2X5   8.25 - 8.30 | JXJ 8.72 - 8.77 |
S/N | 8 3/16 - 8 5/16| LAST     OPEN   | 3X6   8.27 - 8.32 | SXS 8.84 - 8.89 |
1WK | 8 1/8  - 8 1/4 | 8 3/16   8 3/16 | 4X7   8.29 - 8.34 | 2MXM 8.79 - 8.84 |
    |                | TERM FED FUNDS  | 5X8   8.30 - 8.35 | 1YR 8.60 - 8.65 |
1MO | 8 3/16 - 8 5/16| 8 1/4  - 8 3/8  | 6X9   8.32 - 8.37 | 18MO 8.64 - 8.69 |
2MO | 8 3/16 - 8 5/16| 8 1/4  - 8 3/8  | 9X12  7.93 - 7.98 |   MEDIUM TERM    |
3MO | 8 1/4  - 8 3/8 | 8 5/16 - 8 7/16 | 1X7   8.39 - 8.44 | 2 YRS T + 56 - 60 |
4MO | 8 1/4  - 8 3/8 | 8 9/16 - 8 11/16| 2X8   8.37 - 8.42 | 3 YRS T + 63 - 68 |
5MO | 8 5/16 - 8 7/16| 8 3/8  - 8 1/2  | 3X9   8.39 - 8.44 | 4 YRS T + 74 - 78 |
6MO | 8 5/16 - 8 7/16| 8 3/8  - 8 1/2  | 4X10  8.41 - 8.46 | 5 YRS T + 81 - 85 |
9MO | 8 3/8  - 8 1/2 | 8 7/16 - 8 9/16 | 5X11  8.42 - 8.47 | 7 YRS T + 84 - 89 |
1YR | 8 7/16 - 8 9/16| 8 1/2  - 8 5/8  | 6X12  8.45 - 8.50 | 10YRS T + 92 - 96 |
[TELEPHONE NUMBER: 212 - 504 - 2900/SEE PG 317 CAPITAL MKTS -SWAP OPTIONS]
```

TELERATE SYSTEMS

```
01/22        9:57 EST      [LASSER MARSHALL INC. - NEW YORK] PAGE 333
             FED FUNDS O/N |      AGENCY TERM   |     EURODOLLARS      |
             9:50 EST      |      8:59 EST      |     8:59 EST         |
     BID  | 8 3/16         |1MO| 8 1/4 - 8 3/8 |1MO: 8 3/16 - 8 5/16 |
     ASK  | 8 3/16         |2MO| 8 1/4   8 3/8 |2MO: 8 3/16   8 5/16 |
     LAST | 8 3/16         |3MO| 8 5/16  8 7/16|3MO: 8 1/4    8 3/8  |
     OPEN | 8 3/16         |4MO| 8 5/16  8 7/16|4MO: 8 1/4    8 3/8  |
     HIGH | 8 3/16         |5MO| 8 5/16  8 7/16|5MO: 8 1/4    8 3/8  |
     LOW  | 8 3/16         |6MO| 8 3/8   8 1/2 |6MO: 8 5/16   8 7/16 |
          | SHORT DATE EUROS|  | 8 7/16  8 9/16|9MO  8 3/8    8 1/2  |
     O/N : 8 1/8    8 3/16 :  | 8 1/2   8 5/8 |1YR: 8 7/16   8 9/16 |
     T/N : 8 1/8    8 1/4  :  | DOMESTIC TERM |18M: 8 5/8    8 3/4  |
     S/N : 8 3/16   8 5/16 :1MO| 8 1/4   8 3/8|2YR: 8 11/16  8 13/16|
     1WK : 8 3/16   8 5/16 :2MO| 8 1/4   8 3/8|3YR: 8 13/16  9 15/16|
     2WK : 8 3/16 - 8 5/16 :3MO| 8 1/4   8 3/8|4YR: 8 15/16  9 1/16 |
     3WK : 8 3/16 - 8 5/16 :6MO| 8 5/16  8 7/16|5YR: 9        9 1/8 |
     PPY385-7175 ]          |      385-7141   |' [   385-7075  ]    |
```

*   *This page is a transcription of an actual Telerate Systems print-out.*

• DISCOUNT CORPORATION OF NEW YORK FUTURES •

Exhibit 3.7*
Treasury Bill and Eurodollar Futures Prices

```
TELERATE SYSTEMS

01/22      9:56 EST        [   TELERATE FUTURES SERVICE  ]                PAGE 910
|TREASURY BILLS (90 DAYS) --IMM    |    EURODOLLARS--IMM                           |
|         LAST   LOW  HIGH   OPEN CLOSE |        LAST   LOW   HIGH   OPEN CLOSE|
|MAR 90   9262  9262  9266   9265 9263 |MAR 90  9169  9169  9172  72-71   9169 |
|JUN 90  A9276  9276  9279   9276 9274 |JUN 90  9165  9165  9168  67-66   9164 |
|SEP 90                           9278 |SEP 90  9159  9159  9162   9161   9157 |
|DEC 90                           9255 |DEC 90  9137  9137  9140   9140   9136 |
|MAR 91                           9255 |MAR 91  9131  9131  9133   9132   9130 |
|JUN 91  B9267                    9263 |JUN 91  9124  9124  9126   9125   9124 |
|                                      |SEP 91  9121  9121  9124   9123   9121 |
|                                      |DEC 91  9116  9115  9118   9118   9115 |
|                                      |MAR 92  9120  9120  9123   9123   9120 |
|                                      |JUN 92  9116  9116  9119   9119   9116 |
|                                      |SEP 92  9111  9111  9114   9113   9111 |
|                                      |DEC 92  9101  9101  9103   9103   9101 |
|                                      |MAR 93 A9103  9104  9106  05-06   9103 |
|                                      |JUN 93  9099  9099  9100   9100   9098 |
|                                      |SEP 93 B9094                     9093 |
```

*   *This page is a transcription of an actual Telerate Systems print-out.*

• DISCOUNT CORPORATION OF NEW YORK FUTURES •

$$\times [1 + .0835(91/360)]$$
$$\times [1 + .0841(91/360]$$
$$\times [1 + .0863(36/360)] -1\} \times (360/365)$$

$$= .0866$$

or 8.66 percent. At the same time, one-year LIBOR was quoted at 8-9/16, or 8.56 percent. Thus, futures prices in the strip were 10 basis points cheap if the price quotes shown in Exhibits 3.6 and 3.7 were up to the minute. Note that 8.63 percent, which is the futures rate for the three-month period beginning in December, is used as a proxy for the forward rate that would cover the shorter 36-day period that starts in December. This is a standard assumption in calculations like this and is used for the sake of convenience. The calculation could be refined somewhat by reckoning the appropriate forward rate, but little would be gained by the refinement.

In this example, the March to March forward strip rate is:

$$R = (\{[1 + .0831(91/360)]$$
$$\times [1 + .0835(91/360)]$$
$$\times [1 + .0841(91/360)]$$
$$\times [1 + .0863(91/360)]\} - 1) \times (360/364)$$

$$= .0870$$

or 8.7 percent, which is the annual money market rate on the strip and which can be compared with the 8.68 percent offered rate for a March to March swap (see the top entry in the right column of Exhibit 3.6).

Swap Yields versus Strip Rates

Except for quote conventions, swap yields for swaps based on three-month LIBOR and Eurodollar strip rates are measures of the same thing—the fixed rate of return paid on a high-quality private note with a time to maturity equal to the maturity of the swap or the length of the Eurodollar strip.

The quote convention is handled easily. Swap yields typically are quoted on a semiannual bond equivalent yield basis, while Eurodollar strip yields are quoted on a money market basis. A rule of thumb for converting one into the other is:

$$R = [(\,1 + SY/2)^2 - 1] \times (360/365)$$

where R is the Eurodollar strip rate, and SY is the swap yield. One also finds the swap yield represented by the Treasury rate (T) plus a spread (S). Thus, we can restate the expression as:

$$R = \{[\,1 + (T+S)/2]^2 - 1\} \times (360/365)$$

Armed with this expression and any two of the three rates, one can calculate the third. That is, if you know the Eurodollar strip rate and the Treasury yield for a note with a maturity equal to that of the strip, you can calculate the strip rate's spread over the Treasury yield. Similarly, if you know the swap yield (that is, $SY = T+S$), you can calculate the equivalent Eurodollar strip rate.

Pros and Cons of Swaps versus Strips

As we show in Chapter 4, a correctly constructed strip of Eurodollar futures can be made to behave like a generic interest-rate swap.

The most obvious reason for choosing a Eurodollar strip rather than a swap is for better rates. If Eurodollars futures prices are rich—above fair value—selling a strip is better than buying a swap. If Eurodollar futures are cheap, buying a strip is better than selling a swap. This part of the decision is simply a matter of keeping track of the two markets and choosing the market with the best prices.[3]

A second obvious reason is transaction costs, including bid/ask spreads and brokerage. On this score, Eurodollar futures strips have been substantially less costly to execute than interest-rate swaps for the past several years. For one thing, the bid/ask spreads are narrower in the Eurodollar futures market. For another, brokerage is much lower.

A less obvious reason to those who have not been involved in a default or in the dissolution of an intermediary is the reliability

---

3. Discount Corporation of New York Futures issues a daily report called The Short End, which shows the relative richness and cheapness of strips versus swaps. Discount Futures also has PC-based software that allows hedgers and traders to do similar calculations throughout the day. See Appendix C.

or credit worthiness of the other party to the trade. Although there is no explicit exchange of principal in an interest-rate swap, there is credit and default risk. The default in Great Britain by the Hammersmith town council illustrates this point fairly well. The evaporation of Drexel Burnham Lambert, which was an intermediary in an extensive network of swaps, showed how troubles with the intermediary can interrupt the cash flows.

Here, Eurodollar strips have a distinct advantage over swaps. The clearing house of the Chicago Mercantile Exchange (CME) stands between the two sides of the trade, so that the credit risk in a Eurodollar futures strip is the credit risk in the clearing house taken together with the credit risk in the respective clearing members.

At least at this writing (May 1990), Eurodollar strips also enjoy an advantage over swaps in the area of brokerage costs. In the over-the-counter market, the one-way cost of broking a swap is $100 per million per year. At this rate, the full round-turn cost is $200 per million per year, or $600 for a $1 million three-year swap. At the CME, the cost of broking a full three-year swap in the form of 12 Eurodollar futures contracts at $15 per round turn would be only $180.

Also, the offset of longs and shorts in futures offer traders considerably greater flexibility than is available in the swap market. Buying and selling strips of Eurodollar futures does not bloat a bank's balance sheet the way swap trading does, and many banks are feeling the pinch, both in terms of running up against credit lines and in terms of new regulatory capital requirements.

Perhaps the biggest drawback to Eurodollar strips is the steady flow of money back and forth in the form of variation margin. Gains and losses on futures are marked to market daily; payments on swaps are made with a degree of predictable regularity.

Also, Eurodollar futures contracts have expirations extending only to four years and so cannot be used in place of swaps with maturities longer than four years.

CHAPTER 4

Hedging Swaps and Treasuries

We know that interest rate swaps are big business. We know from Chapter 3 that swaps and Eurodollar futures strips are driven by the same kinds of forward short-term interest rates. And we know that Eurodollar futures are both less expensive to trade and offer much more flexibility than interest rate swaps. Thus, there is some mileage to be gained by learning how to incorporate strips of Eurodollar futures into a swap book.

This chapter focuses on how Eurodollar futures fit into the world of interest rate swaps. We also look at the relationship between Eurodollar futures strips and Treasury notes.

Eurodollar futures now trade with quarterly expirations out as far as four years.[1] This makes it possible to create synthetic fixed-rate deposits with maturities extending to just past four years with strips of Eurodollar futures. Traders also can break up the first four years of the yield curve into 16 separate three-month

---

1. By the time this book reaches the market, the Chicago Mercantile Exchange may have added a fifth year, which would allow traders to match the maturity of the Chicago Board of Trade's Five-Year Treasury Note contract.

segments plus a short segment between today and the first futures settlement. These can then be used to create synthetic fixed or variable rate instruments in a huge range of combinations.

As such, Eurodollar futures are a powerful tool for managing short- to intermediate-term interest rate exposure. For that matter, the immodest fans of Eurodollar futures make a convincing case that these contracts were largely responsible for three key money market developments in the 1980s:

- the integration of the world's dollar markets;
- the popularity of interest rate swaps; and
- the emergence of interest rate caps and floors.

We have two objectives in this chapter.

Swaps versus Eurodollar Strips

The first objective is to show how Eurodollar strips can be made to mimic the behavior of interest rate swaps. Once we have done this, it follows that Eurodollar strips can be used to either hedge or replace interest rate swaps. Swap dealers who lean on the Eurodollar futures market for price protection can make better markets. Asset/liability committees that rely on swaps to control risk or reduce funding costs can improve their performance by using Eurodollar strips when futures prices are better (from the bank's perspective) than swap prices. For that matter, we will find that Eurodollar strips can be used to hedge or replace any borrowing with a term up to four years or so.

Treasuries versus Eurodollar Strips

The second objective is to show how Eurodollar strips can be used to trade the credit spread between Treasury and high-quality private paper. Although Eurodollar strips can be used to hedge Treasury notes, Eurodollar futures rates reflect an aspect of interest rate risk that is missing from Treasuries—that is, the credit spread. As a result, a Eurodollar strip hedge for a Treasury note can perform pretty badly.

The deficiency in the hedge, however, can be turned to the advantage of those who have a view on what the credit spread should be and who want a vehicle for trading that view. The Treasury/Eurodollar strip spread is a popular trade, and we show both how the trade should be constructed and how some potentially large pitfalls in the trade can be avoided.

Hedging Swaps

Because the interest rate risk in our swap is tied to three-month LIBOR, Eurodollar futures provide an excellent vehicle for hedging the price exposure in the swap. The hedge is especially good if the rate reset dates correspond exactly or very closely to the settlement dates for Eurodollar futures.

We have already established in Chapter 2 that the key to calculating a correct hedge ratio is to identify the present value of the effect of a change in rates on the price or value of the instrument to be hedged. The chief lesson of this section is that a hedge's robustness depends on how the hedge is constructed. In particular, we find that all correctly calculated hedges work equally well in the face of parallel shifts in the yield curve and changes in the slope of the yield curve.

Hedging against Parallel Shifts in the Yield Curve

The basic steps for finding the number of Eurodollar futures needed to hedge a swap against a parallel shift in the yield curve are:

- find the change in the net present value of the swap for a one-basis-point increase in each of the rates used to value the swap, that is, in the swap yield and in term LIBOR for the first period;
- divide the answer by $25 to find the number of Eurodollar contracts needed.

Consider, for example, a generic swap that pays a fixed rate of nine percent on a quarterly basis against three-month LIBOR flat (that is, pays a variable rate equal to three-month LIBOR). Suppose also that the modified quarterly swap yield and three-month LIBOR start at nine percent. The effect of a one-basis-point increase in the swap yield on the price of the fixed side of the swap can be calculated by subtracting par from the price of the hypothetical note valued at a rate of 9.01 percent. The effect on the price of the fixed side of the swap would be:

$$PV01 = \left\{ \sum_{i=1}^{4} [(2.25)/(1+.0901/4)^i] + (100)/(1+.0901/4)^4 \right\} - 100$$

where 2.25 is the hypothetical quarterly fixed payment and i [= 1 to 4] represents each of the four quarters in the calculation. Performing the calculation, we find:

   PV01 = 99.990539 - 100

         = - 0.009461

or a decrease in the value of the fixed side of a $100 million swap of $9,461. Similarly, the effect on the floating side of the swap would be:

   PV01 = [102.25/(1.022525)] - 100

         = 99.997555 - 100.00000

         = -$.002445 million

or a decrease in the value of the floating side of a $100 million swap of about $2,445.

The effect of the one-basis-point increase in yields for someone who is long the swap (that is, who pays the fixed rate and receives the floating rate) would be a net gain of $7,016. A long swap is equivalent to a short position in the fixed-rate instrument combined with a long position in the floating-rate note. Because the price of the fixed-rate note falls more than the price of the floating-rate note, the gain on the short fixed-rate note position ($9,461) is greater than the loss on the floating-rate note ($2,445). Whoever is short the swap, of course, would lose $7,016 in the face of the same one-basis-point increase in yields.

To hedge against changes in the value of the swap using Eurodollar futures is now a straightforward exercise. We have found that the net present value of a one-basis-point increase in yields is $7,016. We know also that the present value of a one-basis-point increase in LIBOR rates is $25 per futures contract. Thus, the appropriate hedge ratio would be:

Hedge Ratio = PV01 / $25

= $7,016 / $25

= 280.64 contracts

If you were long this swap, you would buy 281 Eurodollar futures to hedge the price risk. The $7,025 [= 281 × $25] you would lose if three-month LIBOR were to rise one basis point would offset almost exactly your $7,016 gain on the swap.

If you were short the swap, you would sell 281 Eurodollar futures.

At this point, there is a question about how to hold your 281 contracts across contract months. One approach is to "stack" the position, which means to hold all of your position in a single contract month. Another would be to spread the contracts out evenly over three or four contracts months to reflect the one-year maturity of the swap.

Either of these approaches will provide an adequate hedge against parallel shifts in the yield curve. As long as all rates rise or fall by the same amount, the gain or loss on the hedge will just offset the loss or gain on the swap. As we will see in the next section, however, these approaches may not provide adequate protection against a shift in the yield curve in which some forward rates are changing more than others.

Hedging against Any Shift in the Yield Curve

In practice, the value of a swap is more sensitive to changes in nearby short-term forward rates than to changes in distant short-term forward rates. Thus, the robustness of a hedge depends on how the contracts are allocated over contract months.

The basic steps for finding the allocation of Eurodollar futures over contract months that will hedge against any shift in the yield curve are:

- express the net present value of the swap as a function of a strip of spot and forward rates;
- find the change in the net present value of the swap for a one-basis-point change in each of the individual spot and forward rates;
- divide each answer by \$25 to find the number of futures needed in each respective contract month.

Consider the same one-year swap used in the hedging example above. If we break up the swap into its four separate parts, we can write the net present value of a long swap position (that is, long the floating side, short the fixed side) as:

$$[100 \, (1 + R/4) - C'/4] \, / \, (1 + R'/4)$$

$$- (C'/4) \, / \, [(1 + R'/4)(1 + F_1/4)]$$

$$- (C'/4) \, / \, [(1 + R'/4)(1 + F_1/4)(1 + F_2/4)]$$

$$- (100 + C'/4) \, / \, [(1 + R'/4)(1 + F_1/4)(1 + F_2/4)(1 + F_3/4)]$$

where C' is the annualized value of the quarterly fixed payment, R is the value of three-month spot LIBOR used to calculate the first payment on the floating side, R' is the current three-month spot rate, and F_1, F_2, and F_3 are the first, second, and third three-month forward rates.

The first part of the expression represents the present value of the hypothetical floating-rate note less the present value of the first hypothetical quarterly coupon payment. The second and third parts represent the contribution of the second and third hypothetical coupon payments to the value of the swap. The fourth expression completes the equation with the value of the fourth hypothetical coupon together with the repayment of the principal on the hypothetical fixed-rate note.

You need good eyes but no heavy mathematics to see that the value of this swap is more sensitive to changes in some rates than in others.

For example, an increase in the current spot rate, R', has no effect on the net present value of the swap if the nominal value of the floating-rate note equals the nominal value of the fixed-rate note.[2] The intuition behind this is that the current spot rate is used to discount both the long position in the floating-rate note *and* the short position in the fixed-rate note. The two effects are a wash.

In contrast, the forward rates, F_1, F_2, and F_3, appear only in the discount factors for payments associated with the fixed-rate side of the swap. Moreover, we see that F_1 enters all of the remaining expressions, while F_3 serves to discount only the payments on the final date. As a result, we should expect to find that the value of the swap is more sensitive to changes in F_1 than to changes in the more distant forward rates F_2 and F_3.

In fact, this is just what we find. If we calculate the change in the value of our $100 million swap for changes in each of the four rates, we get:

PV01(R')   = $0

PV01(F_1) = $2,393

PV01(F_2) = $2,342

PV01(F_3) = $2,292

---

2. Those who are equipped with calculus and blessed with spare time may want to confirm that the effect of an increase in the floating rate, R', equals $-\{(1/4) \times [1/(1 + R'/4)] \times V\}$ where V equals the net present value of the swap. Most swaps are structured so that little or no money changes hands at the outset. That is, they are structured so that their initial net present values are equal to or close to zero. Some swaps are structured to produce a cash payment from one party to the other at the outset. In these cases, a change in the floating rate would have an effect on the value of the swap.

Note that these total $7,027. The difference between this total change and the $7,016 we calculated above is due partly to rounding and partly to the difference between the behavior of quarterly rates and annual swap yields. A one-basis-point change in each of the four quarterly spot or forward rates should produce a more than one-basis-point increase in an annualized swap yield.

Now we see that the value of the swap is sensitive to only three of the four rates that can vary. Moreover, as we expected, the value of the swap is more sensitive to changes in the nearby forward or futures rate, F_1, than to changes in the more distant forward rates.

Further, to the extent the spot and forward rates move in tandem with spot and forward values of three-month LIBOR, we can now construct a hedge that insulates the value of the swap from any change in the yield curve. All we have to do is find the number of futures that will just offset the sensitivity of the swap to each of the three rate changes.

Because our calculations represent present values, this determination is a simple matter of dividing each calculation by $25, which is the present value of a basis point for a futures contract, irrespective of its maturity or expiration. The number of Eurodollar futures we would need in each of the first, second, and third contract months would be:

$2,393 / $25 = 95.72

$2,342 / $25 = 93.68

$2,292 / $25 = 91.68

which totals 281.08 contracts. This is about what we found when we calculated the hedge for a one-basis-point change in the swap yield accompanied by a one-basis-point change in spot LIBOR for the first leg of the swap.

Stacking versus Simple and Complex Strips

What sets this hedge apart from all others is its robustness in the face of unpredictable changes in the slope of the yield curve. Now the practical hedger is faced with a set of choices about how to hedge the swap. The hedger can:

- stack the hedge by holding all contracts in the same contract month;
- buy or sell simple Eurodollar strips in which the total position is allocated evenly over the relevant contract months;
- construct complex Eurodollar strips using weights dictated by the present value of each basis point in the string of relevant forward or futures rates.

Each of these three approaches, which are illustrated in Exhibit 4.1, has its advantages and drawbacks.

For example, the stacking approach is popular because the lead contract month is highly liquid. Large hedges can be executed in a market where the bid/ask spread is only one basis point. One drawback to stacking is that the position must be rolled from one contract month to the next as the hedge ages and the lead contract approaches expiration. Another drawback is that the hedge works only for parallel shifts in the yield curve and is greatly exposed to the risks of non-parallel shifts.

Simple Eurodollar strips, in which the position is divided evenly over the contract months in the swap's horizon, are comparatively easy to execute, although the back months in the strip tend not to be as liquid as the front months. A distinct advantage of the simple strip is that it requires less tending as the hedge ages. Also, even simple strips are more robust than a stacked hedge in the face of changes in the slope of the yield curve.

A complex strip, in which the numbers of contracts held are dictated by the sensitivity of the swap to each contract month's futures rate, provide complete protection against any change in the slope of the yield curve. Further, once the complex strip is in place, it requires less tinkering than the simple strip. On the other hand, complex strips can be slightly more cumbersome to execute than simple strips.

Exhibit 4.1

Stacking, Simple Strips and Complex Strips

Stacking

In a stacked hedge, all contracts are held in the lead month. This approach works for parallel shifts in the yield curve. The contracts are highly liquid but require quarterly rolling as the hedge ages.

Simple Strips

In a simple strip hedge, the total number of contracts is the same as in the stacked hedge, but the contracts are spread evenly over the contract months in the hedge horizon. Simple strips are fairly easy to execute. The back-month contracts are not as liquid as the lead contract, but the hedge requires less rolling as the hedge ages.

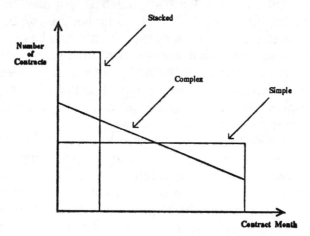

Complex Strips

In a complex strip, each leg of the swap is hedged separately. The total number of contracts is the same as in the stacked and simple strip hedges, but the contracts are weighted according to the present value of a basis point in each leg of the swap. Complex strips are very slightly more difficult to execute than are simple strips, but the hedge requires less tending as the hedge ages.

Rule of Thumb: Hedging the Individual Legs of a Swap

The robust hedges that we have been calculating up to this point assign all of the uncertainty or risk exposure in a swap to changes in the various spot and forward discount rates. While this approach gives solid answers, many people feel more comfortable thinking that the uncertainty in swaps stems from uncertainty about their cash flows.

If we take this approach, we look for hedges against changes in the cash flows rather than against changes in the net present value of the swap. Consider our simple generic swap. The first net cash payment is fixed at the time the deal is struck. The next three net payments depend on realized values of three-month LIBOR. In each case, the nominal value of a basis point change in three-month LIBOR for a $100 million swap is $2,500 if the actual number of days between payments is 90.

The present values of these changes, however, depend on term LIBOR to each payment. The first uncertain payment is made in six months, the second in nine, and the third in twelve. Given the nine percent annual money market rate that we have used in our hedging examples, the values of six-, nine-, and twelve-month LIBOR we would need to discount these nominal cash flows are:

$$R_6 = 100 \times [(1.0225)^2 - 1] \times 2 = 9.101\%$$

$$R_9 = 100 \times [(1.0225)^3 - 1] \times (4/3) = 9.204\%$$

$$R_{12} = 100 \times [(1.0225)^4 - 1] = 9.308\%$$

Given these term LIBOR rates, the present value of a $2,500 change in each of the uncertain cash flows is:

$$PV01(F_1) = \$2,500 / [1+(.09101/2)] = \$2,391$$

$$PV01(F_2) = \$2,500 / [1+(.09204 \times 3/4)] = \$2,339$$

$$PV01(F_3) = \$2,500 / (1+.09308) = \$2,287$$

At \$25 per basis point for each of the futures contracts involved, the number of each contract required would be:

Lead contract   = \$2,391 / \$25 = 95.64

First deferred   = \$2,339 / \$25 = 93.56

Second deferred = \$2,287 / \$25 = 91.48

which totals 280.68 contracts, nearly the same number we obtained with the full-blown discounting method outlined earlier.

Hedge Mismatches and Hedge Management

In practice, swaps do not conform neatly to the expiration cycle for Eurodollar futures. Although the volume of so-called IMM[3] swaps (that is, those tied to futures expiration dates) is not trivial, the bulk of the swap trade is done with reset dates that fall at three-month or six-month intervals after the trade date. Further, although three-month LIBOR is the floating-rate index for many swaps, other short-term rates, including six-month LIBOR, are used widely as well.

As a result, the practical hedger must deal with two kinds of mismatches:

- reset dates versus futures expirations;
- floating index versus three-month LIBOR.

In both cases, the challenge is to find the best Eurodollar match for the actual swap.

Reset Date Mismatch

Examples of the two most common date mismatch problems are shown in Exhibit 4.2.

---

3. IMM stands for the International Money Market, which is a division of the Chicago Mercantile Exchange and is the market in which Eurodollar futures are traded. In some circles, Eurodollar futures are known simply as the IMMs.

Exhibit 4.2

Reset Date Mismatches

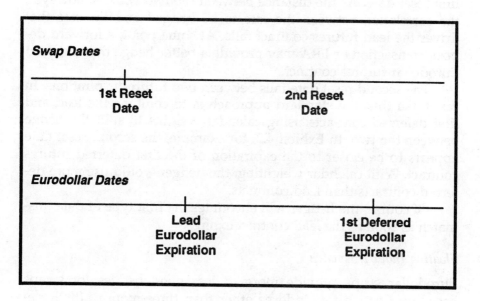

The first reset date on the swap falls before the expiration of the lead Eurodollar futures contract. The problem is that forward LIBOR for the reset date likely will not move in tandem with forward LIBOR for the lead Eurodollar futures expiration.

In this situation, the hedger has two choices, or at least some combination of the two. If the two dates are not very far apart, then the lead contract may well provide a good cross hedge for the first reset date. As the distance between the two widens, however, the correlation between the rate to be hedged and the rate that drives the lead futures contract falls. At some point, a forward deposit transaction or FRA may provide a better hedge than the lead Eurodollar futures contract.

The second reset date falls between two futures expirations. In cases like this, the standard approach is to combine the lead and first deferred contracts using calendar weights to split the hedge between the two. In Exhibit 4.2, for example, the second reset date appears to be closer to the expiration of the first deferred futures contract. With calendar weighting, the hedger would use more deferred contracts than lead contracts.

Of course, the hedger will encounter the first type of date mismatch as soon as the lead contract expires.

Floating Index Mismatch

Eurodollar strips provide more or less good hedges for swaps based on floating-rate indexes other than three-month LIBOR depending on how closely related the rates are. For example, matching six-month LIBOR with Eurodollar futures is comparatively easy because six-month forward rates are forced to conform through arbitrage to the structure of three-month forward rates. Similarly, because LIBOR is a good proxy for a wide range of other private three-month rates (e.g., bankers' acceptances and commercial paper), Eurodollar hedges for swaps involving these indexes can work well, too.

Eurodollar strip hedges can be unreliable hedges for swaps involving highly idiosyncratic rates such as prime or fed funds. The prime rate, for example, is an oddball in the interest rate universe, jumping rather than inching to new levels when a change is required. Thus, even though prime is fairly well related to three-month LIBOR over large swings in rates, the amount of random noise in the spread can dominate the relationship for small rate changes.

Managing a Hedge

Hedges are not static. The rate sensitivity of the swap varies both with the level of rates and with the passing of time. Most fixed-rate instruments, which swaps resemble, exhibit what is called "positive convexity," which means that their prices become more sensitive to yield changes as yields fall and less sensitive to yield changes as yields rise. Because the dollar value of a basis point for a Eurodollar futures contract is $25 no matter what the level of yields, a change in yields may require a change in the size of the hedge position.

Also, the rate sensitivity of a swap varies as it ages. This can be seen in Exhibit 4.3, which shows hedge calculations for a two-year swap at different times. At the outset of the swap, the hedger needs 642 Eurodollar futures. Of these, 97 are in the lead month, 95 in the first deferred month, and so on.

One month later, the number of futures needed to hedge the swap has risen to 650. The reason is that the present value of a basis point change in yields has risen as the reset dates have drawn closer. Recall from Chapter 2 that this is what happened in the problem of locking the cost of funds.

Three months later, however, we find that the number of futures needed to hedge the swap has fallen to 555. This reflects the passing of the first reset date, which contributed the equivalent of roughly 100 Eurodollar futures to the riskiness of the swap. Once this source of uncertainty is gone, the remainder of the swap is less sensitive to rate changes than it was, even at the outset of the swap.

Trading Treasury/Eurodollar Strip Spreads

For the private sector, interest rate risk can be broken down into four categories:

Exhibit 4.3

Effect of Time Passing on a Swap Hedge
(Hedge Ratios for a $100 million 2-Year Swap)

Payment	Nominal Value of an .01	Present Value of an .01 [1]			Hedge Ratio (Number of Eurodollar Futures)			Current Month (Initial Hedge)
		Initial	After 2 Months	After 3 Months	Initial	After 2 Months	After 3 Months	
1	0	0	0	0	0	0	0	—
2	2527.78[2]	2425.98	2458.62	0.00	97	98	0	Lead
3	2527.78	2378.10	2409.45	2425.98	95	96	97	1st Deferred
4	2527.78	2332.07	2362.21	2378.10	93	94	95	2nd Deferred
5	2527.78	2286.60	2318.02	2332.07	91	93	93	3rd Deferred
6	2527.78	2240.55	2270.71	2286.60	90	91	93	4th Deferred
7	2527.78	2196.32	2225.28	2240.55	88	89	90	5th Deferred
8	2527.78	2153.80	2181.65	2196.32	86	87	88	6th Deferred
Total	17694.46	16013.52	16225.94	13859.62	640	648	554	

[1] Assumes flat spot yield curve with LIBOR = 8.30

[2] Equals zero after 3 months

• DISCOUNT CORPORATION OF NEW YORK FUTURES •

- uncertainty about the general level of interest rates;
- uncertainty about the slope of the yield curve;
- uncertainty about the credit spread between high-quality private paper and Treasury instruments; and
- uncertainty about the individual borrower's credit worthiness.

Of the four, the first can be hedged or traded with Treasury bills, notes, and bonds as well as with their associated futures contracts. The third is hard to hedge or trade at all.

The spread over Treasuries that a high-quality borrower must pay lenders to compensate for so-called credit risk is embedded in the yield on an interest rate swap or in a Eurodollar strip rate. For that matter, swap yields are often quoted as the corresponding Treasury rate plus a spread.

Because swap yields and strip rates reflect the combined value of general interest rate levels *and* the credit spread, while Treasury notes reflect only the general interest rate level, swaps and strips can be pretty bad hedges for Treasury securities. Just how much basis risk there might be in cross-hedging swaps with Treasuries is shown in Exhibit 4.4, which charts the credit spread from the beginning of 1988 through June 1990.

The flaw in hedging Treasuries with swaps or strips turns to an advantage, however, for those who have a position on what the credit spread should be. For those who think the credit spread is too small and will widen, a position that is long Treasury notes and either long interest rate swaps or short Eurodollar strips will produce a profit if the credit spread does in fact widen and if the trade is correctly constructed. If Treasury note yields fall more than swap yields or strip rates, gains on the long note position will exceed losses on the short swap or strip position. If Treasury note yields fall, while swap yields or strip rates rise, both legs of the trade will profit. If Treasury note yields rise less than swap yields or strip rates, the losses on the Treasury note position will be more than offset by the gains on the swap or strip.

Similarly, for those who think the credit spread is too large and expect it to narrow, the position can be reversed.

Exhibit 4.4

2-Year Eurodollar Futures Strip — 2-Year Constant Maturity Yield
(Period: January 4, 1988 to November 19, 1990)

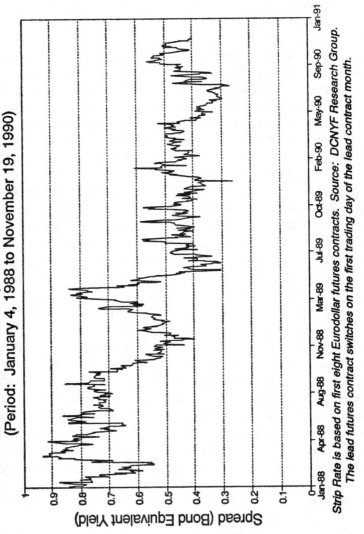

Strip Rate is based on first eight Eurodollar futures contracts. Source: DCNYF Research Group.
The lead futures contract switches on the first trading day of the lead contract month.

To trade the spread effectively requires a clear notion of how the credit spread is measured and how the trade should be constructed to get what one wants out of the trade.

Measuring the Conventional Credit Spread

The conventional measure of the credit spread is the number of basis points over Treasuries needed to produce an equivalent swap yield. Under this convention, the credit spread is quoted in semiannual bond equivalent basis points—that is, on the same basis as the corresponding note yield.

Finding the conventional measure of the credit spread in the swap market is easy because the spread often is quoted as part of the swap yield. For example, Telerate pages 314, 883, and 6492 (among others) show quotes for swaps with maturities ranging from two to ten years as the corresponding Treasury rate (T) plus a spread in semiannual bond equivalent basis points. As shown in Exhibit 2.1 (Chapter 2), the credit spread in a two-year swap was bid at 56 basis points over the two-year Treasury rate and was offered at 60 basis points over. These quotes meant that whoever was making the market would:

- pay 56 basis points over Treasuries fixed to receive LIBOR floating; or
- receive 60 basis points over the two-year Treasury rate to pay LIBOR floating.

Finding the credit spread between Eurodollar strip rates and Treasury yields requires two steps:

- Calculate the annual money market rate for a strip of Eurodollars with an investment horizon equal to the maturity of the note. For example, a two-year strip rate would be needed to compare with the yield on a two-year Treasury note.
- Given the strip rate, calculate the credit spread on a semiannual bond equivalent basis.

For example, with two-month LIBOR at 8-5/16, and the first eight futures rates at:

$$F_1 = 8.31 \quad [= 100 - 91.69]$$
$$F_2 = 8.35 \quad [= 100 - 91.65]$$
$$F_3 = 8.41 \quad [= 100 - 91.59]$$
$$F_4 = 8.63 \quad [= 100 - 91.37]$$
$$F_5 = 8.69 \quad [= 100 - 91.31]$$
$$F_6 = 8.76 \quad [= 100 - 91.24]$$
$$F_7 = 8.79 \quad [= 100 - 91.21]$$
$$F_8 = 8.84 \quad [= 100 - 91.16]$$

the two-year strip rate from January 22, 1990 to January 21, 1992 was 8.85 percent.

At the same time, two-year Treasuries were yielding 8.16 percent at the mid-point of the bid and offer. One way of stating the relationship between a strip yield, Treasury yield, and the credit spread on a semiannual bond equivalent yield basis is:

$$R = \{[1 + (T+S)/2]^2 - 1\} \times (360/365)$$

Given this relationship, $S = 62$ basis points if $R = 8.85$ percent and $T = 8.16$ percent.

Note that here, the Eurodollar strip spread over Treasuries is larger by a few basis points than in the swap market. The difference likely is not large enough to warrant an arbitrage transaction, but might be large enough to induce the trader to buy Eurodollar strips rather than selling an interest rate swap.

Sensitivity to Yield Curve Slope

One nettlesome feature of the conventional measure of the credit spread is that it is sensitive to changes in the slope of the yield curve. A steepening of the yield curve will tend to widen the spread. An inversion of the yield curve will tend to narrow the spread. The following example shows why.

Three LIBOR settings are shown in Exhibit 4.5. In the first, all three-month spot and forward rates extending out to four years are nine percent. In the second, all of the first-year three-month

Exhibit 4.5

Treasury/Eurodollar Strip Spreads

	Yield Curve Slope		
	Flat	Positive	Negative
Forward Rates			
Year 1	9	8	11
Year 2	9	9	10
Year 3	9	10	9
Year 4	9	11	8
Strip Rate	9.18	9.71	9.71
Strip Rate (BEY)	9.10	9.61	9.61
Note Yield	8.00	8.41	8.61
Spread (b.p.)			
Quarterly	108	108	108
Conventional	110	120	100
Note price	100	98.65	97.98

rates are eight percent, all of the second-year three-month rates are nine percent, and so forth. In the third case, the yield curve is inverted, and all of the first-year rates are 11 percent, while all of the fourth-year rates are eight percent.

Note that the Eurodollar strip rate in the first case is 9.18 percent, which reflects the effect of quarterly compounding. Note also that the strip rate in both the second and third cases is 9.71 percent. The rates are the same because strip yield calculations give equal weight, except for slight differences in day counts, to each of the rates in the strip. It doesn't matter, then, whether the yield curve is steep, flat, inverted, or saw-toothed. If the same rates show up the same number of times in two strip-rate calculations, the strip rates will be the same.

For each of these LIBOR settings, we calculated four-year Treasury note yields as follows:

- We subtracted a "pure" credit spread equal to 108 quarterly basis points from each three-month spot or forward LIBOR. This pure credit spread, which we label the quarterly spread, is held constant throughout this exercise.

- Next, we calculated the price of an eight-percent coupon, four-year Treasury note using quarterly three-month spot and forward Treasury rates obtained in the first step. In the first case, for example, all of these quarterly Treasury rates are 7.92 percent. Observe that the note's price is 100 and that its yield on a semiannual bond equivalent basis is eight percent.

- We then calculated the conventional credit spread using the standard conversion formula.

The results of the exercise are striking. In the first case, the conventional spread is 110 basis points, which is almost exactly the same as the "pure" quarterly spread of 108 basis points. The second and third cases, however, produce quite different results. In both cases, the four-year Eurodollar strip rate is 9.71 percent (9.61 percent bond equivalent yield), but the conventional credit spread is 120 basis points for the positively sloped yield curve and only 100 basis points for the negatively sloped curve.

We should have expected results like these. When hedging interest rate swaps, we found that the value of the swap was more sensitive to changes in nearby rates than in deferred rates. Now we find that the same is true for Treasury notes. Raising the fourth-year forward rates to eleven percent while lowering the first-year rates to eight percent reduced the price of our hypothetical eight-percent Treasury note to 98.65. Its yield rose to 8.41 percent. In contrast, raising the first-year rates to eleven percent while lowering the fourth-year rates to eight percent reduced the price to 97.98 and raised its yield to 8.61 percent.

The example makes it clear that Treasury notes are much like swaps in that their prices are more sensitive to changes in nearby forward rates than to changes in distant forward rates. It is this differential sensitivity to rate changes that makes the Treasury/Eurodollar strip spread—as conventionally measured—sensitive to changes in the slope of the yield curve.

This discovery has important implications for trading the Treasury/Eurodollar strip spread.

Trading the Spread

In principle, the credit spread can be traded either with interest rate swaps against Treasuries or with Eurodollar strips against Treasuries. As a practical matter, however, swaps are extraordinarily costly to trade, both in terms of bid/ask spreads and in terms of brokerage.

The costs of trading Eurodollar strips, which can be done with maturities running out to four years, are comparatively low. As a result, the Treasury/Eurodollar strip spread has become a popular trade.

Constructing the Trade

How you approach the trade depends on your objective. We now know that the credit spread as conventionally measured depends both on credit *and* on the slope of the yield curve. Even so, if your objective is to profit from a widening or narrowing of the spread *as conventionally measured*, the correct approach is to buy or sell equally weighted Eurodollar strips against the Treasury position.

If, on the other hand, your objective is to profit from a widening or narrowing of the credit spread, irrespective of the slope of the yield curve, the correct approach is to buy or sell Eurodollar strips that are weighted according to the sensitivity of the Treasury note to changes in each of the Eurodollar futures rates.

The following example illustrates this point.

Suppose that the current interest rate setting is described by the second column of Exhibit 4.5. The LIBOR spot and forward yield curve is positively sloped from eight percent in the first year to eleven percent in the fourth year. The pure quarterly credit spread is 108 basis points, and the conventionally measured credit spread is 121 basis points.

Suppose, too, that you think the conventionally measured credit spread is too narrow and will widen. To trade this spread, you should buy four-year Treasury notes and sell Eurodollar futures against them.

For example, suppose you buy $100 million of a four-year, eight-percent coupon Treasury note. The total dollar value of a basis point for this position is $34,075. At $25 per basis point for a Eurodollar futures contract, you need to sell 1,363 [= $34,075/$25] Eurodollar futures contracts.

How do you distribute the trade over the available contract months?

Two possible Eurodollar strip positions, both calculated just before the expiration of the lead futures contract, are shown in Exhibit 4.6. The first is weighted according to the sensitivity of the note price to each futures rate. (If you are puzzled by the identical weights for pairs of contract months, keep in mind that Treasury coupons are paid semiannually.) The second is a simple unweighted strip. In both cases, the total number of contracts shorted is 1,363. The P/L columns show how each position responds to the yield curve inversion that increases first year rates from eight to eleven percent and decreases fourth year rates from eleven to eight percent.

Trade Performance

The results of the two trades are compared in Exhibit 4.7 for two different outcomes. In one, the pure quarterly credit spread re-

Exhibit 4.6

Eurodollar Hedge P/L for Yield Curve Inversion

Quarter	Weighted Strips	Unweighted Strips	Weighted Hedge P/L (basis points)	Unweighted Hedge P/L (basis points)
1	99	86	742.5	645
2	98	86	735	645
3	94	86	705	645
4	94	85	705	637.5
5	90	85	225	212.5
6	90	85	225	212.5
7	87	85	217.5	212.5
8	87	85	217.5	212.5
9	83	85	-207.5	-212.5
10	83	85	-207.5	-212.5
11	80	85	-200	-212.5
12	80	85	-200	-212.5
13	76	85	-570	-637.5
14	76	85	-570	-637.5
15	73	85	-547.5	-637.5
16	73	85	-547.5	-637.5
Total	1363	1363	722.5	22.5

Exhibit 4.7

Trade Results with Immediate Yield Curve Inversion

Credit Spread Summary

Case	Quarterly Spread		Treasury Note		Conventional Spread	
	Level	Change (basis points)	Price	Yield	Level	Change (basis points)
I	108	0	97.98	8.41	100	-21
II	118	+10	98.32	8.51	111	-10

P/L Comparison

	Weighted Trade		Unweighted Trade	
	Spread Change		Spread Change	
P/L From	0	+10	0	+10
Long Treasuries	-670.0	-330.0	-670.0	-330.0
Short Eurodollar Strip	+722.5	+722.5	+22.5	+22.5
Net	+52.5	+392.5	-647.5	-307.5

mains unchanged at 108 quarterly basis points. In the other, the pure quarterly credit spread increases to 118 quarterly basis points. In both outcomes, the spot and forward LIBOR curve inverts so that first-year rates are now eleven percent while fourth year rates are now eight percent.

Before comparing the trade results, however, consider the effect of each outcome on the conventional Treasury/Eurodollar strip spread. The inversion of the yield curve with no widening of the quarterly credit spread produced a 20-basis-point reduction in the conventional credit spread. The inversion of the yield curve with a 10-basis-point widening of the quarterly credit spread produced a 10-basis-point reduction in the conventional credit spread.

Given the ways we have constructed our trades, we should expect the following outcomes:

- The trade with the weighted Eurodollar strips should show no gain or loss if there is no change in the quarterly credit spread and should make money if the quarterly spread widens.

- The trade with the unweighted Eurodollar strips should lose money if the conventionally measured credit spread narrows.

What we find in Exhibit 4.7 conforms fairly well to these expectations.

The loss on the Treasury note position is roughly offset by the gain on the weighted Eurodollar strip position when there was no change in the quarterly credit spread. (The small net gain in this case reflects small changes in appropriate hedge ratios for a change in yields as large as we are considering here.) Further, the weighted trade made money when the quarterly credit spread widened.

The unweighted trade lost money in both cases, as it should have in the face of a decrease in the credit spread as it is usually measured. Moreover, the amount of money lost is roughly in line with the dollar value of a basis point change in the credit spread.

Reading Credit Spread Charts: A Reminder

Knowing that the spread between Treasury note yields and Euro-dollar strip rates depends on the slope of the yield curve should affect the way a trader looks at a charting of the spread's history. While it is possible to make ad hoc adjustments in the mind's eye for steepening and flattening of the yield curve, the safe route is to calculate the credit spread correctly and to construct any spread trades correctly as well.

CHAPTER 5

Caps, Floors, Collars, and Eurodollar Options

Interest-rate caps began as interest rate guaranties that were bundled together with conventional bank loan agreements. As the business grew, LIBOR became the most widely used reference rate, and the cap parts of the loan agreements occasionally were stripped away and traded as separate items. Today, caps—as well as floors and collars—are bought and sold over the counter as free-standing LIBOR options.[1]

---

1. This chapter and the next presuppose a basic familiarity with option concepts and the use of option pricing models, although much of the substance of these chapters may be accessible to readers who are willing to suspend judgement and take our word on several key points. For those who wish to learn more about option pricing and risk characteristics, we highly recommend our own Options Schools, which are offered regularly throughout the year in Chicago, Hong Kong, London, New York, Singapore, and Tokyo. For the armchair traveller, we recommend Bookstaber's *Option Pricing and Investment Strategies* (Probus, 1987), which contains one of the best practical discussions of option hedging that we have found.

Our goal in this chapter is to lay the groundwork for showing how Eurodollar options and futures can be used to hedge the risk exposure in interest-rate caps and floors. To do this, we will identify the similarities and differences between caps and floors on the one hand and Eurodollar options on the other. In particular, we will show that an interest-rate cap is very much (but not exactly) like a put option on Eurodollar futures. By the same token, we will show that an interest-rate floor is very much like a call option on Eurodollar futures.

We will show how caps and floors can be priced and how their prices respond to:

- changes in the level of interest rates;
- changes in the market's perceptions of interest rate volatility; and
- the passing of time.

Because caps and floors are options, we introduce the standard "Greek alphabet" of option terminology when we explain these effects. The names that option traders give these effects are:

- Delta, which measures the responsiveness of the option's price to a change in the price of the underlying commodity;
- Gamma, which measures the responsiveness of the option's *delta* to changes in the underlying's price. That is, gamma measures the changes in the option's price responsiveness that accompany changes in the underlying's price;
- Zeta (a.k.a. Vega), which measures the responsiveness of the option's price to changes in the market's perceptions about the volatility of the underlying's price; and
- Theta, also known as "time decay," which measures the rate at which an option's price falls as it approaches expiration.

Along the way, we will also show how caps and floors can be combined with floating-rate financing to produce limited risk financing strategies. More advanced strategies are provided in Chapter 8.

An important key to understanding the attractiveness of an option to its holder is that the option represents a right rather than an obligation. For example, a call option gives its holder the right to buy the underlying at a set price within a set span of time. If the market price of the underlying is above the option's exercise or strike price, the option has exercise value and is said to be in the money. If the market price of the underlying is below the call option's exercise or strike price, the option has no exercise value and is said to be out of the money. This arrangement produces an asymmetrical profit-and-loss picture. The option can never be worth less than zero (not counting what was paid for it in the first place); however, at least in the case of a call option, there is no upper limit to how much the option can be worth if it finishes in the money.

The principles are the same but the payoffs are reversed for the holder of a put option, which endows the holder with the right but not the obligation to sell the underlying at a set price within a set time. If the market price of the underlying is below the put's exercise or strike price, the put is said to be in the money. If the market price of the underlying is above the put's strike price, the put is said to be out of the money. As with a call option, a put option can never be worth less than zero. The upper limit on an in-the-money put's value is determined by any limit (for example, zero) on how far the price of the underlying can fall.

The Popularity of Caps

Caps trading is big business. The International Swap Dealers Association (ISDA) reported that roughly $260 billion (notional principal amount) worth of caps, floors, and collars changed hands in 1989. At the end of 1989, the total outstanding value of these various over-the-counter interest rate guaranties was just under $500 billion.

Trading in Eurodollar options, which are the exchange-traded counterparts of caps, floors, and collars, is big business as well. In 1989, six million Eurodollar options were traded on the Chicago Mercantile Exchange (CME). At $1 million notional principal amount per contract, this volume translates into $6 trillion of interest rate guaranties. The outstanding open interest was just over 240 thousand contracts, which translates into a notional principal amount of $240 billion.

The popularity of caps and floors stems from the rich variety of financing structures that they provide. For one thing, many corporate treasurers prefer the risk/reward structure that options provide. In many cases, floating-rate financing combined with insurance against adverse rate moves looks much better than fixed-rate financing. For a fixed price, a cap allows the borrower to take advantage of favorable rate moves while limiting the damage done by an extreme rise in rates. By the same token, an interest-rate floor provides downside rate protection for investors.

Perhaps the most clearly identifiable source of demand for caps was the leveraged buyout market during the mergers and acquisitions frenzy of the late 1980s. Deals financed with floating-rate debt often were required to buy protection against a rise in interest rates. The RJR/Nabisco transaction alone may have accounted for more than $20 billion of caps in 1989.

As with any options, there is no real limit to the ways they can be combined with one another or with their underlying commodity to produce useful payoff structures. An interest-rate floor can be sold to defray the cost of an interest-rate cap. The resulting position is known as a collar. A collar with the same strike or exercise rate for both the cap and the floor behaves like an interest-rate swap and at one time could be used in lieu of swaps to reduce regulatory capital requirements. The cost of a cap can also be reduced by writing a higher strike cap against it. This position, known as a corridor, limits the payoff to the range of rates between the two strikes.

Caps, Floors, and Eurodollar Options

Because LIBOR is the dominant reference rate for these options, Eurodollar options are highly effective tools for either replacing or hedging the risk in caps, floors, and collars. In particular, an interest-rate cap is nearly but not quite the same as a Eurodollar put. An interest-rate floor is roughly the same as a Eurodollar call. A collar is much like a long Eurodollar put combined with a short Eurodollar call.

This chapter focuses on the relationship between caps and floors, which are traded over the counter, and Eurodollar puts and calls, which are traded mainly at the CME. We begin by showing:

- how a cap is structured;
- how to price a cap; and
- how to compare a cap's price and various risk characteristics (i.e., delta, gamma, zeta, and theta) with those of a Eurodollar put.

The lessons learned for caps relate directly to floors and collars.
    Chapter 6 will deal with hedging caps, floors, and collars.

Basic Features of Interest-Rate Caps

An interest-rate cap is like an interest-rate call option. The holder of the cap pays a premium to the writer of the cap. In exchange, the holder is paid money if the underlying interest rate turns out to be higher than the cap, or exercise, rate. If the interest rate turns out to be lower than the cap rate, the holder gets nothing.

An interest-rate cap, then, has all the important features of an option. It has:

- a principal or notional amount;
- an underlying commodity price (actually an underlying interest rate);
- an exercise or strike price (which is really an exercise or strike rate); and
- an expiration date.

In practice, most interest-rate caps are European-style options, which means that they can be exercised only at expiration. Also, caps frequently are traded in strips, which means that a cap may involve a sequence of expiration dates.

An example of a two-year cap rate agreement struck on May 1, 1989 is outlined in Exhibit 5.1. The notional amount of the cap is $100 million. The underlying rate is three-month LIBOR, and the cap rate is nine percent. The settlement or expiration dates range from August 1, 1989 to February 1, 1991. We assume that the rate used to calculate any payment covering the first three months, from May to August 1989, is already known. If so, this two-year cap agreement really comprises a strip of seven rather than eight separate three-month options. In practice, cap traders ignore the first period.

Pricing an Interest-Rate Cap

Interest-rate caps are traded over the counter and are designed to conform, for the most part, to deposit and interest-rate swap settlement conventions. Thus, most caps:

- are European-style options with payoffs determined only at specific settlement or expiration dates;
- determine the size of payoffs using normal money market day count conventions (i.e., actual/360); and
- make payments in arrears (i.e., at the end rather than at the beginning of the settlement period).

The first step in pricing a cap is to break it down into its components. The price of the entire cap is simply the sum of the prices of its individual parts.

The second step is to price each component. How this is done varies from bank to bank. As one would expect, the amount of care that is taken depends largely on how costly it is to not have a good notion of the right price. This is all the more important because caps can have horizons of several years, and the challenges in modelling interest rate volatility over extended periods are formidable.

Exhibit 5.1

CAP Description

Principal Amount	$100 million
Market Index	Three-Month LIBOR
Cap Rate	Nine Percent
Settlement Dates	Quarterly
Period of Agreement	May 1, 1989 - April 30, 1991*

* *First settlement date, August 1, 1989*
First payment date, November 1, 1989
Last settlement date, February 1, 1991
Last payment date, May 1, 1991

Treating Caps as European-Style Eurodollar Puts

We treat the individual legs of a LIBOR-based cap as if they were European-style puts on Eurodollar futures, with an adjustment to accommodate the payment in arrears and the actual/360 day count feature in a cap. By the same token, we treat the separate legs of a LIBOR-based floor as if they were European-style Eurodollar calls. We take this approach in part because it is easy and in part because this is how short-dated caps and floors are handled by a large segment of the market.

To see why a cap is like a Eurodollar put, consider the basic contract terms (Exhibit 5.2) for Eurodollar options, which are traded on the CME. These options are structured so that:

- The holder of a Eurodollar call receives a Eurodollar futures contract if the call is exercised. The holder of a Eurodollar put delivers a Eurodollar futures contract if the put is exercised;

- The Eurodollar futures price is 100 less three-month LIBOR at expiration, where LIBOR is determined by CME surveys of banks in London just before and at the close of trading in the expiring option, which happens at 9:30 a.m. in Chicago.[2]

The resemblance between a three-month LIBOR cap and a Eurodollar put option is illustrated in Exhibit 5.3. In this illustration, we suppose that both options expire at the same time and that the put's strike price is equal to 100 less the cap rate.

Given these simplifying assumptions, we can see that the cap and the Eurodollar put pay off under exactly the same circumstances. If three-month LIBOR at the settlement date of the cap is less than the cap rate, the holder of the cap gets nothing. Of course, if LIBOR is below the cap rate, the Eurodollar futures price will be above the put's strike price, and the put will be worth nothing as well.

---

2. In-the-money Eurodollar options are exercised automatically at expiration and the resulting futures position is marked to market at the final settlement price determined by the CME. For all practical purposes, then, Eurodollar options are cash settled to the CME's final settlement price, with variation margin equal to the option's in-the-money value paid from the short to the long.

Exhibit 5.2

Key Contract Terms for the Chicago Mercantile Exchange's Options on Eurodollar Futures

TERM	Eurodollars
Unit of trading	One Eurodollar futures contract
Tick size	.01
Tick value	$25.00
Delivery months	March, June, September, December
Daily price limit	None
Trading hours (Chicago time)	7:20 a.m. to 2:00 p.m. (Chicago time) 7:20 a.m. to 9:30 a.m. for expiring contract on last trading day
Last trading day	Second London business day before 3rd Wednesday of contract month

• DISCOUNT CORPORATION OF NEW YORK FUTURES •

Exhibit 5.3

Comparing a One-Period Cap on 3-Month LIBOR
with a Put Option on Eurodollar Futures
(Put Strike Price = 100 - Cap Rate)

3-Month Libor at Settlement/Expiration	Value to Put Holder at Expiration	Payment to Cap Holder in Arrears
LIBOR ≤ Cap Rate Futures ≥ Strike Price	0	0
 LIBOR > Cap Rate Futures < Strike Price	Number of Puts Held x (Number of basis points) in the money) x $25	Principal Value x (Reference Rate - Cap Rate) x (Days/360)

On the other hand, if three-month LIBOR is above the cap rate, the holder of the cap receives a cash payment from the seller of the cap. At the same time, if LIBOR is above the cap rate, the Eurodollar futures price will be below the strike price by the same amount that LIBOR exceeds the cap rate, and the put will have value at expiration.

Consider a $1 million, one-period, nine percent cap on three-month LIBOR and a Eurodollar put with a strike price of 91 [= 100 - 9]. As shown in Exhibit 5.4, if three-month LIBOR is eight percent at settlement (expiration in the case of the put), both the cap and the put are worthless. The cap's reference rate is less than the cap rate, and the Eurodollar futures price [92 = 100 - 8] is higher than the put's strike price. Even if three-month LIBOR is nine percent at settlement, neither option has any value at expiration.

If three-month LIBOR is 10 percent at settlement, however, both options have value. The put holder's value comes in the form of an asset whose final market value is equal to $2,500, which is the product of the 100 basis points that the option is in the money and the $25 per basis point (or "tick") set by the CME. The put holder can take that value either by selling the put at expiration, or allowing the put to be exercised automatically and taking a final marking-to-market payment of $2,500 in the form of variation margin.

The cap holder's value comes in the form of a cash payment at the end of the payment period, which in this example is 92 days after the cap's settlement or expiration date. With a principal value of $1 million, the actual cash payment at the end of the 92-day payment period would be $2,555.56.

Thus, except for the day count convention used to calculate the cap payment and the lag in the payment to the cap holder, the cap is worth about the same as the put.

Combining Caps with Floating-Rate Financing

Part of the popularity of caps is that they provide insurance against rising interest rates. How this works is shown in Exhibit 5.5. The upper panel shows the payoff to a long nine percent cap. For rates below nine percent, the buyer of the cap gives up the full

Exhibit 5.4

Comparing a $1 Million, One-Period 9% Cap on 3-Month LIBOR with a 91 Eurodollar Put

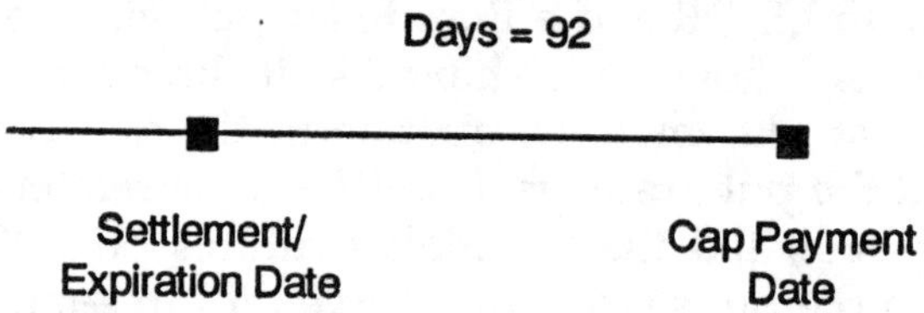

Days = 92

```
■────────────────────────────────■
```

Settlement/   Cap Payment
Expiration Date   Date

At Settlement/ Expiration	At Expiration	At Cap Payment Date
Case 1 3-Month LIBOR = 8%	Put Value = 0	Cap Payment = 0
Case 2 3-Month LIBOR = 9%	Put Value = 0	Cap Payment = 0
Case 3 3-Month LIBOR = 10%	Put Value = 100 x $25 = $2500	Cap Payment = $1 million x (.10 - .09) x (92/360) = $2555.56

Exhibit 5.5

Combining a 9% Cap with Floating-Rate Financing

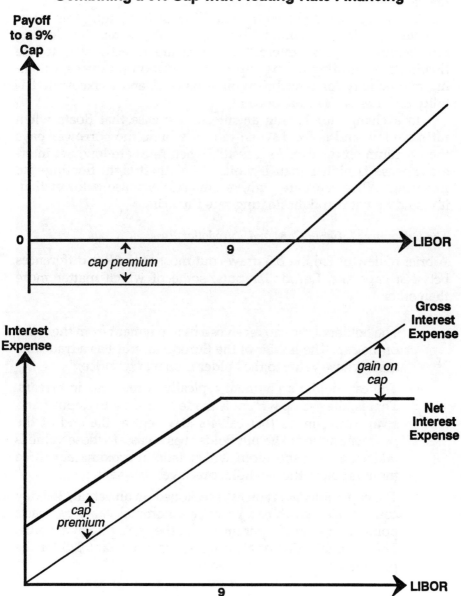

premium. As rates rise above nine percent, the buyer begins to recover the premium. If rates rise far enough, the buyer of the cap makes money.

The lower panel shows the net effect of combining this interest-rate cap with conventional floating-rate financing. The floating rate borrower's gross interest expenses are directly tied to the floating rate. Adding a long cap to this position produces a floating-rate liability for rates below nine percent, and a fixed-rate liability for rates above nine percent.

In exchange for having an interest expense that floats when rates are low and is fixed when rates are high, the borrower pays the premium on the cap. As a result, when rates are low, net interest expense is higher than it would be with straight floating-rate financing. When rates are high, net interest expense is lower than it would be with straight floating-rate financing.

The Differences between Caps and Eurodollar Puts

A brief review of Exhibit 5.3 draws out most of the key differences between caps and Eurodollar puts, some of which matter more than others:

- The holder of the cap receives a cash payment from the seller of the cap. The holder of the Eurodollar put has a tradeable asset whose value to the holder is its market price;

- The cap holder's payment typically is received in arrears. That is, the cash payment is made according to deposit and swap conventions that call for payment at the end of the payment period. The put holder has an asset whose value is taken out at expiration, which falls approximately three months before the cap holder receives payment;

- The cap holder's payment is reckoned on an actual/360 day count basis, which can produce a nominal value per basis point other than $25 per million of the cap's principal value. The nominal value of a basis point is a constant $25 for the put holder.

How to Compare Cap and Eurodollar Put Prices

Just how much these various features of an interest-rate cap affect the cap's price is illustrated in Exhibit 5.6, which shows the price per $1 million notional value of the separate legs of the two-year, nine percent cap described in Exhibit 5.1. To price the cap, we have assumed that spot and forward three-month LIBOR are 8.5 percent so that the cap is 50 basis points out of the money. Also, we have assumed that implied volatility is a constant 15 percent throughout.

The first step in the exercise was to price the separate legs as if they were Eurodollar puts. To make our point, we have priced both American-style and European-style puts. The results are shown in columns (3) and (4). Note that the American-style options, which can be exercised early, tend to be the more valuable of the two.

The second step was to account for the actual/360 day count and the payment in arrears. The effects of these two conventions are shown separately in columns (5) and (6). Because the number of days in a settlement period tends to be greater than 90, the use of the actual/360 day count convention for calculating the cap payment tends to increase the value of the option. The payment in arrears tends to decrease the value of the option by reducing the present value of the payment.

In most instances, the combined effect of these two adjustments is nearly a wash. The combined factor, shown in column (7), is barely different from 1.0. The exception in our example is the leg for which the actual number of days is 89. In this case, both the day count convention and the payment in arrears conspire to reduce the value of the cap. The size of the effect is not very big, however. The difference between the price of the European-style put (28 quarterly basis points) and the price of the cap (27 quarterly basis points) is only one basis point.

Total Price

In practice, Eurodollar option prices are quoted in basis points that are worth $25 each. Cap prices are quoted as a percent of the cap's notional principal value.

Exhibit 5.6

Price of a $1 Million, 2-Year, 9% Cap on 3-Month LIBOR
(Spot, Forward LIBOR = 8.5%)

Settlement (Expiration) Date	Days to Settlement Dates	Days Between Settlement Dates (Days)	Eurodollar Option Price		Day-Count Factor (Days/90)	Discount Factor (1/(1 + R x Days/360)	Combined Factor*	Cap Price
			American Style	European Style				
			(Implied Volatility = 15%)					
	(1)	(2)	(3)	(4)	(5)	(6)	(7)=(5)X(6)	(8)=(4)x(7)
Aug 1, 1989	92	92	.08	.08	1.022	.979	1.001	.08
Nov 1, 1989	184	92	.17	.17	1.022	.979	1.001	.17
Feb 1, 1990	276	92	.24	.23	1.022	.979	1.001	.23
May 1, 1990	365	89	.29	.28	0.989	.979	.968	.27
Aug 1, 1990	457	92	.35	.33	1.022	.979	1.001	.33
Nov 1, 1990	549	92	.39	.37	1.022	.979	1.001	.37
Feb 1, 1990	641	92	.43	.41	1.022	.979	1.001	.41
TOTAL PRICE	X	X	1.95	1.87	X	X	X	1.86

*   Combined factor = Day count factor x Discount factor

•   DISCOUNT CORPORATION OF NEW YORK FUTURES   •

For example, the total price of the cap is shown as 186 quarterly basis points per $1 million of the cap's notional principal value. At $25 per basis point, this amounts to $4,650, which is 0.465 percent of $1 million. In practice, the price of the cap would be quoted as 0.47, or 47 basis points.

Early Exercise

The option prices shown in Exhibit 5.6 make it plain that the distinction between European-style options, which is what caps are, and American-style options, which is what the CME's Eurodollar puts are, can have a big effect on the price. Because these are the two main competing markets for interest-rate guaranties, the difference is important for comparing prices.

Just how much the early exercise feature in the American-style option is worth depends, of course, on the likelihood that the option will be exercised early.[3] The likelihood of early exercise depends on the likelihood that the option will be deep in the money. This depends, of course, on how far the option is in or out of the money and on how much time remains to expiration.

The value of the early exercise feature is shown in Exhibit 5.7, which compares cap (European-style) and put (American-style) prices. The strike on the cap is nine percent, and the exercise price on the put is 91. Prices are shown for three months, one year, and two years to expiration and for options that are 100 basis points out of the money (LIBOR = eight percent), at the money (LIBOR = nine percent), and 100 basis points in the money (LIBOR = ten percent).

The difference in the prices clearly increases as the options go into the money. The difference in the prices also increases as the

---

3. The incentive to exercise a Eurodollar option on a futures contract before it expires stems from the fact that the option has a cash liquidation value that the underlying futures contract does not. Consider, for example, a Eurodollar option that is 200 basis points in the money and has no chance of finishing out of the money. The price of this option will be $5,000 [= 200 × $25] and the option price will move basis point for basis point with the price of the underlying futures contract.

The cost of holding the option is the foregone interest on $5,000. The cost of holding the underlying futures position is the foregone interest on the risk margin, which might be in the neighborhood of $1,000. From the option holder's point of view, the two instruments behave exactly alike, but the option costs more to hold. Thus, the option should be exercised early.

Exhibit 5.7

Comparing the Price of a $1 Million, One-Period, 9% Cap on 3-Month LIBOR with the Price of a 91 Eurodollar Put

(Factor = (92/90)/(1+R/4), Volatility = 15%)

Time to Expiration	Price								
	Out of the Money (LIBOR=8%) (E$ Futures=92)		At the Money (LIBOR=9%) (E$ Futures=91)		In the Money (LIBOR=10%) (E$ Futures=90)	
	Cap	Put	Cap	Put	Cap	Put
3 Months	.02	.02	.26	.26	1.01	1.01
1 Year	.14	.15	.50	.51	1.11	1.15
2 Years	.28	.30	.65	.69	1.19	1.29

time remaining to expiration increases, which makes sense because adding time to the option's life adds to the likelihood that the option will be deep in the money at some time during its life.

Other Real World Considerations

Comparing cap and put prices involves a number of real world considerations that we have not touched on so far. These include:

- differences in expiration dates; and
- differences in reference rates.

Expiration Dates

Because caps are traded over the counter, they can have any settlement dates the traders choose. Eurodollar puts, on the other hand, are traded on the CME and have expirations that conform strictly to the March, June, September, and December quarterly cycle. The option with more time to expiration will be worth more than the option with less, other factors being the same. As a result, an accurate comparison of a cap price with a Eurodollar put price requires an allowance for any differences in times to expiration.

Differences in Reference Rates

Even if the expiration dates for the cap and the Eurodollar put are the same, there remains a small difference in the effective time remaining to expiration. Caps typically use the LIBOR fixing done in the London morning as the reference rate for settlement. The CME establishes its final settlement price on the basis of a LIBOR survey conducted during the London afternoon. The difference is only a few hours, but the resulting rates can be different. The extra few hours alloted the Eurodollar put should impart some small additional amount to its price.

Price Sensitivity

Cap prices respond to the same forces that affect any option's price:

- a change in the price of the underlying commodity—the interest rate in the case of a cap;
- a change in the market's expectations about the volatility that drives the underlying commodity's price—implied interest rate volatility in the case of a cap; and
- a change in the time remaining to expiration.

These depend in turn on the characteristics of the cap including:

- the length of the cap agreement, which determines how many legs there are in the cap and, together with the current date, determines how much time remains to each expiration or settlement date; and
- how much the various legs of the cap are in or out of the money.

Examples of the sensitivity of cap prices to changes in underlying yields, yield volatilities, and the time remaining to expiration or cap dates highlight the importance of each of these factors. It is here that we launch into the "Greek alphabet" of options.

Sensitivity to Changes in Yield Levels (Delta)

A standard approach to measuring the sensitivity of the price of a cap to a change in underlying yields is to assume a parallel, upward shift in the forward or zero-coupon yield curve. That is, each underlying interest rate is increased by the same number of basis points.

For the examples shown in Exhibit 5.8, we have calculated the change in the prices of three different LIBOR-based caps for a 10-basis-point increase in three-month LIBOR. With LIBOR at 8.5 percent initially, the eight percent cap is 50 basis points in the money, the 8.5 percent cap is at the money, and the nine percent cap is 50 basis points out of the money. Exhibit 5.8 shows the prices of the individual legs in quarterly basis points.

Exhibit 5.8

Cap Price Sensitivity to an Increase in LIBOR
(Implied Volatility = 15%)

Settlement Date	8.0% Cap			8.5% Cap			9.0% Cap		
	Price LIBOR=8.5	Price LIBOR=8.6	Price Change	Price LIBOR=8.5	Price LIBOR=8.6	Price Change	Price LIBOR=8.5	Price LIBOR=8.6	Price Change
Aug 1, 1989	.56	.64	+.08	.25	.30	+.05	.08	.11	+.03
Nov 1, 1989	.63	.70	+.07	.35	.40	+.05	.17	.20	+.03
Feb 1, 1990	.68	.75	+.07	.41	.47	+.06	.23	.27	+.04
May 1, 1990	.70*	.76*	+.06	.45*	.50*	+.05	.27*	.31*	+.04
Aug 1, 1990	.75	.81	+.06	.51	.56	+.05	.33	.37	+.04
Nov 1, 1990	.78	.84	+.06	.55	.60	+.05	.37	.41	+.04
Feb 1, 1991	.80	.86	+.06	.58	.63	+.05	.41	.44	+.03
Total	4.90	5.36	+.46	3.10	3.46	+.36	1.86	2.11	+.25

* reflects a combined factor of .965 for day counts and payments in arrears.

• DISCOUNT CORPORATION OF NEW YORK FUTURES •

The in-the-money cap is much more sensitive to the increase in rates than are the at-the-money and out-of-the-money caps. Altogether, the price of the eight percent cap increases from 490 quarterly basis points to 536 for a total change of 46 basis points. In contrast, the price of the 8.5 percent cap increases 36 basis points and the price of the nine percent cap 25 basis points.

Present Value of a Basis Point

If one wants to hedge the yield exposure in a cap, the first step is to translate the change in the cap price into present values. This is easy in our case because we have priced the options as Eurodollar puts. The resulting prices are expressed in quarterly basis points that are worth a constant $25 per basis point. Thus, the 36-basis-point increase in the price of the 8.5 percent cap translates into a present value of $900 [= $25 × 36] increase in the face of a 10-basis-point increase in rates, or $90 per basis point increase in LIBOR for each $1 million notional principal value of the cap.

The second step is to determine the present value of a basis point for the hedging vehicle. We have described how this is done for swaps in Chapters 3 and 4. Once you derive this number, the notional principal amount of the swap required to hedge the cap is simply:

$$\text{Hedge Ratio} = \text{PV01(cap)} \, / \, \text{PV01(swap)}$$

Because this hedge ratio will change as interest rates change and, for away-from-the-money caps, as time passes, this solution is not the end of the hedging problem. Hedges, as we will see, must be adjusted dynamically through time to keep pace with changes in the cap's sensitivity to changes in interest rates.

Cap Deltas (Eurodollar Futures Equivalents)

Getting a handle on the sensitivity of a cap's price to yield changes is easy once the present value of a basis point has been converted into Eurodollar futures equivalents. The only trick in calculating futures equivalents, which is the aggregate delta of the cap, is to remember that we are working with puts. An increase in LIBOR increases the value of a cap while it decreases the price of a Eurodollar futures contract. Because the cap's delta in Eurodollar terms is:

Cap Delta = Change in Cap Price / Change in Futures Price

a cap's delta is negative. In the example above, the change in the cap price was an increase of 36 basis points. The *decrease* in the futures price would have been 10 basis points. The resulting cap delta in Eurodollar terms thus is:

Cap Delta = +36 / -10 = -3.6

Put differently, the price exposure in the cap is the same as the price exposure in a short position of 3.6 Eurodollar futures. To offset the price exposure in a long cap, one would buy 3.6 futures (if one could buy fractions of futures). To offset the price exposure in a short cap, one would sell 3.6 futures.

Cap deltas in Eurodollar futures terms are shown in Exhibit 5.9. As shown there, each $1 million long position in an at-the-money cap is the equivalent of a short position in roughly half of a Eurodollar futures contract. The deltas are smaller than this for an out-of-the-money cap, while the deltas are larger for an in-the-money cap.

The differences in the deltas for the various legs of the cap are worth explaining. Notice, for example, that the deltas of the at-the-money legs are smaller the farther the cap date is in the future. This gentle decline in the deltas reflects the falling present value of a basis point. Cap prices are paid up front, and the delta measures the change in the present value of the cap, not the nominal value of the cap.

Notice, also, that adding time to the cap's life reduces the deltas for those legs of the cap that are in the money and increases the deltas for those legs of the cap that are out of the money. What is really happening here is that both sets of deltas are getting closer to the delta of an at-the-money cap. Although these deltas also reflect changes in the present value of a basis point, the dominant effect is a change in the "effective moneyness" of the various legs as the time to expiration increases. Fifty basis points matter

Exhibit 5.9

Cap Deltas in Eurodollar Futures Terms
(Implied Volatility = 15%)
(Eurodollar Futures = 91.5)

Settlement Date	8.0% Cap (in the money)	8.5% Cap (at the money)	9.0% Cap (out of the money)
Aug 1, 1989	-.78	-.50	-.23
Nov 1, 1989	-.70	-.50	-.30
Feb 1, 1990	-.66	-.49	-.33
May 1, 1990	-.63	-.49	-.35
Aug 1, 1990	-.60	-.48	-.36
Nov 1, 1990	-.58	-.47	-.36
Feb 1, 1991	-.57	-.46	-.37
Total	-4.52	-3.39	-2.30

much more to a three-month option than they do to a two-year option. As a result, the August 1, 1989 legs of the eight percent and nine percent caps are effectively much further away from the money than are the February 1, 1991 legs.

Sensitivity of Cap Deltas to Yield Changes (Gamma)

If caps had deltas that never changed, dealing with the price expo-sure in caps would be simple because hedge ratios would never change. As it is, one of the things that makes options interesting and that puts a challenging spin on the problem of hedging caps is that deltas change to reflect their moneyness. Exhibit 5.9 shows that the prices of in-the-money caps are more sensitive to yield changes than are at-the-money caps. At-the-money caps are, in turn, more sensitive to yield changes than are out-of-the-money caps. Exhibit 5.10 provides a more compact picture of how a cap's sensitivity to changes in yields is affected by the level of yields and the time remaining to expiration.

What these differences mean in practice, of course, is that a cap's delta changes as the underlying yield changes. A rise in the underlying yield takes an out-of-the-money option closer to being at the money, an at-the-money option into the money, and an in-the-money option deeper into the money. In all three cases, the sensitivity of the cap's price to a further increase in yields is higher than before.

Gamma

The name that option traders give this effect is "gamma." The pe-culiarities of gamma that are most important to those running a cap book are these:

- at-the-money caps have higher gammas than do options that are away from the money;
- near-the-money caps that are approaching their settlement dates have higher gammas than do similarly positioned longer-dated caps.

Exhibit 5.10

Cap Deltas

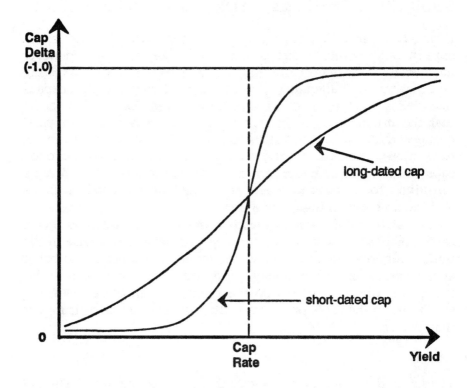

In practice this means that some cap positions will be more difficult to manage than others. Caps that are either deep in the money or deep out of the money will have comparatively stable deltas. Long-dated caps also will have comparatively stable deltas. In contrast, the risk exposure in caps that are near the money and approaching their settlement dates can be brutal to manage because of the wide and rapid swings that even a small change in yields can have on their price sensitivities.

Some notion of just how different caps with different money-ness can be in this regard is provided in Exhibit 5.11. There we show what effect a 10-basis-point change in yields might have on the number of Eurodollar futures needed to hedge the price exposure in a $100 million cap. For this exercise, we consider three different cap rates and three different times to expiration.

The differences are really quite striking.

First consider the state of affairs when the cap date is just five days away. We see here that a 10-basis-point increase in yields has no effect on the hedge ratio for the eight percent (in-the-money) cap or for the nine percent (out-of-the-money) cap. This means that there is no question in people's minds, with only five days left, where these two caps will expire. The eight percent cap is a sure winner (from the holder's point of view), and the only open question is how much the winner will pay. In this case, a long position in the eight percent cap has almost exactly the same exposure as a short position in 100 Eurodollar futures, and this equivalence is not affected by small changes in the level of yields.

The nine percent cap is a sure loser with only five days left. A long position in this cap is the same as no position at all in Eurodollar futures, and this equivalence is not affected by small changes in the level of yields.

The exposure in the 8.5 percent cap, however, is extremely changeable when so little time is left. With LIBOR at 8.5 percent, a long position in $100 million of this cap is equivalent to a short position in 50 Eurodollar futures. A 10-basis-point increase in yields takes this cap into the money and increases its price sensitivity to that of a short position in 75 Eurodollar futures. In other words, a 10-basis-point increase in yields increases the number of Eurodollar futures needed to hedge the position by 25 contracts.

Exhibit 5.11

Change in the Hedge Ratio for a $100 Million Cap in Response to a 10-Basis-Point Increase in Yields
(LIBOR = 8.5%, Volatility = 15%)

Time Left to Settlement Date (days)	Cap Rate		
	8.0%	8.5%	9.0%
5	0	25	0
90	4	7	5
360	2	3	3

*   *Change in the cap's delta for a 10-basis-point increase in the underlying rate, expressed as numbers of Eurodollar futures.*

The practical consequence of such a changeable hedge ratio is that this part of a cap will prove to be very hard to hedge. In the language of option traders, this cap has a lot of gamma. The away-from-the-money caps have no gamma at all.

Adding time to the life of the option affects this characteristic. For example, the price sensitivity of a long-dated, at-the-money option is less changeable than it is for a short-dated, at-the-money option. On the other hand, the price sensitivity of long-term, away-from-the-money positions can be more changeable than the price sensitivity of short-term, away-from-the-money positions.

In all cases, including the longer-dated positions, we see that for any given time remaining to expiration, the variability of price exposure in away-from-the-money caps is less than for at-the-money caps. This is a general rule for all options.

The lessons provided by Exhibit 5.11 are these. Options that are either in or out of the money have more stable hedge ratios than options that are at the money. The difference in hedge ratio stability depends on how much time remains to the cap's settlement and is most pronounced for the short-dated cap. In a nutshell, we find that caps that are both near the money *and* close to their settlement dates will be harder to delta hedge than caps that have either a long time left to settlement or that are well in or out of the money.

The consequences of these differences will be explored further in Chapter 6.

Sensitivity to Changes in Volatility (Zeta/Vega)

Caps are options, and option prices depend on two things for their value:

- the likelihood that the option will end up in the money; and
- the value of the option if it does end up in the money.

Anyone who knows these two things and can calculate a present value can figure out a fair price for the option. Figuring out these two things, however, can be a challenge.

Option Prices and Volatility

To deal with this challenge, modern option pricing theory has fo-
cused on tying the price of an option to the volatility or variability
of the underlying price or interest rate. The theory behind even the
simplest pricing models is rigorous, but the intuition is easy
enough.

Examine the problem of pricing a call option in the two settings shown in Exhibit 5.12. Both situations are the same in all
respects but one. In both cases:

- the underlying price starts at 100;
- the exercise price is 103; and
- the option has four periods to expiration.

The difference between the two cases is that in the first case,
the price can rise or fall by one, while in the second case, the price
can rise or fall by two during any of the four periods remaining to
expiration.

The effect of the higher volatility in the second case on the
price of the call is easy to see.

If the price can change by only one, the call option has only
one opportunity out of 16 to finish in the money. That is, the price
must rise by one in each and every one of the four periods to
finish in the money. If the price ticks down even once, the option
will finish out of the money. Moreover, if it does finish in the
money, its value at expiration is only one [= 104 - 103]. If we ignore the problem of calculating present values, the price of the
option would be:

Call Price = (1/16) × 1

= 1/16

which is simply the probability of finishing in the money multiplied by the option's value if in the money.

If the price can change by two, however, the call option has
five opportunities to finish in the money (there are four ways to

Exhibit 5.12

Volatility and Option Prices

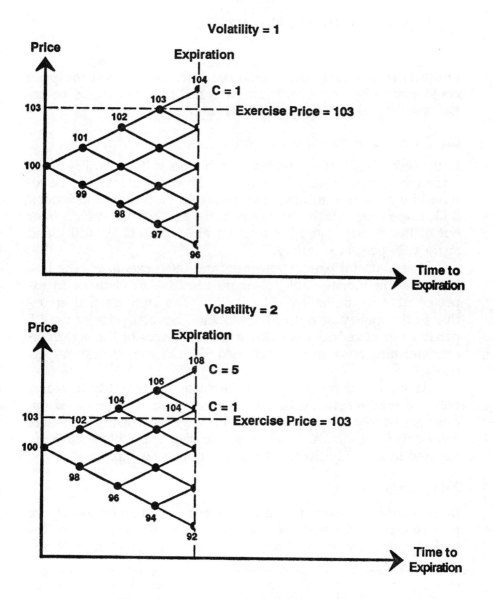

get from 100 to 103). In one of these cases, the call is worth five [= 108 - 103], and in the other four cases, the call is worth one [= 104 - 103]. In this case, the price would be:

$$\text{Call Price } = [(1/16) \times 5] + [(4/16) \times 1]$$
$$= 9/16$$

which is considerably more than the call's price when the price could change by only one. Here, as in real markets, higher potential volatility adds to an option's value.

Cap Prices and Interest Rate Volatility

In the case of caps, the volatility that matters is the volatility of the underlying interest rate. Examples of how cap prices can be affected by a change in interest rate volatility are shown in Exhibit 5.13. These caps, which differ only in the amount that each is in or out of the money, have been priced at 15 percent volatility and again at 20 percent volatility.

Several useful patterns emerge from these examples. The first is that at-the-money caps are more sensitive to changes in expected (that is, implied) yield volatility than are caps that are either in the money or out of the money. The total price of the 8.5 percent cap increased 102 ticks, while the prices of the eight percent and nine percent caps increased 93 ticks and 99 ticks respectively.

Another is that sensitivity to increases in volatility increases with the time remaining to the settlement date. Longer-dated options are simply more responsive to changes in volatility than are short-dated options. As a result, a four-year cap will be far more exposed to volatility changes than will a one-year cap.

Zeta (a.k.a. Vega)

In the world of options trading, the sensitivity of an option's price to a change in the level of implied or expected volatility of the underlying commodity is known as the option's zeta.[4] In practice:

4. Discount Corporation of New York Futures refers to an option's price sensitivity to changes in implied volatility as its zeta. A more common label is vega, but you may encounter any number of other labels in your reading about options.

Exhibit 5.13

Cap Price Sensitivity to an Increase in Volatility
(LIBOR = 15%)

Settlement Date	8.0% Cap			8.5% Cap			9.0% Cap		
	Price Vol=15%	Price Vol=20%	Price Change	Price Vol=15%	Price Vol=20%	Price Change	Price Vol=15%	Price Vol=20%	Price Change
Aug 1, 1989	.56	.63	+.07	.25	.33	+.08	.08	.15	+.07
Nov 1, 1989	.63	.73	+.10	.35	.46	+.11	.17	.27	+.10
Feb 1, 1990	.68	.80	+.12	.41	.55	+.14	.23	.36	+.13
May 1, 1990	.70*	.83*	+.13	.45*	.60*	+.15	.27*	.42*	+.15
Aug 1, 1990	.75	.91	+.16	.51	.68	+.17	.33	.50	+.17
Nov 1, 1990	.78	.95	+.17	.55	.73	+.18	.37	.55	+.18
Feb 1, 1991	.80	.98	+.18	.58	.77	+.19	.41	.60	+.19
Total	4.90	5.83	+.93	3.10	4.12	+1.02	1.86	2.85	+.99

* reflects a combined factor of .968 for day counts and payments in arrears.

• DISCOUNT CORPORATION OF NEW YORK FUTURES •

an option's zeta is the change in the price of the option for a one-percentage-point increase in the expected volatility of the underlying commodity.

For that matter, zeta is a standard measure of risk exposure and is used to determine how exposed a position is to a change in volatility.

The zetas of the caps shown in Exhibit 5.13 are charted in Exhibit 5.14. In both panels, the at-the-money cap is shown to be more sensitive to an increase in volatility than either the out-of-the-money or in-the-money cap. For example, the price of the six-month leg of an 8.5 percent cap would increase by 2.3 quarterly basis points if expected interest rate volatility increased from 15 percent to 16 percent. In contrast, the six-month leg of a nine percent cap would increase by only two basis points, and the six-month leg of an eight percent cap by 1.9 basis points.

We also see that long-dated caps are more sensitive to volatility changes than are short-dated caps. For the at-the-money cap, the zeta of the six-month leg is half again as large as the zeta of the three-month leg. As a general rule:

> the zeta of an at-the-money option is approximately proportional to the square root of the time to the option's expiration.

This is a good rule of thumb but works only for at-the-money options. The relationships for away-from-the-money options are considerably more complex.

The lower panel shows how an increase in interest rate volatility can influence a cap's zeta. For example, we see that the at-the-money cap's zeta is entirely unaffected by the increase in volatility. On the other hand, the higher the level of volatility, the more sensitive prices of the away-from-the-money caps become.

How Volatile Can Interest Rates Be?

For those who are in the business of buying or selling caps, perhaps the most important question to answer is how volatile interest rates can be expected to be over the life of the cap. For example, if volatility is 15 percent, the price of the two-year, 8.5 percent

Exhibit 5.14

Cap Zetas
(LIBOR = 8.5%)

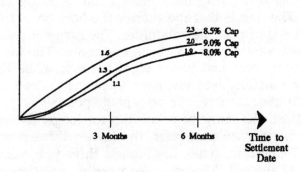

Volatility = 15%

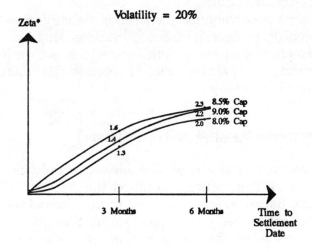

Volatility = 20%

*   *Value shown in basis points*

cap with quarterly settlement dates should be 310 quarterly basis points per $1 million notional value. If volatility is 20 percent, however, the price should be 412 quarterly basis points, roughly 30 percent higher.

An indication of how volatile three-month LIBOR can be is provided in Exhibit 5.15, which shows historical yield volatilities for horizons ranging from one month to five years based on lead Eurodollar futures rates starting in January 1982 and running through June 1990.

A number of striking observations can be made about these volatilities. The first is that the shorter the horizon of the cap, the wider the range of possible volatilities. The range of possible vola-tilities for short-term caps has been enormous. The lowest three-month volatility was just under eight percent, while the highest three-month volatility was just over 44 percent. The range of ob-served volatilities, then, was 36 percentage points.

In contrast, the range of volatilities for longer-dated caps has been fairly narrow. In particular, the lowest three-year volatility was about 17 percent, while the highest three-year volatility was just under 23 percent. The range of possible volatilities was just under six percentage points.

The second observation is the striking stability of average in-terest rate volatility over horizons of various lengths. With the possible exception of a one-month cap, which is a rarity in the market anyway, the average level of interest rate volatility has been close to 19 percent.

Sensitivity to the Passing of Time (Theta)

Why would anyone sell a cap? The answer, simply, is the same reason anyone sells an option—to collect the premium. Collecting the premium, however, is not the end to the transaction. Anyone who sells an option has a potential liability that goes away, if it goes away, only when the option expires. The value of this liabil-ity is the option's price.

Exhibit 5.15

Eurodollar Yield Volatility*
(Percent, January 1982 — June 1990)

Term	Volatility		
	Minimum	Maximum	Average
1 Month	4.2	57.9	18.1
3 Months	7.5	44.4	18.5
6 Months	9.8	36.8	18.9
1 Year	12.2	31.9	19.0
2 Years	14.1	25.7	19.0
3 Years	17.4	22.8	19.2
4 Years	17.4	22.3	19.1
5 Years	17.3	21.5	19.2

* *Based on lead contract futures yield.*

We have already seen that a cap's price is higher the longer its horizon. It follows that a cap's price falls as it approaches its settlement date.

Theta

Option traders call the gradual fall in an option's price as it approaches expiration "theta." Theta typically is defined as the change in the price or value of an option as one day passes.

Theta is also known as "time decay," which is an expression that has a lot of intuitive appeal for people.

Even though options usually are paid for up front, financial economists insist that the proper way to book income from the sale of options is over time as the size of the liability diminishes. In practice, many financial institutions are allowed to book the entire price of an option as current income at the time it is sold, but this practice can lead to serious misunderstandings about the true state of affairs.

For those who care about theta, there are very strong parallels between theta and gamma. In particular, options with a lot of gamma have high rates of time decay. Options with only small amounts of gamma also have low rates of time decay.

As a result, we have the same rule of thumb explaining theta that we use to explain gamma:

> caps that are both near the money and close to their settlement dates will have higher rates of time decay than caps that either have a long time left to settlement or that are in or out of the money.

Interest-Rate Floors

Once you understand the workings of interest-rate caps, interest-rate floors are a breeze. The only difference is that an interest-rate floor is like a Eurodollar call option. Both the similarities and differences between floors and Eurodollar calls are the same as they are between caps and Eurodollar puts.

Interest-rate floors can be priced as if they were European-style calls on Eurodollar futures with appropriate allowances for day counts and payments in arrears. The risk characteristics of interest-rate floors—delta, gamma, zeta, and theta—can be reckoned in the same way.

A comparison of the prices and risk characteristics of interest-rate floors with those for interest-rate caps is provided in Exhibit 5.16.

What is most striking about these examples is that the chief differences between caps and floors are in their prices and deltas. This makes sense. With LIBOR at 8.5 percent, for example, an eight percent cap is 50 basis points in the money while an eight percent floor is 50 basis points out of the money. It stands to reason, then, that the cap should be worth more than the floor. Also, a cap is like a short position in Eurodollar futures, while a floor is like a long position in Eurodollar futures. Thus, it makes sense that cap deltas are negative while floor deltas are positive.

Note that there are almost no differences in how sensitive caps and floors are to changes in volatility or to the passage of time. These similarities stem from what is known as "put/call parity."

Broadly speaking, put/call parity in the world of caps, floors, and swaps, says that a long floor (a call option on Eurodollar futures) combined with a short cap (a put option on Eurodollar futures) behaves like a short swap (a long Eurodollar futures contract).[5]

Combinations of Caps and Floors

Caps and floors can be combined with one another to produce any number of interesting risk/return profiles. Examples of these include:

---

5. For this equivalence to work, the cap, floor, and swap must all have the same reset dates, and the options must be European-style. Put/call parity works less well for Eurodollar options because of their early exercise feature, but this principle provides an extraordinarily useful tool for understanding combinations of options. The time you spend learning about put/call parity will be some of the most valuable minutes you ever spend learning about options.

Exhibit 5.16

Key Features of 1-Period Caps and Floors
(Per $1 Million, LIBOR = 8.5%, Volatility = 15%)

Term and Feature	Cap and Floor Rates					
	8.0%		8.5%		9.0%	
	Cap	Floor	Cap	Floor	Cap	Floor
3 Months						
Price[1]	56	7	25	25	8	57
Delta[2]	-.79	.19	-.50	.48	-.23	.75
Zeta	.01	.01	.02	.02	.01	.01
Theta[3]	-.03	-.03	-.05	-.05	-.03	-.03
1 Year						
Price	72	26	47	47	29	74
Delta	-.63	.29	-.49	.43	-.35	.57
Zeta	.03	.03	.03	.03	.03	.03
Theta	-.02	-.02	-.02	-.02	-.02	-.01
2 Years						
Price	82	40	61	61	44	86
Delta	-.55	.29	-.46	.39	-.37	.48
Zeta	.04	.04	.04	.04	.04	.04
Theta	—	-.01	-.01	-.01	-.01	-.01

1 Quarterly basis points per $1 million principal or notional value.
2 Eurodollar futures delta.
3 Time decay per month.

• DISCOUNT CORPORATION OF NEW YORK FUTURES •

Straddles

- A long position in both a cap and a floor can be used to bet that interest rate volatility will rise.

  Such a position would be like a long straddle or strangle in Eurodollar options.

- A short position in both a cap and a floor can be used to bet that interest rate volatility will fall.

  Such a position would be like a short straddle or strangle in Eurodollar options.

Collars

- A short position in an out-of-the-money interest-rate floor can be used to defray the cost of a long position in an out-of-the-money interest-rate cap.

  The common name for such a position is an interest-rate collar, which allows the interest rate to vary only between the higher cap rate and the lower floor rate.

  The payoff to an interest-rate collar is illustrated in Exhibit 5.17. The effect of combining a collar with conventional floating-rate financing is shown in Exhibit 5.18. The chief virtue of this position is that net financing costs are allowed to float within the band set by the cap and floor rates, while the rates are locked at either the cap or the floor rate if market rates move above or below these bounds.

- A short position in a floor can be combined with a long position in a cap with the same exercise rate to create a synthetic forward deposit or swap. (Remember put/call parity.)

Range forwards

- If the strikes for the cap and the floor in a collar are chosen so that the prices of the two parts are equal but offsetting, the net cost is zero.

Exhibit 5.17

Payoff to a Collar
(Long 9% Cap, Short 7% Floor)

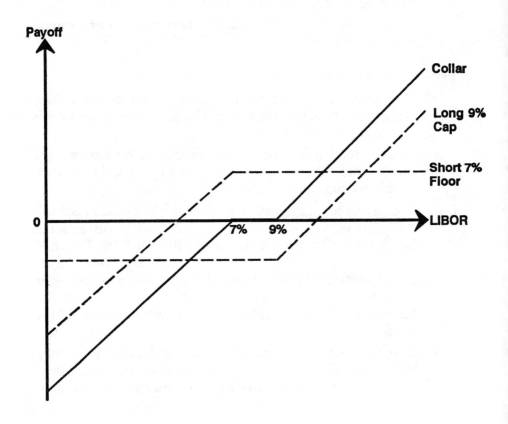

Exhibit 5.18

Combining a Collar with Floating Rate Financing

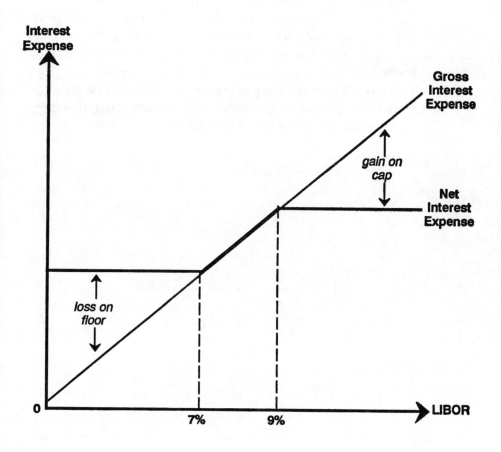

Corridors

- A cap with a high cap rate can be sold to help defray the cost of a cap with a low cap rate. For example, you can sell a cap with a cap rate of 12 percent to offset some of the cost of buying a cap with a cap rate of 10 percent.

  The result is known as a corridor, which fixes the rate paid over the range of rates between the two cap rates. The rate is free to vary below the lower cap rate and above the higher cap rate.

  The payoff to a corridor is shown in Exhibit 5.19. The effect of combining a corridor with conventional floating-rate financing is shown in Exhibit 5.20.

Exhibit 5.19

Payoff to a Corridor
(Long 7% Cap, Short 9% Cap)

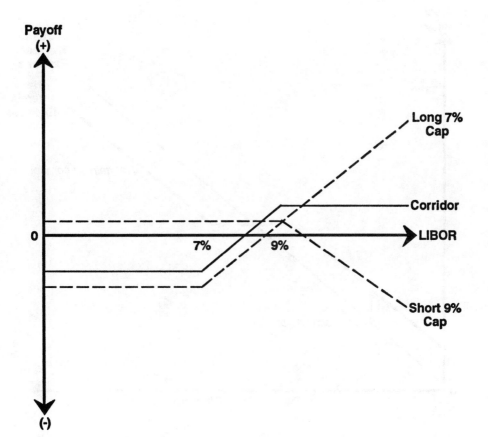

Exhibit 5.20

Combining a Corridor with Floating-Rate Financing

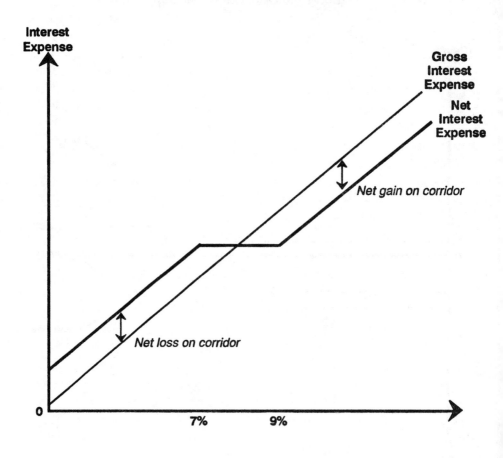

BASIC CAP TERMINOLOGY

Market Index: The interest rate index (along with the maturity) that is being capped. A cap may be set on the following indexes: LIBOR, Treasury Bills, CDs, the prime rate, and others.

Strike (or Cap Rate): The rate that defines the protection level for the holder of the cap. Most often, this level remains constant.

Principal Amount (Notional Amount): The total dollar amount covered in the cap agreement. Most often, this value remains constant over time.

Settlement Dates: The expiration dates of the individual cap options.

Reference Rate: The calculated value of the market index rate on the expiration date. The reference rate determines if the cap option is in or out of the money. This value is dependent upon the source of the rate quotation, the time of the rate quotation, and the method of calculating the rate (average over the period, or single rate).

Settlement Payments: If the reference rate is less than or equal to the cap rate for the period, there is no cash flow between the buyer and the seller of the cap. If the reference rate exceeds the cap rate, the seller of the cap pays the buyer an amount equal to:

(principal value of cap) x (reference rate - cap rate) x [(# of days in reference period)/360]

The two parties must agree upon payment dates.

Reference Period: The number of days between settlement dates (or, in the case of the first period, the number of days between the start date and the first settlement date).

Period of Agreement (Start Date and End Date): The first and last date of the cap agreement.

Fee (or Premium): Bids and offers are quoted in basis points. The total price of the cap is determined by multiplying the quoted price (in percentage terms) by the principal amount of the contract.

For example, a cap might be described by the following information: a 5-year 8% cap on 3-month LIBOR is quoted as 380 (i.e., 3.80%). The fee to cap $10 million in underlying value would be:

(.0380) x ($10,000,000) = $380,000

The cap premium is most often paid up front on a specified date. In some cap agreements, a fraction of the premium is paid each period.

CHAPTER 6

Hedging Caps

The International Swap Dealers Association (ISDA) found that there were nearly half a trillion dollars' worth of caps and floors outstanding in various combinations at the end of 1989. Accordingly, the problem of hedging caps has become big business, especially for those banks that are the mainstay of the business.

The hedger can take either of two broad avenues to deal with the exposure in a cap book. The first is a dynamic hedging strategy in which the hedger offsets the net delta of a cap book. The second is an option replication strategy in which the hedger offsets not only the delta of the cap book, but the gamma, zeta, and theta as well.

Each approach has its virtues and shortcomings, and the purpose of this chapter is to show what those are. In particular, we will show that the dynamic delta hedging strategy has the virtue of being easy and well-understood. The cost of dynamic delta hedging is uncertain, however, and delta hedging does not protect against gapped markets or increases in volatility. Option replication has the virtue of providing a known cost and more complete protection. Its drawback is that it is analytically more difficult, though not impossible, to do.

In the concluding section of this chapter, we will give you a strategy for choosing between the two approaches.

Dynamic Delta Balancing

Before the October 1987 market explosion (a crash for stocks, and a sharp rally in bonds and Eurodollars), dynamic delta balancing was the hedge of choice for those who ran cap books.

Finding a Delta Hedge

The heart of this approach is quite simple. Consider the problem of hedging the nine percent cap described in Exhibit 6.1. This cap is based on three-month LIBOR, which is one of the more widely used reference rates, and has six quarterly settlement dates. The issuer of this cap has effectively sold a strip of puts on Eurodollar futures with exercise prices of 91 [100 - 9]. The price was 17,700 quarterly basis points or 0.44 percent of principal.

The period of agreement runs from June 17, 1987 through March 17, 1989. We chose this cap because it:

- has settlement dates that correspond to IMM settlement dates;
- has settlement dates extending beyond the longest-dated Eurodollar option traded on the Chicago Mercantile Exchange (CME); and
- has settlement dates past the October 1987 stock market crash.

These features make it easy to show how to hedge the cap with futures and make it easy to highlight the potential hazards in dynamic delta hedging.

The risk parameters of this option strip are shown in Exhibit 6.2. In this example, the cap's notional amount is $100 million. Hence, the September 1987 cap option can be treated as a short

Exhibit 6.1
Cap

Cap Rate	9 Percent
Principal Amount	$100,000,000
Market Index	3-Month LIBOR
Settlement Dates	Quarterly
Period of Agreement	June 17, 1987 - March 17, 1989

Exhibit 6.2

Risk Characteristics for Seller of 9% Cap
(in IMM Terms)
June 17, 1987

Risk Characteristic	September 1987	December 1987	March 1988	June 1988	September 1988	December 1988	Total Position
Delta	+6	+19	+26	+32	+37	+40	160
Zeta	-40.5	-144.6	-214.2	-276.4	-327.2	-366.2	-1369.1
Theta	+5.5	+9.5	+8.3	+7.8	+6.9	+6.2	+44.2
Gamma	-1.2	-2.0	-2.1	-1.9	-1.7	-1.6	-10.5
Futures Price	92.61	92.33	92.12	91.94	91.78	91.62	N/A
Options Price (bp)	200	1300	2200	3400	4700	5900	17700

Where
- *Delta* = net futures equivalence
- *Zeta* = change in value of seller's position in basis points given a one-percentage-point increase in implied volatility
- *Theta* = change in option value in bp's given a one-day passage of time
- *Gamma* = change in delta (futures equivalence) given a 10-bp increase in the futures price (that is, a 10-bp decrease in LIBOR)

• DISCOUNT CORPORATION OF NEW YORK FUTURES •

position of 100 SEP 87 91.00 Eurodollar put options. Each of these 100 puts has a delta of -0.06, so that the total delta of the short puts is +6. In other words, because the issuer is short the cap, the issuer's risk exposure is the equivalent of six long futures contracts.

Also, selling options creates negative exposure to zeta. In this case, a zeta of -40.5 in the September 1987 leg of the cap indicates that the seller of the cap loses 40.5 quarterly basis points if implied volatility increases by one percentage point.

Finally, option sellers face positive thetas and negative gammas. The theta for the September 1987 part of the cap is 5.5, which means that the seller earns 5.5 basis points per day in time decay. Similarly, the September 1987 gamma of -1.2 indicates that the current delta of +6 will decrease to +4.8 if Eurodollar futures prices increase by 10 basis points.

The total delta of the cap is 160, which means that the short cap position has the financial risk of being long 160 Eurodollar futures. A delta hedge for this cap, then, requires the hedger to short 160 Eurodollar futures. Exhibit 6.2 also shows that this exposure is spread across six contract months. Because yield curves rarely oblige us with parallel shifts, the prudent hedger would allocate these 160 contracts across the six contracts months in the numbers shown. That is, the hedger would short six September 1987 futures, nineteen December 1987 futures, twenty-six March 1988 futures, and so forth.

Having done so, the hedger is now delta neutral.

Dynamic Rebalancing

The hedger cannot rest, however, because gamma raises its ugly head whenever prices change. Overall, we see that a 10-basis-point increase in Eurodollar futures prices reduces the overall delta of the cap by 10.5 futures equivalents. That is, a fall in LIBOR will leave us overhedged unless we adjust the size of the futures position. In this case, a 10-basis-point increase in Eurodollar prices would call for a 10 or 11 contract reduction in the size of our hedge.

Changes in implied volatility and the passing of time also affect a cap's delta. A cap's delta can be thought of as the probability that the cap will expire in the money. An increase in implied volatility increases people's subjective estimates of the likelihood that an out-of-the-money cap will finish in the money. An increase in implied volatility decreases people's estimates that an in-the-money option will remain in the money until expiration. As time passes, the likelihood that an out-of-the-money option will go into the money falls, and the likelihood that an in-the-money option will stay in the money rises. These changes in a cap's delta require corresponding hedge ratio adjustments.

Once embarked on a strategy of dynamic delta balancing, the hedger must stay on the job, chained to his desk, and manage the position either until all parts of the cap have expired or the hedge is abandoned.

The Cost of Delta Hedging

A widely held fallacy is that delta hedging doesn't cost anything. The source of this fallacy is that no money changes hands when the hedge is established, whereas buying options requires the hedger to pay for protection up front.

Those who hold this fallacy have not thought through the problem of dynamic hedging.

In the above example, the initial hedge required selling 160 Eurodollar futures at various prices ranging from 92.61 for the September 1987 contract to 91.62 for the December 1988 contract. The 10-basis-point increase in Eurodollar prices reduced the cap's delta by 10, which means that the hedger must buy back 10 of the original 160 futures.

Notice that this first adjustment requires the hedger to buy futures at prices 10 basis points higher than the prices at which they were sold.

This sets the stage for a general rule that governs dynamic delta hedging. If you are hedging a short option position, a dynamic delta hedging strategy requires you to:

- buy the underlying commodity (i.e., the underlying) when its price rises; and

- sell the underlying commodity when its price falls.

If we translate this into the language of a conventional formula for trading success, we find that this hedging strategy requires us to:

- buy high;
- sell low.

If this sounds like a formula that will surely cost us money, it is. The only question is how much.

The cost of dynamic delta hedging depends on how often we have to adjust the hedge and at what prices. If prices are highly volatile and bounce around a lot, this approach will be very expensive. If the market is quiet and rates are fairly stable, dynamic delta hedging can be very inexpensive.

In other words, the cost of a dynamic delta hedging strategy depends on how volatile the underlying market turns out to be over the life of the hedge. Because this cannot be known in advance, the cost of delta hedging is uncertain.

The Risks in Delta Hedging

The risks in delta hedging include the possibility that the hedge will cost the hedger more than the gross revenue from the sale of the cap. In option terms, if the actual or realized volatility of the underlying proves greater than the implied volatility at which the option is sold, the transaction will be unprofitable if it is dynamically delta hedged to expiration.

Delta hedging has two other risks as well. Delta hedging a short option position:

- does not protect completely against gapped markets; and
- does not protect at all against an increase in implied volatility.

Only options can do these two things.

As we noted above, one of the reasons we chose this example was that it spanned one of the most dramatic episodes in the history of Eurodollar futures. In the wake of the October 1987 stock market crash, Eurodollar futures rallied sharply. From the close of the market on October 19 to its opening the following day, the price of almost every Eurodollar futures contract increased more than 100 basis points. In addition, implied volatility in the lead contract went from 23 percent to 40 percent in one day.

These were breathtaking changes that had a riveting effect on those who were short delta hedged interest-rate caps.

It was at this time that a large part of the cap market began to consider buying options for protection against gapped markets and adverse volatility changes. This meant replacing dynamic delta hedging strategies with option replication strategies.

Option Replication

At the heart of using option replication strategies to hedge option exposure is the problem of making options with one set of characteristics behave like options with a different set of characteristics. In the case of caps, the hedger knows that options on Eurodollar futures can provide protection against gapped markets (a gamma problem) and protection against adverse volatility moves (a zeta problem). But there is seldom a simple hedge. For one thing, cap dates rarely, if ever, coincide with the expirations of Eurodollar options. For another, caps can have horizons that extend out several years, while Eurodollar options have lives no longer than one-and-a-half years.

How, then, does one use exchange-traded Eurodollar options to mimic the behavior of a cap or a cap book? The next two sections show two ways of approaching this problem.

The first approach handles the hedge by finding a combination of options that offsets the gamma, zeta, and theta of the cap as well as its delta. The virtue of this kind of hedge is that it provides good protection against short-lived shocks like the one that rocked the Eurodollar market after the October 1987 stock market crash. A drawback of this hedge is that it may not be robust.[1]

---

1. The problem addressed in this section was the subject of a Discount Futures research note: Susan Kirshner and Rick McVey, "Hedging Interest Rate Caps: Part I," September 23, 1988.

The second approach deals directly with the problem of finding a robust hedge by requiring the hedge to hold up in the face of large shocks to the underlying price and volatility.[2]

Hedging Gamma, Zeta, and Theta

To see how Eurodollar options can be used to hedge a cap, consider the problem of hedging the risk characteristics shown in Exhibit 6.2. Recall that this cap's strike prices and settlement dates were chosen to correspond closely to IMM settlement dates for Eurodollar options. At the time, Eurodollar options were listed in four contract months at quarterly intervals. Thus, the first four quarters of the cap could be directly and completely hedged by purchasing 100 each of the September 1987, December 1987, March 1988, and June 1988 91.00 Eurodollar puts. The only mismatch in this hedge would be between the European-style options in the cap and the early exercise feature in the Eurodollar options.

If we buy this strip of options, we find ourselves left with the risk exposure shown in Exhibit 6.3. The strip of puts offsets the exposure in the first four quarters of the cap, but leaves us with an exposure in the last two quarters.

How can an effective hedge for these longer-term caps be created when there are no similar exchange-traded options available?

As with the dynamic delta hedging strategy, we can eliminate the yield curve risk by selling Eurodollar futures, but our position still would be left with:

gamma	-3.3 futures
zeta	-693.4 quarterly basis points
theta	+13.1 quarterly basis points

The challenge in offsetting this position is that gamma, zeta, and theta are related to an option's time to expiration and the amount that it is in or out of the money. The effect of time to

---

2. The problem of finding robust hedges was the subject of a Discount Futures research note: Terry Belton, Galen Burghardt, Morton Lane, and Rick McVey, "Hedging Caps (Part II): Robustness," August 14, 1989.

Exhibit 6.3

Hedge Front-Month Cap Options with Eurodollar Options
June 17, 1987

	Risk Characteristic	September 1987	December 1987	March 1988	June 1988	September 1988	December 1988	Total
CAP	Delta	+6	+19	+26	+32	+37	+40	+160
	Zeta	-40.5	-144.6	-214.2	-276.4	-327.2	-366.2	-1369.1
	Theta	+5.5	+9.5	+8.3	+7.8	+6.9	+6.2	+44.2
	Gamma	-1.2	-2.0	-2.1	-1.9	-1.7	-1.6	-10.5
HEDGE (Buy ED 91 Puts)	Delta	-6	-19	-26	-32	0	0	-83
	Zeta	+40.5	+144.6	+214.2	+276.4	0	0	+675.7
	Theta	-5.5	-9.5	-8.3	-7.8	0	0	-31.1
	Gamma	+1.2	+2.0	+2.1	+1.9	0	0	+7.2
RESIDUAL	Delta	0	0	0	0	+37	+40	+77
	Zeta	0	0	0	0	-327.2	-366.2	-693.4
	Theta	0	0	0	0	+6.9	+6.2	+13.1
	Gamma	0	0	0	0	-1.7	-1.6	-3.3

• DISCOUNT CORPORATION OF NEW YORK FUTURES •

expiration on the gamma, zeta, and theta of an at-the-money option are shown, for example, in Exhibit 6.4. Note that the option's zeta increases with time to expiration, while its theta and gamma decrease.

As a result, the longer-dated cap options have larger zetas than the exchange-traded Eurodollar options. Further, the longer-dated cap options have smaller gamma and theta than the Eurodollar options.

In practice, finding the proper combination of exchange-traded options to match the exposure in the longer-dated cap options requires a fair amount of calculation and can be solved on a computer using linear programming techniques. Even so, once a solution has been found, the hedger often will find that the solutions make intuitive sense. For example, one possible option hedge for the back-month cap options is:

Sell 19 September 1987 92.50 calls
Sell 24 September 1987 92.50 puts
Buy   94 June 1988 91.00 calls
Buy   43 June 1988 91.50 calls
Buy 127 June 1988 92.50 puts

The net option characteristics for the residual/hedge position are shown in Exhibit 6.5.

Notice that the back-month (June 1988) Eurodollar options were purchased while front-month (September 1987) Eurodollar options were sold. To see why, assume that only June 1988 Eurodollar options had been bought. If these options had been bought in a quantity that offset the negative zeta of the cap options, the long June 1988 options would have contributed too much positive gamma and too much negative theta. The cap issuer would still need to eliminate the gamma exposure.

Thus, in this case, the cap writer buys more than enough June 1988 Eurodollar options to hedge the cap's level of zeta. The issuer then sells a small number of September 1987 Eurodollar options, which have a lot of gamma and theta but not a lot of zeta, to offset the excess. As shown in Exhibit 6.5, the combined effect of these transactions is to just offset the residual gamma and zeta risk in

Exhibit 6.4

Option Risk Parameters

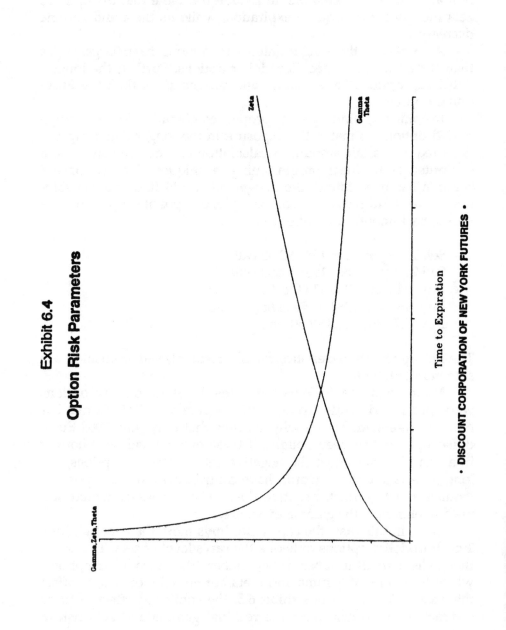

Time to Expiration

Exhibit 6.5

Hedge Residual Risk with Eurodollar Options
June 17, 1987

	Risk Characteristic	September 1987	December 1987	March 1988	June 1988	September 1988	December 1988	Total
RESIDUAL	Delta	0	0	0	0	+37	+40	+77
	Zeta	0	0	0	0	-327.2	-366.2	-693.4
	Theta	0	0	0	0	+6.9	+6.2	+13.1
	Gamma	0	0	0	0	-1.7	-1.6	-3.3
HEDGE	Delta	0	0	0	0	-37	-40	-77
	Zeta	-61.3	0	0	+745.8	0	0	+684.5
	Theta	+6.3	0	0	-19.8	0	0	-13.5
	Gamma	-2.5	0	0	+5.7	0	0	+3.2
NET	Delta	0	0	0	0	0	0	0
	Zeta	-61.3	0	0	+745.8	-327.2	-366.2	-8.9
	Theta	+6.3	0	0	-19.8	+6.9	+6.2	-.4
	Gamma	-2.5	0	0	+.57	-1.7	-1.6	-.1

• DISCOUNT CORPORATION OF NEW YORK FUTURES •

the position. The resulting fully hedged position also has no theta to speak of.

Advantages of a Hedge with Options

To compare this hedge with the original delta hedge, we look at the performance of the cap writer's net position under two extreme conditions:

- yields increase 100 basis points;
- volatility increases by five percent.

Either of these changes would produce a dramatic loss in a cap that has been sold but not hedged.

Gamma Exposure: Yields Up 100 Basis Points

On June 17, the cap writer compares the two methods of hedging his September 1988 and December 1988 cap option exposure. He begins by calculating the current value of these cap options to be 10,600 quarterly basis points (or 106 quarterly basis points per $1 million of the cap). He then values the cap options assuming a 100-basis-point increase in yields. The new value is 19,900 basis points. Since he is short the cap, this amounts to a loss of 9,300 basis points. Note that as rates increased (and as futures prices decreased), the positive delta of the cap increased.

Next, the cap writer calculates the gains offered by the two different hedges:

- The delta-weighted futures hedge of short 37 September 1988 and short 40 December 1988 Eurodollar futures would have gained 7,700 basis points in the face of a 100 basis point increase in yields.
- The exchange-traded option hedge would have gained 9,100 basis points under the same increase in yields.

The difference in the performance of these two positions is the gamma in the options. The delta of a futures contract never changes. It is always 1.0. The delta of the option hedge, on the other hand, increases as the delta of the cap increases.

The bottom line is that the hedge with options out-performed the futures hedge by 1,400 basis points. The two hedges are compared in the upper and lower panels of Exhibit 6.6.

Zeta Exposure: Volatility Up Five Percent

On June 17, the cap writer had a zeta exposure of -693 basis points from the September and December 1988 cap options. If volatility increased by five percentage points, the cap writer would have lost approximately 3,500 basis points [approximately = 693 x 5].

Again, the cap writer calculates the gains offered by the two different hedges:

- The delta-weighted futures position has no zeta at all and provided no gain from the change in implied volatility.
- The hedge with real options, which was net long zeta, would have produced a 3,500-basis-point gain.

Thus, the hedge with the exchange-traded options would have out-performed the futures hedge by 3,500 basis points. This is because a futures hedge has no zeta and can provide no protection against adverse changes in implied volatility. Real options can offer zeta protection.

The Importance of Robustness

The hedge we constructed in the previous section was designed to neutralize the cap's delta, gamma, zeta, and theta. The resulting hedge proved to be far superior in two key respects to a hedge that neutralized only the cap's delta.

A drawback to the approach we took in the previous section is that the hedge was not designed to be robust. Delta, gamma, zeta, and theta provide a useful summary of the risk exposure in a cap for a particular set of circumstances; however, they do not capture all the risk. Large changes in one or more of the key underlying variables and the passing of time can have substantial ef-

Exhibit 6.6

Hedge with Futures
Change in Value in Basis Points

yields up 100 b.p.		volatility up 5%
CAP	-9300	-3500
HEDGE	+7700	0
	-------	-------
NET	-1600	-3500

Hedge with Exchange-Traded Eurodollar Options
Change in Value in Basis Points

yields up 100 b.p.		volatility up 5%
CAP	-9300	-3500
HEDGE	+9100	+3500
	-------	-------
NET	- 200	0

fects on a cap's risk profile. To find a robust hedge, you must look beyond these four risk parameters.

A good hedge should work well over time and over a wide range of combinations of large changes in both futures prices and volatilities. Moreover, a good hedge should require comparatively little tinkering.

Our chief purpose in this section is to describe a methodology for constructing such hedges. Two examples will help demonstrate the importance of building robustness into a surrogate option hedge.

Example 1: Matching Zeta Profiles

Consider an 11 percent cap, which is equivalent to a Eurodollar put with an exercise price of 89.00. Suppose also that futures are trading currently at 90.50 so that the cap is 150 basis points out of the money. For the sake of concreteness, let the zeta of the cap at the current futures price be 35, as shown in Exhibit 6.7.

How should the seller of such a cap hedge against volatility exposure? Both calls and puts are available at a wide range of strike prices, and any long option will provide positive zeta. Is any one or combination of available exchange-traded options better than any other?

The answer is yes.

Consider first the 90.50 calls and puts, which are at the money and as a result have larger zetas than options at any other strike. With these, the hedger could obtain the necessary zeta with a smaller number of contracts than with options at any other strike.

The resulting hedge, however, would not be robust. That is, the zeta of options at the 90.50 strike would offset the zeta of the cap only as long as the futures price stayed at 90.50. At any other price, there would be a zeta mismatch between the cap and the hedge.

As shown in Exhibit 6.7, the problem stems from the relationship between an option's zeta (or gamma or theta) and the amount it is in or out of the money. An option's zeta is largest when it is at the money. The 90.50 options in the hedge, for example, have their greatest zeta at the current futures price. The cap, however, has its greatest zeta at the lower futures price of 89.00. If futures prices

Exhibit 6.7

Zeta Profile Mismatch

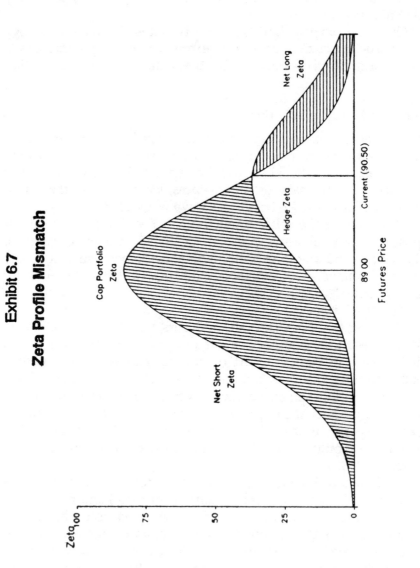

Cap Portfolio Zeta

Net Short Zeta

Hedge Zeta

Net Long Zeta

$Zeta_{100}$

75

50

25

0

89 00

Current (90.50)

Futures Price

fall, the hedge will fall short of providing protection against changes in implied volatility. If futures prices rise, the hedge will provide too much protection.

The most robust hedge against the volatility exposure in this cap would be provided by 89.00 options if they were available. These would gain and lose zeta in exactly the right amounts as the futures price rises or falls. The hedger would need more of these options, of course, because their zeta at the current futures price of 90.50 would be smaller than the zeta of the 90.50 options. Thus, the better match is obtained at a higher cost in terms of the total number of contracts traded.

In some instances, a cap is too far out of the money to match exactly with exchange-traded options. When faced with this problem, the hedger can keep the damage down by matching the moneyness of the hedge as closely as possible to the moneyness of the cap. For example, if the 89.00 strike is not trading, the hedger might be forced to choose the 89.50 strike. The match would not be perfect but it would still be better than the match provided by the 90.50 strike.

Example 2: Short-Dated Caps

A good local hedge also may not hold up over time. This problem is especially acute with very short-dated options. As shown earlier in Exhibit 6.4, the gamma, zeta, and theta characteristics of options all vary with time to expiration. Moreover, these parameters change more quickly, at least for an at-the-money option, as the option approaches expiration.

As a result, a surrogate option hedge for a very short-dated, over-the-counter (OTC) option that works well one day will deteriorate rapidly as the OTC option approaches expiration. For example, as shown in Exhibit 6.4, the gamma and theta of an expiring at-the-money option will quickly run off to infinity as it approaches expiration while its zeta will drop rapidly to zero. In contrast, although the gamma and theta of a longer-dated option will rise and its zeta fall as time passes, these changes occur more slowly. Thus, anyone hedging a very short-dated option with substantially longer-dated, exchange-traded options must either look past today to a specific hedging horizon or be prepared to adjust the surrogate option hedge—as we say about voting in Chicago—both early and often.

Finding Robust Hedges

Ideally, we want to find hedges that work no matter what happens. As a practical matter, we focus on:

- Changes in the level of yields as large as two standard deviations in either direction. This reflects the cap's delta profile and shows the effect of yields rising or falling while volatility remains unchanged;

- Changes in the level of volatility as large as two standard deviations in either direction. This reflects the cap's zeta profile and shows the effect of volatilities rising or falling while yields remain unchanged;

- Combined changes in yields and volatilities; and

- Changes in the slope of the yield curve as measured by the spread between lead and deferred contract futures prices.

Altogether, including the possibility of nothing happening except the passing of time, our search for a robust hedge covers 15 possible interest rate, volatility, and yield curve scenarios.

For each of these scenarios, we calculate the gain or loss on the cap. We then find the combination of futures and options, subject to certain constraints, that best offsets those gains and losses.[3]

Non-Parallel Shifts in Implied Volatility

All of the work we have done on the maturity structure of volatility suggests that short-term volatilities are more changeable than

---

3. The particular algorithm we use finds the optimal hedge by searching among alternative combinations of available Eurodollar futures and options. The weights on the various futures and options in the hedge are chosen to minimize the sum of squared deviations between the hedge and cap payoffs subject to a constraint on total transaction costs. The transaction cost constraint is represented by a limit on the number of contracts, long or short, that the hedge is allowed to use. In addition, for simplicity and ease of execution, a constraint also is placed on the number of distinct option series allowed in the solution. One could also allow for contract liquidity by permitting bid/ask spreads to be reckoned among the costs of the hedge.

long-term volatilities.[4] Exhibit 6.8 confirms similar behavior for implied volatilities.

For example, the daily standard deviation of implied volatility for one-month options is shown to be 1.1 percentage points around an average implied volatility of 16.2 percent. In contrast, the daily standard deviation of implied volatility for nine-month options is only 0.5 percentage points around an average implied volatility of 20.1 percent. In other words, one-month implied volatilities are more than twice as variable as nine-month implied volatilities.

There are two practical consequences of gearing hedges to standard deviations of outcomes:

- the range of volatilities scanned for near-dated options is wider than the range of volatilities scanned for longer-dated options; and
- the range of volatilities scanned for long-horizon hedges is wider than the range of volatilities scanned for short-horizon hedges.

To illustrate the first point, suppose that you want to hedge against a two-percentage-point swing in nine-month volatilities using one-month options. In constructing a hedge, you would consider a 4.4-percentage-point swing in one-month volatilities. This feature of our hedge design is especially important when exchange-traded options with comparatively short expirations are used to cross-hedge the volatility exposure in an interest rate cap with comparatively long expirations.

Our approach to picking volatility scenarios also ties the range of implied volatilities (and futures prices) to the length of the hedging horizon. For example, the range of probable outcomes is roughly five times wider for a one-month hedging horizon than it is for a one-day hedging horizon. Thus, a hedge that would cover 95 percent of the one-day risk in a nine-month option would have to work over a range of implied volatilities from 19.1 percent to 21.1 percent (that is, 20.1 percent plus or minus two standard

---

4. Evidence of this will be provided in the concluding section of this chapter.

Exhibit 6.8

Variability of Eurodollar Implied Volatilities
(March 1985 to June 1989)

Time to Expiration (months)	Average Implied Volatility	Standard Deviation of 1-Day Changes in Implied Volatility*
1	16.2	1.1
3	18.1	0.7
6	20.1	0.6
9	21.0	0.5

Source: *DCNYF Database*

* *Evaluated at the average level of implied volatility.*

• DISCOUNT CORPORATION OF NEW YORK FUTURES •

deviations). For a 30-day hedging horizon, the appropriate range of implied volatilities would be from 15.1 percent to 25.1 percent.

Typical Structure of a Hedge

In the cap market, reset dates often do not correspond to the expirations of Eurodollar futures and options. Either the dates fall on a different day in the expiration month or in a different month altogether, or the reset dates extend further than the longest-dated Eurodollar option.

Exhibit 6.9 summarizes the possible mismatches between a cap's settlement dates and the expiration dates available for Eurodollar futures and options. Any cap or book of caps can be segregated into options having three different kinds of expiration dates:

- short-dated options that expire before any available exchange-traded option;
- mid-dated options that expire in between the settlement dates of two exchange-traded options; and
- long-dated options that expire after any available exchange-traded options.

Referring again to Exhibit 6.4, the difficulty in using exchange-traded options to hedge caps stems from the fact that zeta, gamma, and theta depend on an option's time remaining to expiration. Thus, you cannot hedge options with one expiration solely with options with another expiration. The resulting hedge will either have too much of one characteristic or too little of another.

Part of the answer to this problem was illustrated in the previous section where a long-dated cap was hedged with long options in the farthest-dated Eurodollar option and with short options in the nearest-dated Eurodollar option. The reasoning behind this combination was that the long-dated options provided the zeta exposure while the short-dated options helped to offset the excessive gamma and theta.

Generally, the typical structure of a hedge for a cap is as follows:

Exhibit 6.9

Cap Settlement Dates

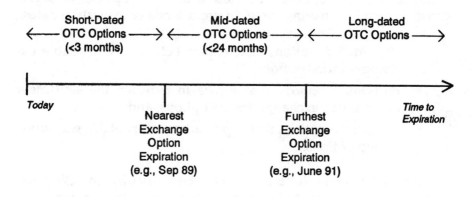

- hedge the short-dated options of the cap with long positions in the lead month exchange-traded options and short positions in the longer-dated options;

- hedge the mid-dated options of the cap with long positions in exchange-traded options that straddle the expiration of the OTC option;

- hedge the long-dated options of the cap with long positions in the longest-dated, exchange-traded options and short positions in shorter-dated options.

When you look at the whole cap, of course, some of the long and short positions of the hedge will cancel each other. Nonetheless, the basic structure of a hedge for a cap using exchange-traded contracts will typically involve combinations of both long and short positions in Eurodollar options.

Example of Hedging a Three-Year Cap

We can illustrate these concepts with the following example of an 8.75 percent three-year quarterly cap on three-month LIBOR with its first settlement in 45 days. (See Exhibit 6.10.) We assume that the first available Eurodollar option contract expires in 90 days so that none of the settlement dates on the cap correspond to expiration dates available for IMM Eurodollar options. Moreover, this cap has options expiring in all three expiration classes—short, mid, and long.

For illustrative purposes, we will first show how a hedge might be constructed if it were designed to deal separately with each of the three types of options embedded in the cap. Such an approach would be suitable only for the simplest hedging problems, but it has the advantage of highlighting the reasoning behind the hedge for a more complicated position. In practice, anyone with a complex book of caps would hedge the book as a whole. Thus, we will also construct a hedge for the cap as a whole and compare the result with the combined hedges for the individual parts of the cap.

Exhibit 6.10

Cap

Cap Rate **Principal Amount** **Market Index** **Settlement Dates**	8.75 Percent $100,000,000 3-Month LIBOR Quarterly, Aug 1, 1989 - May 1, 1992
Settlement Dates **of Available IMM** **Eurodollar Options**	Quarterly, Sep 1989 - June 1991

Hedging the Long-Dated Options

The long-dated portion of the cap consists of four options expiring from August 1, 1991 to May 1, 1992. The hedge we constructed for these options was designed so that no rebalancing would be required for at least one year. Our optimization results suggested the following hedge:

Buy 301 June 1991   90.75   puts
Buy 27 June 1991   90.75   calls
Buy 140 June 1991   91.75   puts
Sell 104 September 1990   90.75   puts
Sell 27 June 1992   futures

Hedges for long-dated options tend to hold up reasonably well over time because their risk characteristics change fairly slowly. Exhibit 6.11 illustrates this point by comparing the net gains and losses on the hedged long-dated options with those resulting if the portfolio were left unhedged. Over a 45-day period (columns 4 and 5), the worst case scenario is only an 11-tick loss per million ($27,500 per $100 million cap) on the hedged portfolio and a 335-tick loss on the unhedged options. After one year, which was the target horizon for this hedge, the hedged position could lose as much as 53 ticks if yields and volatilities both increased two standard deviations. In the same scenario, however, the unhedged options would have lost 1,238 ticks per million or a little over $3 million on a $100 million portfolio.

Two properties of the hedge contribute to its robustness. One is that the strikes for the options in the hedge surround the strike price of the cap fairly closely. This reflects the point made earlier that a properly constructed hedge ought to reflect the moneyness of the cap. Because the hedge constructed here does so, it provides substantial protection against changes in volatility even if futures prices move considerably.

Exhibit 6.11

Hedging the Long-Dated Portion of a Cap
with Exchange-Traded Options
(P/L in quarterly ticks; 1 tick = $2,500 on $100 Million Cap Portfolio)

Yield & Volatility Scenarios	One Year Horizon P/L		45 Day Horizon P/L	
	Unhedged Cap	Hedged Cap	Unhedged Cap	Hedged Cap
No Change	+47	-12	+4	-2
Yield				
+2 Std. Deviation	-1022	+25	-238	+8
+1	-372	-18	-105	+1
-1	+241	-7	+92	-3
-2	+299	+10	+159	-2
Volatility				
+2 Std. Deviation	-273	-37	-94	-6
+1	-82	-23	-42	-4
-1	+134	-2	+44	0
-2	+192	+8	+79	+2
Yield/Volatility				
+2/+2 Std. Deviation	-1238	-53	-335	+3
+2/-2	-1005	+42	-169	+14
-2/+2	+148	-31	+73	-8
-2/-2	`+311	+17	+220	+4
Yield Curve Slope				
Steepen 1 Std. Deviation	-286	-45	-153	-11
Flatten 1 Std. Deviation	+240	0	+128	+3
Average Absolute Error[1]	393	22	129	5
Maximum Loss	1238	53	335	11

[1]   *Absolute value of P/L over all scenarios*

• DISCOUNT CORPORATION OF NEW YORK FUTURES •

The other property is that the hedge uses futures to deal with the two scenarios that allow for changes in the slope of the yield curve. Exchange-traded Eurodollar futures are available for settlement up to four years in the future, while options are available only one-and-a-half years.[5] One of the risks of relying solely on shorter-dated options to hedge longer-dated caps is that spreads between long- and short-term forward rates can change. This risk can be reduced by combining back-month futures contracts, whose expiration dates more closely match the settlement dates of the long-dated parts of the cap, with back-month call options. Similarly, one can combine calls with interest rate swaps or U.S. Treasury securities to handle caps extending beyond four years. Combining call options with either futures or swaps is a way of synthetically creating a longer-dated put option that provides better protection against yield curve slope changes.

We should stress that robust hedges like these can have apparent risk exposure if they are evaluated in the conventional way. For example, the current delta of the hedged position in this case would be -4.3. The reason for this imbalance is that the hedge was designed with a one-year horizon in mind, and the deltas of the various options in the position will change as they age.

Also, a practical consequence of our approach to choosing volatility scenarios is that the hedged position will have a slight negative zeta. Because we scan over a wider range of implied volatilities in the nearby months than we do in the distant months, we need less long zeta in the hedge to counterbalance the short zeta in the longer-dated OTC options.

Hedging the Mid-Dated Options

Hedges for mid-dated OTC options are probably the most straightforward to construct since they simply involve buying put options in the contract months that straddle the settlement date. Exhibit 6.12 shows the effect of such a hedge for the portion of the cap

---

5. The hedging examples used in this chapter were prepared when the CME still listed Eurodollar options with expirations out to two full years. The two most distant contract months have since been discontinued so that the longest dated option has no more than 18 months remaining to expiration.

Exhibit 6.12

Hedging a Mid-Dated Portion of a Cap
with Exchange-Traded Options
(Cap Settles November 1, 1989)
(P/L in quarterly ticks; 1 tick = $2,500 on $100 Million Cap Portfolio)

Yield & Volatility Scenarios	90 Day Horizon		45 Day Horizon	
	Unhedged Cap	Hedged Cap	Unhedged Cap	Hedged Cap
No Change	+15	0	+6	0
Yield				
+2 Std. Deviation	-132	0	-81	-1
+1	-46	-2	-30	-1
-1	+35	+2	+26	+1
-2	+37	-1	+34	0
Volatility				
+2 Std. Deviation	+2	0	-6	+1
+1	+9	0	+1	0
-1	+20	+1	+11	0
-2	+23	+1	+15	-1
Yield/Volatility				
+2/+2 Std. Deviation	-134	+1	-87	+1
+2/-2	-132	0	-79	-1
-2/+2	+36	+1	+29	+1
-2/-2	`+37	-1	+36	0
Yield Curve Slope				
Steepen 1 Std. Deviation	+6	+1	0	+1
Flatten 1 Std. Deviation	+22	0	+12	-1
Average Absolute Error[1]	46	1	30	1
Maximum Loss	134	2	87	1

[1]   Absolute value of P/L over all scenarios

• DISCOUNT CORPORATION OF NEW YORK FUTURES •

settling on November 1, 1989. The hedge, which was designed so that no rebalancing would be needed for at least 90 days, is:

Buy 27 September 1989 91.00 puts
Buy 76 December 1989 91.25 puts

This hedge is not much different from one that might be constructed simply by using calendar days to weight the two adjacent contract months. The main difference is that hedges for those parts of the cap expiring in the middle of two IMM expiration dates will be slightly more robust if a greater weight is placed on the back-month contract. This is because the risk parameters of the front-month options begin to change more quickly than those on the cap so that the effectiveness of the hedge is reduced.

At some point, of course, the shorter-dated exchange option expires. In this case, the September 1989 puts expire on Monday, the 18th. At that time, the problem becomes one of hedging a short-dated cap.

Hedging the Short-Dated Options

We can illustrate the problem of hedging short-dated options by constructing one for the cap expiring August 1, 1989. The best hedge is:

Buy 124 September 1989 91.25 puts
Buy 12 September 1989 91.25 calls
Sell 15 June 1990 91.25 puts

The reasoning behind this hedge is the same as that previously discussed for long-dated caps. If the August settlement had been hedged simply by buying September Eurodollar puts, the mismatch in expiration dates would produce a net position that is either short gamma, long zeta, or both. One way to offset this residual risk is to increase the number of front-month options purchased and to sell back-month options.

Finding robust hedges for short-dated caps becomes increasingly more difficult as the mismatch between expiration dates worsens. As Exhibit 6.13 indicates, the hedge for a 45-day option

Exhibit 6.13

Hedging the Short-Dated Portion of a Cap
with Exchange-Traded Options
(P/L in quarterly ticks; 1 tick = $2,500 on $100 Million Cap Portfolio)
(P/L at Cap Expiration)

Yield & Volatility Scenarios	Cap Expires in 45 Days		Cap Expires in 15 Days	
	Unhedged Cap	Hedged Cap[1]	Unhedged Cap	Hedged Cap[2]
No Change	+22	+10	+13	+9
Yield				
+2 Std. Deviation	-95	-1	-53	-8
+1	-35	-4	-20	-3
-1	+22	-4	+13	-3
-2	+22	-1	+13	-8
Volatility				
+2 Std. Deviation	+22	+24	+13	+20
+1	+22	+16	+13	+14
-1	+22	+6	+13	+5
-2	+22	+2	+13	+1
Yield/Volatility				
+2/+2 Std. Deviation	95	+1	-53	0
+2/-2	-95	0	-53	-13
-2/+2	+22	+1	+13	-1
-2/-2	`+22	0	+13	-13
Yield Curve Slope				
Steepen 1 Std. Deviation	+18	+9	+12	+10
Flatten 1 Std. Deviation	+22	+8	+13	+7
Average Absolute Error[3]	37	6	21	8
Maximum Loss	95	4	53	13

[1] *Buy 124 Sep '89 91.25 Puts; Buy 12 Sep '89 91.25 Calls; Sell 15 June '90 91.25 Puts*
[2] *Buy 124 Sep '89 91.25 Puts; Buy 19 Sep '89 91.25 Calls; Sell 7 June '90 91.00 Puts*
[3] *Absolute value of P/L over all scenarios.*

• DISCOUNT CORPORATION OF NEW YORK FUTURES •

using three-month and longer-dated Eurodollar options appears to work reasonably well (columns 2 and 3). The worst case scenario for the hedged portfolio after 45 days is only a four-tick loss. This is less than one-twentieth the maximum loss realized by the unhedged portfolio.

The hedge is less impressive when a 15-day option is hedged with three-month options (columns 4 and 5). Compared to the 45-day cap, this hedge requires a larger number of front-month contracts and a scaling back in the number of back-month contracts sold. While the hedge certainly reduces the risk in the cap, the reduction appears to be relatively modest.

One reason for the modest reduction in risk is that with a 15-day horizon, less is likely to go wrong with an unhedged portfolio; that is, there is less risk to reduce. A second reason is that when there is a large mismatch between the settlement date of the cap and the expiration date of the nearest exchange-traded option, hedging an expiring option can actually increase risk by making the position more sensitive to unusual changes in the shape of the yield curve or in the maturity structure of implied volatility. We assume, for example, that implied volatilities all rise or fall by the same number of standard deviations. We know, however, that there is slippage in this relationship that will cause the actual hedge to be riskier than it seems on paper.

In these cases, inexpensive robust hedges usually don't exist. Depending on the risk preferences of the cap writer, the best strategies are to leave the cap unhedged, delta hedge the cap with futures, or sell the cap to someone else.

Combined Hedge

As a general rule, the best hedge for a cap will not be the simple sum of hedges for the individual options embedded in the cap. This reflects the fact that some of the risks in the separate options in the cap offset one another. As a result, less expensive and more reliable hedges can usually be constructed when the interactions between the various options are taken into account.

The combined hedge that appears to work reasonably well for the three-year cap is:

Buy 365   September 1989   91.25   puts
Sell 59   September 1989   90.75   calls
Buy 649   June 1991   91.00   puts
Buy 135   June 1991   91.50   calls
Sell 91   June 1992   futures

The hedge involves buying the longest-dated options, buying and selling front-month options, and selling longer-dated futures.[6]

An interesting feature of this hedge is the absence of options with intermediate expirations. This reflects, in part, the interaction between the three parts of the cap. Hedges for the short-dated and long-dated parts of the cap required short positions at intermediate expirations to balance the characteristics of long positions in the shortest-dated and longest-dated exchange-traded options. Hedges for the mid-dated parts of the cap required long positions at intermediate expirations. In this case, these requirements appear to be offsetting.

Also note that the hedge relies fairly heavily on the use of front-month options. The obvious disadvantage in using these options is that they will have to be replaced fairly soon. On the other hand, front-month options usually have the advantage of being relatively liquid so that bid/ask spreads tend to be small. If the costs of rolling the options over into the next expiration exceed the benefits of greater liquidity, the hedger might choose to restrict the hedge to somewhat longer-dated options.

Exhibit 6.14 summarizes the risk parameters of the cap writer's position, which shows that this particular position is nearly flat in all four important dimensions.

Exhibit 6.15 shows the net profit-and-loss after 45 days, which was the target horizon for this hedge. For comparison, we also show the gains and losses associated with hedging the cap using only futures (column 4, Exhibit 6.15). As the table shows, the futures hedge is not robust to large changes in price or volatility. By contrast, the hedge constructed using options appears to hold up fairly well. The worst case scenario for the unhedged cap is a

---

6. As noted above, the CME now list Eurodollar options with expirations out to 18 months. Given the options that are available now, a new solution to this hedge likely would replace the June 1991 options with December 1990 options.

Exhibit 6.14

Risk Summary for Combined Hedge

	Cap	Hedge	Total
Delta	+564.3	-565.9	-1.6
Gamma	-29.1	29.4	0.3
Zeta	-40.6	39.8	-0.8
Theta	+0.8	-0.9	0.1

Delta = *net futures equivalence*
Gamma = *change in delta given a 10-bp increase in the futures price*
Zeta = *change in value of cap writer's position in ticks given a one-percentage-point increase in implied volatility One tick = $2,500 on $100 million cap*
Theta = *change in value of cap writer's position in ticks given a one-day passage of time*

• DISCOUNT CORPORATION OF NEW YORK FUTURES •

Exhibit 6.15

Combined Hedge for Cap
(P/L in quarterly ticks; 1 tick = $2,500 on $100 Million Cap Portfolio)
(P/L after 45 Days)

Yield & Volatility Scenarios	Unhedged Cap	Hedged Cap	Memo: Delta Hedged with Futures
No Change	+49	+4	+49
Yield			
+2 Std. Deviation	-826	+1	-161
+1	-341	-5	-19
-1	+291	-7	-12
-2	+457	0	-130
Volatility			
+2 Std. Deviation	-175	+14	-175
+1	-55	+8	-55
-1	+139	+1	+139
-2	+217	0	+217
Yield/Volatility			
+2/+2 Std. Deviation	-1029	-3	-364
+2/-2	-688	+4	-22
-2/+2	+277	-7	-309
-2/-2	+578	+10	-8
Yield Curve Slope			
Steepen 1 Std. Deviation	-243	+4	+18
Flatten 1 Std. Deviation	+282	+4	+21
Average Absolute Error[1]	376	5	113
Maximum Loss	1029	7	364

[1] *Absolute value of P/L over all scenarios*

• DISCOUNT CORPORATION OF NEW YORK FUTURES •

1,029-tick loss per $1 million cap. Using futures reduces this loss to 364 ticks, while the worst case scenario for the options hedge is only a seven-tick loss.

Yield Curve Slope Risk

In the previous section, yield curve slope risk was eliminated with a two-step procedure that worked by first delta hedging the longer-dated part of the cap with futures and then using options to eliminate the residual risk. The two-step procedure is an alternative that may be appropriate for hedgers who are especially concerned about yield curve risk. The solution described in this section, by contrast, relies less heavily on futures.

Part of the difference between the two solutions may simply reflect the fact that the yield curve scenarios described above are not rich enough to adequately characterize a broad array of possible yield curves. Moreover, our optimization algorithm places restrictions on the number of different hedging instruments allowed so that it precludes complex solutions involving futures with many different expiration dates. The relatively few futures contracts in the above solution also highlights a distinct disadvantage of the two step procedure. Using futures and calls to synthetically create puts requires a larger number of contracts, and therefore greater transaction costs, than purchasing puts outright. As a result, the two-step procedure usually provides better protection against unusual changes in the shape of the yield curve but only at the cost of a less robust hedge in other scenarios or greater transaction costs.

Hedge Error versus Hedge Cost

As one might expect, tighter hedges can be achieved at a higher cost. This point is illustrated in Exhibit 6.16, which shows the relationship between hedge error (for which we use average absolute error) and the number of contracts used in the hedge. As shown in Exhibit 6.15, the average absolute hedge error was 376 ticks for the completely unhedged portfolio. In contrast, our hedge, which used a total of 1,300 contracts, had a hedge error of only five ticks.

As Exhibit 6.16 illustrates, hedge error decreases as the number of contracts used in constructing the hedge increases. There

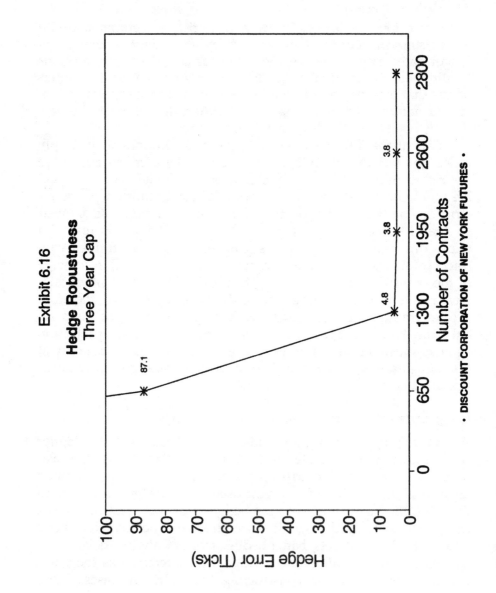

Exhibit 6.16

Hedge Robustness
Three Year Cap

• DISCOUNT CORPORATION OF NEW YORK FUTURES •

are, however, substantial decreasing returns to scale. Cutting the number of contracts in the hedge to 650 increases the hedging error to 87 ticks. Doubling the number of contracts to 2,600 reduces the hedge error by less than one tick. Faced with such a tradeoff, it is the hedger who must choose the hedge that strikes the best balance between hedge error and transaction costs.

Managing Hedges over Time

The most important issue remaining is how to manage most efficiently a cap or book of caps over time. This issue raises a number of questions about rebalancing rules, which in turn raises questions about appropriate hedging horizons. Although the hedging horizons used in this section vividly illustrate how robust a hedge can be over time, the horizons themselves are almost certainly not optimal.

When to Hedge with Futures and When to Hedge with Options

Until now, we have been absorbed in the technical side of hedging caps. Now we turn to the practical economic question of when one should hedge with options and when one should hedge with futures. The decision belongs to the hedger, of course, but the answer should hinge, at least in part, on the relative costs of these two strategies.

We showed at the outset of this chapter that the cost of a dynamic delta balancing strategy depends on realized volatility. Realized volatility is a measure of how volatile the underlying market turns out to be over the life of the hedge. If the market turns out to be highly volatile, the delta hedge will be costly. If the market turns out to be quiet, the delta hedge will be cheap.

What is the alternative? The chief alternative, and the one we have spent the most time on in this chapter, is to buy options. What does this cost? The cost of buying real options depends on implied volatility. Implied volatility is a measure of how volatile people expect the underlying market to be. If people expect the market to be highly volatile, a real option hedge will be expensive. If people expect the market to be quiet, a real option hedge will be cheap.

How can the hedger choose between the two? The work we have done on the maturity structure of volatilities can shed some light on how to answer this question. In Exhibit 6.17, we show how volatile LIBOR has been over various horizons during the time from January 1982 through June 1990.[7] For example, we find that the lowest one-year historical volatility observed during this period was 12 percent. The highest one-year historical volatility was 32 percent. For caps with a five-year horizon, historical volatilities ranged from 17 percent on the low end to 22 percent on the high end.

With these historical volatilities as background, consider the following two situations.

The first corresponds to the weeks following the October 1987 stock market crash. At that time, implied volatilities in Eurodollar options with nearly a year remaining to expiration were trading at levels over 30 percent. Given the range of historical volatilities shown in Exhibit 6.17, this would appear to be high.[8] During the entire period from 1982 on, there has not been one episode in which historical volatility was as high as this level of implied volatility, not even the period including the crash.

The hedger can now ask, "What are the chances that a dynamic delta balancing hedge will cost more than a real option hedge?" Another way of asking the same question is, "What are the chances that realized volatility will be higher than the current level of implied volatility?" In this instance, if history is any guide, the answer is that the chances appear to be very small indeed. As a result, the hedger should lean toward a dynamic delta hedging strategy.

The second situation corresponds to the end of June 1990. At that time, implied volatilities in Eurodollar options with nearly

---

7. This table also appeared in Chapter 5.
8. The correct reference point would have been the range of historical volatilities that had been observed as of this date. As a practical matter, the volatilities in Exhibit 6.17 are not especially sensitive to the date.

Exhibit 6.17

Eurodollar Yield Volatility
(Percent, January 1982 to June 1990)

Term	Volatility		
	Minimum	Maximum	Average
1 Month	4.2	57.9	18.1
3 Months	7.5	44.4	18.5
6 Months	9.8	36.8	18.9
1 Year	12.2	31.9	19.0
2 Years	14.1	25.7	19.2
3 Years	17.4	22.8	19.2
4 Years	17.4	22.3	19.1
5 Years	17.3	21.5	19.2

* *Based on lead contract futures yield.*

nine months remaining to expiration were trading below 12 percent. Given the range of historical volatilities shown in Exhibit 6.17, this would appear to be low. Suppose the hedger now asks, "What are the chances that a dynamic delta balancing hedge will cost more than a real option hedge?" In this case, the answer would appear to be "very high." For that matter, the probability of a dynamic delta hedging strategy costing more than an option replication strategy would seem to be nearly one. Thus, the hedger should lean toward a hedge with real options.

In most cases, the answer is less clear. Implied volatilities in Eurodollar options and caps rarely trade at such extreme levels. More often, both implied and historical volatilities lie within the range of historical experience. When they do, the hedger's choice is not clear-cut. Rather, the best hedging approach may require a blending of the two strategies, tilting the mix toward the less expensive and away from the more expensive as the levels of implied volatilities rise and fall.

CHAPTER 7

Practical Considerations

A cademics have known for some time that futures are not the same as forwards. Apart from credit considerations, the chief difference between the two is that gains and losses on futures are settled at the end of every day in cash. Forward contracts rarely have this mark-to-market provision. Even so, it is standard practice in the futures industry to price futures as if they were forwards. For example, the fair value calculations done in Chapter 2 and the Eurodollar strip rate calculations done in Chapter 3 treat futures this way. And, for most commodities, pricing futures as if they were forwards is just fine.

Treating Eurodollar futures as if they were forward contracts, however, can lead to serious pricing errors.[1] The effect of financing variation margin at high rates when yields rise and at low rates when yields fall produces a substantial bias in favor of the short and against the long for Eurodollar futures that have horizons of two or more years. For example, at Eurodollar rates around eight percent and at reasonable levels of yield volatility, the value of the financing bias can be as much as eight basis points on a four-year Eurodollar strip. On a single strip of 16 contracts, eight basis points is worth $3,200. This is serious money.

This chapter will focus on the source and size of the pricing bias and on the implications for banks and other institutions that use Eurodollar futures as an integrated part of their balance sheets. We will show that Eurodollar futures are generally rich when one takes the financing bias into account. For that matter, if Eurodollar strips trade either at or near their fair values as fair values are usually calculated, a short strip is almost always better than a long swap.

Also, our experience indicates that a wide range of financial institutions structure their internal financing arrangements in a way that the richness is not apparent to individual traders. In particular, we find that a surprisingly large number of banks do not charge their traders the current overnight market rate for funds. As we show in this chapter, then, Eurodollar futures will not seem expensive to the traders for these banks even though they are expensive to the bank. In other words, a substantial part of the financial community may not be taking full advantage of what Eurodollar futures can do.

---

1. The material in this chapter was first released in our research note, Belton and Burghardt, "The Financing Bias in Eurodollar Futures Prices," March 22, 1990. Since then, we have heard from a number of banks indicating that our reasoning is correct and that our estimates of the pricing bias are in the right direction although they may be overstated. We found that each bank had done its own homework along similar lines and considered the mispricing of Eurodollar futures to be an opportunity as long as it lasts. At the same time, because each bank felt very proprietary about its work, we were not able to reconcile our results with theirs. We suggest that each bank that has anything more than a trivial Eurodollar position follow the competition's lead and do its own homework.

The Bias in Interest-Rate Futures

Ignoring the effect of daily variation margin payments on interest-rate futures can lead to serious mispricings because of the strong correlation between gains and losses and the interest rates at which those gains and losses can be invested or financed.

For example, a long Eurodollar futures position loses money when yields rise, so that losses must be financed at high rates. A long Eurodollar futures position makes money when yields fall, so that gains are invested at low rates. (See Exhibit 7.1.) On average, then, the interest expense on losses exceeds the interest income on gains. The net result is a distinct disadvantage to being long Eurodollar futures and a corresponding advantage to being short.

To compensate for this imbalance, the futures price must be lower than it otherwise would be. Or, to achieve the same result, the implied futures rate must be higher than the corresponding forward rate. Just how much lower or higher depends, among other things, on how volatile interest rates are expected to be and on how much time remains to the final settlement of the Eurodollar futures contract.

Determining the size of this financing bias requires extensive computer simulations that allow us to capture the effect of interest rate variability over the life of a Eurodollar futures contract. In the next section, we will use a simplified example to outline the problem.

Where Does the Bias Come From?

To see why the daily settlement of gains and losses can affect Eurodollar futures prices, consider the interest rate picture shown in Exhibit 7.2. This exhibit shows a set of possible interest rates starting with a current spot rate of 10 percent. To keep things simple, we assume that in each of two periods rates can either rise or fall 100 basis points, each with a 50 percent probability. At the end of the first period, we see that the spot rate can be either 11 percent or 9 percent. At the end of the second period, the spot rate can be either 12, 10, or 8 percent.

Exhibit 7.1

Variation Margin Financing Bias for Eurodollar Futures

Yield Change	Cash Flow on Long Position	Financing Condition
Yields Up	Cash Paid Out	Borrow at High Rate
Yields Down	Cash Received	Invest at Low Rate

Exhibit 7.2

Financing Variation Margin on Eurodollar Futures

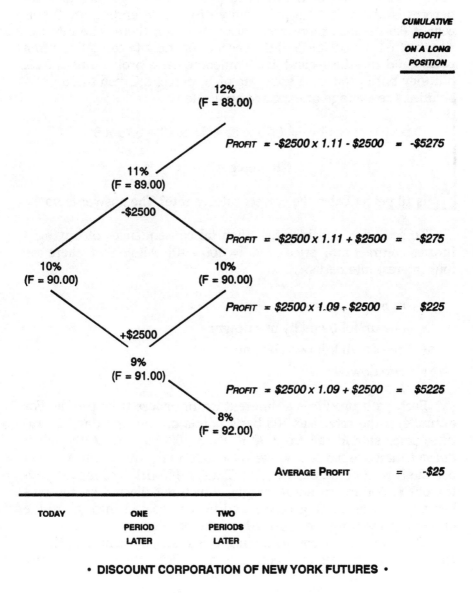

*CUMULATIVE
PROFIT
ON A LONG
POSITION*

12%
(F = 88.00)

PROFIT = -$2500 x 1.11 - $2500 = -$5275

11%
(F = 89.00)

-$2500

PROFIT = -$2500 x 1.11 + $2500 = -$275

10%   10%
(F = 90.00)   (F = 90.00)

PROFIT = $2500 x 1.09 - $2500 = $225

+$2500

9%
(F = 91.00)

PROFIT = $2500 x 1.09 + $2500 = $5225

8%
(F = 92.00)

AVERAGE PROFIT   =   -$25

TODAY   ONE   TWO
               PERIOD   PERIODS
               LATER   LATER

• DISCOUNT CORPORATION OF NEW YORK FUTURES •

The correct forward rate for a situation like this is simply the expected spot rate at the end of the second period. Given our 50 percent probability assumption, the probability of getting to 12 percent is 0.25 [= 0.5 × 0.5], which is the probability of the rate rising two periods in a row. The probability of getting to eight percent is also 0.25. The probability of the rate ending at 10 percent is 0.5 because there are two ways to get there. The rate can rise the first period and fall the second, or the rate can fall the first period and rise the second. Each outcome has a probability of 0.25, but they both produce a spot rate of 10 percent. Given these probabilities, the average or expected spot rate is:

Expected spot rate $= 0.25 \times 12 + 0.5 \times 10 + 0.25 \times 8$

$$= 10 \text{ percent}$$

Is 10 percent also the correct futures rate? The answer is no.

To see why, consider the financial consequences of buying a futures contract at a price of 90 [= 100 - 10]. Altogether, there are four interest rate paths:

- two ups;
- one up followed by one down;
- one down followed by one up;
- two downs.

Each path produces a different profit or loss time profile. For example, if the rate rises 100 basis points on the first day, the futures price should fall from 90 to 89, a 100-tick loss. Although it doesn't matter what tick value we use to make our point, we will use the conventional $25 per tick. Thus, a 100-tick loss means paying out $2,500 in variation margin, which is collected by the broker, paid to the clearing house, and in turn passed through to the broker representing the short side of the position.

There are two ways to finance this cash payment, but the financial consequences are about the same. First, the long can draw down or deplete existing cash balances that are earning appropriate short-term money market rates. In this case, we assume the long gives up the opportunity to invest $2,500 at 11 percent. Second, the long can borrow the cash and pay an appropriate short-term money market rate to finance the borrowing. In this case, the long must pay 11 percent. In either case, the total cost of having to pay out $2,500 at the end of the first period will be $2,775 [= $2,500 × 1.11] by the end of the second period.

Using this reasoning, we can work out the total gains and losses along each interest rate path:

- Two up days

  Profit = -$2,500 × (1.11) - $2,500 = -$5,275

- One up day/one down day

  Profit = -$2,500 × (1.11) + $2,500 = -$275

- One down day/one up day

  Profit = $2,500 × (1.09) - $2,500 = +$225

- Two down days

  Profit = $2,500 × (1.09) + $2,500 = +$5,225

Even a cursory inspection shows that the losses are bigger than the gains. On average, this position will lose money. The expected value of the loss is:

$$-\$25 = -\$5,275/4 + -\$275/4 + \$225/4 + \$5,225/4$$

assuming a probability of one-fourth for each outcome.

Note, too, that the short's perspective is just the opposite. If the futures contract can be sold at 90, the expected profit is $25.

If the futures contract is priced at 90, the immediate implication of this expected loss is that the futures price, which we found by subtracting the correct forward yield from 100, is too high. If our standard for a "fair" futures price is that the expected profit from holding either a long or a short position should be zero, then the futures price must be lower.

In this simple setting, where the value of a tick was $25, the futures price should be about 89.99. Stated differently, the futures yield should be 10.01, which is higher than the correct forward rate.

How Big is the Bias?

To get a better grip on what the financing bias should be, we undertook extensive simulations to capture the three most important variables:

- interest rate volatility;
- futures contract horizon; and
- correlation between futures rates and overnight financing rates.

Increases in any of these three key variables should increase the bias.

Our results are shown in Exhibits 7.3 through 7.5.

Our Best Estimate of the Bias

Exhibit 7.3 shows our best guess about how many basis points are needed to compensate the long for the financing bias at three levels of yield volatility and for contract horizons ranging from three months to five years.

The key assumptions underlying Exhibit 7.3 are:

- gains and losses are financed overnight at the federal funds rate; and
- the correlation between fed funds and Eurodollar rates is 88 percent (our estimate based on historical data from January 1985 through February 1990).

Exhibit 7.3

Theoretical Rate Spreads
Futures Rate Less Implied Forward Rates
(basis points)

Time to Expiration	Eurodollar Yield Volatility		
	15%	20%	25%
3 months	0	0	0.1
6 months	0.2	0.3	0.5
1 year	0.7	1.2	2.0
2 years	2.8	5.2	8.2
3 years	6.7	11.9	18.9
4 years	12.0	21.6	34.1
5 years	19.0	34.1	53.9

Assumes variation margin on futures is financed at fed funds rate. Relationship between fed funds and Eurodollar futures estimated econometrically.

• **DISCOUNT CORPORATION OF NEW YORK FUTURES** •

Exhibit 7.4

Observed Rate Spreads
Eurodollar Futures Rate Less Implied Forward Rates
(basis points, 1/2/90 to 3/8/90)

Contract Month	Rate Spreads				Average Mispricing
		Observed			
	Theoretical*	Average	Smallest	Largest	(Theoretical-Average)
June '90	0.0	5.4	-6	20	-5.4
September '90	0.3	9.4	1	31	-9.1
March '91	1.2	-2.6	-33	24	3.8
March '92	5.2	-19.2	-36	7	24.4
March '93	11.9	-18.1	-56	2	30.0
December '93	21.6	2.4	-29	28	19.2

*   *Assumes 20 percent yield volatility*

• DISCOUNT CORPORATION OF NEW YORK FUTURES •

Exhibit 7.5

Observed Rate Spreads
Eurodollar Strip Rate Less Swap Rate
(basis points, 1/2/90 to 3/8/90)

| Term | Rate Spreads | | | | Average Mispricing |
| | Theoretical | Observed | | | |
		Average	Smallest	Largest	(Theoretical-Average)
2 years	2.1	-2.0	-12	7	4.1
3 years	4.6	-1.6	-11	9	6.2
4 years	8.1	-1.6	-14	12	9.7

The most striking conclusions to be drawn from Exhibit 7.3 are:

- The financing bias is trivial for contracts with horizons less than one year. Regardless of the level of volatility, the bias is less than two basis points.

- The bias is highly sensitive to increases in the horizon for longer dated contracts.

  At 20 percent yield volatility, the theoretical spread is 12 basis points for a three-year contract and 22 basis points for a four-year contract.

- The bias is highly sensitive to increases in volatility for longer dated contracts.

  The theoretical spread for a four-year contract is 12 basis points at 15 percent yield volatility. At 20 percent yield volatility, the theoretical spread is 22 basis points.

Implications for Traders and Hedgers

How well do observed spreads between Eurodollar futures rates and their corresponding forward rates compare with the spreads needed to compensate for the financing bias? Exhibit 7.4 compares the theoretical spread at 20 percent yield volatility with observed spreads for various individual contract months during the first three months of 1990.

The right column of Exhibit 7.4 shows in basis points the difference between the theoretical spread and the average observed spread. A positive spread can also be read as the amount by which the futures contract is overpriced. For example, the March 1992 contract appears to have been overpriced by 24 basis points on average over the first two-and-a-half months of this year. The September 1990 contract, on the other hand, seems to have been an average of nine basis points cheap (that is, underpriced) over the same period.

On average, we find that the near-dated futures contracts are underpriced while the long-dated contracts are overpriced. Most of this mispricing, though, is in the spread between the Eurodollar futures rate and the implied forward rate. Only a small part is due to the financing bias.

A different picture emerges when we compare Eurodollar strip rates with interest-rate swap rates. Exhibit 7.5 shows the theoretical spread for two-year, three-year, and four-year Eurodollar strips together with observed spreads in the swap market.

Here we find that the average mispricing increases with the term of the strip and that most of the mispricing is due to a failure to take the financing bias into account.

Are the mispricings large enough to worry about? Probably.

The mispricing on a Eurodollar strip applies to every contract in the strip. Thus, on a four-year Eurodollar strip, each basis point is worth $400 [= $25 × 4 contract months × 4 years] per million. At this rate, a 10-basis-point mispricing on a $50 million strip is worth $200,000.

This is serious money and has important implications for traders and hedgers. For example, given the choice between selling a strip of Eurodollar futures and entering into a long swap (to pay fixed and receive floating rates), selling the Eurodollar strip would seem to be more profitable than buying the swap by a substantial margin.

Sensitivity to Rate Correlations and Yield Levels

Exhibit 7.6 shows that the theoretical bias is sensitive to the correlation between financing rates and Eurodollar futures rates. As expected, higher correlations require bigger adjustments. Note that our best estimates of the bias (Exhibit 7.3) correspond fairly closely to those shown here for a 90 percent correlation.

Exhibit 7.7 shows that the theoretical bias depends also on the starting level of yields. For any given level of relative yield volatility, the bias is considerably larger at a high starting yield than at a low starting yield.

Exhibit 7.6

Effect of Yield Correlation* on Theoretical Rate Spread
(basis points)

Low Yield Volatility (15%)

Time to Expiration	Correlation			
	1.0	0.9	0.8	0.7
6 months	0.2	0.2	0.2	0.1
1 year	0.8	0.7	0.6	0.6
2 years	3.2	2.9	2.6	2.3
3 years	7.6	6.9	6.1	5.4
4 years	13.7	12.5	11.1	9.8
5 years	21.6	19.8	17.7	15.5

High Yield Volatility (20%)

Time to Expiration	Correlation			
	1.0	0.9	0.8	0.7
6 months	0.4	0.3	0.3	0.3
1 year	1.4	1.3	1.1	1.0
2 years	5.9	5.4	4.8	4.2
3 years	13.6	12.4	11.1	9.7
4 years	24.6	22.5	20.2	17.7
5 years	38.8	35.8	32.2	28.4

*   Correlation between Eurodollar rate and overnight financing rate

• DISCOUNT CORPORATION OF NEW YORK FUTURES •

Exhibit 7.7

Effect of Yield Level on Theoretical Rate Spread*
(basis points)

Time to Expiration	Yield Level (percent)		
	8.5	10.5	12.5
3 months	0.0	0.1	0.2
6 months	0.3	0.5	0.7
1 year	1.3	2.0	2.9
2 years	5.4	8.4	11.8
3 years	12.4	19.1	27.3
4 years	22.5	34.6	49.6
5 years	35.8	55.2	79.0

* *Assumes 20 percent yield volatility and .90 correlation between Eurodollar rate and overnight financing rate.*

Implications for Banks

The importance of the net effect of financing variation margin on long-dated Eurodollar positions should not be lost on those who set internal pricing policies for banks and other financial institutions.

The pricing bias is in the eye of the beholding trader. If the trader's financing costs are highly correlated with LIBOR, the trader will find that the bias has a measurable effect on his net income. If, as is true for some financial institutions, the trader's financing costs are largely unrelated to LIBOR, the trader will feel almost none of the effects of the financing bias.

In both instances, the trader can be expected to make optimal use of Eurodollar futures from his own perspective. Only in the first instance, though, in which the trader's financing costs mirror his bank's financing costs, will the trader's use of futures be optimal for the bank as well. In the second, the trader will, on balance, have a position that is either too long or that is not short enough to maximize the bank's expected income.

In principle, dealing with this problem is straightforward. Traders can be expected to deal with the financing bias optimally from the bank's perspective if their financing costs are made to be the same as the bank's.

Any other financing policy will produce less than optimal results.

CHAPTER 8

Options on Swaps

Options on swaps ("swaptions") were a natural progression once caps had become firmly entrenched in the market for Eurodollar derivatives. While caps are big business, options on swaps are becoming big business. Approximately $70 billion of these options were traded in 1989, leaving $80 billion in outstanding notional principal amount at the end of the year.

The driving force behind the growing popularity of options on swaps seems to be the extraordinary flexibility that they offer in the world of corporate finance. We will show, for example, that options on swaps can be used to transform callable debt into fixed-rate debt and fixed-rate debt into callable debt. As a result, corporate treasurers have a wider range of financing tools available to them than they had with the conventional tool kit.

As is often the case when there are more than two ways to do the same thing, one way can be cheaper. In this case, it appears that some of the early interest among traders in options on swaps came from outright arbitrage opportunities. For example, there appear to have been instances in which options on swaps carried a higher price than the options embedded in conventional callable corporate notes and bonds. In such cases, companies have been able to sell callable debt and sell options on swaps. The final result, as we will show in this chapter, is straight fixed-rate financing at a lower rate than is available in the fixed-rate debt market.

Even though pure arbitrage is a fleeting thing, the flexibility afforded by options on swaps make them an extremely desirable financing tool. As a result, the innovation is likely to remain after the free income has gone away.

What Are Options on Swaps?

Two major types of options on swaps have evolved. These are:

- an option to enter into a swap at some time in the future; and
- an option to cancel a swap at some time in the future.

Unfortunately, no consistent names for these two types of options have emerged. To help us with the material in this chapter, though, we will adopt the terminology summarized in Exhibit 8.1.

Swaptions

In general, a swaption is an option to enter into a swap. For our purposes, we will distinguish between call swaptions and put swaptions as follows:

- A call swaption is the right to enter into a swap to receive fixed and pay floating rates.
- A put swaption is the right to enter into a swap to pay fixed and receive floating rates.

Of course, if you have sold either of these options, you are obliged to enter into the other side of the transaction if the option is exercised.

This convention has the advantage of making swaptions behave like Treasury note or bond options. With a call swaption, you

Exhibit 8.1

Types of Options on Swaps

Call Swaption -	the right to receive a fixed rate in a swap.
Put Swaption -	the right to pay a fixed rate in a swap.
Callable Swap -	a swap in which the fixed rate payor has the right to terminate the swap.
Putable Swap -	a swap in which the fixed rate receiver has the right to terminate the swap.

have the right to enter into a swap that pays you a predetermined fixed rate while you pay the floating market rate. The value of this right will go up if interest rates fall. This is true as well for a call option on a Treasury note. Thus, call swaptions and calls on Treasury notes should both rise in value as interest rates fall and fall in value as interest rates rise.

With a put swaption, you have the right to enter into a swap that allows you to pay a predetermined fixed rate while you receive the floating market rate. The value of this right will go up if interest rates rise. The same is true, of course, for a put option on a Treasury note.

The drawback to this convention is that if you exercise a call swaption, you establish a short position in a swap. Similarly, if you exercise a put swaption, you establish a long position in a swap.

At this writing (July 1990), there is no clear-cut agreement on terminology in the market. For example, we polled six major participants in the swaptions market and found four in favor of the convention we will use in this chapter. Two favored reversing the nomenclature so that exercising a call swaption would leave you with a long swap while exercising a put swaption would leave you with a short swap.

We also found that everyone dealt with this difference of opinion by specifying explicitly whether the option permitted the holder to pay fixed or receive fixed in the swap. This approach, while cumbersome, has the highly prized virtue of being clear.

Cancelable Swaps

In a cancelable swap, one of the counterparties has the option or right to cancel the swap at some time before the maturity of the swap contract. For example, you may enter into a five-year swap with the right to terminate the swap three years from now, or two years before the maturity of the swap. The convention we will follow here for naming such swaps is consistent with our naming of swaptions. That is:

- A callable swap is a swap in which the side paying fixed (and receiving floating) has the right to terminate the swap.

Stated differently, if you pay fixed in a callable swap, you are long the option. If you receive fixed in a callable swap, you are short the option.

- A putable swap is a swap in which the side receiving fixed (and paying floating) has the right to terminate the swap.

Stated differently, if you pay floating in a putable swap, you are long the option. If you receive floating in a putable swap, you are short the option.

These conventions fit with our distinction between call swaptions and put swaptions.

Consider a five-year swap, callable in three years. If you are paying fixed in this arrangement, you have the right to terminate the swap three years from now. Three years from now, what remains of the original five-year swap is a two-year swap in which you are paying fixed. Exercising your right to cancel the swap is the same as establishing an offsetting swap in which you receive fixed.

A callable swap, then, is equivalent to a position in a straight five-year swap in which you pay fixed combined with a three-year call swaption on a two-year swap. By the same token, a five-year swap, putable in three years, is equivalent to a straight five-year swap in which you pay floating combined with a three-year put swaption on a two-year swap.

Maturities

Swaptions and cancelable swaps typically trade with maturities and expirations in multiples of years and can be quoted in much the same way as forward-rate agreements (FRAs). That is, the first number in the description indicates how many years there are until the option can be exercised. The difference between the first and second numbers indicates the term of the swap if the option is exercised.

For example, a 3x5 swaption is the right to establish a two-year swap three years from now. A 5x10 swaption is the right to establish a five-year swap five years from now.

The same approach can be used to describe cancelable swaps. For example, a 3x5 cancelable swap is a five-year swap that may be terminated by one of the counterparties after three years. A 5x10 cancelable swap is a 10-year swap that may be terminated after five years.

American- versus European-style options

Options that trade over the counter tend to be European-style, which means that they can be exercised only on particular dates. The exceptions are American-style options, which can be exercised anytime up to and including expiration. Options on swaps are often a hybrid of the two.

Applications of Options on Swaps

Swaptions and cancelable swaps have become popular partly because of their flexibility. They have also attracted attention because they have, from time to time, allowed institutions to take advantage of perceived mispricings in the callable debt market.

Callable debt is a standard part of the corporate finance tool kit. With a callable note or bond, the issuer retains the right to buy back the issue at some time in the future at an agreed-upon price. That is, the issuer holds a call option. As a result, the issuer's position can be viewed as a short position in a conventional non-callable, fixed-rate note and a long position in a call option on that note.

Whoever owns the callable issue, of course, is long the equivalent of a non-callable, fixed-rate note and is short the call option. The net value of the position must reflect the value of the short call. As a result, the price of the callable issue will be lower than the price of the non-callable issue by the value placed on the call option.

With the advent of swaptions, we find that the same position can be assembled from components rather than bought off the shelf. For example, the corporate borrower has a choice between issuing callable debt on the one hand and issuing straight, non-callable debt combined with a long swaption on the other. If the swaption has the same expiration and strike price characteristics as the option embedded in the callable issue, the two approaches provide the same financial characteristics.

If the callable debt market and the swaptions market are not integrated fully, however, the prices of the two options need not be the same. If they are not, the stage is set for pure arbitrage.

Two examples will help show how options on swaps fit into the corporate finance world and how one can profit from relative mispricings in the callable debt and swap options markets.

Example 1: Create Synthetic Five-Year, Fixed-Rate Financing

Consider the following problem. A company really wants straight five-year debt. The obvious approach would be to issue a five-year, fixed-rate, non-callable note directly. An alternative to this approach would be to:

- issue a five-year, fixed-rate note, callable by the issuer after three years; and
- sell a 3x5 call swaption.

In the second approach, the issuer has the option to call its debt after three years and is, as a result, long a call option. The issuer then offsets the long call embedded in the callable note by selling an equivalent option in the swap market. The net result is the equivalent of a fixed-rate, non-callable note.

To see why the second approach is like the first, consider how the second approach plays out as yields rise and fall. As shown in Exhibit 8.2, if yields rise, the market price of the note will be lower than the price at which the issuer can call the note. With no incentive to call the note, the issuer leaves the note outstanding and continues to pay the fixed rate until the note matures. At the same time, if rates have risen, the call swaption is out of the money as well. Thus, the swaption expires worthless, and the issuer has taken in the premium.

The net result is that the issuer pays a fixed rate for the full five years.

Exhibit 8.2

Synthetic Noncallable Fixed Rate Debt
(Issue 5-Year Debt Callable after 3 Years,
and Sell a 3 x 5 Call Swaption)

Year 3 Scenario	Callable Debt	3x5 Call Swaption	Net Financing
Yields Up	Issuer does not call debt. Pay fixed rate for 5 years.	Counterparty does not exercise option.	Pay fixed rate for 5 years.
Yields Down	Issuer calls debt. Pay fixed rate for first 3 years; pay floating rate for last 2 years.	Counterparty exercises option. Receive floating and pay fixed in swap for last 2 years.	Pay fixed rate for 5 years.

Next consider what happens if yields fall. In this case, the issuer calls the debt and can pay floating for the last two years of what would have been the note's life. At the same time, the counterparty to the call swaption would have exercised the option. The fall in rates imparts value to the right to receive fixed and pay floating in the swap valuable and sends the call swaption into the money. From the issuer's standpoint, this works out well because the floating receipts on the swap will offset the interest payments on two years' worth of floating-rate financing. The two years of fixed payments on the swap will fill in the remaining two years of the note's life.

Either way, whether rates rise or fall, the issuer pays fixed for five years. Thus, the issuer has created a synthetic fixed-rate note.

The cost of this synthetic fixed-rate financing depends, of course, on the prices placed on the two options. For example, the price at which the note was sold originally will be less than the price of the straight, non-callable note. The difference was the price the issuer had to pay for the embedded call option. If this is smaller than the price at which the issuer can sell the 3x5 call swaption, the net result is a higher issuing price for the synthetic note than for the conventional fixed-rate note. Put differently, the all-in or total interest cost of the synthetic note would be lower than with the conventional note.

It is worth noting that if the prices of identical call options are different in the two markets, a company with no interest in issuing debt might still be interested in these markets. For example, if the price of a synthetic note is enough higher than the price of a conventional note to justify the trouble, the company could use its financing facilities to sell the synthetic and buy a conventional fixed-rate note. The net result would be offsetting positions, and the company can take out the different between the two prices, or, put differently, the spread between the two rates.

Example 2: Create Synthetic Floating-Rate Financing

For a slightly more concrete example, consider a company with floating-rate, LIBOR-based assets that wants floating rate liabilities. For the sake of this example, suppose that its choices are:

- to borrow floating at LIBOR less 30 basis points; or
- to create a synthetic floating-rate liability.

The first alternative suggests that the issuer has extraordinarily good credit. The second alternative could take any number of forms. One would be to issue a five-year note, callable in three years, and to pay floating in a 3x5 callable swap.

In particular, suppose that the issuer can sell a five-year note, callable in three years, at 55 basis points over the yield on five-year Treasuries. Suppose further that the issuer can pay floating in the 3x5 callable swap and receive fixed payments at 100 basis points over the five-year Treasury yield.

The resulting cash flows for the first three years of this transaction are illustrated in Exhibit 8.3. On the note, the issuer pays the five-year Treasury rate plus 55 basis points. On the swap, the issuer pays LIBOR on the floating side and receives the five-year Treasury rate plus 100 basis points on the fixed side. When netted, the fixed receipts are 45 basis points higher than the fixed payments. Thus, the issuer has a fixed 45 basis points income for three years that can be used to reduce the floating-rate interest expense.

For the first three years of this arrangement, the issuer's net interest expense is LIBOR less 45 basis points.

What happens over the last two years of the arrangement's life depends on what happens to rates. As shown in Exhibit 8.4, if rates fall, the swap is not canceled and the note is not called. Life goes on as before, and the issuer's net interest expense is still 45 basis points under LIBOR.

If rates rise, on the other hand, both options are exercised. The swap is canceled by the counterparty to the swap, and the issuer calls the note. What is left is simply a floating-rate payment at whatever floating rate is available to the issuer at the time. If we assume that the issuer can still obtain financing at 30 basis points under LIBOR, then that is the floating rate during the last two years if interest rates fall.

In this example, the synthetic floating-rate note is clearly better than five years of straight floating-rate financing. The best thing that can happen is that the issuer reduces the cost of floating-rate financing by 15 basis points. The worst is that the swap is

Exhibit 8.3

Cash Flows for Synthetic Floating-Rate Note
(Years 1 to 3)

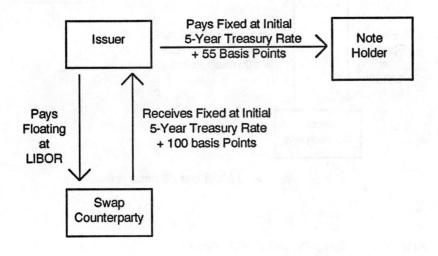

Net = LIBOR less 45 basis points

Exhibit 8.4

Cash Flows for Synthetic Floating-Rate Note
(Years 4 and 5)

Rates Up: Swap Not Canceled, Note Not Called

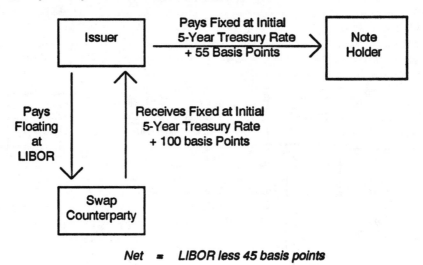

Net = LIBOR less 45 basis points

Rates Down: Swap Canceled, Note Called

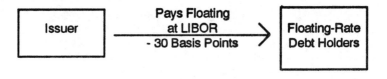

Net = LIBOR less 30 basis points

canceled, the note is called, and the issuer is thrown back into the floating-rate debt market on exactly the same terms that would have been available in any case.

Perhaps the only drawback to this arrangement, apart from the usual credit risks inherent in over-the-counter transactions, is that the issuer closes off any possibility of benefitting from a further improvement in the market's perceptions of the issuer's credit standing. The rate is locked at 45 basis points under LIBOR in the case of the synthetic floating-rate note, while the spread is variable in the conventional floating-rate debt market. Of course, the issuer's credit could worsen, in which case locking the spread would prove to be a good thing.

Swaption/Cancelable Swap Parity

These two examples highlight an interesting and very useful relationship between swaptions and cancelable swaps. At least for European-style options, swaps, swaptions, and cancelable swaps can be combined in any number of combinations to produce useful outcomes. For example, a cancelable swap can be combined with a generic swap to create a swaption. Consider:

- paying fixed in a 3x5 callable swap and paying floating in a generic five-year swap is the same as being long a 3x5 call swaption;
- paying floating in a 3x5 putable swap and receiving floating in a five-year generic swap is the same as a 3x5 put swaption.

The truth of these statements is shown in Exhibit 8.5, which shows what happens to the cash flows on the three different instruments—all of which have the same fixed rate—as interest rates rise and fall.

For example, during the first three years of the call swaption's life, there are no cash flows, except for the premium or price paid for the option. The same is true for the combination of a short generic swap (in which you pay floating and receive fixed) and the

Exhibit 8.5

Swaption - Cancellable Swap Parity

Callable

Year	Rate Scenario	Long 3x5 Call Swaption		Short 5-Year Swap	Pay Fixed 3x5 Callable Swap		Swap & Callable Swap Cash Flow
		Action	Cash Flow		Action	Cash Flow	
1-3	Up or down		None	Receive fixed Pay floating		Pay fixed Receive floating	None
4-5	Up	Don't exercise	None	Receive fixed Pay floating	Don't cancel	Pay fixed Receive floating	None
4-5	Down	Exercise	Receive fixed Pay floating	Receive fixed Pay floating	Cancel	None	Receive fixed Pay floating

Putable

Year	Rate Scenario	Long 3x5 Put Swaption		Long 5-Year Swap	Pay floating 3x5 Putable Swap		Swap & Putable Swap Cash Flow
		Action	Cash Flow		Action	Cash Flow	
1-3	Up or down		None	Pay fixed Receive floating		Pay floating Receive fixed	None
4-5	Up	Exercise	Pay fixed Receive floating	Pay fixed Receive floating	Cancel	None	Pay fixed Receive floating
4-5	Down	Don't Exercise	None	Pay fixed Receive floating	Don't Cancel	Pay floating Receive fixed	None

• DISCOUNT CORPORATION OF NEW YORK FUTURES •

3x5 callable swap (in which you pay fixed and receive floating). The cash flows net out to zero.

If rates rise, there are still no cash flows in either case. You do not exercise the call swaption, and so you end up without a swap position. At the same time, you do not cancel the callable swap, so that its cash flows continue to offset the cash flows of the generic swap.

If rates fall, you exercise your call swaption so that you receive fixed and pay floating for two years. If you had the combination instead, you would find it worthwhile to cancel the callable swap, which would leave you receiving fixed and paying floating for the last two years of the generic swap's life.

Walking through these same steps should convince you that a 3x5 put swaption is the same as a long five-year generic swap (in which you pay fixed and receive floating) combined with paying floating in a 3x5 putable swap.

Once you have convinced yourself that these combinations work, you will find that any other set of combinations will work. For example, as shown in Exhibit 8.6, a long generic swap combined with a call swaption is the same as paying fixed in a callable swap. Combining a put swaption with a putable swap can create a synthetic generic swap. Similarly, drawing on the power of put/call parity, a long call swaption can be combined with a short put swaption to create a synthetic deferred generic swap.

The combinations are endless, and it is this kind of combining and recombining that can produce interesting financing opportunities. We have read extensive examples of financial products that banks have developed using swaps and swaptions, and it is clear from what we have read that bank product development groups have a lot of fun looking for new ways to do things.

Implications for Pricing Cancelable Swaps

One very useful side benefit of swaption/cancelable swap parity is that the value of a cancelable swap can be derived easily from the value of a swaption with the same underlying terms. The reason is that the generic swap has no value at the time it is originated. That is, if you know how to price a swaption, you also know how to price the corresponding cancelable swap.

Exhibit 8.6

Examples of Swaption/Cancellable Swap Parity

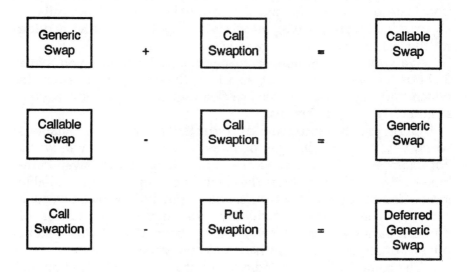

Pricing Options on Swaps

In practice, fees for options on swaps are set in one of two ways. For swaptions, as with caps, prices are usually set as an upfront fee and expressed as a percent of the notional principal amount. The option embedded in a cancelable swap can be priced either by setting the fixed-rate payment above (in the case of a callable swap) or below (in the case of a putable swap) the fixed rate on a generic swap, or by charging an upfront fee equal to the present value of these premiums or discounts.

Options on swaps are sensitive to the same kinds of variables as are caps, but with an interesting twist. A cap typically is a strip of options on a sequence of short-period forward rates. A swap option is a single option on a strip of forward rates. As a result, swaption prices are sensitive to:

- the term of the swap;
- how much the swaption is in or out of the money;
- the market's assessment about the general level of yield volatility; and
- whether the swaption can be exercised at multiple points in time (as with American-style options) or only at expiration (as with European-style options).

Theoretical prices for three different at-the-money call swaptions (callable swaps) under different volatility and exercise assumptions are shown in Exhibit 8.7. These prices are expressed as a percent of the notional principal amount of the underlying swap. Note in particular that:

- there is little or no difference between the prices of American-style and European-style swaptions if volatility is low;
- the difference between American-style and European-style options can be large if volatility is high, and the longer the term of the swap, the larger the difference;

Exhibit 8.7

Callable Swap and Swaption Pricing
At-the-Money Option[1]
Up Front Premium as a Percent of Notional Principal Amount

Term of Swap	American Style Yield Volatility		European Style Yield Volatility	
	10%	13%	10%	13%
3x5	.74%	1.33%	.74%	.87%
4x7	.96	1.83	.96	1.20
5x10	1.76	2.98	1.73	2.01

[1] *Fixed rate payor pays same rate as on a generic swap.   Assumes semi-annual pay swap.*

- fees on longer-dated swaptions are more sensitive to increases in volatility than are fees on short-dated swaptions; and

- fees on European-style swaptions are less sensitive to changes in volatility than are American-style swaptions.

Exhibit 8.8 presents the same theoretical prices, but expresses them for callable swaps as the difference between the fixed rate on the callable swap and the fixed rate on a generic swap. This quote convention is not possible for call swaptions, of course, because there may never be a swap in place.

Price Sensitivity of Callable Swaps

A callable swap will respond differently than will a generic swap to changes in the level of rates and the market's perceptions of rate volatility. These differences are illustrated in Exhibit 8.9 for swaps and callable swaps with terms ranging from five to ten years. In each case you are long the swap, which means that you are paying the fixed rate and receiving the floating rate. With the callable swap, you also have the right to cancel the swap. The notional principal amounts are $100 million in all cases.

Consider, then, the difference between a generic five-year swap and the 3x5 callable swap. Because you are paying fixed and receiving floating in the swap, an increase in yields will increase the value of the swap to you. This increase, which is shown as "delta" in Exhibit 8.9, is $34.6 thousand for the five-year generic swap.

An increase in rates, however, takes your long call option out of the money. As a result, the value of your call option is falling while the value of the swap is increasing. The net change in the price of the callable swap, then, is an increase of only $26.1 thousand for the 3x5 callable swap.

Exhibit 8.8

Callable Swap Pricing
Semi-Annual Swaps
(Basis Point Premium Over Generic Swap)

Term of Swap	American Style Yield Volatility		European Style Yield Volatility	
	10%	13%	10%	13%
3x5	24 bp	42 bp	24 bp	28 bp
4x7	22	45	22	30
5x10	35	61	35	42

Exhibit 8.9

Risk Parameters
Swaps versus Callable Swaps[1]
($100 Million Notional Principal Amount)

	5 Year 3x5		7 Year 4x7		10 Year 5x10	
	Callable	Generic	Callable	Generic	Callable	Generic
Delta[2]	26.1	34.6	36.1	45.8	40.4	59.2
Gamma[3]	-3.6	0.2	0.3	0.6	-2.5	1.0
Zeta (Vega)[4]	91	0	167	0	224	0

[1]   *At-the-money callable swap with fixed rate set equal to fixed rate on generic swap.*

[2]   *Change in the value of a long swap (in $000) for a one-basis-point increase in yields.*

[3]   *Change in delta for a 10-basis-point decrease in yields*

[4]   *Change in the value of a long swap (in $000) for a one-percentage-point increase in yield volatility*

We also see in Exhibit 8.9 that generic and callable swaps are different in two other respects, one measured by gamma, the other by zeta.[1]

For example, if rates were 10 basis points lower, the gamma of the 3x5 callable swap indicates that its price would be less sensitive to a one-basis-point increase in yields than it was. The reason is that as rates fall, the call option is taken into the money and the value of the call option becomes more sensitive to a change in rates. Thus, with rates 10 basis points lower, we find that the price of the callable swap would increase only $22.5 thousand [= $26.1 - $3.6] in response to a one-basis-point increase in yields. In contrast, the value of the generic swap would rise $34.8 thousand [= 34.6 + $0.2] in response to the same one-basis-point increase in rates.

The differences in price sensitivity between generic and callable swaps is illustrated further in Exhibit 8.10. Changes in the price of the generic swap are charted by the dotted line, while changes in the price of the callable swap are charted by the solid line. The difference between the two price lines is the value of the call option, which becomes more valuable as rates fall and less valuable as rates rise. If rates are high enough, of course, the call would be deep out of the money and worthless. Once the call is worthless, the callable swap and the generic swap would behave the same way in response to changes in the level of yields.

The callable swaps respond to the market's views on rate volatility, while the generic swaps do not. This difference reflects the sensitivity of option prices to changes in expectations about the general level of rate volatility. Options have this sensitivity; swaps do not. As a result, because you are long the option, a one-percentage-point increase in the level of yield volatility would increase the value of the $100 million, 3x5 callable swap by $91,000. The value of the generic swap would be unaffected.

---

1. Generic and callable swaps also will have different time decay characteristics. The call swaption, for example, will lose value as time passes because the call option will lose time value.

Exhibit 8.10

3 x 5 Callable Swap versus Noncallable 5-Year Swap
(Fixed Rate Payor Pays 5-Year Treasury + 70 bp vs. LIBOR Flat)

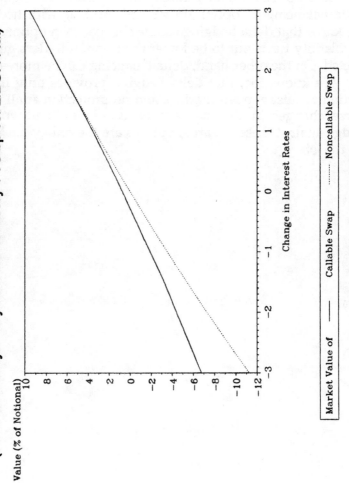

Value (% of Notional)

Change in Interest Rates

| Market Value of | Callable Swap | Noncallable Swap |

• **DISCOUNT CORPORATION OF NEW YORK FUTURES** •

Hedging Options on Swaps

The hedging issues here are much the same as those we faced in the problem of hedging caps. Although the details are different, the broad questions still boil down to an initial decision between dynamic delta hedging and option replication.

Strips of Eurodollar futures can be effective hedging tools for delta balancing an option on a swap. And, as with hedging caps, we know that delta hedging can be cheaper than option replication if volatility turns out to be lower than option traders generally expected. On the other hand, delta balancing can be more expensive.

We know, too, that delta hedging provides only limited protection against gapped markets and no protection at all against adverse changes in the market's expectations about volatility. To hedge against these hazards, options are the only vehicles that can do the job.

CHAPTER 9

SLICs, BICs, and GICs

Guaranteed investment contracts (GICs) have been part of the stock in trade of the insurance industry for years. GICs were designed mainly for qualified retirement plans such as 401(k)s, and this remains their primary function. Beginning in 1987, banks and savings and loan associations entered the business with bank investment contracts (BICs) and savings and loan investment contracts (SLICs). In all, the total volume of BICs, GICs, and SLICs outstanding is estimated at this writing to be well in excess of $100 billion.[1]

At the heart of a GIC is an interest rate guaranty. Many GICs extend this guaranty to any money added during a prespecified period, and many GICs allow money to be withdrawn without penalty. Such GICs contain embedded call and put options. That is, the right to deposit money at a guaranteed rate is likely to be exercised whenever market rates fall below the guaranteed rate. In

---

1. The material for this chapter first appeared in Terry Belton and Galen Burghardt, "SLICs, BICs, and GICs," Discount Corporation of New York Futures Research Note, August 27, 1990.

this sense, the opportunity to add money is like a call option on an interest-bearing note. The right to withdraw money is likely to be exercised whenever market rates rise above the guaranteed rate. Thus, withdrawal rights are like put options.

As we will see, the options in GICs, BICs, and SLICs are not especially easy to price. Easy to price or not, the options are there and pose serious problems for hedgers. A short position in GICs is exposed to sharp swings in deposit rates and to increases in deposit rate volatility. Thus, the hedging problems that arise in this market are much like those faced by any hedger that is short interest rate options.

Our goal in this chapter is to describe an approach for pricing these interest rate options and to map out some possible strategies for hedging the interest rate risk in GICs.

What Are GICs, BICs, and SLICs?

GICs, BICs, and SLICs are really nothing more than negotiated term deposits. GICs are issued by insurance companies and are the oldest of the three products. BICs and SLICs, which appeared first in 1987, are essentially the same as GICs except that they are issued by commercial banks and savings and loans. Unlike GICs, then, BICs and SLICs are backed by federal deposit insurance.

Because GICs are negotiated contracts, their terms can vary widely from one contract to the next. A description of some of the key negotiating points follows.

Bullet GICs versus Window GICs

A bullet GIC is a simple, old-fashioned term deposit. It is characterized by a single lump sum deposit that earns a guaranteed interest rate until a known maturity date. No money can be added to a bullet GIC after the initial lump sum has been invested.

A window GIC usually requires an initial lump sum deposit, but allows for additional deposits to be made over some period of time at the guaranteed interest rate. Typically, this "window" runs from six months to a year. For example, a four-year GIC with a one-year window allows the participants in the plan to make additional contributions at the guaranteed rate any time during the first year of the contract.

Withdrawal and Transfer Provisions

Most window GICs have provisions that allow for the early withdrawal or transfer of deposits. In some cases, GICS allow for full withdrawal or transfer without penalty at any time. In other cases, the contract provisions place restrictions on the ability of plan participants to move their funds. For example, many plans allow participants to transfer funds to an equity fund but not to a competing money market or bond fund that is part of the same 401(k) plan.

The combination of window provisions and early withdrawal rights means that GICs contain valuable interest rate options:

- The window that allows for continued deposits at the investor's discretion represents a valuable call option. The option has value to the investor because, when market yields fall, the investor can pay par for a position in a fixed income fund whose cash flows are worth more than par.

- The early withdrawal provisions, by contrast, provide the investor a valuable set of put options. These options have value because, when market yields rise, the investor can transfer funds out of the GIC and receive par value, even though the market value of the fund may be below par.

Altogether, a window GIC is an instrument that is partly a term deposit and partly a position in interest rate options. The investor owns these options. The issuer of the GIC is short these options.

GICs that contain window and withdrawal provisions are thus exposed to the same kinds of risks as any outright option position. That is, the issuer is exposed to sharp, gapped moves in market interest rates. Further, the issuer is exposed to increases in both actual and expected interest rate volatility.[2]

---

2. See Chapter 6 on hedging interest-rate caps for an illustration of these perils.

Bullet GICs and Eurodollar Futures

Those who issue bullet GICs are exposed to fluctuations in interest rates primarily because they guarantee the rate on the GIC before the funds are actually paid by the investor. As a result, the issuer may incur a loss if yields fall after the forward commitment has been made, but before the funds are received and invested.

For bullet GICs, eliminating the interest rate risk from a forward rate commitment is a relatively straightforward matter. A commonly used strategy is to:

- establish a long position in Eurodollar futures, a strip of Eurodollar futures, or Treasury note futures to lock in the return to a forward investment that will be made when the funds are received; and
- lift the hedge when the funds are received and invest in an asset with a duration that matches the duration of the GIC portfolio.

A strip of Eurodollar futures is often an excellent hedging vehicle for forward rate commitments on bullet GICs with maturities up to four years. A Eurodollar strip is a futures position that contains one each of the contracts in a sequence of contract months. For example, a one year strip might contain one each of the September 1991, December 1991, March 1992, and June 1992 contracts.

The reason for chaining together Eurodollar futures in this fashion is that a strip is a way to synthetically create a longer term forward deposit rate. One-year strips behave much like forward deposits and can be used to lock in the return on a one-year asset. Two-year strips behave like two-year forward deposits. At present, one can construct Eurodollar strips up to four years long.[3]

Calculating the correct number of futures contracts needed to hedge a forward rate commitment on a bullet GIC is relatively easy. Consider, for example, a one-week forward rate commitment on a $10 million three-year bullet GIC where the proceeds are to be invested in a three-year bullet loan.

3. See Chapter 3 for an explanation of how to calculate the term yield on a strip of Eurodollar futures.

Since the loan has a single payment after three years, its duration is three years, and a one-basis-point increase in rates will cause its market value to decline by about .03 percent [= .01 × Duration/100] of $10 million, or $3,000. Thus, the dollar value of a basis point on the asset is $3,000.

By design, the dollar value of a basis point on a Eurodollar futures contract is $25 so that every one-basis-point decrease in the Eurodollar futures rate produces a $25 gain for the long and a corresponding $25 loss for the short. Since the issuer will incur a loss on its portfolio if yields fall, a long position in Eurodollar futures is needed and the total number of contracts needed would be:

$$\text{Hedge Ratio} = (\$3,000 \ / \ \$25) = 120 \text{ contracts}$$

The only remaining issue is how to allocate the contracts across contract months. If all 120 contracts were stacked in the lead contract, the hedge would provide adequate protection only against parallel shifts in the yield curve. By evenly allocating the contracts among the first 12 contract months, however, a synthetic three-year forward deposit rate is created that will better reflect the yield on the three-year asset that is being hedged. Hence, a robust hedge for locking in the return on the $10 million three-year loan is a long position in 10 Eurodollar futures contracts in each of the first 12 contract months.[4]

Window GICs and Eurodollar Futures and Options

Although hedging bullet GICs is relatively easy, window GICs can present a real challenge to the hedger.

The key to successfully hedging a portfolio funded with GICs is in forecasting accurately the sensitivity of deposits and withdrawals to future changes in interest rates. Once this is done, the issuer needs to:

- estimate the effect of a change in yields on the market value of a GIC and on the market value of the assets funded by the GIC;

---

4. See Chapter 4 for more on the question of matching yield curve exposure.

- estimate the effect of a change in yield volatility on the market value of a GIC and on the market value of the assets funded by the GIC; and

- find suitable combinations of futures and options to hedge the net exposure in the position to changes in yield levels and yield volatilities.

Deposits and Withdrawals

The biggest stumbling block to reckoning the sensitivity of a GIC's price to a change in the level of yields is the problem of determining the sensitivity of deposits and withdrawals to yield changes. The answer depends in part on the contract's provisions.

For example, in a contract with fairly limited withdrawal and deposit provisions, the running net deposit position may differ from the initial lump sum deposit by only 10 to 15 percent in either direction, no matter what the level of interest rates.

With liberal deposit and withdrawal/transfer provisions, large yield decreases have triggered net deposits in some plans that have been more than twice as large as the initial lump sum deposit. Large yield increases have triggered withdrawals equal to as much as half the initial lump sum contribution.

The answer also depends in part on the awareness of the participants in the plan. From this standpoint, GICs have a great deal in common with mortgages. That is, among those who invest in GICs, the range of market awareness and financial understanding can vary widely for plan to plan. As a result, the flows of deposits and withdrawals for two plans with identical features can differ significantly from each other.

In practice, most underwriters use whatever historical data are available to forecast net deposit flows when pricing a GIC.

Example of a Deposit and Withdrawal Schedule

Exhibit 9.1 provides an example of how deposits and withdrawals might be affected by changes in the level of rates. The left column shows possible changes in the level of market interest rates. The next two columns show possible responses to those rate changes.

Consider first the schedule of deposits. With no change in rates, deposits are added to the initial lump sum contribution at a rate equal to 10 percent per year. That is, if the initial investment was $100 million, the issuer of the GIC in this example can expect an additional $10 million to be deposited over the course of a one-year window. A 50 basis point increase in rates will slow deposit inflows to $2 million; a 50-basis-point decrease in rates will accelerate deposit inflows to $20 million.

Consider next the schedule of withdrawals. Our hypothetical schedule shows money being taken out at a rate of 10 percent if yields remain unchanged. This is consistent with changes in the investment or spending requirements of the various individuals participating in the contract. On balance, the withdrawals in this case just offset the deposits, so that the size of the fund remains unchanged if rates do not change. A rise in rates should accelerate the pace of withdrawals. A fall in rates should slow withdrawals.

Interest Rate Sensitivity of a GIC

The sensitivity of net deposits to changes in yields has a direct effect on how the market value of the GIC responds to changes in interest rates.

The relationship between price and yield is shown for both a bullet GIC and a window GIC in Exhibit 9.2. The price/yield relationship for the bullet GIC displays the kind of so-called positive convexity that is normal for a fixed-rate note or term deposit. That is, its price becomes more sensitive to yield changes as yields fall and less sensitive as yields rise.

The window GIC has similar properties but the effect of changing yields is much more pronounced. As yields fall, the call options embedded in the contract go in the money. The increase in the value of this right reflects the increase in the difference between the GIC's guaranteed rate and the market rate as the market rate falls. To the issuer of the GIC, this represents a cost.

As yields rise, the right to redeem funds at par kicks in and causes withdrawals on the window GIC to accelerate. That is, an increase in yields sends the embedded put options into the money. The gains on these options offset somewhat the declining value of the deposit so that the window GIC outperforms the bullet GIC.

Exhibit 9.1

Baseline Deposit and Withdrawal Schedules
Benefit-Responsive GICs

Change in Market Interest Rates (basis points)	Incremental Deposits[1]	Withdrawals[2]
+300	0 %	38 %
+200	0	30
+100	0	25
+50	2	15
0	10	10
-50	20	1
-100	40	0
-200	60	0
-300	75	0

[1]   *Contributions at an annual rate as a percent of initial lump sum.*

[2]   *Withdrawals at an annual rate as a percent of initial lump sum. Withdrawals constrained so that they cannot exceed initial lump sum.*

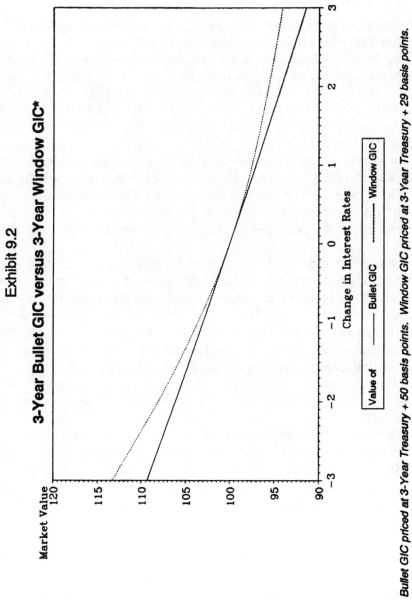

Exhibit 9.2

3-Year Bullet GIC versus 3-Year Window GIC*

Market Value

Change in Interest Rates

Value of   —— Bullet GIC   ········ Window GIC

* Bullet GIC priced at 3-Year Treasury + 50 basis points. Window GIC priced at 3-Year Treasury + 29 basis points.

· DISCOUNT CORPORATION OF NEW YORK FUTURES ·

In a nutshell, then, the window GIC outperforms the bullet GIC from the investor's standpoint, irrespective of whether rates go up or down. To compensate the issuer for selling such a wonderful asset, window GICs are issued at lower guaranteed rates than those that can be obtained on bullet GICs.

GIC Duration

In addition to their effect on convexity, the embedded options in a window GIC also affect the duration of a GIC.

As Exhibit 9.3 illustrates, the duration of a window GIC with no withdrawal rights will exceed the maturity of the GIC. This reflects the fact that the window feature of the GIC resembles a long call option. Thus the duration of the GIC will be a weighted sum of the duration of a bullet GIC plus the duration of a call option.

In contrast, the duration of a GIC with both window and early withdrawal provisions can be above or below the maturity of the GIC. Since the withdrawal features of a GIC resemble a long put option, and since put options are bearish instruments, the puts work to offset the positive duration of the window feature of the GIC.

One point that is obvious from Exhibit 9.3 is that both the duration of a GIC and the value of the embedded interest rate options are quite sensitive to assumptions about the sensitivity of net deposit flows to changes in interest rates. For example, we estimate that a three-year window GIC with no provisions for early withdrawal would have an effective duration of 3.6 years using the baseline deposit assumptions of Exhibit 9.1. Halving the assumption on deposit inflows reduces this duration estimate to 3.3 years, resulting in about a 10 percent reduction in the appropriate hedge ratio.

The value of the embedded interest rate options, shown in the bottom row of the table, also appear quite sensitive to deposit and withdrawal assumptions. The estimated costs of the embedded options range from a low of five basis points to a high of about 21 basis points, depending on the GIC's features and assumptions about deposit flows.

Exhibit 9.3

GIC Duration
3-Year GIC

		1-Year Window		Window & Withdrawal	
	Bullet GIC	Baseline	50% of Baseline	Baseline	50% of Baseline
Duration	3.0	3.6	3.3	3.1	3.1
Eurodollar Futures Hedge Ratio[1]	12.0	14.4	13.2	12.4	12.4
Estimated Spread to 3-Year Treasury[2]	50	41	45	29	40
Estimated Spread Relative to Bullet GIC	-	9	5	21	10

[1] *Number of Eurodollar futures contracts needed to hedge a forward rate commitment on a $1 million lump sum investment*

[2] *Estimated spread to 3-year Treasury required in order for GIC to be priced at par. Estimated from DCNYF's Option Adjusted Spread (OAS) pricing model*

• DISCOUNT CORPORATION OF NEW YORK FUTURES •

Hedging the Embedded Options in a GIC

One of the big differences between bullet GICs and window GICs is that bullet GICs only have exposure to the level of interest rates. Window GICs also have exposure to the level of interest rates; however, like other interest rate options, GICs are exposed to changes in the volatility of interest rates.

The first step in successfully managing the interest rate risk in a portfolio funded by window GICs is to assess the sensitivity of the portfolio to changes in both the level and volatility of interest rates.

Exhibit 9.4 summarizes the interest rate risk for a noncallable bond portfolio funded by a three-year window GIC. The portfolio was designed to be duration neutral so that the value of the portfolio is immunized against small changes in interest rates. In addition to the duration of the portfolio, we also show other risk measures that option traders traditionally use to assess risk in their portfolios. These measures indicate that although the portfolio is duration neutral, it is exposed to large changes in interest rates, and to changes in the volatility of rates.

Zeta

Because the GIC issuer has effectively written both interest rate puts and calls, the issuer is exposed to increases in the market's assessment of interest rate volatility. The -22.6 zeta shown in Exhibit 9.4 indicates that a one-percentage-point increase in the market's assessment of yield volatility (implied volatility) will decrease the value of the $10 million portfolio by $22.6 thousand.

Gamma

The portfolio's negative gamma means that the net duration of the portfolio decreases as yields fall and increases as yields rise. As yields fall, deposit inflows accelerate and the duration of the GIC increases relative to the duration of the noncallable bond. As yields rise, withdrawals accelerate and the duration of the GIC decreases relative to the duration of the bond portfolio.

Exhibit 9.5 illustrates the effect of negative gamma on the portfolio by plotting the net gains and losses on the portfolio over

Exhibit 9.4

Risk Parameters for a
$10 Million Noncallable Fixed Rate Bond Portfolio
Funded by 3-Year GIC

	Bond Portfolio	GIC	Net Position of Issuer
Duration	3.1	3.1	0
Delta[1]	3.1	3.1	0
Gamma[2]	0.1	1.0	-0.9
Zeta[3]	0	22.6	-22.6

[1]   *Change in the market value of the position (in $000) for a one-basis-point increase in yields.*

[2]   *Change in delta for a 100-basis-point decrease in yields.*

[3]   *Change in value of position for a one-percentage-point increase in yield volatility.*

a three-month horizon against yield changes ranging between plus and minus two percentage points. The gains and losses include the net coupon income earned on the portfolio plus changes in the market value of the portfolio.

As the chart vividly illustrates, this is a position that is short volatility. As market yields rise, the value of the assets and liabilities both fall, but the value of the assets fall faster than the value of the GIC. By contrast, as market yields fall, the value of both assets and liabilities rise, but the value of the GIC rises faster than the value of the assets. Like any delta-neutral short option position, this position makes money only if rates are stable. If rates either increase substantially or decrease substantially, the position is a loser.

As discussed in Chapter 6 on hedging caps, there are two ways to hedge a duration neutral position that has negative gamma such as that shown in Exhibit 9.5. The first is to pursue a dynamic futures strategy, which essentially involves adjusting the size of a futures hedge to match the changing price sensitivity of the portfolio. Generally speaking, this will entail buying futures as yields fall (and prices rise) and selling them as yields rise (and prices fall). The cost of this strategy depends on how volatile interest rates are over the life of the hedge.

The second approach to hedging the negative gamma in a portfolio funded by window GICs is to add a long position in options to the hedge. Exhibit 9.6 illustrates the effect of such a strategy for the three-year GIC portfolio. The hedge was constructed on June 21, 1990 when December 1990 Eurodollar futures were trading slightly below 92. The hedge comprises long positions in December 1990 Eurodollar puts and calls.

Over the scenarios examined, the hedge looks impressive. As yields rise, the gains on the puts in the hedge accelerate in a manner that offsets the effects of the withdrawal provisions on the GIC. As yields fall, the gains on the calls offset the effects of the window provisions on the GIC. Finally, under stable interest rates, the positive coupon income on the portfolio offsets the time decay on the options in the hedge.

Exhibit 9.5

Net P/L on Noncallable Bond Portfolio Funded by 3-Year GIC*

Duration Neutral Portfolio

P/L over 3-Month Horizon

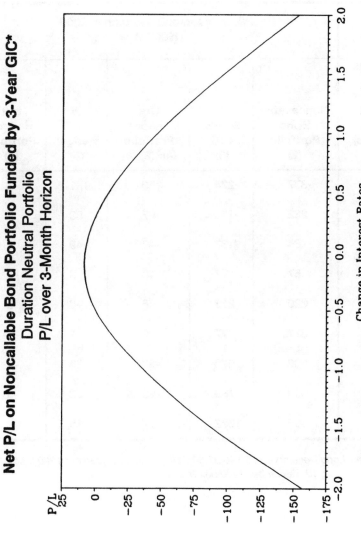

Change in Interest Rates

Assumes yield on bond portfolio exceeds yield on GIC by 30 basis points.

• **DISCOUNT CORPORATION OF NEW YORK FUTURES** •

Exhibit 9.6

Net P/L on $10 Million Portfolio
Hedged with Eurodollar Options
(June 21, 1990)

Change in Interest Rates (basis points) (1)	P/L over 3-month Horizon in $000 ($000's)				
	Noncallable Bond Portfolio (2)	3-Year GIC (3)	Net Unhedged Portfolio (4)=(2)-(3)	Hedge[1] (5)	Net Hedged Portfolio (6)
+200	-377	-224	-153	151	-2
+150	-232	-135	-97	99	2
+100	-84	-37	-47	49	2
+50	67	77	-10	9	-1
0	220	213	8	-8	0
-50	377	377	0	-1	-1
-100	536	573	-37	35	-2
-150	699	789	-90	93	3
-200	865	1022	-157	155	-2

[1]   *Hedge = Long December 1990 40 91.50 Calls; Long 41 December 1990 92.50 Puts;*
Long 10 December 1990 93.00 Calls.

• DISCOUNT CORPORATION OF NEW YORK FUTURES •

Reality Check

It's worth noting that the price paid for an option-based hedge provides a useful check on whether the window GIC is fairly priced. If the embedded options in the GIC are fairly priced by the issuer, the hedged portfolio ought to produce adequate profits (that is, approximately risk-free rates of return) over a wide range of scenarios. If the hedged portfolio systematically produces losses, however, the window GICs are underpriced and likely are a bad deal for issuers but a good opportunity for investors. If the hedged portfolio systematically produces profits greater than those on a relatively risk-free asset, the window GICs are overpriced and represent a profit opportunity for the issuer.

CHAPTER 10

Hedging the Price Risk in ARMs

One of the important trends in the mortgage industry in recent years has been the growing role played by adjustable rate mortgages (ARMs). ARM originations in the primary market have averaged about one-half of all conventional loan originations over the past few years. In the secondary market, the growth of ARM securities, while not spectacular, has at least become respectable. In 1989, the volume of ARM securities issued by the Federal Home Loan Mortgage Corporation (Freddie Mac) and the Federal National Mortgage Association (Fannie Mae) exceeded $30 billion.

The attractive feature of ARMs for certain investors is their potential price stability. ARMs have coupons that can be adjusted up or down as interest rates rise or fall. As a result, ARM prices should rise less rapidly than the prices of fixed-rate mortgages when yields are falling and fall less rapidly when yields are rising.

Even so, most ARMs are structured so that their prices respond quite sharply to large changes in yields. During the first three months of 1989, for example, prices of some cost of funds index (COFI) ARMs fell by as much as three points as short-term

269

interest rates rose. From early 1988 to early 1989, moreover, some issues lost as much as six percent of their value. A good picture of the potential price risk in ARMs is provided by Exhibit 10.1, which plots the prices of a Fannie Mae COFI ARM security against the level of three-month LIBOR from January 1988 to May 1989.

As a result, ARMs have proven to have greater price risk than many investors thought they would have. Moreover, short-term interest rates show no signs of becoming any less volatile than they have been over the past several years, which suggests that some ARMs will continue to have significant price volatility.

The purpose of this chapter is to explain why ARM prices are as volatile as they are and to map out possible strategies for hedging the risk in an ARM portfolio using interest rate futures and options.

ARM Securities

The most widely used vehicles for investing in ARMs in the secondary market are securities issued by the Government National Mortgage Association (Ginnie Mae), Fannie Mae, and Freddie Mac. Most of these securities have coupons that are tied either to the one-year constant maturity Treasury index or to the San Francisco Federal Home Loan Bank Cost of Funds Index. Some important characteristics of two of the more active ARM programs are shown in Exhibit 10.2.

Although ARM securities differ in a variety of details, nearly all of them share a number of fundamental characteristics. For example:

- Coupons are set equal to the index rate (e.g., one-year Treasury rate) plus a margin.
- Coupons are adjusted periodically. One-year Treasury ARM coupons typically are adjusted each year, while COFI ARM coupons typically are adjusted monthly.
- There are limits on how much the rate can be adjusted. Treasury ARMs usually have both annual caps (e.g., 200 basis points) and lifetime caps (e.g., 600 basis points) on how

Exhibit 10.1

FNMA COFI ARM Prices
January 1988 - May 1989

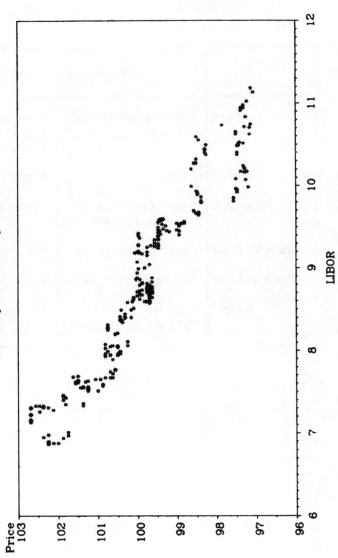

· DISCOUNT CORPORATION OF NEW YORK FUTURES ·

Exhibit 10.2

Comparison of FNMA COFI ARM and FHLMC
One Year Treasury Indexed ARM Securities

	FHLMC 1-Year Treasury	FNMA COFI
Index	1-Year Constant Maturity Treasury	San Francisco Federal Home Loan Bank
Rate Adjustment Interval	1 Year	1 Month
Lifetime Caps	Typically six percent above initial coupon	13 percent or higher
Periodic Caps	Two percentage points	N/A
Periodic Floor	Two percentage points	N/A
Margin	Typically 150-225 basis points	125 basis points

much the rate can be either raised or lowered. COFI ARMs usually have only lifetime caps.

- ARMs can be prepaid at any time before maturity without penalty.

Why are Treasury ARM Prices So Volatile?

The combined effect of the restrictions on how much ARM coupons can be adjusted in response to changes in the level of yields and the borrower's ability to prepay the mortgage at any time creates a security that behaves less like a pure floating rate note and more like a short-term, fixed-rate mortgage. For that matter, an ARM can be thought of as a floating-rate note that contains a number of interest-rate options. For example:

- The annual and lifetime caps are valuable to the borrower because they provide insurance against large increases in interest rates. In effect, such interest-rate caps are the same as put options on interest-bearing securities. The borrower owns these puts. The lender or investor is the writer of these puts. Like interest rate put options, caps become more valuable as rates rise. They become less valuable as rates fall.

- The annual floors provide the lender with the equivalent of call options that are in the money whenever the interest rate is lower than the floor rate. The investor owns these calls. The borrower is the writer of these calls.

- The right to prepay without penalty gives the borrower a call option. The lender is the writer of the call.

Altogether, the position of the lender or someone who invests in a one-year Treasury ARM is:

- long a one-year floater;
- short cap options;
- long floor options;

• short prepayment options;

and the price of the ARM is:

ARM Price =   One-year floater price
                  – Price of cap options
                  + Price of floor options
                  – Price of prepayment option

As a practical matter, whenever the floor option goes into the money, borrowers tend to exercise their prepayment options. As a result, only the first two items on the list matter much. Further, because ARMs have frequently been written at teaser rates that are below market, interest-rate floors have rarely been binding.

The effect of the cap options on the behavior of an ARM price is illustrated in Exhibit 10.3. The dashed line represents the price of a one-year floater priced originally at par. The solid line represents the price of a one-year Treasury ARM with a seven percent initial coupon, 175 basis point margin, an annual cap of two percentage points and a lifetime cap of six percentage points above the initial coupon (that is, a 13 percent lifetime cap).

The prices of the two instruments respond quite differently to changes in the level of interest rates, particularly in response to increases in interest rates. The difference, of course, is the change in the value of the interest-rate caps. As rates rise, the caps either restrict or threaten to restrict the upward adjustment of the coupon. The value of this restriction, which is a boon to the borrower and a burden to the lender, naturally rises as rates rise. As a result, the price of the ARM falls faster than the price of the floater. For example, the distance between the price of the floater and the price of the ARM increases from *AB* to *CD* if rates rise 200 basis points. In contrast, the options become less valuable as rates fall. As a result, the distance between the floater and ARM price decreases from *AB* to *EF* if rates fall 200 basis points.

In the parlance of the bond markets, this slowing of the increase in ARM prices as interest rates fall is known as "negative convexity," which is a property shared by any position that contains short options. In contrast, non-callable Treasury securities ex-

Exhibit 10.3

Price-Yield Curve of One Year Treasury ARM

(ARM Coupon=7, Margin=1.75, Annual Cap=2.0, Lifecap=13, 12 months to reset)
July 1990

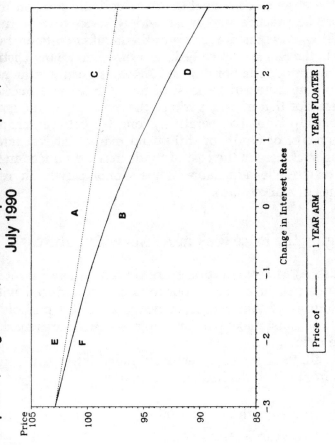

Price of ——— 1 YEAR ARM .... 1 YEAR FLOATER

• DISCOUNT CORPORATION OF NEW YORK FUTURES •

hibit "positive convexity," which means that the rate of price increase accelerates as interest rates fall.

COFI ARMs

The chief differences between COFI ARMs and Treasury ARMs are the index rate, the frequency with which the coupon is reset, and the absence of annual or other periodic caps on many COFI ARMs. In practice, the most widely used cost of funds index (COFI) is a weighted average of the liability costs of thrift institutions in the San Francisco Federal Home Loan Bank District.

The price behavior of COFI ARMs is greatly influenced by the relationship between the cost of funds index and market rates of interest. For that matter, perhaps the most important aspect of this relationship is the comparatively long lag between changes in the average cost of funds for thrifts and market interest rates. The resulting stickiness in the cost of funds index produces an ARM coupon that, while adjustable, adjusts only slowly in response to changes in market rates.

Hedging the Price Risk in ARMs with Futures

Because ARM security prices are driven largely by interest rates, the price risk in an ARM portfolio can be reduced with interest rate futures. If you choose to hedge an ARM portfolio with futures, you must make two key choices—the futures market and the hedge ratio.

In all, there are seven actively traded interest-rate futures contracts from which the hedger can choose:

- three-month Treasury bills
- two-year Treasury notes
- five-year Treasury notes
- ten-year Treasury notes
- long-term Treasury bonds

- three-month Eurodollars
- municipal bonds

These offer a wide range of characteristics in key areas such as:

- maturity (or duration)
- credit
- convexity

Each contract offers advantages and disadvantages for anyone hedging an ARM portfolio. For example, the Treasury contracts capture the level and slope of a relatively risk-free yield curve. The Eurodollar contract captures the effect of spreads between Treasury and non-Treasury securities. The municipal bond contract offers a substantial degree of negative convexity.

Conventional Wisdom

A standard approach to hedging ARMs has been to sell three-year or other short-term Treasury notes against portfolios of ARM securities. These hedges, however, have often proved ineffective, and there is a growing sense in the mortgage industry that there is no effective or reliable hedge for ARMs.

The argument in favor of using Treasury notes to hedge ARMs was based chiefly on similarities in relative price sensitivity to changes in the general level of yields. There are, however, at least two arguments against using Treasury notes as a hedge for ARMs:

- treasury notes exhibit positive convexity while ARMs exhibit negative convexity;
- ARM prices are sensitive to the changes in the spread between Treasury and non-Treasury securities.

How important these arguments are is an empirical question.

Eurodollars May Offer a Better Fit

An indication of the relative importance of the various characteristics of competing financial instruments is provided by Exhibit 10.4, which reports price correlations (both levels and changes) between a Fannie Mae COFI ARM and the six most actively traded interest-rate futures contracts available on U.S. exchanges. Because two-year note futures only began trading in June 1990, we've omitted them from the analysis. What we find is that, over the period examined, the three-month Eurodollar futures contract would have been the best hedging vehicle. For that matter, a strip of Eurodollar futures might have proven to be better than a single contract month because it would more closely reflect the behavior of one and two year rates and might more closely approximate the duration of a COFI ARM. Given the wide range of available alternatives, the choice of a hedging vehicle is a matter that deserves careful consideration.

Although the superior performance of the Eurodollar contract might seem odd, there are two plausible reasons for this result:

- Eurodollar futures have no convexity, and in this sense would be superior to Treasury notes or futures on Treasury notes, which exhibit positive convexity;
- Eurodollar futures are sensitive to the spread between Treasury and non-Treasury securities.

The zero convexity of Eurodollar futures reflects the design of the contract. The value of a Eurodollar futures contract changes by $25 for every one-basis-point change in the underlying futures rate irrespective of the level of yields. By contrast, Treasury notes become more sensitive to changes in yields as yields fall.

If Eurodollar futures really do offer a potentially better fit, there remains the problem of determining the appropriate hedge ratio.

Exhibit 10.4

Correlations Between FNMA COFI ARM Prices
and 1st Deferred Contract Futures Prices
January 1988 - May 1989

Futures Contract	Correlation Coefficients		
	Price Level	1-Month Price Change	3-Month Price Change
Eurodollar	.94	.40	.61
Treasury Bill	.93	.35	.49
5-Year Treasury Note	.67	.32	.47
10-Year Treasury Note	.24	.28	.52
Treasury Bond	-.25	.26	.58
Municipal Bond	-.81	.20	.57

• DISCOUNT CORPORATION OF NEW YORK FUTURES •

Hedge Ratio

Since ARM prices fall as interest rates rise, a short position in futures can be used to offset the losses. The key to constructing a hedge is to have a futures position whose change in value is equal but opposite to the change in the value of the ARM portfolio.

How many Eurodollar futures contracts should the hedger sell? The answer depends on the value and effective duration of the ARM portfolio. Effective duration is the percent change in the price of a security in response to a 100-basis-point change in interest rates, calculated for a range of interest rates around its current yield. By convention, effective duration frequently is quoted in years to be consistent with traditional duration measures.

For example, at current rates (July 1990), the effective duration of a new eight percent one-year Treasury ARM is about 1.80 years. Thus, a 100-basis point increase in interest rates would cause the price of the ARM to fall by about 1.8 percent, or $180,000 on a $10 million market value ARM portfolio.

The effective duration of a Eurodollar contract is 0.25 years. The nominal size of a Eurodollar contract is $1 million, so that a 100-basis-point increase in interest rates would cause the value of a single futures contract to fall by $2,500. This can be turned into a gain by shorting the contract, and the number of contracts needed to offset the loss in the ARM portfolio would be 72 [= $180,000/$2,500].

In general, the number of futures contracts to sell against a long ARM portfolio is:

$$\text{Hedge Ratio} = (D_{ARM} \times V_{ARM}) / (D_f \times V_f)$$

where D represents effective duration and V represents market or portfolio equivalent value. In the case of the $10 million ARM portfolio with an effective duration of 1.80, the appropriate hedge ratio using Eurodollar futures is

$$\text{Hedge Ratio} = (1.8 \times \$10) / (0.25 \times \$1)$$

$$= 72$$

Hedge Ratios for Various ARMs

All ARMs are not alike, of course, and the effective durations of ARMs can vary widely depending on their key characteristics. To illustrate, Exhibit 10.5 provides effective duration estimates for a short but varied list of Treasury and COFI ARMs.

The range of effective durations is fairly wide. The information in Exhibit 10.5, which is based on the yield curve that prevailed on July 18, 1990, does a good job of illustrating the importance of different ARM characteristics. For example, the highest duration ARM on the list is a one-year Treasury ARM with a seven percent coupon, a margin of 175 basis points and 12 months until the next adjustment date. Shortening the length of the time until the next adjustment date to six months reduces the ARM's duration from 2.15 years to 1.76 years. Increasing the ARM's coupon from 7 percent to 9.25 percent also reduces the ARM's effective duration, in this case from 2.15 years to 1.54 years.

The range of durations in Exhibit 10.5 makes it clear that the appropriate hedge for an ARM portfolio depends on the composition of the portfolio.

Improving the Hedge with Options

One of the problems with hedging ARMs with Eurodollar futures is that the hedge is likely to perform poorly if rates move by a large amount. This is especially likely to be a problem for Treasury ARMs with below-market coupons that are bound effectively by annual caps. For such ARMs, the cap options, which are roughly the equivalent of puts on Eurodollar futures, are at or in the money and exert a considerable influence on the ARM's price behavior.

The effect of large changes in yields on the performance of the Eurodollar futures hedge is illustrated in Exhibit 10.6. The importance of negative convexity in the ARMs is clear. Decreases in yields produce smaller and smaller incremental gains to the ARM portfolio, while increases in yields produce larger and larger incremental losses. In contrast, the incremental gains and losses on the

Exhibit 10.5
Prices and Durations for Alternative ARM Securities
July 18, 1990

Index	Coupon	Margin	Months to Reset	Price (32nds)	Effective Duration
1-Year Treasury[1]	7.0	1.75	12	98 - 01	2.15
"	7.0	1.75	6	99 - 05	1.76
"	7.75	2.125	12	100 - 04	1.94
"	7.75	2.125	6	100 - 02	1.55
"	8.0	2.0	12	100 - 05	1.80
"	8.0	2.0	6	100 - 00	1.37
"	9.25	2.25	12	102 - 10	1.54
"	9.25	2.25	6	102 - 21	1.10
11th District COFI	9.42	1.25	1	101 - 05	1.86

[1]   FHLMC 1-Year Treasury ARMs with 2 percent annual caps and lifetime caps equal to 600 basis points above coupon.

Exhibit 10.6

Hedging Treasury ARMs with Eurodollar Futures
(Instantaneous Rate Shock)

($10 Million ARM portfolio: Hedge = -72 Eurodollar futures)
(ARM coupon = 8.0 percent; margin =2.0; months to reset =12)

Change in Interest Rates (Basis Points)	P/L on ARM Portfolio ($ 000's)	P/L on Short Eurodollar Futures ($ 000's)	Net P/L on Hedged Portfolio ($ 000's)
-300	453	-540	-87
-200	311	-360	-49
-100	163	-180	-17
-50	85	-90	-5
0	0	0	0
+50	-93	90	-3
+100	-197	180	-17
+200	-436	360	-76
+300	-715	540	-175

Eurodollar futures position is the same no matter how widely yields swing. As a result, when yields are rising, the accelerating losses on the ARM portfolio are only partly offset by the gains on the short futures position. When yields are falling, on the other hand, the losses on the Eurodollar position more than offset the decelerating gains on the ARM portfolio.

Supplementing the Hedge with Puts

The hedge can be improved by buying something with the right convexity. As we noted above, Eurodollar put options behave very much like the options that are embedded in an ARM. Thus, we should be able to improve the hedge by buying Eurodollar puts.

The machinery for finding the right combination is fairly complicated, but the effect of finding the right combination on the performance of the hedge is illustrated clearly in Exhibit 10.7, where gains and losses are shown for both the hedged and unhedged ARM portfolio over a three-month horizon. The size of the short futures position in the hedge has been scaled back to 59 contracts from 72 contracts. The difference has been made up with 38 long December Eurodollar puts with an exercise price of 90.75.

The contribution of the puts to the hedged portfolio matches quite well the gains and losses on the ARM. As interest rates fall, the short futures and long puts lose money at a rate that tracks the gains on the ARM portfolio. As interest rates rise, the long puts go in the money and the gains accelerate at a pace that keeps up with the accelerating losses on the ARM portfolio. Finally, when rates are stable, the puts lose money from time decay, but the ARM portfolio realizes more than offsetting gains as the coupon reset date is approached.

Real versus Synthetic Puts

In practice, there are two ways to buy puts. One is to buy real puts for which one pays the full premium at the outset. The other is to adjust the size of the Eurodollar futures position to match the changing price sensitivity of the ARM portfolio.

Exhibit 10.7

Hedging Treasury ARMs with Eurodollar Futures and Options
($10 Million ARM portfolio:
Hedge =-59 ED futures, +38 DEC 90.75 ED puts)
(ARM coupon = 8.0 percent; margin = 2.0; months to reset = 12)
P/L over 3-month Horizon[1]

Change in Interest Rates (Basis Points)	P/L on ARM Portfolio ($ 000's)	P/L on Hedge			Net P/L on Hedged Portfolio ($ 000's)
		Futures ($000's)	Options ($000's)	Combined ($ 000's)	
-300	435	-443	-2	-445	-10
-200	310	-295	-2	-297	+13
-100	184	-148	-1	-149	+35
-50	117	-74	-1	-75	+42
0	44	0	-1	-1	+43
+50	-39	74	0	74	+35
+100	-133	148	8	156	+23
+200	-355	295	76	371	+16
+300	-620	443	170	613	-8

[1]   *Assumes ARM financed at 8 percent repo rate*

The second of these strategies, which is a popular way of hedging interest-rate caps traded in the over-the-counter market, can be thought of as buying a synthetic put. Such a strategy, however, has two distinct drawbacks. The first is that such a hedge is exposed to large and sudden changes in yields that would prevent smooth and continuous adjustments in the hedge ratio. Exhibit 10.6 provides an indication of the losses the hedger would sustain if interest rates were to move too far and too fast to allow the hedger to adjust.

The second potential drawback to pursuing a dynamic hedging strategy is that the final cost of the strategy depends on how volatile the interest rate market turns out to be. If markets are quiet, few adjustments will be needed, and the dynamic strategy will prove to be inexpensive. If markets turn out to be highly volatile, however, several adjustments will be needed—all requiring the hedger to either buy high or sell low—and the costs of the strategy will prove to be high.

In a nutshell, then, a dynamic futures hedging strategy can be less expensive than the outright purchase of real options if markets turn out to be quieter than expected, but a dynamic hedging strategy is exposed to gapping markets and to large, unexpected increases in market volatility.

Further Considerations

We have outlined what we think is a workable approach to hedging ARM portfolios. The approach is based on properly estimating the sensitivity of ARM prices to changes in interest rates and finding appropriate combinations of futures and options to match the price exposure in ARMs. Further, we find that while ARM hedges involving the sale of Treasury notes have proven to be unreliable, the Eurodollar futures and options market may well be a workable, superior alternative.

Two caveats, however, are in order.

Other Sources of Risk

First, there are other sources of risk in an ARM portfolio. In addition to changes in the general level and volatility of yields, ARM prices are subject to:

- changes in the slope of the yield curve because of the effect on prepayments; and
- surges in the volume of ARMs offered for sale.

The first of these complicates the problem of finding a robust hedge for an ARM portfolio but is not insurmountable given the interest-rate futures instruments that are available.

The second is a source of risk that cannot be hedged with conventional futures. As with any cross-hedge—in this case, hedging ARM price risk with futures on interest-bearing instruments other than ARMs—there is no effective way to hedge risks that are peculiar to the instrument itself. For example, if a large S&L finds it necessary to dump a large stock of ARMs on the market, ARM prices will almost certainly fall without any accompanying fall in the prices of other interest-bearing instruments.

Basis Risk

All hedgers face basis risk. Because of the independent forces that operate on ARMs and on the Eurodollar market, gains and losses will not always be offsetting. Moreover, the hedger often will find small gains or small losses on both legs of the portfolio—the ARMs and the Eurodollar futures and options. As a result, a hedged ARM portfolio will prove to be more volatile on some days than an unhedged portfolio. The hedge pays off, however, if interest rates rise significantly. When this happens, basis risk is outweighed by the fundamental driving force that interest rates exert over ARM prices.

If You Decide to Hedge

You need access to two things if you wish to hedge a portfolio of ARM securities:

- an up-to-date ARM pricing model, which is necessary for calculating effective durations; and
- an optimization model for finding the combination of futures and options that best fits the price risk in an ARM portfolio.

As shown earlier in this chapter, the range of durations for ARM securities is wide, and the duration of any given ARM security depends on its own particular characteristics. In practice, the price sensitivity of an ARM security can be calculated only with the help of a sophisticated pricing model. Many such models are available, including the one we use at Discount Futures. The addendum on how ARMs are priced at the end of this chapter lays out the basic structure of these models and provides an illustration of how the models work.

The pricing models are necessary to find a good hedge. To find a superior hedge, one also needs a good optimization model and reliable option pricing capacity to select the correct mix of futures and options from the entire constellation of available contracts. Discount Futures has this capacity, which we can use to help you construct hedges for your ARM portfolios.

Addendum
How ARMs are Priced

The challenge in pricing and hedging ARMs lies in valuing the various call and put options that are embedded in ARMs. Because these options are inter-related and because many of the options have extremely long times remaining to expiration, conventional option pricing models are not up to the task. Elaborate simulation models have been erected in their place that are better suited to the task but that require a higher level of financial sophistication than do the conventional models.

The models used by Discount Futures and others in pricing ARMs and other mortgages are complex in practice, but the basic structure of the models can be reduced to two basic stages:

- *Capturing the volatility of interest rates in a way that is consistent with the current term structure of Treasury yields and the observed volatility of interest rates;*

- *Capturing the financial realities of ARMs including limitations on coupon adjustments and prepayments.*

Stage I: Constructing the Interest Rate Distribution

We know that interest rates are volatile. The purpose of the first stage is to describe interest rate volatility in a way that meets two reality checks:

- *The distribution of interest rate paths must be consistent with the current term structure of zero-coupon Treasury yields;*

- *The resulting volatility of interest rates must be consistent with observed short-term interest rate volatility.*

How this is done can be illustrated with a very simple binomial depiction of interest rate volatility, which is illustrated in the insert.

Basic setting

As shown in panel A, the current one-year Treasury rate is 10 percent and, by the beginning of the next year, can either increase to R_u with a probability of 1/2 or decrease to R_d with a probability of 1/2.

The market data with which we have to reconcile R_u and R_d are shown in panel B. The current one-year zero-coupon Treasury price is 90.91, which gives us the current one-year Treasury rate of 10 percent. The current two-year zero-coupon Treasury price is 82, which gives us a current two-year Treasury rate of 10.4 percent and a forward one-year Treasury rate of 10.87 percent. One-year interest rate volatility is 20 percent.

With this as the basic setting, the problem is to find values for R_u and R_d that are consistent with a two-year zero-coupon Treasury price of 82 and one-

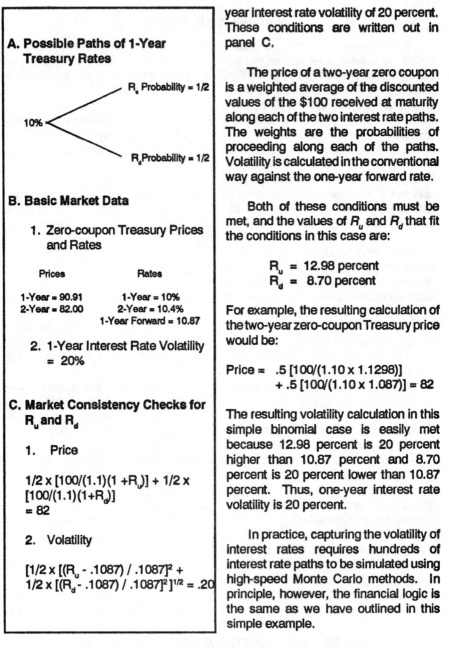

A. Possible Paths of 1-Year Treasury Rates

R_u Probability = 1/2

10%

R_d Probability = 1/2

B. Basic Market Data

1. Zero-coupon Treasury Prices and Rates

Prices	Rates
1-Year = 90.91	1-Year = 10%
2-Year = 82.00	2-Year = 10.4%
	1-Year Forward = 10.87

2. 1-Year Interest Rate Volatility = 20%

C. Market Consistency Checks for R_u and R_d

1. Price

$1/2 \times [100/(1.1)(1 + R_u)] + 1/2 \times [100/(1.1)(1+R_d)]$
$= 82$

2. Volatility

$[1/2 \times [(R_u - .1087) / .1087]^2 + 1/2 \times [(R_d - .1087) / .1087]^2]^{1/2} = .20$

year interest rate volatility of 20 percent. These conditions are written out in panel C.

The price of a two-year zero coupon is a weighted average of the discounted values of the $100 received at maturity along each of the two interest rate paths. The weights are the probabilities of proceeding along each of the paths. Volatility is calculated in the conventional way against the one-year forward rate.

Both of these conditions must be met, and the values of R_u and R_d that fit the conditions in this case are:

$$R_u = 12.98 \text{ percent}$$
$$R_d = 8.70 \text{ percent}$$

For example, the resulting calculation of the two-year zero-coupon Treasury price would be:

Price = .5 [100/(1.10 x 1.1298)]
      + .5 [100/(1.10 x 1.087)] = 82

The resulting volatility calculation in this simple binomial case is easily met because 12.98 percent is 20 percent higher than 10.87 percent and 8.70 percent is 20 percent lower than 10.87 percent. Thus, one-year interest rate volatility is 20 percent.

In practice, capturing the volatility of interest rates requires hundreds of interest rate paths to be simulated using high-speed Monte Carlo methods. In principle, however, the financial logic is the same as we have outlined in this simple example.

Pricing Other Securities

Once the interest rate paths have been generated, they can be used to price other securities. The simplest security to price is a pure floater, which should trade at par.

Floater

Consider a pure floater that accrues interest at 10 percent in year 1 and at whatever the one-year rate is one year hence. At the end of year 2, the bond will have paid a total of

$$\$100 \ (\ 1.10) \times (1 + R_u)$$
$$= \$100(1.10)(1.1298) = \$124.28$$

If rates rise and a total of

$$\$100 \ (\ 1.10) \times (1 + R_d)$$
$$= \$100(1.10)(1.087) = \$119.57$$

If rates fall. The theoretical model price for this security would be:

$$\text{Price} = 0.5 \ [\$124.28/(1.10)(1.1298)]$$
$$+ \ 0.5 \ [\$119.57/(1.10)(1.087)]$$
$$= \$100$$

Capped floater

Apart from prepayments, the most distinguishing feature of an ARM is the cap on coupon adjustments. The effect of a cap on the floater is to reduce the present value of the cash flow along the path where rates rise. A floater with a cap of 11 percent, for example, would pay only

$$\$100 \ (\ 1.10) \times (1.11) = \$122.10$$

by the end of year 2 if one-year market rates rise to 12.98 percent. The value of this security would then be:

$$\text{Price} = 0.5 \ [\ \$122.10/(1.10)(1.1298)]$$
$$+ \ 0.5 \ [\ \$119.57/(1.10)(1.087)]$$
$$= 99.12.$$

As we would expect, the effect of the cap is to reduce the price of the security. In this case, the cap is estimated to cost the investor 0.88 percent.

Stage II: Pricing ARMs

Once the distribution of interest rate paths is generated, the next stage is to calculate the likely cash flows from an ARM security along each path. This first requires assigning a unique coupon path to each interest rate path. Then, we must forecast prepayments along each path. In the model we use, ARM prepayments depend mainly on the age of the loan and the spread between the ARM coupon and the fixed-rate mortgage rate that is also generated by the model in each period. The parameters of our prepayment model were estimated from historical data on about 600,000 adjustable rate mortgages originated since 1980.

APPENDIX A

International Bank
Deposit Futures

Exhibit A.1-1

Futures Contract Specifications

	Eurodollars			
Contract Term	Chicago Mercantile Exchange (CME)	Singapore International Monetary Exchange (SIMEX)	London International Financial Futures Exchange (LIFFE)	Tokyo International Financial Futures Exchange (TIFFE)
Unit of Trading	$1,000,000	Same as CME	Same as CME	Same as CME
Price Quote	100 - annualized futures interest rate	Same as CME	Same as CME	Same as CME
Tick Size	.01 (1 basis point)	Same as CME	Same as CME	Same as CME
Tick Value	$25	Same as CME	Same as CME	Same as CME
Delivery Months	March, June, September, December	Same as CME	Same as CME	Same as CME
Last Trading Day	Second London Business Day before the third Wednesday of the delivery month	Same as CME	Same as CME	Two business days before the third Wednesday of each contract month. If this third Wednesday follows on a bank holiday in New York City, the last trading day will be one business day prior to the third Wednesday.
Final Settlement Price	100 - spot LIBOR as determined by CME bank survey	Same as CME	100 - spot LIBOR as determined by LIFFE bank survey	100 - spot TIBOR as determined by a Tokyo bank survey
Trading Hours	7:20 a.m. to 2:00 p.m. (Chicago time) 7:20 a.m. to 9:30 a.m. for expiring contract on last trading day	7:45 a.m. to 5:20 p.m. (Singapore time)	8:30 a.m. to 4:00 p.m. and 4:25 P.M. to 6:00 p.m. (London time)	9:00 a.m. to 12:00 p.m. and 1:30 p.m. to 3:30 p.m. (Tokyo time)

Exhibit A.1-2

Futures Contract Specifications

Short Sterling	EuroDeutschemarks			EuroYen		Pibor
London International Financial Futures Exchange (LIFFE)	Singapore International Monetary Exchange (SIMEX)	LIFFE	MATIF	Tokyo International Financial Futures Exchange (TIFFE)	SIMEX	MATIF
£500,000	DM 1,000,000	DM 1,000,000	DM 1,000,000	¥100,000,000	¥100,000,000	Ff 5,000,000
100 - annualized interest rate	100-annualized interest rate	100-annualized interest rate	100-annualized interest rate	100-annualized interest rate	100-annualized interest rate	100-annualized interest rate
.01 (1 basis point)	.01 (1 basis point)	.01 (1 basis point)	.01 (1 basis point)	.01 (1 basis point)	.01 (1 basis point)	.01 (1 basis point)
£12.50	DM 25	DM 25	DM 25	¥2,500	¥2,500	Ff 125
March, June, September, December	March, June, September, December	March, June, September, December	March, June, September, December	March, June, September, December	March, June, September, December	March, June, September, December
Third Wednesday of Delivery Month	Second London business day immediately preceding the third Wednesday of the contract month	Two business days prior to the third Wednesday of the delivery month	Two business days prior to the third Wednesday of the delivery month	Two banking days prior to the third Wednesday of the contract month	Second SIMEX business day prior to the third Wednesday of the contract month	Second business day before the 11th Thursday of each quarter of the calendar year
100 - spot short sterling LIBOR rate as determined by a LIFFE bank survey	Same as LIFFE	100 - 3mo EuroDM LIBOR rate as determined by a LIFFE bank survey	100 - 3mo EuroDM PIBOR rate as determined by a MATIF bank survey	100 - 3mo Euroyen TIBOR rate as determined by a TIFFE bank survey	100 - 3mo Euroyen SIBOR rate as determined by a SIMEX bank survey	100 - PIBOR rate as determined by ASB bank survey
8:20 am- 4:05 pm (London time)	8:15 am - 5:30 pm (Singapore time)	8:00 am -4:10 pm (London time)	8:30 am -4:00 pm (Paris time)	9:00 am -12:00 pm and 1:30 pm - 3:30 pm (Tokyo time)	8:00 am -5:00 pm (Singapore time)	8:30 am - 4:00 pm (Paris time)

Exhibit A.2-1

Average Daily Trading Volume
(Actual Contracts)

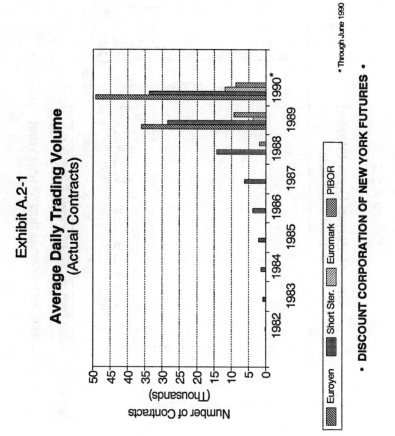

* Through June 1990

Euroyen   Short Ster.   Euromark   PIBOR

• DISCOUNT CORPORATION OF NEW YORK FUTURES •

Exhibit A.2-2

End-of-Period Open Interest
(Actual Contracts)

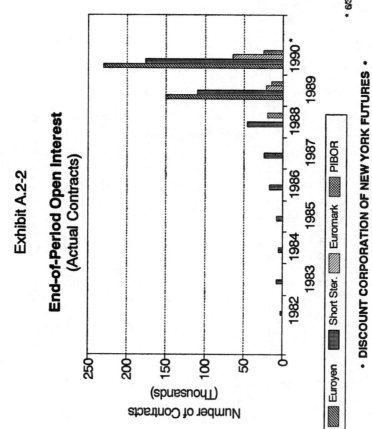

• DISCOUNT CORPORATION OF NEW YORK FUTURES •

* 6/30/90

APPENDIX B

Cash/Futures Arbitrage Transactions

In Chapter 2, we showed that selling overvalued futures could reduce the cost of borrowing and that buying undervalued futures could increase the rate of return to investing. We also argued that the sheer force of banks looking constantly for the lowest cost of funds or the highest rate of return on assets should work to keep futures prices in line with their theoretical fair values. In the academic literature, the act of choosing the best place to do something that you are going to do anyway is called one-way arbitrage. And, in the world of Eurodollar futures, one-way arbitrage seems to suffice to keep futures in line with cash.

Nevertheless, some readers will find it worthwhile to work through the two-way arbitrage transactions that serve as a backstop for the more common one-way transactions.

In a two-way arbitrage transaction, the bank does not borrow short and sell futures in lieu of borrowing long. Rather, the bank would borrow short, sell futures, and *lend* long. If the futures price is sufficiently overvalued, the combined effect of borrowing at LIBOR, selling the overvalued futures, and lending at LIBID is a pure arbitrage profit. That is, the bank assumes little or no risk and can take out a spread from the mispricing.

To see how, consider first the possibilities if futures were trading above their fair value. In particular, suppose that futures with two months to expiration were trading at 91.90. Given the values of LIBOR and LIBID shown in Exhibit 2.6, a bank could:

- borrow for two months at LIBOR (8-5/16)
- sell 10 Eurodollar futures at 91.90
- lend for five months at LIBID (8-1/4)

Exhibit B.1 shows how this transaction plays out.

At the outset, the bank borrows and lends exactly the same amounts of money so that the net cash flow is zero. Two months later, the final settlement price for Eurodollar futures at expiration is 91.70, which means that the bank has taken in $5,000 [= -10 x -20 x $25] in variation margin on the short futures position. That is, the bank was short 10 contracts, the futures price fell 20 basis points, and each basis point was worth $25.

At the two-month mark, the bank can combine the $5,000 in variation margin with a loan for $9,995,000 to pay off the $10,000,000 due on the two-month loan. Once again, the cash flows are a wash.

At the five-month mark, we see that the bank can use the proceeds of its original five-month loan to pay off the amount due on the three-month loan that it took out at the expiration of the futures contract. Thus, the cash flows wash out here as well.

This shows that the bank can piece together a riskless position that includes a short position in overpriced Eurodollar futures and break even without risk. If the futures price had been above 91.90, the bank could have made money without risk. Thus, there are powerful forces that will keep the futures price from rising above 91.90, which can be thought of as an upper boundary, or arbitrage bound.

Exhibit B.1

Futures Price Above Fair Value
(Futures trading at 91.90 = 100 - 8.10)

Today

- Bank borrows $9,863,353 (= 10,000,000/1.013854) for two months at LIBOR (8-5/16)

- Bank sells 10 E$ futures at 91.90 (= 100 - 8.10)

- Bank lends $9,863,353 for five months at five-month LIBID (8-1/4)

> Net Cash Flow = 0

Two Months Later (Futures settle at 91.70 = 100 - 8.30)

- Bank repays $10,000,000 on two-month loan

- Bank receives $5,000 from short futures

- Bank borrows $9,995,000 for three months at LIBOR (8.30)

> Net Cash Flow = 0

Five Months Later

- Bank receives $10,202,406 (= 9,863,353 x 1.034375) from five-month loan

- Bank repays $10,202,404 (= 9,995,000 x 1.02075) on three-month loan

> Net Cash Flow = 0

A similar exercise shows what can happen if Eurodollar futures are underpriced. Exhibit B.2 shows the outcome of a sequence of arbitrage transactions that begins with the bank:

- lending for two months at LIBID (8-3/16)
- buying 10 Eurodollar futures at 91.50
- borrowing for five months at LIBOR (8-3/8)

The reasoning that ran through the example of overpriced Eurodollar futures runs through this example as well. At the two-month mark, the Eurodollar futures price has risen to settle at 91.70, which produces a profit of $5,000. The $5,000 in variation margin can be added to the proceeds of the original loan and invested at three-month LIBID (8.175 percent if the spread between LIBOR and LIBID hasn't changed). Then, at the five-month mark, the proceeds of this investment can be used to pay off the original five-month borrowing.

All along the way, the cash flows wash. The bank breaks even without risk. At any price below 91.50, the bank would make money. Thus, powerful forces are at work here as well to keep the price from falling below 91.50, which would be the lower boundary or arbitrage bound in this example.

Exhibit B.3 shows that futures mispricings fall into two sorts. One sort includes mispricings that are large enough to induce a banker to buy or sell futures in lieu of lending or borrowing over some horizon in the cash market but too small to precipitate full scale arbitrage. The other includes mispricings that are large enough to induce a bank to do both sides of the arbitrage. Given the bid/ask spreads used in constructing our examples, we find that the range of prices within which futures can vary without triggering two-way arbitrage is 20 basis points on either side of fair value. Such a range is wider than the mispricings that we typically observe in practice.

We should note, too, that boundaries between one-way and two-way arbitrage opportunities shown in Exhibit B.3 is narrower than it is in practice. The examples do not allow for the costs of putting on an arbitrage position. While the futures side of an arbi-

Exhibit B.2

Futures Price Below Fair Value
(Futures trading at 91.50 = 100 - 8.50)

Today

- Bank lends $9,865,377 for two months at two-month <u>LIBID</u> (8-3/16)

- Bank buys 10 E$ futures at 91.50 (= 100 - 8.50)

- Bank borrows $9,865,377 for five months at five-month <u>LIBOR</u> (8-3/8)

> Net Cash Flow = 0

Two Months Later (Futures settle at 91.70 = 100 - 8.30)

- Bank receives $10,000,000 from original loan

- Bank receives $5,000 from long futures

- Bank lends $10,005,000 at three-month LIBID (e.g., 8.175%)

> Net Cash Flow = 0

Five Months Later

- Bank receives $10,209,477 (= 10,005,000 x 1.0204375)

- Bank repays $10,209,640 (= 9865,377 x 1.034896)

> Net Cash Flow = 0

Conclusion

Given the bid/ask spreads in the term deposit market, <u>active arbitrage</u> is profitable if the futures rate differs from the fair value of LIBOR by <u>more than</u> 20 basis points.

• **DISCOUNT CORPORATION OF NEW YORK FUTURES** •

Exhibit B.3

Cash/Futures Arbitrage Ranges
(2-Month LIBOR = 8-5/16, 2-Month LIBID = 8-3/16)
(5-Month LIBOR = 8-3/8, 5-Month LIBID = 8-1/4)

Futures Rate	Bank Action		
Above Fair Value	Bank lends short, buys E$ futures and borrows long		strong (two-way) arbitrage
	Bank lends short and buys E$ futures rather than lending long	8.50%	weak (one-way) arbitrage
Fair Value		8.30%	
Below Fair Value	Bank borrows short and sells E$ futures rather than borrowing long		weak (one-way) arbitrage
		8.10%	
	Bank borrows short, sells E$ futures and lends long		strong (two-way) arbitrage

trage transaction is cheap to do, the cash side is costly because it uses up credit lines with other banks and limits flexibility. Including these costs in the equation would widen the gap between the upper and lower boundaries.

APPENDIX C

The Short End Reports and Software

Discount Corporation of New York Futures uses two tools—both called The Short End—to compare the cost of funds across deposit, swap, and futures markets.

The first is a daily report that is produced and distributed at 6:30 a.m. Chicago time, before the futures market in Chicago opens. This report uses Eurodollar futures prices available from LIFFE and shows the relative richness or cheapness of Eurodollar futures against spot LIBOR rates and the swap market. A sample Short End report is shown in Exhibit C.1.

The second is PC-based software, which can be used to compare the relative richness or cheapness of the competing markets throughout the trading day. In particular, The Short End:

- performs rich/cheap analysis of all traded Eurodollar futures

Exhibit C.1

THE SHORT END
Friday, November 16, 1990 6:30 a.m. CST

EURODOLLAR FUTURES STRIPS, SWAPS, AND SPOT LIBOR
(Annual Money Market Rates A/360 days)

Term	Futures Strip Rate	Spot LIBOR	SWAP RATE (Pay Fixed)	Strip vs. LIBOR	Strip vs. Swap
1 year	7.92	8.00		8 b.p. rich	
2 year	8.14	8.25	8.20	11 b.p. rich	6 b.p. rich
3 year	8.42	8.50	8.44	8 b.p. rich	2 b.p. rich
4 year	8.64	8.69	8.65	5 b.p. rich	1 b.p. rich

FORWARD STRIPS

			Implied Forward		
RED*	8.43	8.54	8.43	11 b.p. rich	fair
GREEN**	9.01	9.03	8.95	2 b.p. rich	6 b.p. cheap
BLUE***	9.29	9.26	9.28	3 b.p. cheap	1 b.p. cheap

*   , EDZ91, EDH92, EDM92, EDU92
** , EDZ92, EDH93, EDM93, EDU93
*** , EDZ93, EDH94, EDM94, EDU94

FAIR VALUES OF EURODOLLAR AND ONE MONTH LIBOR FUTURES

Contract	Fair Value	Last on LIFFE	
ED Dec 90	92.04	92.10	6 b.p. rich
ED Mar 91	92.21	92.44	23 b.p. rich
ED Jun 91	92.36	92.47	11 b.p. rich
ED Sep 91	92.22	92.36	14 b.p. rich
		IMM SETTLE	
EM Nov 90	92.05	92.08	3 b.p. rich
EM Dec 90	91.61	91.83	22 b.p. rich
EM Jan 91	92.22	92.32	10 b.p. rich
EM Feb 91	92.35	92.35	fair
EM Mar 91	92.21	92.37	16 b.p. rich

DATA

EURODOLLAR FUTURE (LIFFE)

Z90	92.10	M92	91.69	Z93	91.07
H91	92.44	U92	91.57	H94	91.05
M91	92.47	Z92	91.38	M94	90.98
U91	92.36	H93	91.33	U94	90.94
Z91	92.11	M93	91.24
H92	91.92	U93	91.18

CASH LIBOR CURVE

O/N	8 1/16	6 Mo.	8
1 Wk.	7 15/16	9 Mo.	8
1 Mo.	7 15/16	1 Yr.	8
2 Mo.	8 3/16	18 Mo.	8 1/8
3 Mo.	8 1/16	2 Yr.	8 1/4
4 Mo.	8	3 Yr.	8 1/2
5 Mo.	8	4 Yr.	8 11/16

These are only indications and should not be construed to represent market quotations.

• **DISCOUNT CORPORATION OF NEW YORK FUTURES** •

- calculates Eurodollar futures strip rates
- compares Eurodollar futures strip rates with the time deposit and swap markets
- analyzes swap yields and strip rates as spreads over Treasury yields
- calculates weighted hedges for Eurodollar futures against Treasury notes
- calculates forward rates
- facilitates strip trading by converting bid and offered prices on Eurodollar futures into strip yields
- employs Discount Futures' proprietary estimates of futures mispricings.

Sample screens are shown in Exhibit C.2.

Exhibit C.2

Sample Screens from
The Short End Software

Data Tables Calculators Help Quit

─────────Eurodollar Futures Fair Values on 11/15/90─────────

Contract	Remaining Trade Days	Actual Price	Fair Value	Adjusted Fair Value
Dec 90	33	92.10	92.04 (6)	92.04 (6)
Mar 91	124	92.44	92.21 (23)	92.21 (23)
Jun 91	215	92.47	92.36 (11)	92.36 (11)
Sep 91	306	92.36	92.19 (17)	92.17 (19)
Dec 91	397	92.08	91.60 (48)	91.58 (50)
Mar 92	488	91.88	91.69 (19)	91.66 (22)
Jun 92	579	91.67	91.91 (-24)	91.87 (-20)
Sep 92	670	91.55	91.72 (-17)	91.67 (-12)
Dec 92	761	91.36	91.24 (12)	91.17 (19)
Mar 93	852	91.31	91.28 (3)	91.20 (11)
Jun 93	943	91.22	91.33 (-11)	91.23 (-1)
Sep 93	1034	91.16	91.22 (-6)	91.10 (6)
Dec 93	1125	91.05	90.96 (9)	90.82 (23)
Mar 94	1216	91.03	91.04 (-1)	90.88 (15)
Jun 94	1307	90.96	91.13 (-17)	90.94 (2)
Sep 94	1405	90.92	91.03 (-11)	90.82 (10)

──<F1>-Help; <Ctrl-F>-Futures; <Ctrl-L>-LIBOR; <ESC>-Exit──
Copyright (C) 1990 Discount Corporation of New York Futures

Data Tables Calculators Help Quit
──────── The Short End (Version 1.00) ────────

─────────Eurodollar Futures Strips (6-month increments)─────────
Strip Rates (A/360)

From→ To↓	901115	910515	911115	920515	921115	930515	931115	940515
910515	7.89							
911115	7.92	7.66						
920515	7.95	7.99	8.04					
921115	8.16	8.14	8.40	8.44				
930515	8.27	8.37	8.51	8.77	8.74			
931115	8.44	8.48	8.70	8.81	9.01	8.91		
940515	8.53	8.64	8.77	8.97	9.02	9.18	9.06	
941115	8.65	8.71	8.90	9.00	9.16	9.17	9.31	9.17

──<F1>-Help; <↓,↑,F2>-Analysis; <F3>-BEY; <F4>-Build; <Ctrl-F,L,S>-Data; <ESC>──

──── Copyright (C) 1990 Discount Corporation of New York Futures ────

· DISCOUNT CORPORATION OF NEW YORK FUTURES ·

Appendix D

ISDA Standard Swap Documentation

Code of

Standard Wording, Assumptions and Provisions for Swaps

1986 Edition

INTERNATIONAL SWAP DEALERS ASSOCIATION, INC.

TABLE OF CONTENTS

ARTICLE 12

PAYMENTS ON EARLY TERMINATION

ARTICLE 13

SUBMISSION TO JURISDICTION

ARTICLE 14

NOTICES

ARTICLE 15

REPRESENTATIONS

ARTICLE 16

AGREEMENTS

ARTICLE 17

SPECIFIED ENTITIES

ARTICLE 18

CROSS BORDER PROVISIONS

ARTICLE 19

CERTAIN PROVISIONS RELATING TO TAX MATTERS

ARTICLE 20

MISCELLANEOUS

PREFACE TO THE CODE OF STANDARD WORDING, ASSUMPTIONS AND PROVISIONS FOR SWAPS, 1986 EDITION

The International Swap Dealers Association, Inc. ("ISDA") is pleased to publish the 1986 Edition of the Code of Standard Wording, Assumptions and Provisions for Swaps (the "1986 Code"). The publication of the 1986 Code represents an important step forward in the efforts that began in late 1983 to standardize and simplify rate swap documentation, efforts which led to the publication one year ago of the 1985 Edition of the Code (the "1985 Edition"). As was foreseen at the time the 1985 Edition was published, the rate swap market has continued the rapid growth and development that have characterized it since its inception. At the same time, certain new trends and practices have emerged from the ever-increasing volume of transactions.

It is against this background that the 1986 Code is published. The 1985 Edition has been well received and widely used by market participants, including large and small market makers and end users. As a logical extension of its predecessor, the 1986 Code addresses a number of subjects on which the 1985 Edition was silent. The rate swap market has now developed sufficiently to enable the Documentation Task Force of ISDA to reach agreement on standard language to be included in the Code to cover matters as diverse as compounding of floating amounts, events of default and termination events, standard representations and agreements, and a range of cross border and tax-related matters.

The approach that has been taken with respect to these new subjects is a familiar one: the 1986 Code creates presumptions as to certain matters, which the parties are free to vary; it provides a menu of choices as to other matters; and as to still other matters it provides only a framework without any suggested solutions.

Users will find that the 1986 Code, by introducing a distinction between a "rate swap agreement" and a "rate swap transaction", will better accommodate both those agreements that relate to a series of transactions treated as an integrated whole and those single-swap agreements that govern only one rate swap transaction. Those who have worked with the 1985 Edition will find a transition to the 1986 Code an easy matter. Those who prefer to continue using the 1985 Edition can rest assured that the original edition of the Code will serve them well in future transactions. The basic rate setting provisions of the 1985 Edition remain unchanged in the 1986 Code.

Parties may in their agreement adopt all or any portion of either the 1985 Edition or the 1986 Code and, of course, they may specify any variations or additions they desire to the provisions of either edition.

Unlike the 1985 Edition of the Code, which was viewed upon its publication as a first step in the effort to develop a standard vocabulary for rate swaps, the 1986 Code is intended to be a comprehensive Code for dollar rate swaps that will remain unchanged for the foreseeable future. The Documentation Task Force of ISDA now will turn its attention to other projects, such as the development of standard documentation for currency swap transactions and suggested standard form agreements and confirmation telexes for various types of rate swap and currency swap transactions.

GUIDE TO THE CODE OF SWAPS

1986 Edition

This Guide illustrates how the Code of Standard Wording, Assumptions and Provisions for Swaps, 1986 Edition (the "1986 Code"), can be used to simplify greatly the documentation of a rate swap. The 1986 Code can be used for fixed-to-floating rate swaps and for floating-to-floating rate swaps, whether simple or complex.

The 1985 Edition of the Code covered two principal subjects that continue to be essential parts of the 1986 Code: cash flows of a rate swap (Code Articles 1 through 10) and calculation of amounts payable upon early termination of a rate swap (Code Articles 11 and 12). These provisions have been refined in the 1986 Code to facilitate the use of integrated master agreements and to provide for compounding of Floating Amounts. The 1986 Code also adds many important new provisions, including definitions of various possible Events of Default and Termination Events (Code Sections 11.7 and 11.8), a list of representations (Code Article 15), a list of agreements (Code Article 16), definitions relating to Specified Entities, which are designed to simplify documentation for rate swaps in which a party's obligations are guaranteed or supported in some way by another entity (Code Article 17), cross border provisions (Code Article 18), and withholding tax provisions (Code Article 19).

Like the 1985 Edition, the 1986 Code is not a contract. The payment obligations of the parties to a rate swap arise from the terms of their agreement. Parties may adopt the 1986 Code (or, if they prefer, may adopt the 1985 Edition of the Code) in its entirety as the general basis of their contract, either in a master agreement or in an agreement for an individual rate swap. They may also incorporate certain portions of either edition of the Code without incorporating others. In either case, they may specify variations in or additions to the provisions they incorporate. Express provisions in a contract always will override anything to the contrary in the Code.

On many points, the 1986 Code creates a rule to apply in the absence of any express provision by the parties in their agreement. On other points, the 1986 Code creates a menu of choices for use by the parties in deciding a particular matter. Such menu choices are intended only to suggest possible provisions to be considered by the parties and are not required to be included in any particular contract.

I. USING THE 1986 CODE TO ESTABLISH THE CASH FLOWS OF A TYPICAL RATE SWAP

If parties incorporate the 1986 Code into an agreement, they need only specify a few brief payment terms. This aspect of the Code remains unchanged in the 1986 Code. For example, for a "plain-vanilla" rate swap involving an exchange of semiannual fixed payments for semiannual floating payments, with the Floating Rate reset at the beginning of each semiannual period, only the following terms need be specified:

- Fixed Rate Payor and Floating Rate Payor. Code Sections 2.1 and 2.2.
- Effective Date. Code Section 3.2.

- Termination Date. Code Section 3.3.
- Notional Amount. Code Section 4.3.
- Payment Dates. Code Section 4.5.
- Fixed Amounts (or Fixed Rate). Code Sections 5.1 and 5.2.
- Floating Rate Option (and, for some options, a Designated Maturity). Code Section 7.1.
- Reset Dates. Code Section 6.3(b).
- Calculation Agent. Code Section 4.8.

After specifying these terms, each party readily knows the dates on which payments are due, the exact amount of each fixed payment and how the exact amount of each floating payment is to be calculated. Each semiannual Payment Date automatically becomes the first day of a Calculation Period. The Calculation Period lasts until the next Payment Date. In this case, each Payment Date is also a Period End Date. Code Section 4.6(a). Payment Dates that would otherwise fall on nonbanking days are adjusted automatically by the Code (with alternative adjustments possible). Code Section 4.5.

If the Fixed Amount is not a specified amount, it will be determined for each Calculation Period on the basis of the following formula:

$$\text{Fixed Amount} = \text{Notional Amount} \times \text{Fixed Rate} \times \text{Portion of year covered by the Calculation Period}$$

For this formula, the parties must specify the Notional Amount and the Fixed Rate. The Code tells how days in a year are to be counted for purposes of applying the Fixed Rate, but parties may easily vary the Code's provision. Code Section 5.2(b).

The Floating Amount will be determined for each Calculation Period on the basis of the following formula:

$$\text{Floating Amount} = \text{Notional Amount} \times (\text{Floating Rate} \pm \text{Spread}) \times \text{Portion of year covered by the Calculation Period}$$

For this formula, the parties must specify the Notional Amount and the Spread, if there is one, and must select a Floating Rate Option to be used in determining the Floating Rate. The method for applying the Floating Rate to the portion of the year covered by the Calculation Period is set forth in the Code but may be modified by the parties. Code Section 6.3(f).

The Code sets forth seven Floating Rate Options:
- LIBOR (the London Interbank Offered Rate)
- Prime
- Treasury Bill
- CD
- Commercial Paper
- Federal Funds
- Bankers Acceptance

There are two basic ways of determining each Floating Rate Option—either by referring to a widely available source, such as the Reuters Screen or a Federal Reserve publication, or by obtaining quotations from participants in the relevant market.

Reset Dates for a rate swap are the days on which the Floating Rate changes, which in a typical rate swap will be a day near the start of each Calculation Period.

II. CHANGES IN THE 1986 CODE FROM THE 1985 EDITION RELEVANT TO CASH FLOWS OF A RATE SWAP

Articles 1 through 10 of the 1986 Code remain substantially unchanged from the same Articles of the 1985 Edition. The principal refinements in these provisions are:

● **Rate Swap Agreement and Rate Swap Transaction.** The 1985 Edition included a single basic definition of the term "rate swap". The 1986 Code creates a distinction between two concepts: "Rate Swap Agreement" and "Rate Swap Transaction". Code Sections 1.1 and 1.2. A Rate Swap Agreement is defined as an agreement that governs one or several Rate Swap Transactions. The new approach accommodates what has become the prevailing practice of executing master agreements that cover multiple transactions. It also facilitates the provisions of the 1986 Code (discussed below) which presume that an early termination will apply simultaneously to all transactions under a given Rate Swap Agreement and that permit termination payments to be calculated on an aggregate basis.

● **Trade Date.** A new term "Trade Date" was added as Code Section 3.4 to refer to the day on which the parties enter into a Rate Swap Transaction as opposed to the Effective Date or the time the Rate Swap Transaction is fully documented. This term should facilitate use of the new representations and agreements contained in the 1986 Code because users of the 1986 Code may require that representations and warranties be true as of the Trade Date for each Rate Swap Transaction.

● **Compounding.** The 1986 Code contains new provisions to cover compounding of Floating Amounts, a matter not dealt with in the 1985 Edition. Code Article 6. Compounding involves dividing each Calculation Period into a series of "Compounding Periods" and adding up the individual Compounding Period Amounts for all such Compounding Periods, with each Compounding Period Amount taking account of compounding of the Compounding Period Amounts for prior Compounding Periods in that same Calculation Period.

● **Corresponding Payment Dates.** New Section 9.3 of the 1986 Code addresses situations in which Payment Dates coincide for two or more Rate Swap Transactions governed by the same Rate Swap Agreement. This Section provides that if "Net Payments—Corresponding Payment Dates" is specified by the parties, then payments will be netted among the various Rate Swap Transactions for which Payment Dates coincide.

● **Conditions Precedent.** Changes have been made to Code Section 10.2 which have the effect of relieving a party of the duty to make any fixed or floating payments under a Rate Swap Agreement if there is any Event of Default (or incipient Event of Default) with respect to the other party under the Rate Swap Agreement, even if the Event of Default does not relate to the transaction for which the fixed or floating payment is due. This change is intended to help implement the concept that all Rate Swap Transactions under a single master agreement are part of a single, integrated agreement.

III. USING THE CODE FOR OTHER RATE SWAPS

In addition to facilitating the "plain-vanilla" rate swaps described in Part I of this Guide, the 1986 Code includes many terms and provisions that are useful for more complicated rate swaps:

● **Different Payment Dates.** Under the Code, the parties can make payments at different times simply by distinguishing "Party A Payment Dates" from "Party B Payment Dates".

● **More Frequent Reset Dates.** Instead of specifying a day near the start of each Calculation Period as the Reset Date for a rate swap, parties can provide for the Floating Rate to be reset more frequently than once every Calculation Period—every three months, monthly, weekly or daily. When there is more than one Reset Date for a Calculation Period, parties may specify a method (or may use the method provided in the Code) for combining the rates determined on the various Reset Dates in calculating the Floating Rate for that Calculation Period. Code Sections 6.3(a) (iii)-(v).

● **Delayed Payment.** By specifying "Delayed Payment" in a rate swap, parties may defer the Payment Date for each Calculation Period by five banking days (or any other period they specify). Code Section 4.5(c). The Delayed Payment option is useful for rate swaps involving weekly or daily Reset Dates. Amounts due may be calculated prior to the day of payment, while at the same time the appropriate rate for a Reset Date occurring near the end of the Calculation Period may be taken into account.

● **Rate Cut-off Date.** As an alternative to Delayed Payment in rate swaps involving weekly or daily Reset Dates, parties may use a "Rate Cut-off Date" to "freeze" the Floating Rate toward the end of the Calculation Period for the purpose of calculating the Floating Amount. Code Section 6.3(d).

● **Two Floating Rate Payors.** The Code can be used for rate swaps in which both parties pay based upon a floating rate simply by combining the appropriate terms with the names of the parties: "Party A Floating Rate Option", "Party A Reset Dates", etc.

● **Compounding.** As explained in Part II of this Guide, new provisions in the 1986 Code permit compounding of Floating Amounts. Code Article 6.

IV. EARLY TERMINATION

The 1986 Code, like its predecessor, contemplates that parties may wish to designate a date for settling out, on a "lump-sum" basis, amounts payable under a rate swap if a default or other event identified in their contract as permitting early termination occurs. A date designated in this manner is called an "Early Termination Date".

"Event of Default" and "Termination Event" are defined in the 1986 Code by means of a list of terms describing typical events that might be specified by the parties to a rate swap. As is true for all "menus" of choices in the Code, the events described in Code Section 11.7 and Section 11.8 are only possibilities and are not required to be included in a particular contract. The parties to a rate swap are free to specify events of default and termination events not described in the Code. Events that were considered by the drafters but not defined in the 1986 Code include cross-default, insolvency, judgment lien, material adverse change, merger or sale of assets without consent and revocation of authorizations.

Code Section 11.10, which is new in the 1986 Code, provides that, with respect to any Event of Default or Termination Event, the parties can agree that the event will not be deemed to occur until the end of a specified "Cure Period" or until after notice is given, or both. If the parties so specify, only after this period has elapsed or notice has been given can an Early Termination Date be designated. The 1986 Code also contemplates that parties may, if they wish, agree not to designate an Early Termination Date as a result of illegality or the imposition of withholding taxes without first attempting to eliminate the illegality or taxes by assigning the agreement or affected transaction to another branch, office or affiliate. Code Sections 11.6 and 18.3. (See the discussion in Part VI below.)

The early termination provisions of the 1986 Code do not address the requirements for notice of an Early Termination Date or the treatment of unpaid amounts for Calculation Periods that ended on or before the Early Termination Date. These points should be addressed in each Rate Swap Agreement. In addition, parties may wish to indicate in their Rate Swap Agreement whether certain payment obligations survive the termination of the Rate Swap Agreement (such as the obligation to pay default interest pursuant to Section 10.3 of the Code, the obligation to pay expenses pursuant to Section 12.7 of the Code, the obligation to compensate the other party for losses arising from currency translation under Section 18.1 of the Code, and the tax gross-up obligation under Section 19.1 of the Code).

Article 12 of the 1986 Code continues to provide three different approaches to settling out on the Early Termination Date the loss or profit arising from an early termination:

(1) "Agreement Value" fixes the loss or profit on the basis of quotations from market makers in the rate exchange market for a replacement transaction that would generate the same payment streams as the transaction being terminated.

(2) "Formula" calculates loss or profit on the basis of hypothetical alternative borrowings and investments available on the Early Termination Date.

Adjustments for an element of fault or differences in creditworthiness of the parties may be made by specifying spreads above or below the relevant borrowing and investment rates.

(3) "Indemnification" allows the parties to calculate damages on the basis of a general indemnity.

In selecting an approach to damages, the parties should indicate whether the amount calculated is to be recovered on a "fault" or a "no-fault" basis. For that purpose, the Code provides three applications of each approach:

(1) If the parties specify "Agreement Value", "Formula" or "Indemnification" but say nothing about "Two Way Payments", payment will be made on a "fault" basis. The party suffering the greater loss will recover only if it cannot be held accountable for the event that caused the early termination. If neither party is at fault, recovery will be based on "Two Way Payments".

(2) If the parties add the term "Two Way Payments", payment will be made on a "no-fault" basis. The party suffering the greater loss will recover without regard to accountability for the early termination.

(3) If the parties add the term "Limited Two Way Payments", recovery will depend on the nature of the event giving rise to the early termination. Recovery will be made on the basis of (1) above if termination is the result of an Event of Default and on the basis of (2) above if termination is the result of a Termination Event.

Article 12 generally provides that the party not accountable for the event giving rise to the early termination of the rate swap will be the one that determines the amount, if any, payable on the Early Termination Date. If, however, neither party can be held accountable or the parties are both accountable, then each party will determine the relevant amount and payment will be based on the average of the amounts determined.

V. CHANGES IN THE 1986 CODE FROM THE 1985 EDITION RELEVANT TO EARLY TERMINATION

In addition to adding a list of potential Events of Default and Termination Events, the 1986 Code makes the following changes in Code Articles 11 and 12:

● **Early Termination Date.** As rewritten in the 1986 Code, Code Section 11.1 presumes that upon an Early Termination Date the parties to a Rate Swap Agreement will settle out their payment obligations for all Rate Swap Transactions governed by that Rate Swap Agreement, whether or not the Event of Default or Termination Event relates to all the transactions. The parties can vary this presumption by providing that "Limited Early Termination" applies to a particular Event of Default or Termination Event; in that case, only the Rate Swap Transactions affected by the event are terminated. "Limited Early Termination" most likely would be used for Termination Events such as "Illegality" and "Tax Event".

● **Right to Terminate.** New Code Section 11.6 sets forth presumptions that the party with a right to declare an Early Termination Date if a Termination Event occurs is (i) a party affected by the event if it is a "Tax Event", (ii) either party if the event is "Illegality" and (iii) otherwise the party that is not affected by the event.

● **Immediate Early Termination Date.** Parties can specify in their Rate Swap Agreement that if a particular Event of Default or Termination Event (*e.g.*, bankruptcy or insolvency) happens, an Early Termination Date will occur immediately, without it having to be designated by the appropriate party and without any other action. Amounts due upon immediate early termination will be determined as of the day on which the Early Termination Date occurred or as soon thereafter as practicable. Code Section 11.1.

● **Alternative Measures of Damages.** Whereas the 1985 Edition provided that "Formula" was the automatic fall-back for "Agreement Value" as the measure of damages, the 1986 Code requires parties using "Agreement Value" to specify an alternative measure of damages. Code Section 12.2. This recognizes that many ISDA members have a preference for "Indemnification" as a fall-back because of its simplicity. The 1986 Code also presumes that "Indemnification" is to be the automatic fall-back for "Formula". Code Section 12.2.

● **Aggregation.** Many institutions using master agreements currently provide in their agreements that if an Early Termination Date occurs and as a result the entire master agreement is to be terminated, termination payments will be calculated for each transaction governed by that Rate Swap Agreement and the amounts so calculated will be aggregated to determine the amount actually payable on the Early Termination Date. The 1986 Code now accommodates this approach by permitting parties to specify that "Aggregation" applies to the measure of damages they have selected. Code Section 12.3. If Aggregation is not specified, termination payments will be determined and paid separately for each of the transactions being terminated, as is presumed to be the case under the 1985 Edition. The 1986 Code contains new definitions of "Aggregate Market Quotation", "Aggregate Loss" and "Aggregate Formula Settlement Amount" that would be used to determine termination payments for Rate Swap Agreements to which Aggregation applies. Code Sections 12.4(c), 12.5(b) and 12.6(a)(i).

● **Formula.** Many users found the "Formula" provisions in the 1985 Edition difficult to comprehend because of their complexity. These provisions have been reorganized in the 1986 Code and several subheadings and explanatory sentences have been added in an effort to guide readers through the definitions. Code Section 12.6. It is hoped that, as revised, the provisions will be easier to follow. No changes have been made in the substance of the Formula.

VI. NEW PROVISIONS IN THE 1986 CODE

As discussed in Part IV of this Guide, the 1986 Code includes a new menu of Events of Default and Termination Events. The 1986 Code also covers the following new subjects not included in the 1985 Edition:

● **Representations.** Article 15 of the 1986 Code sets forth standard representations which the parties can incorporate in their Rate Swap Agreement if they wish. Code Section 15.1(a) contains certain "Basic Representations" intended to cover the basic corporate matters relevant to a Rate Swap Transaction. Code Section 15.1 also includes certain other nontax representations: absence of Events of Default or Termination Events; absence of litigation questioning or affecting the legality, validity or enforceability of the Rate Swap Agreement or Credit Support Document or affecting the party's ability to perform; accuracy of financial information included in SEC filings; and accuracy of other specified information. Any applicable nontax representations are presumed to be made at the time the party enters into the Rate Swap Agreement and repeated on the Trade Date of each Rate Swap Transaction and at any other specified time. Of course, parties are free to make additional representations not included in Code Article 15. Tax representations are set forth separately in Code Article 19.

● **Agreements.** Under the 1986 Code, parties may incorporate into their Rate Swap Agreement any of the specified standard agreements. The nontax agreements relate to maintaining of authorizations and complying with laws, furnishing of annual financial statements, furnishing of quarterly financial statements, furnishing of regular public reporting documents, furnishing of other specified information, and the giving of notice of Events of Default or Termination Events. Code Article 16. The tax covenants are contained in Code Section 19.4 and include covenants to provide Form 1001 or Form 4224, to provide required or reasonably requested tax forms and to give notice of events that would nullify the other party's tax gross-up obligation.

● **Specified Entities.** The new concept "Specified Entity" is useful for rate swaps in which a party's obligations are guaranteed or supported in some way by an affiliate or other entity. The affiliate or other entity would be a "Specified Entity" for the party, as defined in Code Article 17, and could easily be included in representations or agreements using the terms defined in Code Articles 15 and 16. If the parties so specify, certain Events of Default and Termination Events would be triggered by the occurrence of the event in question with respect to the Specified Entity (for example, a misrepresentation by a guarantor or affiliate).

● **Cross Border Provisions.** The 1986 Code includes new provisions covering payment in a contractually specified currency (Code Section 18.1), waiver of immunities (Code Section 18.2) and assignment to avoid "Illegality" or a "Tax Event" (Code Section 18.3). Under Code Section 18.3, if the parties to a rate swap specify "Assignment To Avoid Illegality" or "Assignment To Avoid a Tax Event", upon the occurrence of what would otherwise be a Termination Event for illegality or taxes, the affected party must use reasonable efforts to assign the Rate Swap Agreement to another office, branch or affiliate to avoid the illegality or withholding taxes, subject to the other party's consent. The Rate Swap Agreement may further provide that this assignment obligation is a "two-way" obligation so that, if the affected party is unable to assign the Rate Swap Agreement, the nonaffected party will, if requested, use reasonable efforts to assign the Rate Swap Agreement. Aside from this provision for assignment to avoid "Illegality" or "Tax Events", the general subject of assignment of rate swaps is not addressed in the 1986 Code.

● **Withholding Tax Gross-Up.** The 1986 Code includes new provisions that apply where a party making a payment is legally required to withhold "Taxes" from the payment. Code Section 19.1(b) requires the party making such withholding to gross up the amount of the payment for any amount it withholds on account of "Indemnifiable Taxes" (generally, taxes imposed by a jurisdiction with which the payee has no connection). Under Code Section 19.1(c), however, a party is released from its gross-up obligation with respect to Indemnifiable Taxes that result from a breach by the other party of a "Payee Tax Representation" or a "Tax Covenant" made by the other party (unless the breach results from a "Change in Tax Law" and the parties have specified that the representation or covenant is subject to the occurrence of a "Change in Tax Law").

CODE OF STANDARD WORDING, ASSUMPTIONS
AND PROVISIONS FOR SWAPS, 1986 EDITION

Any or all provisions of this Code may be incorporated into a document by wording in the document indicating that, or the extent to which, the document is subject to the Code of Standard Wording, Assumptions and Provisions for Swaps, 1986 Edition (as published by the International Swap Dealers Association, Inc.). All provisions of this Code so incorporated in a document will be applicable to that document unless otherwise provided in that document, and all terms defined in this Code and used in provisions of this Code that are incorporated by reference in a document will have the respective meanings set forth in this Code unless otherwise provided in that document. Any term used in a document will, when combined with the name of a party, have meaning in respect of the named party only.

The parties to a Rate Swap Agreement may, but need not, include in the Rate Swap Agreement any of the matters or terms covered by this Code, and a Rate Swap Agreement need not be limited to the matters or terms covered by this Code.

ARTICLE 1
CERTAIN GENERAL DEFINITIONS

Section 1.1. Rate Swap Agreement. "Rate Swap Agreement" means an agreement (however designated) governing one or more Rate Swap Transactions.

Section 1.2. Rate Swap Transaction. "Rate Swap Transaction" means a rate exchange or swap transaction.

Section 1.3. Dollar. "Dollar" and "$" each means the lawful currency of the United States of America.

Section 1.4. New York Banking Day. "New York Banking Day" means any day other than a Saturday, a Sunday or a day on which commercial banks in New York City are required or authorized to be closed.

Section 1.5. London Banking Day. "London Banking Day" means any day on which dealings in deposits in Dollars are transacted in the London interbank market.

Section 1.6. Business Day. "Business Day" means any day other than a Saturday, a Sunday or a day on which commercial banks in the city specified by the parties (or, if a city is not specified, New York City) are required or authorized to be closed.

ARTICLE 2
PARTIES

Section 2.1. Fixed Rate Payor. "Fixed Rate Payor" means, in respect of a Rate Swap Transaction, a party obligated to make payments from time to time during the Term of the Rate Swap Transaction of amounts calculated by reference to a fixed per annum rate.

Section 2.2. Floating Rate Payor. "Floating Rate Payor" means, in respect of a Rate Swap Transaction, a party obligated to make payments from time to time during the Term of the Rate Swap Transaction of amounts calculated by reference to a floating per annum rate.

ARTICLE 3

TERM

Section 3.1. Term. "Term" means the period commencing on the Effective Date of a Rate Swap Transaction and ending on the Termination Date of the Rate Swap Transaction.

Section 3.2. Effective Date. "Effective Date" means the date specified as such for a Rate Swap Transaction, which date is the first day of the Term of the Rate Swap Transaction.

Section 3.3. Termination Date. "Termination Date" means the date specified as such for a Rate Swap Transaction, which date is the last day of the Term of the Rate Swap Transaction.

Section 3.4. Trade Date. "Trade Date" means, in respect of a Rate Swap Transaction, the date on which the parties enter into the Rate Swap Transaction.

ARTICLE 4

CERTAIN DEFINITIONS RELATING TO PAYMENTS

Section 4.1. Fixed Amount. "Fixed Amount" means, in respect of a Rate Swap Transaction, an amount that, subject to Sections 9.2, 9.3 and 10.2 of this Code, is payable by a Fixed Rate Payor on an applicable Payment Date and determined by reference to a Calculation Period as provided in Article 5 of this Code.

Section 4.2. Floating Amount. "Floating Amount" means, in respect of a Rate Swap Transaction, an amount that, subject to Sections 9.2, 9.3 and 10.2 of this Code, is payable by a Floating Rate Payor on an applicable Payment Date and determined by reference to a Floating Rate Option and a Calculation Period as provided in Article 6 of this Code.

Section 4.3. Notional Amount. "Notional Amount" means, in respect of any Calculation Period for a Rate Swap Transaction, the amount specified as such for the Rate Swap Transaction.

Section 4.4. Eurodollar Convention. "Eurodollar Convention" means, with respect to either Payment Dates or Period End Dates for a Rate Swap Transaction, that such Payment Dates or Period End Dates will be each day during the Term of the Rate Swap Transaction that numerically corresponds to the preceding applicable Payment Date or Period End Date, as the case may be, in the calendar month that is the specified number of months after the month in which the preceding applicable Payment Date or Period End Date occurred (or, in the case of the first applicable Payment Date or Period End Date, the day that numerically corresponds to the Effective Date in the calendar month that is the specified number of months after the month in which the Effective Date occurred), except that (a) if there is not any such numerically corresponding day in the calendar month in which a Payment Date or Period End Date, as the case may be, should occur, then the Payment Date or Period

2

End Date will be the last day that is a New York Banking Day and a London Banking Day in that month, (b) if a Payment Date or Period End Date, as the case may be, would otherwise fall on a day that is not a New York Banking Day and a London Banking Day, then the Payment Date or Period End Date will be the first following day that is a New York Banking Day and a London Banking Day unless that day falls in the next calendar month, in which case the Payment Date or Period End Date will be the first preceding day that is a New York Banking Day and a London Banking Day and (c) if the preceding applicable Payment Date or Period End Date, as the case may be, occurred on the last day in a calendar month that was a New York Banking Day and a London Banking Day, then all subsequent applicable Payment Dates or Period End Dates, as the case may be, prior to the Termination Date will be the last day that is a New York Banking Day and a London Banking Day in the month that is the specified number of months after the month in which the preceding applicable Payment Date or Period End Date occurred.

   Section 4.5. Payment Date. "Payment Date" means, in respect of a Rate Swap Transaction,

   (a) if "Delayed Payment" or "Early Payment" is not specified for the Rate Swap Transaction and Payment Dates are specified or otherwise predetermined for the Rate Swap Transaction, each day during the Term of the Rate Swap Transaction so specified or predetermined and the Termination Date;

   (b) if "Delayed Payment" or "Early Payment" is not specified for the Rate Swap Transaction and the parties specify that Payment Dates will occur in accordance with the Eurodollar Convention at a specified interval of calendar months, each day during the Term of the Rate Swap Transaction at the specified interval, determined in accordance with the Eurodollar Convention, and the Termination Date;

   (c) if "Delayed Payment" is specified for the Rate Swap Transaction and Period End Dates are established for the Rate Swap Transaction, each day that is five New York Banking Days after an applicable Period End Date or after the Termination Date; or

   (d) if "Early Payment" and a period of days are specified for the Rate Swap Transaction and Period End Dates are established for the Rate Swap Transaction, each day that is the specified number of days before an applicable Period End Date or before the Termination Date;

except that, in the case of subsections (a), (c) and (d) above, an adjustment will be made if any Payment Date would otherwise fall on a day that is not a New York Banking Day (or, if a party to the Rate Swap Transaction is obligated to pay Floating Amounts calculated by reference to any "LIBOR" Floating Rate Option, any Payment Date would otherwise fall on a day that is not a New York Banking Day and a London Banking Day), so that

   (e) if (i) the "Following Banking Day" convention is specified for the Rate Swap Transaction or (ii) an applicable convention is not specified, the Payment Date will be the first following day that is a New York Banking Day (and, if any "LIBOR" Floating Rate Option applies to the Rate Swap Transaction, a London Banking Day);

   (f) if the "Modified Following Banking Day" convention is specified for the Rate Swap Transaction, the Payment Date will be the first following day that is a

New York Banking Day (and, if any "LIBOR" Floating Rate Option applies to the Rate Swap Transaction, a London Banking Day) unless that day falls in the next calendar month, in which case the Payment Date will be the first preceding day that is a New York Banking Day (and, if any "LIBOR" Floating Rate Option applies to the Rate Swap Transaction, a London Banking Day); or

(g) if the "Preceding Banking Day" convention is specified for the Rate Swap Transaction, the Payment Date will be the first preceding day that is a New York Banking Day (and, if any "LIBOR" Floating Rate Option applies to the Rate Swap Transaction, a London Banking Day).

Section 4.6.   Period End Date.   "Period End Date" means, in respect of a Rate Swap Transaction,

(a) if Period End Dates are not established for the Rate Swap Transaction, each Payment Date during the Term of the Rate Swap Transaction;

(b) if Period End Dates are specified or otherwise predetermined for the Rate Swap Transaction, each day during the Term so specified or predetermined; or

(c) if it is specified for the Rate Swap Transaction that Period End Dates will occur in accordance with the Eurodollar Convention and an interval of calendar months is specified, and if "Delayed Payment" or "Early Payment" is specified for the Rate Swap Transaction, each day during the Term at the specified interval, determined in accordance with the Eurodollar Convention;

except that, in the case of subsection (b) above, an adjustment may be made if any Period End Date would otherwise fall on a day that is not a New York Banking Day (or, if a party to the Rate Swap Transaction is obligated to pay Floating Amounts calculated by reference to any "LIBOR" Floating Rate Option, any Period End Date would otherwise fall on a day that is not a New York Banking Day and a London Banking Day), so that

(d) if "No Adjustment of Period End Dates" is specified for the Rate Swap Transaction, an adjustment will not be made, notwithstanding that the Period End Date occurs on a day that is not a New York Banking Day (or a London Banking Day);

(e) if (i) the "Following Banking Day" convention is specified for the Rate Swap Transaction or (ii) an applicable convention is not specified, the Period End Date will be the first following day that is a New York Banking Day (and, if any "LIBOR" Floating Rate Option applies to the Rate Swap Transaction, a London Banking Day);

(f) if the "Modified Following Banking Day" convention is specified for the Rate Swap Transaction, the Period End Date will be the first following day that is a New York Banking Day (and, if any "LIBOR" Floating Rate Option applies to the Rate Swap Transaction, a London Banking Day) unless that day falls in the next calendar month, in which case the Period End Date will be the first preceding day that is a New York Banking Day (and, if any "LIBOR" Floating Rate Option applies to the Rate Swap Transaction, a London Banking Day); or

(g) if the "Preceding Banking Day" convention is specified for the Rate Swap Transaction, the Period End Date will be the first preceding day that is a

4

New York Banking Day (and, if any "LIBOR" Floating Rate Option applies to the Rate Swap Transaction, a London Banking Day).

Section 4.7. Calculation Period. "Calculation Period" means, in respect of a Rate Swap Transaction, each period from, and including, one Period End Date to, but excluding, the next following applicable Period End Date during the Term of the Rate Swap Transaction, except that (a) the initial Calculation Period for each party to the Rate Swap Transaction will commence on, and include, the Effective Date, and (b) the final Calculation Period for each party to the Rate Swap Transaction will end on, but exclude, the Termination Date.

Section 4.8. Calculation Agent. "Calculation Agent" means the party to a Rate Swap Transaction (or a third party) designated as such for the Rate Swap Transaction and responsible for (a) calculating the applicable Floating Rate, if any, for each Calculation Period or Compounding Period, (b) calculating any Floating Amount payable in respect of each Calculation Period, (c) calculating any Fixed Amount payable in respect of each Calculation Period, (d) giving notice to the parties to the Rate Swap Transaction on the Calculation Date for each Calculation Period, specifying (i) the date for payment in respect of such Calculation Period, (ii) the party or parties required to make the payment or payments then due, (iii) the amount or amounts of the payment or payments then due and (iv) reasonable details as to how such amount or amounts were determined and (e) if, after such notice is given, there is a change in the number of days in the relevant Calculation Period and the amount or amounts of the payment or payments due in respect of that period, promptly giving the parties to the Rate Swap Transaction notice of such changes, with reasonable details as to how such changes were determined. Whenever the Calculation Agent is required to select banks or dealers for the purpose of calculating a Floating Rate, the Calculation Agent will make such selection in good faith for the purpose of obtaining a representative rate that will reasonably reflect conditions prevailing at the time in the relevant market.

Section 4.9. Calculation Date. "Calculation Date" means, for any Calculation Period, the earliest day on which it is practicable to provide the notice that the Calculation Agent is required to give in respect of that Calculation Period, and in no event later than the close of business on the Business Day next preceding the Payment Date in respect of that Calculation Period.

ARTICLE 5
FIXED AMOUNTS

Section 5.1. Calculation of a Fixed Amount. The Fixed Amount for each applicable Payment Date in respect of any Calculation Period will be

(a) if an amount is specified for the Rate Swap Transaction as the Fixed Amount payable in respect of that Calculation Period, such amount; or

(b) if an amount is not specified for the Rate Swap Transaction as the Fixed Amount payable in respect of that Calculation Period, an amount calculated on a formula basis in respect of that Calculation Period as follows:

$$\begin{matrix} \text{Fixed} \\ \text{Amount} \end{matrix} = \begin{matrix} \text{Notional} \\ \text{Amount} \end{matrix} \times \begin{matrix} \text{Fixed} \\ \text{Rate} \end{matrix} \times \begin{matrix} \text{Fixed Rate} \\ \text{Day Count} \\ \text{Fraction} \end{matrix}$$

Section 5.2. Certain Definitions Relating to Fixed Amounts. For purposes of the calculation of a Fixed Amount:

(a) "Fixed Rate" means the per annum rate specified as such for the Rate Swap Transaction, expressed as a decimal.

(b) "Fixed Rate Day Count Fraction" means

(i) if (A) "Actual/365" is specified for a Rate Swap Transaction as the applicable Fixed Rate Day Count Fraction or (B) an applicable Fixed Rate Day Count Fraction is not specified, the actual number of days in the Calculation Period in respect of which payment is being made divided by 365 (or, if any portion of that Calculation Period falls in a leap year, the sum of (X) the actual number of days in that portion of the Calculation Period falling in a leap year divided by 366 plus (Y) the actual number of days in that portion of the Calculation Period falling in a nonleap year divided by 365);

(ii) if "Actual/360" is specified for a Rate Swap Transaction as the applicable Fixed Rate Day Count Fraction, the actual number of days in the Calculation Period in respect of which payment is being made divided by 360; or

(iii) if "30/360" or "360/360" is specified for a Rate Swap Transaction as the applicable Fixed Rate Day Count Fraction, the number of days in the Calculation Period in respect of which payment is being made (calculated on the basis of a year of 360 days with 12 30-day months) divided by 360.

ARTICLE 6

FLOATING AMOUNTS

Section 6.1. Calculation of a Floating Amount. The Floating Amount for each applicable Payment Date in respect of any Calculation Period for a Rate Swap Transaction will be

(a) if Compounding is specified, an amount equal to the sum of the Compounding Period Amounts for each of the Compounding Periods in that Calculation Period; or

(b) if Compounding is not specified, an amount calculated on a formula basis in respect of that Calculation Period as follows:

$$
\begin{array}{ccccc}
\text{Floating} & & \text{Notional} & & \text{Floating} & & \text{Floating} \\
\text{Amount} & = & \text{Amount} & \times & \text{Rate} & \times & \text{Rate} \\
& & & & \pm \text{Spread} & & \text{Day Count} \\
& & & & & & \text{Fraction}
\end{array}
$$

Section 6.2. Calculation of a Compounding Period Amount. The Compounding Period Amount for any Compounding Period for a Rate Swap Transaction will be an amount calculated on a formula basis in respect of that Compounding Period as follows:

$$
\begin{array}{ccccc}
\text{Compounding} & & \text{Adjusted} & & \text{Floating} & & \text{Floating} \\
\text{Period} & = & \text{Notional} & \times & \text{Rate} & \times & \text{Rate} \\
\text{Amount} & & \text{Amount} & & \pm \text{Spread} & & \text{Day Count} \\
& & & & & & \text{Fraction}
\end{array}
$$

Section 6.3. Certain Definitions Relating to Floating Amounts. For purposes of the calculation of a Floating Amount:

(a) "Floating Rate" means, in respect of any Calculation Period or Compounding Period for a Rate Swap Transaction, a per annum rate, expressed as a decimal, equal to

(i) if a per annum rate is specified for the Rate Swap Transaction as the Floating Rate applicable in respect of that Calculation Period or Compounding Period, the Floating Rate so specified;

(ii) if only one Reset Date is established for the Rate Swap Transaction during (or with respect to) that Calculation Period or Compounding Period, the Relevant Rate for that Reset Date;

(iii) if more than one Reset Date is established for the Rate Swap Transaction during (or with respect to) that Calculation Period or Compounding Period and the "Unweighted Average Rate" method of calculation is specified, the arithmetic mean of the Relevant Rates for each of these Reset Dates;

(iv) if more than one Reset Date is established for the Rate Swap Transaction during (or with respect to) that Calculation Period or Compounding Period and the "Weighted Average Rate" method of calculation is specified, the arithmetic mean of the Relevant Rates in effect for each day in that Calculation Period or Compounding Period, calculated by multiplying each Relevant Rate by the number of days such Relevant Rate is in effect, determining the sum of such products and dividing such sum by the number of days in the Calculation Period or Compounding Period; or

(v) if more than one Reset Date is established for the Rate Swap Transaction during (or with respect to) that Calculation Period or Compounding Period and neither the "Unweighted Average Rate" nor the "Weighted Average Rate" method of calculation is specified, a Floating Rate determined (A) as if "Weighted Average Rate" had been specified as the applicable method of calculation if the applicable Floating Rate Option is a "Prime" or "Federal Funds" Floating Rate Option and (B) as if "Unweighted Average Rate" had been specified as the applicable method of calculation if any other Floating Rate Option is applicable.

(b) "Reset Date" means each day specified as such (or determined pursuant to a method specified for such purpose) for the Rate Swap Transaction, except that an adjustment will be made if any Reset Date would fall on a day that is not a New York Banking Day (or, if the Floating Amount is being calculated by reference to any "LIBOR" Floating Rate Option, any Reset Date would fall on a day that is not a New York Banking Day and a London Banking Day), so that the Reset Date will be the first preceding day that is a New York Banking Day (and, if the Floating Amount is being calculated by reference to any "LIBOR" Floating Rate Option, a London Banking Day).

(c) "Relevant Rate" means (subject to the effect of any applicable Rate Cut-off Date), for any day, a per annum rate, expressed as a decimal, equal to

(i) if such day is a Reset Date, the rate determined with respect to that day for the specified Floating Rate Option as provided in Article 7 of this Code; or

(ii) if such day is not a Reset Date, the Relevant Rate determined pursuant to clause (i) above for the next preceding Reset Date.

(d) "Rate Cut-off Date" means each day specified as such (or determined pursuant to a method specified for such purpose) for the Rate Swap Transaction. The Relevant Rate for each Reset Date in the period from, and including, a Rate Cut-off Date to, but excluding, the next applicable Period End Date (or, in the case of the last Calculation Period, the Termination Date) will (solely for purposes of calculating the Floating Amount payable on the next applicable Payment Date) be deemed to be the Relevant Rate in effect on that Rate Cut-off Date.

(e) "Spread" means the per annum rate, if any, specified as such for the Rate Swap Transaction (expressed as a decimal). For purposes of determining a Floating Amount or a Compounding Period Amount , if positive the Spread will be added to the Floating Rate and if negative the Spread will be subtracted from the Floating Rate.

(f) "Floating Rate Day Count Fraction" means, in respect of any Calculation Period or Compounding Period, (i) if any "Treasury Bill" Floating Rate Option is specified as the applicable Floating Rate Option, the actual number of days in that Calculation Period or Compounding Period divided by 365 (or, if any portion of that Calculation Period or Compounding Period falls in a leap year, the sum of (A) the actual number of days in that portion of the Calculation Period or Compounding Period falling in a leap year divided by 366 plus (B) the actual number of days in that portion of the Calculation Period or Compounding Period falling in a nonleap year divided by 365) and (ii) in all other cases, the actual number of days in that Calculation Period or Compounding Period divided by 360.

Section 6.4. Certain Additional Definitions Relating to Compounding. For purposes of the calculation of a Floating Amount where "Compounding" is specified:

(a) "Compounding Period" means, in respect of a Calculation Period, each period from, and including, one Compounding Date to, but excluding, the next following applicable Compounding Date during that Calculation Period, except that (i) each initial Compounding Period for a Rate Swap Transaction will commence on, and include, the Effective Date and (ii) each final Compounding Period for a Rate Swap Transaction will end on, but exclude, the Termination Date.

(b) "Compounding Date" means each day during the Term of a Rate Swap Transaction specified as such (or determined pursuant to a method specified for such purpose) for the Rate Swap Transaction, except that, if the Period End Date for any Calculation Period is subject to adjustment in accordance with Section 4.6 of this Code, each applicable Compounding Date in that Calculation Period will be subject to adjustment in the same manner as such Period End Date.

(c) "Adjusted Notional Amount" means (i) in respect of the first Compounding Period in any Calculation Period, the Notional Amount for that Calculation Period and (ii) in respect of each succeeding Compounding Period in that Calculation Period, an amount equal to the sum of the Notional Amount for that Calculation Period and the Compounding Period Amounts for each of the previous Compounding Periods in that Calculation Period.

ARTICLE 7

CALCULATION OF RATES FOR CERTAIN FLOATING RATE OPTIONS

Section 7.1. Floating Rate Options. For purposes of determining a Relevant Rate:

(a) "LIBOR" means that the rate in respect of a Reset Date will be determined on the basis of the offered rates for deposits in Dollars for a period of the Designated Maturity commencing on that Reset Date which appear on the Reuters Screen LIBO Page as of 11:00 a.m., London time, on the day that is two London Banking Days preceding that Reset Date. If at least two such offered rates appear on the Reuters Screen LIBO Page, the rate in respect of that Reset Date will be the arithmetic mean of such offered rates. If fewer than two offered rates appear, the rate in respect of that Reset Date will be determined as if the parties had specified "LIBOR (Reference Banks)" as the applicable Floating Rate Option.

(b) "LIBOR (Reference Banks)" means that the rate in respect of a Reset Date will be determined on the basis of the rates at which deposits in Dollars are offered by the Reference Banks at approximately 11:00 a.m., London time, on the day that is two London Banking Days preceding that Reset Date to prime banks in the London interbank market for a period of the Designated Maturity commencing on that Reset Date and in a Representative Amount. The Calculation Agent will request the principal London office of each of the Reference Banks to provide a quotation of its rate. If at least two such quotations are provided, the rate in respect of that Reset Date will be the arithmetic mean of the quotations. If fewer than two quotations are provided as requested, the rate in respect of that Reset Date will be the arithmetic mean of the rates quoted

9

by major banks in New York City, selected by the Calculation Agent, at approximately 11:00 a.m., New York City time, on that Reset Date for loans in Dollars to leading European banks for a period of the Designated Maturity commencing on that Reset Date and in a Representative Amount.

(c) "Prime" means that the rate for a Reset Date will be the rate set forth in H.15(519) for that day opposite the caption "Bank Prime Loan". If on the Calculation Date for a Calculation Period such rate for a Reset Date in that Calculation Period is not yet published in H.15(519), the rate for that Reset Date will be the arithmetic mean of the rates of interest publicly announced by each bank that appears on the Reuters Screen NYMF Page as such bank's prime rate or base lending rate as in effect for that Reset Date as quoted on the Reuters Screen NYMF Page on that Reset Date or, if fewer than four such rates appear on the Reuters Screen NYMF Page for that Reset Date, the rate determined as if the parties had specified "Prime (Reference Banks)" as the applicable Floating Rate Option.

(d) "Prime (Reference Banks)" means that the rate for a Reset Date will be the arithmetic mean of the rates of interest publicly announced by each Reference Bank as its prime rate or base lending rate as in effect for that day. Each change in the prime rate or base lending rate of any bank so announced by such bank will be effective as of the effective date of the announcement or, if no effective date is specified, as of the date of the announcement.

(e) "Treasury Bill" means that the rate for a Reset Date on which United States Treasury bills are auctioned will be the rate set forth in H.15(519) for that day opposite the Designated Maturity under the caption "U.S. Government Securities/Treasury Bills/Auction Average (Investment)". If on the Calculation Date for a Calculation Period United States Treasury bills of the Designated Maturity have been auctioned on a Reset Date during that Calculation Period but such rate for such Reset Date is not yet published in H.15(519), the rate for that Reset Date will be the Bond Equivalent Yield of the auction average rate for these Treasury bills as announced by the United States Department of the Treasury. If United States Treasury bills of the Designated Maturity are not auctioned during any period of seven consecutive calendar days ending on and including any Friday and a Reset Date would have occurred if such Treasury bills had been auctioned during that seven-day period, a Reset Date will be deemed to have occurred on the day during that seven-day period on which such Treasury bills would have been auctioned in accordance with the usual practices of the United States Department of the Treasury, and the rate for that Reset Date will be determined as if the parties had specified "Treasury Bill (Secondary Market)" as the applicable Floating Rate Option (unless it is indicated for the Rate Swap Transaction that weeks in which United States Treasury bills of the Designated Maturity are not auctioned will be ignored, in which case there will not be any Reset Date during that seven-day period).

(f) "Treasury Bill (Secondary Market)" means that the rate for a Reset Date will be the Bond Equivalent Yield of the rate set forth in H.15(519) for that day opposite the Designated Maturity under the caption "U.S. Government Securities/Treasury Bills/Secondary Market". If on the Calculation Date for a Calculation Period such rate for a Reset Date in that Calculation Period is not yet

10

published in H.15(519), the rate for that Reset Date will be the Bond Equivalent Yield of the arithmetic mean of the secondary market bid rates of the Reference Dealers as of approximately 3:30 p.m., New York City time, on that day for the issue of United States Treasury bills with a remaining maturity closest to the Designated Maturity.

(g) "CD" means that the rate for a Reset Date will be the rate set forth in H.15(519) for that day opposite the Designated Maturity under the caption "CDs (Secondary Market)". If on the Calculation Date for a Calculation Period such rate for a Reset Date in that Calculation Period is not yet published in H.15(519), the rate for that Reset Date will be the rate set forth in Composite 3:30 P.M. Quotations for U.S. Government Securities for that day in respect of the Designated Maturity under the caption "Certificates of Deposit". If on the Calculation Date for a Calculation Period the appropriate rate for a Reset Date in that Calculation Period is not yet published in either H.15(519) or Composite 3:30 P.M. Quotations for U.S. Government Securities, the rate for that Reset Date will be determined as if the parties had specified "CD (Reference Dealers)" as the applicable Floating Rate Option.

(h) "CD (Reference Dealers)" means that the rate for a Reset Date will be the arithmetic mean of the secondary market offered rates of the Reference Dealers as of 10:00 a.m., New York City time, on that day for negotiable certificates of deposit of major United States money market banks with a remaining maturity closest to the Designated Maturity and in a Representative Amount.

(i) "Commercial Paper" means that the rate for a Reset Date will be the Money Market Yield of the rate set forth in H.15(519) for that day opposite the Designated Maturity under the caption "Commercial Paper". If on the Calculation Date for a Calculation Period such rate for a Reset Date in that Calculation Period is not yet published in H.15(519), the rate for that Reset Date will be the Money Market Yield of the rate set forth in Composite 3:30 P.M. Quotations for U.S. Government Securities for that day in respect of the Designated Maturity under the caption "Commercial Paper" (with a Designated Maturity of one month or three months being deemed to be equivalent to a Designated Maturity of 30 days or 90 days, respectively). If on the Calculation Date for a Calculation Period the appropriate rate for a Reset Date in that Calculation Period is not yet published in either H.15(519) or Composite 3:30 P.M. Quotations for U.S. Government Securities, the rate for that Reset Date will be determined as if the parties had specified "Commercial Paper (Reference Dealers)" as the applicable Floating Rate Option.

(j) "Commercial Paper (Reference Dealers)" means that the rate for a Reset Date will be the Money Market Yield of the arithmetic mean of the offered rates of the Reference Dealers as of 11:00 a.m., New York City time, on that day for commercial paper of the Designated Maturity placed for industrial issuers whose bond rating is "Aa" or the equivalent from a nationally recognized rating agency.

(k) "Federal Funds" means that the rate for a Reset Date will be the rate set forth in H.15(519) for that day opposite the caption "Federal Funds (Effective)". If on the Calculation Date for a Calculation Period such rate for a

Reset Date in that Calculation Period is not yet published in H.15(519), the rate for that Reset Date will be the rate set forth in Composite 3:30 P.M. Quotations for U.S. Government Securities for that day under the caption "Federal Funds/ Effective Rate". If on the Calculation Date for a Calculation Period the appropriate rate for a Reset Date in that Calculation Period is not yet published in either H.15(519) or Composite 3:30 P.M. Quotations for U.S. Government Securities, the rate for that Reset Date will be determined as if the parties had specified "Federal Funds (Reference Dealers)" as the applicable Floating Rate Option.

(l) "Federal Funds (Reference Dealers)" means that the rate for a Reset Date will be the arithmetic mean of the rates for the last transaction in overnight Federal funds arranged by each Reference Dealer prior to 9:00 a.m., New York City time, on that day.

(m) "Bankers Acceptance" means that the rate for a Reset Date will be the Money Market Yield of the rate set forth in H.15(519) for that day opposite the Designated Maturity under the caption "Bankers Acceptances (Top Rated)". If on the Calculation Date for a Calculation Period such rate for a Reset Date in that Calculation Period is not yet published in H.15(519), the rate for that Reset Date will be determined as if the parties had specified "Bankers Acceptance (Reference Dealers)" as the applicable Floating Rate Option.

(n) "Bankers Acceptance (Reference Dealers)" means that the rate for a Reset Date will be the Money Market Yield of the arithmetic mean of the offered rates of the Reference Dealers as of the close of business in New York City on that day for top-rated bankers acceptances of the Designated Maturity and in a Representative Amount.

Section 7.2. Certain Published and Displayed Sources.

(a) "H.15(519)" means the weekly statistical release designated as such, or any successor publication, published by the Board of Governors of the Federal Reserve System.

(b) "Composite 3:30 P.M. Quotations for U.S. Government Securities" means the daily statistical release designated as such, or any successor publication, published by the Federal Reserve Bank of New York.

(c) "Reuters Screen LIBO Page" means the display designated as page "LIBO" on the Reuter Monitor Money Rates Service (or such other page as may replace the LIBO page on that service for the purpose of displaying London interbank offered rates of major banks).

(d) "Reuters Screen NYMF Page" means the display designated as page "NYMF" on the Reuter Monitor Money Rates Service (or such other page as may replace the NYMF page on that service for the purpose of displaying prime rates or base lending rates of major United States banks).

Section 7.3. Certain General Definitions Relating to Floating Rate Options.

(a) "Representative Amount" means, for purposes of any Floating Rate Option for which a Representative Amount is relevant, an amount that is representative for a single transaction in the relevant market at the relevant time.

12

(b) "Designated Maturity" means the period of time specified as such for a Rate Swap Transaction.

(c) "Reference Banks" means (i) for purposes of the "LIBOR (Reference Banks)" Floating Rate Option, four major banks in the London interbank market and (ii) for purposes of the "Prime (Reference Banks)" Floating Rate Option, three major banks in New York City, in each case selected by the Calculation Agent.

(d) "Reference Dealers" means (i) for purposes of the "Treasury Bill (Secondary Market)" Floating Rate Option, three primary United States Government securities dealers in New York City, (ii) for purposes of the "CD (Reference Dealers)" Floating Rate Option, three leading nonbank dealers in negotiable Dollar certificates of deposit in New York City, (iii) for purposes of the "Commercial Paper (Reference Dealers)" Floating Rate Option, three leading dealers of commercial paper in New York City, (iv) for purposes of the "Federal Funds (Reference Dealers)" Floating Rate Option, three leading brokers of Federal funds transactions in New York City and (v) for purposes of the "Bankers Acceptance (Reference Dealers)" Floating Rate Option, three leading dealers of bankers acceptances in New York City, in each case selected by the Calculation Agent.

(e) "Bond Equivalent Yield" means, in respect of any security with a maturity of six months or less, the rate for which is quoted on a bank discount basis, a yield (expressed as a percentage) calculated in accordance with the following formula:

$$\text{Bond Equivalent Yield} = \frac{D \times N}{360 - (D \times M)} \times 100$$

where "D" refers to the per annum rate for the security, quoted on a bank discount basis and expressed as a decimal; "N" refers to 365 or 366, as the case may be; and "M" refers to, if the Designated Maturity approximately corresponds to the length of the Calculation Period in respect of which the Bond Equivalent Yield is being calculated, the actual number of days in that Calculation Period and, otherwise, the actual number of days in the period from, and including, the applicable Reset Date to, but excluding, the day that numerically corresponds to that Reset Date (or, if there is not any such numerically corresponding day, the last day) in the calendar month that is the number of months corresponding to the Designated Maturity after the month in which that Reset Date occurred.

(f) "Money Market Yield" means, in respect of any security with a maturity of six months or less, the rate for which is quoted on a bank discount basis, a yield (expressed as a percentage) calculated in accordance with the following formula:

$$\text{Money Market Yield} = \frac{D \times 360}{360 - (D \times M)} \times 100$$

where "D" refers to the per annum rate for the security, quoted on a bank discount basis and expressed as a decimal; and "M" refers to, if the Designated Maturity approximately corresponds to the length of the Calculation Period in respect of which the Money Market Yield is being calculated, the actual number of days in that Calculation Period and, otherwise, the actual number of days in the period from, and including, the applicable Reset Date to, but excluding, the day that numerically corresponds to that Reset Date (or, if there is not any such numerically corresponding day, the last day) in the calendar month that is the number of months corresponding to the Designated Maturity after the month in which that Reset Date occurred.

Section 7.4. Corrections to Published and Displayed Rates. For purposes of determining the Relevant Rate for any day

(a) in any case where the Relevant Rate for a day is based on information obtained from any published or displayed source (including, without limitation, H.15(519) or Composite 3:30 P.M. Quotations for U.S. Government Securities), that Relevant Rate will be subject to the corrections, if any, to that information subsequently published or displayed by that source within 30 days of that day;

(b) in any case where the Relevant Rate for a day is based on information obtained from any source used because H.15(519) is not yet available, that Relevant Rate will (except in the case of rates based on quotations from Reference Banks or Reference Dealers) be subject to correction based upon the applicable rate, if any, subsequently published in H.15(519) within 30 days of that day; and

(c) in the event that a Fixed Rate Payor or Floating Rate Payor for any Rate Swap Transaction notifies the other party to the Rate Swap Transaction of any correction referred to in subsection (a) or subsection (b) above no later than 10 New York Banking Days after the expiration of the 30-day period referred to in such subsection, an appropriate amount will be payable as a result of such correction (whether such correction is made or such notice is given before or after the Termination Date of the Rate Swap Transaction), together with interest on that amount at a rate computed on the basis of the "Federal Funds" Floating Rate Option with daily Reset Dates for the period from, and including, the day on which, based on such correction, a payment in the incorrect amount was first made to, but excluding, the day of payment of the refund or payment resulting from such correction.

ARTICLE 8

ROUNDING

All percentages resulting from any calculations referred to in this Code will be rounded upwards, if necessary, to the next higher one hundred-thousandth of a percentage point (*e.g.*, 9.876541% (or .09876541) being rounded to 9.87655% (or .0987655)), and all Dollar amounts used in or resulting from such calculations will be rounded to the nearest cent (with one half cent being rounded up).

ARTICLE 9

GROSS PAYMENTS AND NET PAYMENTS

Section 9.1. Gross Payments. "Gross Payments" means that, subject to Section 10.2 of this Code, each Fixed Amount and each Floating Amount is to be paid in full on the applicable Payment Date.

Section 9.2. Net Payments. "Net Payments" means that, subject to Section 10.2 of this Code, (a) on any Payment Date when amounts would otherwise be payable in respect of a Rate Swap Transaction by each of two parties to the other, neither party will be obligated to make a payment of any such amount to the other party, but if the amount that would have been payable by one party exceeds the amount that would have been payable by the other party, the party by which the larger amount would have been payable will be obligated to pay to the other party the excess of the larger amount over the smaller amount and (b) on any Payment Date when a Fixed Amount or Floating Amount would be payable in respect of a Rate Swap Transaction by only one party, such amount is to be paid in full by that party.

Section 9.3. Net Payments—Corresponding Payment Dates. "Net Payments—Corresponding Payment Dates" means that "Net Payments" will be applicable and that, subject to Section 10.2 of this Code, on any day when amounts would (after giving effect to Section 9.2 of this Code) otherwise be payable under a Rate Swap Agreement by each of two parties to the other, neither party will be obligated to make a payment of any such amount to the other party, but if the aggregate amount that would have been payable by one party exceeds the aggregate amount that would have been payable by the other party, the party by which the larger aggregate amount would have been payable will be obligated to pay to the other party the excess of the larger aggregate amount over the smaller aggregate amount.

Section 9.4. Payment Basis If Not Specified. If a payment basis is not specified for a Rate Swap Transaction, payments will be made as if "Net Payments" had been specified.

ARTICLE 10

PAYMENTS

Section 10.1. Payment Procedures. Payments in respect of a Rate Swap Transaction will be timely if made in same day funds not later than 2:00 p.m., local time at the designated place of payment, on the day on which they are due. Any amount due on a day on which banks are not open for business in the designated place of payment will be payable (without interest) on the first following day on which banks are open in that place.

Section 10.2. Conditions Precedent. Each obligation of each party to a Rate Swap Agreement to pay any amount due under the Rate Swap Agreement in respect of any Calculation Period is subject to (a) the condition precedent that no Event of Default (as defined in Section 11.2 of this Code), or event that with the giving of notice or lapse of time (or both) would become an Event of Default, in respect of the other party has occurred and is continuing and (b) each other applicable condition precedent specified in the Rate Swap Agreement.

Section 10.3. Default Rate. "Default Rate" means, in respect of a Rate Swap Transaction, the rate specified as such for the Rate Swap Transaction; if a Default Rate is specified, a party that defaults in the payment of any amount due will, to the extent permitted by law, be required to pay interest on such amount to the other party, on demand, for the period from, and including, the original due date for payment to, but excluding, the date of actual payment at the Default Rate (using the same Floating Rate Day Count Fraction that would apply under this Code if such Default Rate were a Floating Rate and such period were a Calculation Period).

ARTICLE 11
EARLY TERMINATION

Section 11.1. **Early Termination Date.** "Early Termination Date" means a Business Day on which the parties to a Rate Swap Agreement will settle out, on a "lump-sum" basis, their payment obligations for the Rate Swap Transactions governed by that Rate Swap Agreement (or, if the Early Termination Date occurs as the result of an Event of Default or Termination Event to which the parties have specified that "Limited Early Termination" applies, their payment obligations for the Rate Swap Transactions governed by that Rate Swap Agreement and affected by that Event of Default or Termination Event) in respect of each Calculation Period for any such Rate Swap Transaction that would, but for the occurrence of the Early Termination Date, end after the Early Termination Date. Subject to any conditions to designation of an Early Termination Date set forth in a Rate Swap Agreement, a party to a Rate Swap Agreement may designate an Early Termination Date (a) if an Event of Default in respect of the other party has occurred and is continuing at the time the Early Termination Date is designated or (b) if a Termination Event in respect of either party has occurred and is continuing at the time the Early Termination Date is designated and the party has the right to designate an Early Termination Date as provided in Section 11.6 of this Code or in the Rate Swap Agreement. If an Early Termination Date is designated in accordance with the preceding sentence, the Early Termination Date will occur on the date so designated, whether or not the Event of Default or Termination Event is continuing on the Early Termination Date; *provided, however,* if the Rate Swap Agreement specifies that upon the occurrence of a particular Event of Default or Termination Event "Immediate Early Termination" will occur, the Early Termination Date will occur immediately upon the occurrence of such Event of Default or Termination Event, without any Early Termination Date being designated and without any other action being taken by either party to the Rate Swap Agreement, and the amount payable pursuant to Article 12 of this Code will be determined as of such Early Termination Date or as soon thereafter as practicable, regardless of when either party learns of the occurrence of the Event of Default or Termination Event, and will be paid promptly after notice of the amount due and owing under Article 12 of this Code. A party entitled to designate an Early Termination Date in accordance with this Section 11.1 may do so by giving to the other party to the Rate Swap Agreement such notice as the Rate Swap Agreement requires (specifying in reasonable detail in such notice the basis upon which it is given).

Section 11.2. **Event of Default.** "Event of Default" means, in respect of a party and a Rate Swap Agreement (or, in the case of an Event of Default to which "Limited Early Termination" applies, a Rate Swap Transaction governed by that Rate

16

Swap Agreement and affected by that Event of Default), any event specified in that Rate Swap Agreement as an Event of Default in respect of that party.

Section 11.3. Termination Event. "Termination Event" means, in respect of a party and a Rate Swap Agreement (or, in the case of a Termination Event to which "Limited Early Termination" applies, a Rate Swap Transaction governed by that Rate Swap Agreement and affected by that Termination Event), any event specified in that Rate Swap Agreement as a Termination Event in respect of that party.

Section 11.4. Defaulting Party. "Defaulting Party" means the party in respect of which an Event of Default has occurred.

Section 11.5. Affected Party. "Affected Party" means each party in respect of which a Termination Event has occurred.

Section 11.6. Right To Terminate Following Termination Events. Upon the occurrence of a Termination Event in respect of a party and a Rate Swap Agreement (or, if "Limited Early Termination" applies, a Rate Swap Transaction), (a) if such Termination Event is a "Tax Event", a party that is an Affected Party will have the right to designate an Early Termination Date, (b) if such Termination Event is "Illegality", either party will have the right to designate an Early Termination Date and (c) otherwise, the party that is not the Affected Party will have the right to designate an Early Termination Date. If the Rate Swap Agreement specifies "Assignment To Avoid Illegality" or "Assignment To Avoid a Tax Event", an Early Termination Date may not be designated as a result of "Illegality" of the type described in Section 11.8(a)(i) of this Code or a "Tax Event" unless the applicable provisions of Section 18.3 of this Code have been complied with.

Section 11.7. Specifying Events of Default and Termination Events. The parties to a Rate Swap Agreement may specify as Events of Default or Termination Events such events as they may agree. Such events may, but need not, include any of the events described in this Section and need not be limited to the events described in this Section. If used for purposes of specifying Events of Default or Termination Events in a Rate Swap Agreement, the following terms will, subject to the passage of any applicable cure period or the giving of any applicable notice specified in that Rate Swap Agreement, have the indicated meanings in respect of a party:

(a) "Breach of Covenant" means failure by the party to comply with or perform any agreement or obligation (not including an obligation to make a payment or to give notice of an Event of Default or Termination Event and not including any Tax Covenant) to be complied with or performed by the party in accordance with the Rate Swap Agreement.

(b) "Credit Support Default" means (i) default by the party or any applicable Specified Entity with respect to any obligation which the party (or such Specified Entity) has under any Credit Support Document relating to the Rate Swap Agreement or to any Rate Swap Transaction governed by the Rate Swap Agreement or (ii) the expiration or termination of such Credit Support Document, or the ceasing of such Credit Support Document to be in full force and effect, prior to the Termination Date of each Rate Swap Transaction governed by the Rate Swap Agreement and to which the Credit Support Document applies without the written consent of the other party to the Rate

17

Swap Agreement or (iii) the party (or such Specified Entity) repudiates, or challenges the validity of, such Credit Support Document.

(c) "Default Under Specified Swaps" means the occurrence of an event of default in respect of the party or any applicable Specified Entity under any Specified Swap that, following the giving of any applicable notice and the lapse of any applicable grace period, has resulted in the designation or occurrence of an Early Termination Date in respect of that Specified Swap.

(d) "Failure To Give Notice of Events of Default or Termination Events" means failure by the party to notify the other party of the occurrence of an Event of Default or Termination Event in respect of the party within 10 days after the occurrence of such Event of Default or Termination Event.

(e) "Failure To Pay" means failure by the party to pay, when due, any amount required to be paid by it under the Rate Swap Agreement.

(f) "Failure To Pay Under Specified Swaps" means failure by the party or any applicable Specified Entity to pay, when due, following the giving of any applicable notice and the lapse of any applicable grace period, an amount to be paid by the party (or such Specified Entity) under any Specified Swap.

(g) "Misrepresentation" means a representation (other than a Payee Tax Representation or a representation that the party is "Exempt From Withholding") made or repeated or deemed to have been made or repeated by the party or any applicable Specified Entity in the Rate Swap Agreement or any Credit Support Document relating to the Rate Swap Agreement proves to have been incorrect or misleading in any material respect when made or repeated or deemed to have been made or repeated.

(h) "Tax Misrepresentation" means a Payee Tax Representation or a representation that the party is "Exempt From Withholding" made or repeated or deemed to have been made or repeated by the party proves to have been incorrect or misleading in any material respect on the Trade Date of any Rate Swap Transaction governed by the Rate Swap Agreement.

Section 11.8. Specifying Termination Events. If used for purposes of specifying Termination Events in a Rate Swap Agreement (in addition to or in lieu of any of the events described in Section 11.7 of this Code or in addition to such other events as the parties may agree), the following terms will, subject to the passage of any applicable cure period or the giving of any applicable notice specified in that Rate Swap Agreement, have the indicated meanings in respect of a party:

(a) "Illegality" means, due to the adoption of, or any change in, any applicable treaty, law, rule or regulation after the Trade Date of a Rate Swap Transaction governed by the Rate Swap Agreement or due to the promulgation of, or any change in, the interpretation by any court, tribunal or regulatory authority with competent jurisdiction of any applicable treaty, law, rule or regulation after the Trade Date of that Rate Swap Transaction, it becomes unlawful for the party (i) to perform any absolute or contingent obligation to make a payment or to receive a payment in respect of that Rate Swap Transaction or to comply with any other material provision of the Rate Swap Agreement relating to that Rate Swap Transaction or (ii) to perform, or for any applicable Specified Entity to perform, any absolute or contingent obligation which the party (or such Specified Entity) has under any Credit Support Document relating to that Rate Swap Transaction.

(b) "Tax Event" means the occurrence in respect of a party of any event specified in the Rate Swap Agreement as a Tax Event. If used for purposes of specifying Tax Events in the Rate Swap Agreement, the following terms will have the indicated meanings in respect of the party referred to below as an "Affected Party":

(i) "Tax Event upon Payment of Additional Amounts" means that an Affected Party determines that it is required to pay to the other party an additional amount in respect of an Indemnifiable Tax as provided in Section 19.1 (b) of this Code (except in respect of default interest).

(ii) "Tax Event upon Substantial Likelihood of Gross-up" means that, in the written opinion of independent legal counsel of recognized standing, there is a substantial likelihood that an Affected Party will be required on the next succeeding Payment Date to pay to the other party an additional amount in respect of an Indemnifiable Tax as provided in Section 19.1 (b) of this Code (except in respect of default interest) and such substantial likelihood results from either (A) a Change in Tax Law or (B) an action taken by a taxing authority, or brought in a court of competent jurisdiction, on or after the Trade Date of a Rate Swap Transaction governed by the Rate Swap Agreement (regardless of whether such action was taken or brought with respect to a party to the Rate Swap Agreement).

Section 11.9. Certain General Definitions Relating to Events of Default and Termination Events.

(a) "Credit Support Document" means any agreement or instrument which is specified as such in a Rate Swap Agreement.

(b) "Indemnifiable Tax" and "Change in Tax Law" have the meanings set forth in Section 19.5 of this Code.

(c) "Specified Entity" has the meaning set forth in Section 17.1 of this Code.

(d) "Specified Swap" means, for purposes of an Event of Default or Termination Event specified in a Rate Swap Agreement, any rate swap, rate cap, currency exchange transaction or similar transaction specified or described as such in that Rate Swap Agreement with respect to a party to that Rate Swap Agreement (or any applicable Specified Entity) and that Event of Default or Termination Event.

Section 11.10. Cure Period and Notice. For purposes of determining whether, and when, an Event of Default or Termination Event has occurred

(a) if a Rate Swap Agreement does not specify, in respect of a party and an Event of Default or Termination Event, a period of days to be the applicable "Cure Period" and does not specify "After Notice", such Event of Default or Termination Event in respect of that party will arise immediately upon the occurrence of the event or commencement of the condition giving rise to the Event of Default or Termination Event;

(b) if the Rate Swap Agreement specifies, in respect of a party and an Event of Default or Termination Event, a period of days to be the applicable "Cure

Period" and specifies "After Notice", such Event of Default or Termination Event in respect of that party will arise the specified period of days after notice of the event or condition giving rise to the Event of Default or Termination Event is given to the party by the other party to the Rate Swap Agreement if such event or condition is continuing after such period has elapsed;

(c) if the Rate Swap Agreement specifies, in respect of a party and an Event of Default or Termination Event, a period of days to be the applicable "Cure Period" but does not specify "After Notice", such Event of Default or Termination Event in respect of that party will arise the specified period of days after the occurrence of the event or commencement of the condition giving rise to the Event of Default or Termination Event if such event or condition is continuing after such period has elapsed; and

(d) if the Rate Swap Agreement specifies, in respect of a party and an Event of Default or Termination Event, "After Notice" but does not specify a period of days to be the applicable "Cure Period", such Event of Default or Termination Event in respect of that party will arise immediately upon notice of the event or condition giving rise to the Event of Default or Termination Event being given to the party by the other party to the Rate Swap Agreement if such event or condition is continuing at the time such notice is given.

ARTICLE 12

PAYMENTS ON EARLY TERMINATION

Section 12.1. **Measures of Damages.** For purposes of determining the amount payable on an Early Termination Date (or, if Immediate Early Termination applies, promptly after notice of the amount due and owing) in respect of a Rate Swap Transaction or a Rate Swap Agreement, as the case may be,

(a) "Agreement Value" means that on the Early Termination Date (or, if Immediate Early Termination applies, promptly after notice of the amount due and owing), if there is a Defaulting Party or only one Affected Party, that party will be obligated to make a payment to the other party in the amount, if any, by which the Market Quotation determined by the other party exceeds zero. If "Agreement Value" is the applicable measure of damages and notice of the Early Termination Date is given as a result of a Termination Event but there is more than one Affected Party, the payment to be made will be determined as if the parties had specified "Agreement Value—Two Way Payments" as the applicable measure of damages.

(b) "Agreement Value—Limited Two Way Payments" means that on the Early Termination Date (or, if Immediate Early Termination applies, promptly after notice of the amount due and owing), if there is a Defaulting Party, that party will be obligated to make a payment to the other party in the amount, if any, by which the Market Quotation determined by the other party exceeds zero. If notice of the Early Termination Date is given as the result of a Termination Event, the payment to be made will be determined as if the parties had specified "Agreement Value—Two Way Payments" as the applicable measure of damages.

(c) "Agreement Value—Two Way Payments" means that on the Early Termination Date (or, if Immediate Early Termination applies, promptly after notice of the amount due and owing), (i) if there is a Defaulting Party or only one Affected Party, that party will, if the Market Quotation determined by the

20

other party exceeds zero, pay the amount of such excess to the other party, and the other party will, if the Market Quotation determined by it is less than zero, pay the amount of such deficiency to the Defaulting Party or the Affected Party, as the case may be, and (ii) if there is more than one Affected Party, each party will determine a Market Quotation, and the party with the lower Market Quotation will pay an amount equal to one-half of the difference between the two Market Quotations to the party with the higher Market Quotation.

(d) "Indemnification" means that on the Early Termination Date (or, if Immediate Early Termination applies, promptly after notice of the amount due and owing), if there is a Defaulting Party or only one Affected Party, that party will be obligated to make a payment to the other party in an amount equal to the positive amount, if any, of the other party's Loss. If "Indemnification" is the applicable measure of damages and notice of the Early Termination Date is given as the result of a Termination Event but there is more than one Affected Party, the payment to be made will be determined as if the parties had specified "Indemnification—Two Way Payments" as the applicable measure of damages.

(e) "Indemnification—Limited Two Way Payments" means that on the Early Termination Date (or, if Immediate Early Termination applies, promptly after notice of the amount due and owing), if there is a Defaulting Party, that party will be obligated to make a payment to the other party in an amount equal to the positive amount, if any, of the other party's Loss. If notice of the Early Termination Date is given as the result of a Termination Event, the payment to be made will be determined as if the parties had specified "Indemnification—Two Way Payments" as the applicable measure of damages.

(f) "Indemnification—Two Way Payments" means that each party will determine its Loss, and on the Early Termination Date (or, if Immediate Early Termination applies, promptly after notice of the amount due and owing), the party with the Loss that is less will be obligated to make a payment to the party with the Loss that is greater in an amount equal to one-half of the difference between their Losses.

(g) "Formula" means that on the Early Termination Date (or, if Immediate Early Termination applies, promptly after notice of the amount due and owing), if there is a Defaulting Party or only one Affected Party, that party will be obligated to make a payment to the other party in an amount equal to the excess, if any, of the Formula Settlement Amount of the Defaulting Party or Affected Party, as the case may be, over the Formula Settlement Amount of the other party. If "Formula" is the applicable measure of damages and notice of the Early Termination Date is given as the result of a Termination Event but there is more than one Affected Party, the payment to be made will be determined as if the parties had specified "Formula—Two Way Payments" as the applicable measure of damages.

(h) "Formula—Limited Two Way Payments" means that on the Early Termination Date (or, if Immediate Early Termination applies, promptly after notice of the amount due and owing), if there is a Defaulting Party, that party will be obligated to make a payment to the other party in an amount equal to the excess, if any, of the Formula Settlement Amount of the Defaulting Party over the Formula Settlement Amount of the other party. If notice of the Early Termination Date is given as the result of a Termination Event, the payment to be made will be determined as if the parties had specified "Formula—Two Way Payments" as the applicable measure of damages.

(i) "Formula—Two Way Payments" means that on the Early Termination Date (or, if Immediate Early Termination applies, promptly after notice of the amount due and owing) the Formula Settlement Amounts of the parties will be netted, and the party with the higher Formula Settlement Amount will be obligated to make a payment to the party with the lower Formula Settlement Amount in an amount equal to the difference between their Formula Settlement Amounts.

Section 12.2. Alternative Measures of Damages. If for any reason the amount payable in respect of an Early Termination Date cannot be determined, or is not determined, pursuant to the applicable measure of damages, (a) if "Agreement Value", "Agreement Value—Limited Two Way Payments" or "Agreement Value—Two Way Payments" is specified as the applicable measure of damages, the amount payable in respect of the Early Termination Date will be determined on the basis of the alternative measure of damages specified by the parties or (b) if "Formula", "Formula—Limited Two Way Payments" or "Formula—Two Way Payments" is specified as the applicable measure of damages, the amount payable in respect of the Early Termination Date will be determined on the basis of "Indemnification", "Indemnification—Limited Two Way Payments" or "Indemnification—Two Way Payments", respectively, as the alternative measure of damages.

Section 12.3. Aggregation. If "Aggregation" is specified in a Rate Swap Agreement in respect of a measure of damages or an alternative measure of damages, (a) all references to "Market Quotation" in Section 12.1 of this Code will be deemed references to "Aggregate Market Quotation", all references to "Formula Settlement Amount" in Section 12.1 will be deemed references to "Aggregate Formula Settlement Amount", and all references to "Loss" in Section 12.1 will be deemed references to "Aggregate Loss", and (b) if "Formula", "Formula—Limited Two Way Payments" or "Formula—Two Way Payments" is the applicable measure of damages, the amount of any damages determined on that basis will be increased or reduced, as appropriate, by an amount determined on the basis of "Indemnification", "Indemnification—Limited Two Way Payments" or "Indemnification—Two Way Payments", respectively, applying Aggregation, for all Rate Swap Transactions for which there is more than one Floating Rate Payor.

Section 12.4. Certain Definitions Relating to Agreement Value.

(a) "Market Quotation" means, with respect to a Rate Swap Transaction and a party to the Rate Swap Transaction making the determination, an amount (which may be negative) determined on the basis of quotations from Reference Market-makers for the Dollar amount that would be payable on the Early Termination Date, either by the party to the Rate Swap Transaction making the determination (to be expressed as a positive amount) or to such party (to be expressed as a negative amount), in consideration of an agreement between such party and the quoting Reference Market-maker and subject to such documentation as they may in good faith agree, with a Term commencing on the Early Termination Date (unless the Effective Date has not yet occurred, in which case the Term of such agreement will commence on the Effective Date), that would have the effect of preserving for such party the economic equivalent of the payment obligations of the parties in respect of each Calculation Period for that Rate Swap Transaction that would, but for the occurrence of the Early

Termination Date, end after the Early Termination Date (excluding any unpaid amounts in respect of any Calculation Period ended on or prior to the Early Termination Date but otherwise including, without limitation, any amounts that would, but for the occurrence of the Early Termination Date, have been payable (assuming each applicable condition precedent had been satisfied) on the next applicable Payment Date in respect of any Calculation Period in which the Early Termination Date occurs). The party making the determination (or its agent) will request each Reference Market-maker to provide its quotation as of 11:00 a.m., New York City time, on the Early Termination Date (or, if Immediate Early Termination applies, as of a time as soon thereafter as practicable). If more than three such quotations are provided, the Market Quotation will be the arithmetic mean of the quotations, without regard to the quotations having the highest and lowest values. If exactly three such quotations are provided, the Market Quotation will be the quotation remaining after disregarding the quotations having the highest and lowest values. If fewer than three quotations are provided, the Market Quotation in respect of the Rate Swap Transaction will not be determined for either party and the alternative measure of damages will apply.

(b) "Reference Market-makers" means four leading dealers in the relevant rate swap market selected by the party determining a Market Quotation in good faith from among dealers of the highest credit standing which satisfy all the criteria that such party applies generally at the time in deciding whether to offer or to make an extension of credit.

(c) "Aggregate Market Quotation" means, with respect to a Rate Swap Agreement and a party, the sum of the Market Quotations (both positive and negative) determined by such party for all Rate Swap Transactions governed by that Rate Swap Agreement with respect to which an Early Termination Date has occurred and for which a Market Quotation is determined, plus, for each Rate Swap Transaction governed by that Rate Swap Agreement with respect to which an Early Termination Date has occurred and for which a Market Quotation is not, or cannot be, determined, (i) if "Formula", "Formula—Limited Two Way Payments" or "Formula—Two Way Payments" is the alternative measure of damages specified by the parties, (A) in respect of each Rate Swap Transaction for which there is not a Floating Rate Payor or there is only one Floating Rate Payor, an amount (whether positive or negative) equal to the other party's Formula Settlement Amount less such party's Formula Settlement Amount and (B) in respect of each Rate Swap Transaction for which there is more than one Floating Rate Payor, an amount equal to such party's Loss, or (ii) if "Indemnification", "Indemnification—Limited Two Way Payments" or "Indemnification—Two Way Payments" is the alternative measure of damages specified by the parties, an amount equal to such party's Loss.

Section 12.5. Certain Definitions Relating to Loss.

(a) "Loss" means, with respect to a Rate Swap Transaction and a party, an amount equal to the total amount (expressed as a positive amount) required, as determined as of the Early Termination Date (or, if Immediate Early Termination applies, as of a time as soon thereafter as practicable) by the party in good faith, to compensate the party for any losses and costs (including loss of bargain and costs of funding but excluding attorneys' fees and other out-of-pocket expenses) that it may incur as a result of the early termination of the obligations of the parties in respect of the Rate Swap Transaction. If a party determines that it would gain or benefit from the early termination of the obligations of the parties in respect of the Rate Swap Transaction, such party's Loss will be an amount (expressed as a negative amount) equal to the amount of the gain or benefit as determined by that party.

(b) "Aggregate Loss" means, with respect to a Rate Swap Agreement and a party, the sum of such party's Losses (both positive and negative) for all Rate Swap Transactions governed by that Rate Swap Agreement with respect to which an Early Termination Date has occurred and for which a Loss is determined.

Section 12.6.   Certain Definitions Relating to Formula.

(a) *General Definitions.*

(i) "Aggregate Formula Settlement Amount" means, with respect to a Rate Swap Agreement and a party, the sum of such party's Formula Settlement Amounts for all Rate Swap Transactions governed by that Rate Swap Agreement with respect to which an Early Termination Date has occurred and for which there is not a Floating Rate Payor or there is only one Floating Rate Payor and for which the Formula Settlement Amount can be determined for each party.

(ii) "Current Value" means, in respect of any amount, the value of that amount on the Early Termination Date after discounting that amount on a semiannual basis from the originally scheduled date for payment on the basis of the Treasury Rate.

(iii) "Treasury Rate" means a per annum rate (expressed as a semiannual equivalent and as a decimal and, in the case of United States Treasury bills, converted to a Bond Equivalent Yield) determined to be the per annum rate equal to the semiannual equivalent yield to maturity for United States Treasury securities maturing on the Termination Date, as determined by interpolation between the most recent weekly average yields to maturity for two series of United States Treasury securities, (A) one maturing as close as possible to, but earlier than, the Termination Date and (B) the other maturing as close as possible to, but later than, the Termination Date, in each case as published in the most recent H.15(519) (or, if a weekly average yield to maturity for United States Treasury securities maturing on the Termination Date is reported in the most recent H.15(519), as published in H.15(519)).

(b) *Definitions Relating to the Basic Formula.*

(i) "Formula Settlement Amount" means, with respect to a Rate Swap Transaction and a party, the sum of such party's (A) Current Calculation Period Adjustment (if the Early Termination Date is not an applicable Period End Date) and (B) Cost of Termination.

(ii) *Definitions Relating to the Current Calculation Period Adjustment.*

(A) "Current Calculation Period Adjustment" means, with respect to a Rate Swap Transaction and a party, the sum of (I) the Adjusted Fixed Amount, if such party is a Fixed Rate Payor, or the Adjusted Floating Amount, if such party is a Floating Rate Payor, and (II) the Redeployment Adjustment, if applicable.

(B) "Adjusted Fixed Amount" means, in respect of a Rate Swap Transaction and a Fixed Rate Payor, an amount equal to:

(I) if the Fixed Amount payable by the Fixed Rate Payor in respect of the Calculation Period in which the Early Termination Date occurs is a specified amount, such amount multiplied by a fraction the numerator of which is the actual number of days in the period from, and including, the most recent applicable Period End Date (or, if the Early Termination Date occurs before the first applicable Period End Date, from, and including, the Effective Date for the Rate Swap Transaction) to, but excluding, the Early Termination Date and the denominator of which is the actual number of days in the applicable Calculation Period in which the Early Termination Date occurs; or

(II) if the Fixed Amount payable by the Fixed Rate Payor is determined on a formula basis, an amount determined on that basis, as specified for the Rate Swap Transaction, for a hypothetical Calculation Period from, and including, the most recent applicable Period End Date (or, if the Early Termination Date occurs before the first applicable Period End Date, from, and including, the Effective Date for the Rate Swap Transaction) to, but excluding, the Early Termination Date.

(C) "Adjusted Floating Amount" means, in respect of a Rate Swap Transaction and a Floating Rate Payor, an amount determined to be the Floating Amount that would be payable by the Floating Rate Payor, computed on the basis of the applicable Floating Rate Option, the applicable Spread, if any, and the other variables specified for the Rate Swap Transaction, for a hypothetical Calculation Period from, and including, the most recent applicable Period End Date (or, if the Early Termination Date occurs before the first applicable Period End Date, from, and including, the Effective Date for the Rate Swap Transaction) to, but excluding, the Early Termination Date (except that if no Reset Date would otherwise occur during this hypothetical Calculation Period, the first day of this hypothetical Calculation Period will be deemed to be a Reset Date).

(D) A Redeployment Adjustment will be calculated only for a Rate Swap Transaction in which each Floating Rate is determined by reference to a single Reset Date for the Calculation Period to which the Floating Rate applies, and if positive the Redeployment Adjustment will be included in the Current Calculation Period Adjustment of the Fixed Rate Payor, and if negative the Redeployment Adjustment will be included (but as a positive amount) in the Current Calculation Period Adjustment of the Floating Rate Payor. "Redeployment Adjustment" means, with respect to a Rate Swap Transaction and a party for which it is applicable, an amount equal to the product of (I) the Notional Amount, (II) the Redeployment Rate and (III) a fraction, the numerator of which is the number of days remaining (from, and including, the Early Termination Date) in the Calculation Period in which the Early Termination Date occurs and in respect of which a Floating Amount would have been payable (assuming each applicable condition precedent had been satisfied) had the Early Termination Date not occurred and the denominator of which is the denominator of the Floating Rate Day Count Fraction that would otherwise have been applicable to that Calculation Period, after discounting that product, on a semiannual basis, from the Payment Date in respect of that Calculation Period to the Early Termination Date on the basis of the Treasury Rate.

(E) "Redeployment Rate" means a per annum rate (which may be positive or negative), expressed as a decimal, equal to (I) a hypothetical Relevant Rate for the Early Termination Date computed as if the Early Termination Date were a Reset Date and as if the Designated Maturity were approximately equal to the length of the period from the Early Termination Date to the next scheduled Payment Date but otherwise on the basis of the applicable Floating Rate Option and the other variables specified for the Rate Swap Transaction, less (II) the Floating Rate utilized to calculate the Adjusted Floating Amount.

(iii) *Definitions Relating to Cost of Termination for Future Calculation Periods.*

(A) "Cost of Termination" means (I) in respect of a Rate Swap Transaction and a Fixed Rate Payor, the Fixed Rate Payor's Discounted Remaining Fixed Amount Payments and (II) in respect of a Rate Swap Transaction and a Floating Rate Payor, the Alternative Financing Costs adjusted to give effect to the Floating Rate Spread Adjustment, if applicable.

(B) "Discounted Remaining Fixed Amount Payments" means, in respect of a Rate Swap Transaction and a Fixed Rate Payor, an amount equal to the sum of the Current Values of the Fixed Amounts (after subtracting, in the case of the next scheduled Fixed Amount, the Adjusted Fixed Amount if the Early Termination Date does not coincide with an applicable Period End Date) that would have been payable (assuming each applicable condition precedent had been satisfied) by the Fixed Rate Payor after an Early Termination Date if the Early Termination Date had not occurred.

(C) "Alternative Financing Costs" means, in respect of a Rate Swap Transaction, an amount which equals (I) if "Formula" is the applicable measure of damages and the Defaulting Party or Affected Party is a Fixed Rate Payor or "Formula—Limited Two Way Payments" is the applicable measure of damages and the Defaulting Party is a Fixed Rate Payor, the sum of the Current Values of each payment of interest the Floating Rate Payor would receive after the Early Termination Date (after subtracting from any such payment of interest any amount earned in respect of any period prior to the Early Termination Date) from an Alternative Fixed Rate Investment, (II) if "Formula" is the applicable measure of damages and the Defaulting Party or Affected Party is a Floating Rate Payor or if "Formula—Limited Two Way Payments" is the applicable measure of damages and the Defaulting Party is a Floating Rate Payor, the sum of the Current Values of each payment of interest the Fixed Rate Payor would pay for an Alternative Fixed Rate Borrowing and (III) if "Formula—Limited Two Way Payments" is the applicable measure of damages and the Early Termination Date occurs as the result of a Termination Event or if "Formula—Two Way Payments" is the applicable measure of damages, the arithmetic mean of the amounts described in clauses (I) and (II) above, unless a Treasury Rate Spread is expressly provided for the purpose of this clause (III), in which case Alternative Financing Costs

26

will be the amount described in clause (I) above (adjusted to give effect to that Treasury Rate Spread).

(D) "Alternative Fixed Rate Borrowing" means, in respect of a Rate Swap Transaction, at the option of the Fixed Rate Payor, either

(I) a loan in a principal amount equal to the Notional Amount that is or could have been obtained by the Fixed Rate Payor on the Early Termination Date, maturing on (or as close as possible to) the Termination Date and bearing interest payable semiannually (with a short first period, if necessary) at a per annum rate equal to (x) if a Treasury Rate Spread is expressly provided for the purpose of this clause (I), the Treasury Rate adjusted to give effect to that Treasury Rate Spread, (y) if a Treasury Rate Spread is not expressly provided for the purpose of this clause (I) and the Fixed Rate Payor has actually obtained such a loan, the actual fixed rate of interest the Fixed Rate Payor is required to pay for it and (z) if a Treasury Rate Spread is not expressly provided for the purpose of this clause (I) and the Fixed Rate Payor has not actually obtained such a loan, the arithmetic mean of the rates that two banks of nationally recognized standing in the United States, selected by the Fixed Rate Payor in good faith, estimate to be the lowest fixed rate of interest at which the Fixed Rate Payor could have borrowed such a loan on the Early Termination Date from responsible lenders or, if the Fixed Rate Payor is a bank, funded such a loan on the Early Termination Date in the London interbank market; or

(II) if a Treasury Rate Spread is not expressly provided for such purpose and the Fixed Rate Payor is a bank subject to the reserve requirements and insurance assessments described below, certificates of deposit of the Fixed Rate Payor in an amount equal to the Notional Amount which are or could have been issued by the Fixed Rate Payor on the Early Termination Date, with repayment of principal due on (or as close as possible to) the Termination Date and bearing interest payable semiannually (with a short first period, if necessary) at a per annum rate equal to the sum of (x) the quotient of (1) the arithmetic mean of the respective bid rates quoted to the Fixed Rate Payor as of 11:00 a.m., New York City time, on the Early Termination Date by each of three certificate of deposit dealers in New York City of recognized standing selected by the Fixed Rate Payor in good faith for the purchase at face value of such certificates of deposit, divided by (2) one minus the maximum aggregate reserve requirements (expressed as a decimal) imposed under Regulation D of the Board of Governors of the Federal Reserve System on nonpersonal time deposits of $100,000 or more having a maturity similar to such certificates of deposit, as in effect on the Early Termination Date, plus (y) the net assessment rate per annum payable to the Federal Deposit Insurance Corporation (or any successor) for the insurance of domestic deposits of the Fixed Rate Payor during the calendar year in which the Early Termination Date occurs, as determined by the Fixed Rate Payor on the Early Termination Date.

(E) "Alternative Fixed Rate Investment" means, in respect of a Rate Swap Transaction, an investment in United States Treasury securities in a principal amount equal to the Notional Amount maturing on (or as close as possible to) the Termination Date which are or could have been purchased by the Floating Rate Payor on the Early Termination Date, yielding interest at a per annum rate equal to, at the option of the Floating Rate Payor, either (I) if the Floating Rate Payor has actually made such an investment, the per annum rate equal to the semiannual equivalent yield to maturity of such securities (expressed as a decimal and, in the case of United States Treasury bills, converted to a Bond Equivalent Yield), or (II) if the Floating Rate Payor has not actually made such an investment, the Treasury Rate, in either case plus or minus the Treasury Rate Spread, if applicable.

(c) *Definitions Relating to Certain Adjustments to the Basic Formula.*

(i) A Treasury Rate Spread will be used only if the parties to a Rate Swap Transaction specify a rate to be used for that purpose in determining Alternative Financing Costs under clause (III) of Section 12.6 (b) (iii) (C) of this Code, an Alternative Fixed Rate Borrowing under Section 12.6 (b) (iii) (D) of this Code or an Alternative Fixed Rate Investment under Section 12.6 (b) (iii) (E) of this Code. "Treasury Rate Spread" means, in respect of any calculation for which it is applicable, the per annum rate, if any, specified as such for the Rate Swap Transaction (expressed as a decimal). For purposes of applying a Treasury Rate Spread, if positive the Treasury Rate Spread will be added to the Treasury Rate or other rate to which it is applicable and if negative the Treasury Rate Spread will be subtracted from that rate.

(ii) *Definitions Relating to a Floating Rate Spread Adjustment.*

(A) A Floating Rate Spread Adjustment will be calculated only for a Rate Swap Transaction in which the Floating Amount reflects a Spread specified by the parties. "Floating Rate Spread Adjustment" means an amount equal to the Discounted Remaining Spread Amounts. In computing the Cost of Termination, the Floating Rate Spread Adjustment will be added to the Alternative Financing Costs if the Spread is positive and subtracted from the Alternative Financing Costs if the Spread is negative.

(B) "Discounted Remaining Spread Amounts" means, in respect of a Rate Swap Transaction, an amount equal to the sum of the Current Values of the Spread Amounts (after subtracting, if the Early Termination Date does not coincide with an applicable Period End Date, that portion, if any, of the Adjusted Floating Amount attributable to the Spread from the Spread Amount determined in respect of the Calculation Period in which the Early Termination Date occurs) computed for each Calculation Period ending after the Early Termination Date in respect of which a Floating Amount would have been payable (assuming each applicable condition precedent had been satisfied) if the Early Termination Date had not occurred.

(C) "Spread Amount" means, in respect of a Rate Swap Transaction and a Calculation Period, an amount equal to the product of (I) the Notional Amount, (II) the Spread (for such purpose deemed to be positive) and (III) the Floating Rate Day Count Fraction that would otherwise have been applicable to that Calculation Period.

Section 12.7. Limited Indemnification for Expenses. A Defaulting Party (unless the appropriate measure of damages contemplates "Two Way Payments") and, if there is only one Affected Party, the Affected Party (unless the appropriate measure of damages contemplates "Limited Two Way Payments" or "Two Way Payments") will, on demand, indemnify and hold harmless the other party for and against all reasonable out-of-pocket expenses, including attorneys' fees and all stamp, registration, documentation or similar taxes or duties, incurred by such other party by reason of the enforcement and protection of its rights under a Rate Swap Agreement or by reason of the early termination of the Rate Swap Agreement or any Rate Swap Transaction governed by that Rate Swap Agreement, including, but not limited to, costs of collection.

Section 12.8. Statement of Calculations. A party to a Rate Swap Agreement requesting payment of any amount under Article 12 of this Code will provide to the other party a statement in reasonable detail showing the calculation of such amount (including all relevant quotations). Absent written confirmation of a quotation obtained in determining a Market Quotation or Alternative Financing Costs from the source providing such quotation, the records of the party obtaining such quotation will be conclusive evidence of the existence and accuracy of such quotation.

ARTICLE 13

SUBMISSION TO JURISDICTION

Section 13.1. Submission to Jurisdiction. With respect to any claim arising out of a Rate Swap Agreement, (a) each party irrevocably submits to the nonexclusive jurisdiction of the courts of the State of New York and the United States District Court located in the Borough of Manhattan in New York City, and (b) each party irrevocably waives any objection which it may have at any time to the laying of venue of any suit, action or proceeding arising out of or relating to the Rate Swap Agreement brought in any such court, irrevocably waives any claim that any such suit, action or proceeding brought in any such court has been brought in an inconvenient forum and further irrevocably waives the right to object, with respect to such claim, suit, action or proceeding brought in any such court, that such court does not have jurisdiction over such party.

Section 13.2. Jurisdiction Not Exclusive. Nothing in this Code will be deemed to preclude either party to a Rate Swap Agreement from bringing an action or proceeding in respect of the Rate Swap Agreement in any other jurisdiction.

ARTICLE 14

NOTICES

Section 14.1. Notices. Any notice or communication in respect of a Rate Swap Agreement will be sufficiently given to a party if in writing and delivered in person, sent by certified or registered mail (airmail if overseas) or the equivalent (with return receipt requested) or by overnight courier or given by telex (with answerback received) addressed to the party at its address or telex number provided for that purpose.

Section 14.2. Effectiveness of Notice. A notice or communication will be effective, if delivered by hand or sent by overnight courier, on the day it is delivered (or if that day is not a day on which commercial banks are open for business in the city specified in the address for notice provided by the recipient (a "Local Banking Day"), or if delivered after the close of business on a Local Banking Day, on the first following day that is a Local Banking Day), if sent by telex, on the day the recipient's answerback is received (or if that day is not a Local Banking Day, or if after the close of business on a Local Banking Day, on the first following day that is a Local Banking Day) or, if sent by certified or registered mail (airmail if overseas) or the equivalent (return receipt requested), three Local Banking Days after dispatch if the recipient's address for notice is in the same country as the place of dispatch and otherwise seven Local Banking Days after dispatch (or, in either case, if delivered after the close of business on a Local Banking Day, on the first following day that is a Local Banking Day).

Section 14.3. Addresses. Either party by notice to the other may designate additional or different addresses or telex numbers for subsequent notices or communications.

ARTICLE 15

REPRESENTATIONS

Section 15.1. Representations of the Parties. On the date as of which it enters into a Rate Swap Agreement, on the Trade Date of each Rate Swap Transaction governed by the Rate Swap Agreement and at any additional times specified in the Rate Swap Agreement, each party makes to the other party and to any Specified Entity of the other party the applicable representations specified in that Rate Swap Agreement. If used for purposes of specifying representations in a Rate Swap Agreement, the following terms will have the indicated meanings in respect of a party to the Rate Swap Agreement:

(a) "Basic Representations" means that the party represents that: (i) it is duly organized, validly existing and in good standing under the laws of the jurisdiction of its organization or incorporation; (ii) it has the power to execute and deliver the Rate Swap Agreement and any other documentation relating to the Rate Swap Agreement that it is required by the Rate Swap Agreement to deliver and to perform its obligations under the Rate Swap Agreement and any obligations it has under any Credit Support Document and has taken all necessary action to authorize such execution and delivery and performance of such obligations; (iii) its execution and delivery of the Rate Swap Agreement and any other documentation relating to the Rate Swap Agreement that it is required by the Rate Swap Agreement to deliver and its performance of its obligations under the Rate Swap Agreement and any obligations it has under any Credit Support Document do not violate or conflict with any law, rule or regulation applicable to it, any provision of its charter or by-laws (or comparable constituent documents), any order or judgment of any court or other agency of government applicable to it or any of its assets or any contractual restriction binding on or affecting the party or any of its assets; (iv) all authorizations of and exemptions,

30

actions or approvals by, and all notices to or filings with, any governmental or other authority that are required to have been obtained or made by the party at the time this representation is made with respect to the Rate Swap Agreement or any Credit Support Document to which it is a party have been obtained or made and are in full force and effect and all conditions of any such authorizations, exemptions, actions or approvals have been complied with; and (v) each of the Rate Swap Agreement and any Credit Support Document to which it is a party constitutes the party's legal, valid and binding obligation, enforceable against the party in accordance with its terms (subject to applicable bankruptcy, reorganization, insolvency, moratorium or similar laws affecting creditors' rights generally and subject, as to enforceability, to equitable principles of general application (regardless of whether enforcement is sought in a proceeding in equity or at law)).

(b) "Absence of Certain Events" means that the party represents that no event or condition has occurred that constitutes (or would with the giving of notice or passage of time or both constitute) an Event of Default or, to the party's knowledge, a Termination Event with respect to the party, and no such event would occur as a result of the party's entering into or performing its obligations under the Rate Swap Agreement or any Credit Support Document to which it is a party.

(c) "Absence of Litigation" means that the party represents that there is not pending or, to the party's knowledge, threatened against the party or any of its Affiliates any action, suit or proceeding at law or in equity or before any court, tribunal, governmental body, agency or official or any arbitrator that purports to draw into question, or is likely to affect, the legality, validity or enforceability against the party of the Rate Swap Agreement or any Credit Support Document to which it is a party or the party's ability to perform its obligations under the Rate Swap Agreement or such Credit Support Document.

(d) "Accuracy of Financial Information" means that the party represents that all financial information furnished to the other party to the Rate Swap Agreement pursuant to Section 16.1(a), 16.1(b) or 16.1(c) of this Code, or included in any report on Form 10-K, Form 10-Q or Form 8-K (or any successor form) filed by the party with the Securities and Exchange Commission which is furnished by the party to the other party to the Rate Swap Agreement, is, as of its date, true, accurate and complete in every material respect.

(e) "Accuracy of Specified Information" means that the party represents that all applicable information that is furnished in writing by or on behalf of the party to the other party to the Rate Swap Agreement and is identified in the Rate Swap Agreement is, as of the date of the information, true, accurate and complete in every material respect.

ARTICLE 16

AGREEMENTS

Section 16.1. Agreements of the Parties.   Each party to a Rate Swap Agreement agrees to perform any additional obligations specified in that Rate Swap Agreement as agreements in respect of that party for so long as the party has any obligations under the Rate Swap Agreement or under any Credit Support Document. If used for purposes of specifying agreements in a Rate Swap Agreement, the following terms will have the indicated meanings in respect of a party to the Rate Swap Agreement:

(a) "Furnish Annual Financial Statements" means that the party agrees to furnish to the other party, as soon as available and in any event within 120 days (or as soon as practicable after becoming publicly available) after the end of each of its fiscal years, a copy of the annual report of the party (or of such other entity as is specified in the Rate Swap Agreement) containing audited consolidated financial statements for such fiscal year certified by independent certified public accountants and prepared in accordance with accounting principles that are generally accepted in the country in which the party (or such entity) is organized.

(b) "Furnish Quarterly Financial Statements" means that the party agrees to furnish to the other party, as soon as available and in any event within 60 days (or as soon as practicable after becoming publicly available) after the end of each of its fiscal quarters, unaudited consolidated financial statements of the party (or of such other entity as is specified in the Rate Swap Agreement) for such quarter prepared in accordance with accounting principles that are generally accepted in the country in which the party (or such entity) is organized and on a basis consistent with that of the annual financial statements of the party (or such entity).

(c) "Furnish Investor Reports and Regular Public Reporting Documents" means that the party agrees to furnish to the other party, promptly after public availability, each regular financial or business reporting document that is (i) distributed or made generally available by the party (or by such other entity as is specified in the Rate Swap Agreement) to its shareholders or investors or (ii) filed by the party (or such entity) with such regulatory authorities as are specified in the Rate Swap Agreement and made available for public inspection.

(d) "Furnish Specified Information" means that the party agrees to furnish to the other party, upon request or as provided in the Rate Swap Agreement, such information as is specified in the Rate Swap Agreement as required to be so furnished.

(e) "Give Notice of Default and Certain Events" means that the party agrees, upon learning of the occurrence of any event or commencement of any condition that constitutes (or that with the giving of notice or passage of time or both would constitute) an Event of Default or Termination Event with respect to the party, promptly to give the other party notice of such event or condition (or, in lieu of giving notice of such event or condition in the case of an event or condition that with the giving of notice or passage of time or both would constitute an Event of Default or Termination Event with respect to the party, to cause such event or condition to cease to exist before becoming an Event of Default or Termination Event).

(f) "Maintain Authorizations and Comply with Laws" means that the party agrees (i) to maintain in full force and effect all authorizations of and exemptions, actions or approvals by, and all filings with or notices to, any governmental or other authority that are required to be obtained or made by the party with respect to the Rate Swap Agreement or any Credit Support Document to which it is a party and will use all reasonable efforts to obtain or make any that may become necessary in the future and (ii) to comply in all material respects with all applicable laws, rules, regulations and orders to which it may be subject if failure so to comply would materially impair its ability to perform its obligations under the Rate Swap Agreement or any Credit Support Document to which it is a party.

ARTICLE 17
SPECIFIED ENTITIES

Section 17.1. Definition of Specified Entity. "Specified Entity" means an entity specified as such in a Rate Swap Agreement with respect to a party to that Rate Swap Agreement and one or more Events of Default, Termination Events, representations, or agreements or other obligations.

Section 17.2. Definition of Affiliate. "Affiliate" of a party means any entity controlled, directly or indirectly, by the party, any entity that controls, directly or indirectly, the party or any entity under common control with the party. For purposes of this definition, "control" of an entity or of a party means ownership of a majority of the voting power of the entity or party.

Section 17.3. Representations and Agreements by Specified Entities. If a Rate Swap Agreement or an instrument or agreement relating to a Rate Swap Agreement indicates that any representation or agreement of a kind referred to in Section 15.1, 16.1, 19.2, 19.3 or 19.4 of this Code is made by any Specified Entity, for purposes of the Specified Entity's representation or agreement, all references to "the party" in Section 15.1, 16.1, 19.2, 19.3 or 19.4 will be deemed references to "the Specified Entity" and, if the Specified Entity is not a party to the Rate Swap Agreement, all references to "the Rate Swap Agreement" in Section 15.1, 16.1, 19.2, 19.3 or 19.4 will be deemed references to "the instrument or agreement executed by the Specified Entity in connection with the Rate Swap Agreement".

Section 17.4. Performance of Obligations by Specified Entities. If an obligation of a party under a Rate Swap Agreement is fully performed for the party by an applicable Specified Entity that is a party to a Credit Support Document or a party to the Rate Swap Agreement, such obligation will be deemed to have been fully performed by the party.

ARTICLE 18
CROSS BORDER PROVISIONS

Section 18.1. Payment in the Contractual Currency. To the extent permitted by applicable law, any obligation to make payments under a Rate Swap Agreement or Credit Support Document in any currency (the "Contractual Currency") will not be discharged or satisfied by any tender in any currency other than the Contractual Currency, except to the extent such tender results in the actual receipt by the party to which payment is owed, acting in a reasonable manner and in good faith in converting the currency so tendered into the Contractual Currency, of the full amount in the Contractual Currency of all amounts due in respect of the Rate Swap Agreement or Credit Support Document. If for any reason the amount in the Contractual Currency so received falls short of the amount in the Contractual Currency due in respect of the Rate Swap Agreement or Credit Support Document, the party or Specified Entity required to make the payment will, to the extent permitted by applicable law, immediately pay such additional amount in the Contractual Currency as may be necessary to compensate for the shortfall. If for any reason the amount in the Contractual Currency so received exceeds the amount in the Contractual Currency due in respect of the Rate Swap Agreement or Credit Support Document, the party receiving the payment will refund promptly the amount of such excess. To the extent permitted by applicable law, the obligation to pay an additional amount in accordance with the second preceding sentence will be enforceable as a separate and independent cause of action for the purpose of recovery in the Contractual Currency of such additional amount, will apply notwithstanding any indulgence granted by the party to which payment is owed and will not be affected by judgment being obtained for any other sums due in respect of the Rate Swap Agreement or Credit Support Document.

To the extent permitted by applicable law, if any judgment or order expressed in a currency other than the Contractual Currency is rendered (a) for the payment of any amount owing in respect of a Rate Swap Agreement or Credit Support Document, (b) for the payment of any amount relating to any early termination in respect of a Rate Swap Agreement or any breach of a Credit Support Document or (c) in respect of a judgment or order of another court for the payment of any amount described in clause (a) or clause (b) above, the party seeking recovery, after recovery in full of the aggregate amount to which such party is entitled pursuant to the judgment or order, will be entitled to receive immediately from the other party, or from the applicable Specified Entity required to make such payment, the amount of any shortfall of the Contractual Currency received by such party as a consequence of sums paid in such other currency and will refund promptly to the other party, or such Specified Entity, any excess of the Contractual Currency received by such party as a consequence of sums paid in such other currency, if such shortfall or such excess arises or results from any variation between the rate of exchange at which the Contractual Currency is converted into the currency of the judgment or order for the purposes of such judgment or order and the rate of exchange at which such party is able, acting in a reasonable manner and in good faith in converting the currency received into the Contractual Currency, to purchase the Contractual Currency with the amount of the currency of the judgment or order actually received by such party. The term "rate of exchange" includes, without limitation, any premiums and costs of exchange payable in connection with the purchase of or conversion into the Contractual Currency.

Section 18.2.   Waiver of Immunities.   Each party or Specified Entity entering into a Rate Swap Agreement or Credit Support Document irrevocably waives, to the fullest extent permitted by applicable law, with respect to itself and its revenues and assets, all immunity on the grounds of sovereignty or other similar grounds from (a) suit, (b) jurisdiction of any court, (c) attachment of its assets (whether before or after judgment) and (d) execution of judgment to which it might otherwise be entitled in any suit, action or proceeding relating to the Rate Swap Agreement or Credit Support Document in the courts of any jurisdiction and irrevocably agrees, to the extent permitted by applicable law, that it will not claim any such immunity in any such suit, action or proceeding.

Section 18.3.   Assignment To Avoid Illegality or a Tax Event.

(a) If (i) Illegality occurs and a Rate Swap Agreement specifies "Assignment To Avoid Illegality" or (ii) a Tax Event occurs and the Rate Swap Agreement specifies "Assignment To Avoid a Tax Event", the Defaulting Party or, if there is only one Affected Party, the Affected Party will have the obligation to use all reasonable efforts (which shall not require the party to incur a loss) to make within 30 days, subject to the consent of the other party (which consent will not be withheld if the other party's policies in effect at the time would permit it to enter into a Rate Swap Agreement with the proposed assignee), an assignment of its rights and delegation (and transfer) of its obligations under the Rate Swap Agreement (or, if "Limited Early Termination" applies, its rights and obligations under the Rate Swap Agreement in respect of all Rate Swap Transactions governed by the Rate Swap Agreement and affected by the Illegality or Tax Event) to another of its offices, branches or Affiliates for the purpose of causing such Illegality or Tax Event to cease to exist, so long as such assignment and delegation will not create another Illegality or Tax Event. If the Defaulting Party or, if there is only one Affected Party, the Affected Party is not able to make such an assignment and delegation for such purpose after a reasonable effort to do so, and if the Rate Swap Agreement specifies that "Two Way Assignment" applies to Assignment To Avoid Illegality (in the case of Illegality) or Assignment To Avoid a Tax Event (in the case of a Tax Event), the Defaulting Party or the Affected Party may, for such purpose, request the other party to assign its rights and delegate its obligations under the Rate Swap Agreement (or, if "Limited Early Termination" applies, its rights and obligations under the Rate Swap Agreement in respect of all Rate Swap Transactions governed by the Rate Swap Agreement and affected by the Illegality or Tax Event) to another of its offices, branches or Affiliates for the purpose of causing such Illegality or Tax Event to cease to exist, so long as such assignment and delegation will not create another Illegality or Tax Event. Upon such request, such other party will have the obligation to use all reasonable efforts (which shall not require such other party to incur a loss) to make such an assignment and delegation within 30 days, subject to the consent of the Defaulting Party or the Affected Party (which consent will not be withheld if the Defaulting Party's or the Affected Party's policies in effect at the time would permit it to enter into a Rate Swap Agreement with the proposed assignee). Any such assignment and delegation will become effective upon (A) delivery to the nonassigning party of notice of the assignment and delegation and evidence reasonably satisfactory to such nonassigning party that the assignee and delegatee has, pursuant to such assignment and delegation, legally and effectively accepted all the rights, and assumed all the obligations, of the assigning and delegating party under the Rate Swap Agreement (or, if "Limited Early Termination" applies, its rights and obligations under the Rate Swap Agreement in respect of all Rate Swap Transactions governed by the Rate Swap Agreement and affected by the Illegality or Tax Event), (B) the nonassigning party's written consent to the assignment, (C) delivery to the nonassigning party of (I) a letter of credit, guarantee or other Credit Support Document satisfactory to the nonassigning party, if the nonassigning party's policies in effect at the time would require such a letter of credit, guarantee or other Credit Support Document in connection with a Rate Swap Agreement with the proposed assignee, and (II) such tax forms, certificates and opinions as the nonassigning party may reasonably request and (D) payment by the Defaulting Party or the Affected Party to the other party of all reasonable costs incurred by such other party in connection with the assignment and delegation (including but not limited to attorneys' fees and any costs of negotiating or executing Credit Support Documents). Upon the effectiveness of any such assignment and delegation as provided in this Section, the assigning and delegating party will be released from all its obligations under the Rate Swap Agreement (or, if "Limited Early Termination" applies, its obligations under the Rate Swap Agreement in respect of all Rate Swap Transactions governed by the Rate Swap Agreement and affected by the Illegality or Tax Event) except as otherwise expressly provided in connection with such assignment and delegation.

(b) In the event that clause (i) or clause (ii) of the first sentence of Section 18.3 (a) of this Code is applicable and there is more than one Affected Party, each party will use all reasonable efforts to reach agreement within 30 days on action to be taken for the purpose of causing the Illegality or the Tax Event to cease to exist, which action may require one party or both parties to effect an assignment and delegation on the basis described in Section 18.3 (a) of this Code, and the parties will share equally the costs incurred in connection with any such assignment and delegation.

Section 18.4. Definitions of "Illegality" and "Tax Event". For purposes of Section 18.3, the terms "Illegality" and "Tax Event" have the meanings set forth in Section 11.8 (a) (i) and Section 11.8 (b) of this Code, respectively.

ARTICLE 19
CERTAIN PROVISIONS RELATING TO TAX MATTERS

Section 19.1. Tax Gross-Up.

(a) All payments under a Rate Swap Agreement are to be made without any deduction or withholding for or on account of any Tax except as provided in this Section 19.1.

(b) Subject to Section 19.1 (c) of this Code, if a party to a Rate Swap Agreement is required by any applicable law, rule or regulation to make any deduction or withholding for or on account of any Tax from any payment to be made by it under the Rate Swap Agreement, then that party (the "Withholding Party") will (i) promptly notify the other party (the "Taxed Party") of such requirement, (ii) pay to the relevant authorities the full amount required to be deducted or withheld (including the full amount required to be deducted or withheld from any additional amount paid by the Withholding Party to the Taxed Party pursuant to this Section 19.1 (b)) promptly upon the earlier of determining that such deduction or withholding is required or receiving notice that such amount has been assessed against the Taxed Party, (iii) promptly forward to the Taxed Party an official receipt (or a certified copy), or other documentation acceptable to the Taxed Party, evidencing such payment to such authorities and (iv) if such Tax is an Indemnifiable Tax, pay to the Taxed Party, in addition to the payment to which the Taxed Party is otherwise entitled under the Rate Swap Agreement, such additional amount as is necessary to ensure that

36

the net amount actually received by the Taxed Party (free and clear of Indemnifiable Taxes, whether assessed against the Withholding Party or the Taxed Party) will equal the full amount the Taxed Party would have received had no such deduction or withholding been required.

(c) A party to a Rate Swap Agreement will not be required to pay any additional amount to the other party pursuant to Section 19.1 (b) of this Code to the extent that such additional amount would not be required to be paid but for (i) the failure of a Payee Tax Representation made by the other party to be accurate and true or (ii) the failure by the other party to comply with or perform any Tax Covenant made by it in the Rate Swap Agreement. However, the preceding sentence will not apply to a failure with respect to a Payee Tax Representation or Tax Covenant that is specified in the Rate Swap Agreement to be subject to the occurrence of a "Change in Tax Law", if such failure would not have occurred but for a Change in Tax Law.

(d) If (i) a party to a Rate Swap Agreement (the "Withholding Party") is required by any applicable law, rule or regulation to make any deduction or withholding from a payment received by the other party (the "Taxed Party") for or on account of a Tax in respect of which the Withholding Party would not be required to pay an additional amount to the Taxed Party pursuant to Section 19.1 (b) of this Code, (ii) the Withholding Party does not so deduct or withhold and (iii) a liability resulting from such Tax is assessed directly against the Withholding Party, then, except to the extent the Taxed Party has satisfied or then satisfies the liability resulting from such Tax, the Taxed Party promptly will pay to the Withholding Party the amount of such liability (including any related liability for interest, but including any related liability for penalties only if the Taxed Party has agreed to "Give Notice of Breach of Payee Tax Representation or Tax Covenant" and has failed to comply with or perform such agreement).

Section 19.2. Payee Tax Representations. At all times during the Term of any Rate Swap Transaction governed by a Rate Swap Agreement, each party makes to the other party and to any Specified Entity of the other party the representations specified in that Rate Swap Agreement as "Payee Tax Representations" in respect of that party. If used for purposes of specifying Payee Tax Representations in the Rate Swap Agreement, the following terms will have the indicated meanings in respect of a party to the Rate Swap Agreement:

(a) "Effectively Connected" means that the party represents that, if it is acting through a branch, agency or office in the United States of America (including only the States and the District of Columbia) in respect of a Rate Swap Transaction governed by the Rate Swap Agreement, any payment received or to be received by it in connection with the Rate Swap Transaction is effectively connected with its conduct of a trade or business in the United States.

(b) "Eligible for Treaty Benefits" means that the party represents that it is fully eligible for the benefits (if any) of the "Business Profits" or "Industrial and Commercial Profits" provision, as the case may be, the "Interest" provision, and the "Other Income" provision (if any), of the Specified Treaty with respect to any payment described in such provisions and received or to be received by it in connection with a Rate Swap Transaction governed by the Rate Swap Agreement.

(c) "Ordinary Business Use" means that the party represents that each payment received or to be received by it in connection with a Rate Swap

Transaction governed by the Rate Swap Agreement relates to the regular business operations of the party (and not to an investment of the party).

(d) "Qualify as Business Profits" means that the party represents that each payment received or to be received by it in connection with a Rate Swap Transaction governed by the Rate Swap Agreement (other than default interest) qualifies as "business profits" or "industrial and commercial profits", as the case may be, under the Specified Treaty.

Section 19.3. Withholding Tax Representation. If a Rate Swap Agreement specifies "Exempt from Withholding" in respect of a party (the "first party"), then on the date as of which it enters into a Rate Swap Agreement, on the Trade Date of each Rate Swap Transaction governed by the Rate Swap Agreement, and at any additional times specified in the Rate Swap Agreement, the first party represents to the other party and to any Specified Entity of the other party that the first party is not required by any law, rule or regulation of the jurisdiction (a) of the first party's incorporation, organization, management and control, or seat, (b) where a branch or office through which the first party is acting for purposes of the Rate Swap Agreement is located or (c) in which the first party executes the Rate Swap Agreement, to make any deduction or withholding for or on account of any Tax from any payment (other than default interest) to be made by the first party to the other party under the Rate Swap Agreement. In making this representation the first party may rely on (i) the accuracy of any Payee Tax Representations and the satisfaction of any Tax Covenants made or deemed to be made by the other party under the Rate Swap Agreement and (ii) the accuracy and effectiveness of any document provided by the other party pursuant to any Tax Covenant.

Section 19.4. Tax Covenants. Each party to a Rate Swap Agreement agrees to perform any additional obligations specified in that Rate Swap Agreement as "Tax Covenants" in respect of that party for so long as the party has any obligations under the Rate Swap Agreement or under any Credit Support Document. If used for purposes of specifying Tax Covenants in the Rate Swap Agreement, the following terms will have the indicated meanings in respect of a party to the Rate Swap Agreement:

(a) "Give Notice of Breach of Payee Tax Representation or Tax Covenant" means that the party agrees to give notice of any failure described in the first sentence of Section 19.1 (c) of this Code with respect to any Payee Tax Representation or Tax Covenant made or deemed to have been made by the party, promptly upon learning of such failure.

(b) "Provide Form 1001" or "Provide Form 4224" means that the party agrees to Provide Tax Forms and to complete, accurately and in a manner reasonably satisfactory to the other party, and to execute and deliver to the other party, a United States Internal Revenue Service Form 1001 or 4224 (as the case may be), or any successor form, (i) before the first Payment Date under the Rate Swap Agreement, (ii) promptly upon reasonable demand by the other party and (iii) promptly upon learning that any such form previously provided by the party has become obsolete or incorrect.

(c) "Provide Tax Forms" means that the party agrees to complete, accurately and in a manner reasonably satisfactory to the other party, and to execute, arrange for any required certification of, and deliver to the other party (or to such government or taxing authority as the other party reasonably directs), any form or document that may be required or reasonably requested in order to allow the other party to make a payment under the Rate Swap Agreement without any deduction or withholding for or on account of any Tax or with such deduction or withholding at a reduced rate, promptly upon the earlier of (i) reasonable demand by the other party and (ii) learning that the form or document is required.

Section 19.5.　Certain Definitions Relating to Tax Matters.

(a) "Specified Treaty" means the treaty specified as such in a Rate Swap Agreement with respect to one or more Payee Tax Representations.

(b) "Change in Tax Law" means the enactment, promulgation, execution or ratification of, or any change in or amendment to, any treaty, law, regulation or ruling (or in the application or official interpretation of any treaty, law, regulation or ruling) that occurs on or after the Trade Date of any Rate Swap Transaction governed by a Rate Swap Agreement.

(c) "Tax" means any present or future tax, levy, impost, duty, charge, assessment or fee of any nature (including interest, penalties and additions thereto) that is imposed by any government or other taxing authority in respect of a payment under a Rate Swap Agreement, other than a stamp, registration, documentation or similar tax.

(d) "Indemnifiable Tax" means any Tax other than a Tax that would not be imposed in respect of a payment under a Rate Swap Agreement but for a present or former connection between the jurisdiction of the government or taxing authority imposing such Tax and the recipient of such payment (including, without limitation, a connection arising from such recipient being or having been a citizen or resident of such jurisdiction, or being or having been organized, present or engaged in a trade or business in such jurisdiction, or having or having had a permanent establishment or fixed place of business in such jurisdiction, but excluding a connection arising solely from such recipient having executed, delivered, performed its obligations or received a payment under, or enforced, the Rate Swap Agreement).

ARTICLE 20

MISCELLANEOUS

Section 20.1.　No Waiver of Rights.　A failure or delay in exercising any right, power or privilege in respect of a Rate Swap Agreement will not be presumed to operate as a waiver, and a single or partial exercise of any right, power or privilege will not be presumed to preclude any subsequent or further exercise of that right, power or privilege or the exercise of any other right, power or privilege.

Section 20.2.　Counterparts.　A Rate Swap Agreement and each Credit Support Document or other written agreement relating to the Rate Swap Agreement may be executed in counterparts, each of which will be deemed an original.

Section 20.3.　Governing Law.　A Rate Swap Agreement and each Credit Support Document or other written instrument or agreement relating to the Rate Swap Agreement will, unless otherwise expressly provided, be governed by and construed in accordance with the laws of the State of New York, without reference to choice of law doctrine.

Section 20.4.　Headings.　The article and section headings used in this Code or in a Rate Swap Agreement are for convenience of reference only and are not to affect the construction of or be taken into consideration in interpreting this Code or any Rate Swap Agreement.

INDEX OF TERMS

User's Guide to the

Standard Form Agreements

1987 Edition

INTERNATIONAL SWAP DEALERS ASSOCIATION, INC.

TABLE OF CONTENTS

I. INTRODUCTION

This Guide describes how the standard form agreements published by the International Swap Dealers Association, Inc. ("ISDA") can be used by participants in the swap market to document interest rate swaps, currency exchanges and cross-currency interest rate swaps. There are two forms, entitled "Interest Rate Swap Agreement" and "Interest Rate and Currency Exchange Agreement", which differ principally in the types of transactions to which each is suited. The forms are complete contracts which are designed to reflect general market practice and, it is believed, provide a fair basis on which participants in the market may enter into swap transactions.

Publication of these forms represents a major step forward in the efforts that began in late 1983 to standardize and simplify swap documentation. These efforts, prompted by the rapid growth and development of the swap market, began with the publication in the fall of 1985 of the Code of Standard Wording, Assumptions and Provisions for Swaps (the "Code") and continued with the publication of the 1986 Edition of the Code, which expanded the coverage of the Code to include subjects not dealt with in the 1985 Edition. The standard form agreements represent the next step in that process.

The forms were developed during the second half of 1986 and early 1987 by working groups in New York and London of the Documentation Task Force of ISDA. These working groups consisted of representatives of many of the commercial, investment and merchant banks which are ISDA members, as well as their counsel. In addition, comments were solicited from several companies and governmental agencies worldwide which participate in the interest rate and currency swap markets. During the first half of 1987, the Documentation Task Force developed the 1987 Interest Rate and Currency Exchange Definitions (the "Currency Definitions") for use in conjunction with the Interest Rate and Currency Exchange Agreement.

It is hoped that the use of these forms will allow swap participants to simplify and accelerate the process of documenting swaps. In particular, use of the forms should significantly reduce time spent reviewing and negotiating mechanical provisions and enable the parties to concentrate on business terms. In addition, the forms are designed to allow users to modify any provisions as they think necessary, as described below. Copies of the forms, the Code and the Currency Definitions may be obtained from ISDA (telephone (212) 972-3088).

Part II of this Guide gives an overview of how to use the forms. For those who want a more detailed explanation of the forms, Part III contains a section-by-section guide to the provisions.

A Note on Copyright

ISDA consents to and encourages the use and photocopying of these forms for the preparation of swap agreements. ISDA does not, however, consent to the reproduction of either form for purposes of public distribution or sale.

II. THE FORMS—An Overview

A. Description of the Forms

Both of the forms are master agreements which can govern multiple swap transactions. The economic terms of each swap transaction are documented in a separate confirmation (a "Confirmation") which constitutes a supplement to the agreement. In the case of each form, the basic text and all the Confirmations form one agreement. The two forms are described below:

1. *The Code-based Form.* The "Interest Rate Swap Agreement" is an agreement for U.S. dollar-denominated interest rate swaps. It incorporates by reference the 1986 Edition of the Code with certain modifications and is intended to be used with the Code. (All references hereinafter to the Code are to the 1986 Edition of the Code.) It is governed by the law of the State of New York. It is referred to in this Guide as the "Code-based form".

2. *The Multi-currency Form.* The "Interest Rate and Currency Exchange Agreement" is an agreement for interest rate swaps in any currency as well as currency swaps and cross-currency interest rate swaps. It does not incorporate the Code by reference but contains provisions virtually identical to the Code provisions contained in the Code-based form, except that the form does not include provisions comparable to Articles 2 through 8 of the Code, which set forth how fixed and floating amounts are calculated and provide definitions of various floating rate options. Instead, Confirmations under the Multi-currency form incorporate the Currency Definitions, which set forth provisions comparable to those Articles of the Code. This form of agreement can be governed by New York law or English law at the election of the parties. It is referred to in this Guide as the "Multi-currency form".

There are no substantive differences in the two forms, other than minor ones necessitated by the multi-currency aspects of the Multi-currency form and differences in the jurisdiction and governing law sections. These differences are noted in Part III of this Guide.

The choice as to which form to use is likely to depend primarily on the type of transactions the parties expect to enter into, because most of the differences between the forms are related to the type of transaction.

Parties who wish to continue to use and develop their own forms are free to borrow from or adapt the ISDA forms as they wish.

B. How to Use the Forms

The forms are structured as complete contracts. Each contains payment provisions, representations, agreements, events of default, provisions for early termination, cross-border provisions and other provisions typically found in swap contracts.

To use the forms, users need only fill in identifying information in the main text and complete the schedule (the "Schedule") attached to each form. Users may also note on the Schedule whether certain optional provisions in the forms will apply. The items that must be addressed by users and the optional provisions are highlighted in part III of this Guide. Users may also alter or amend the provisions of the forms as they wish. Amendments can be made by specifying additional or alternative provisions in the Schedule. Deletions can be made either by a statement in the Schedule or by crossing out a provision in the main text.

Users of the forms should employ the printed version and should not retype the main text of each form (see the note on copyright in Section I of this Guide). This guarantees to each party that the language corresponds to the standard forms and thereby reduces the time and expense involved in reviewing documentation prepared by another party. Such benefits are dramatically lessened if the forms are retyped. It is advantageous to use the printed forms even if users wish to make additions or deletions, for this enables them to focus on the necessary changes.

The Schedules are designed to be filled out as printed or retyped as users may choose. It may be more practical to retype the Schedule where significant additions are made.

The Code-based form includes an Exhibit setting forth a form of telex and/or letter agreement which may be used as a Confirmation for individual swap transactions under that form. The Currency Definitions include an Exhibit setting forth a form of telex and/or letter agreement which may be used as a Confirmation for individual swap transactions under the Multi-currency form. The actual telexes or letter agreements used to confirm particular swaps would be prepared by the parties by following the appropriate form, with such changes as are appropriate.

III. USING THE FORMS—A Section-by-Section Guide

The following is a section-by-section guide to using the forms. It highlights the items which the parties must specify in the Schedule and those which must be completed in the main text. It also explains certain provisions, including the optional provisions included in the forms, and explains, in a few instances, certain alternatives to provisions included in the forms. Unless otherwise noted, comments apply to both forms and references to a particular section are references to that section in each form.

A. Organization of the Forms

To the extent possible, the order of provisions and the enumeration of sections are the same in the two forms. Certain tax provisions are consolidated in Section 12 of the Code-based form because it is expected that this form will be frequently used in transactions involving two United States parties where withholding tax issues will not be of concern. The comparable provisions are included in appropriate sections throughout the Multi-currency form (see for example the Payments, Representations and Agreements sections). Certain other differences in the texts and in enumeration of sections result from the incorporation by reference of the Code in the Code-based form.

B. Identifying Information and Signatures

The name of each party and, if desired, the form and jurisdiction of its organization must be filled in on the first page of the main text as well as in the heading of the Schedule. The form must be dated on the first page and in the heading of the Schedule. The name of each party and the names and titles of signatories must be filled in on the signature page. Additional signatures may be added on that page as necessary. The main text of the agreement must be signed; the Schedule may, but need not, be signed.

C. Section 2—Payments

1. *Payments.* Most payment terms will be set forth in the individual Confirmations. (See Section III(O) of this Guide.)

2. *Bank Accounts.* Each agreement contemplates that the parties will specify accounts for payments under each swap in the individual Confirmation or in some other notice. (See Section 2(a).) Of course, the parties may if they wish specify the accounts in the Schedule. The forms provide that the parties may change a specified account upon five days notice. In the Code-based form, the new account must be in the same country.as the prior account (for the convenience of the other party and to minimize any possible adverse withholding tax risks). There is no such restriction in the Multi-currency form in recognition of the fact that an account in a swap involving the European Currency Unit or certain other currencies may need to be moved to a different country under certain circumstances. (See Section 2(b). See also Section III(O)(4) of this Guide.)

3. *Netting.* Each form provides that payments due on the same date in the same currency under a given swap will be netted. Each agreement also enables the parties to elect that, when payment dates on two or more swaps coincide, the payments due under those swaps on the same day and in the same currency will be netted. This choice may be made by specifying in the Schedule that "Net Payments—Corresponding Payment Dates" will apply. (See Section 2(c) and the Schedule.) The parties can also specify that this election will take effect at a later date if time is needed to make the necessary administrative arrangements. Alternatively, the parties may subsequently elect to apply "Net Payments—Corresponding Payment Dates" by stating this in a Confirmation.

4. *Calculation Agent.* The parties should specify the Calculation Agent in the Schedule or in each Confirmation. (The Code and the Currency Definitions define the term Calculation Agent and set forth such agent's duties and obligations.) When using the Code-based form, parties can specify the Calculation Agent in the space provided in the Schedule (or by adding the term to a Confirmation). When using the Multi-currency form, parties can specify the Calculation Agent in the space provided in each Confirmation (or by specifying in the Schedule the party which will be the Calculation Agent).

5. *Deduction or Withholding for Taxes.* Section 19.1 of the Code contains the provisions of the Code-based form comparable to those in Section 2(d) of the Multi-currency form. See Section III(K) of this Guide for a discussion of tax matters.

6. *Default Interest.* See Section III(N)(2) of this Guide regarding default interest.

7. *Multibranch Parties.* Each form is also designed to permit one or both of the parties to make and receive payments through more than one branch or office. See Section III(I) of this Guide.

4

D. Section 3—Representations

1. *General.* Section 3 contains the parties' representations (except for the representation of any Multibranch Party contained in Section 10 and except, in the case of the Code-based form, for tax representations). Users may specify additional or different representations (or make deletions) in the Schedule. Sections 3(e) and (f) of the Multi-currency form refer to any tax representations specified by the parties in the Schedule. See Section III(K) of this Guide for a discussion of these tax representations and the comparable representations in the Code-based form. All representations are repeated as of each date on which the parties enter into a swap (other than tax representations given by a party in its capacity as a payee, which are made continuously).

2. *Accuracy of Information.* The representation in Section 3(d) applies only to information specified in the Schedule. Parties should specify in the Schedule the documents or other information as to which this representation is made.

E. Section 4—Agreements

1. *General.* Section 4 contains the parties' supplemental agreements (except that in the Code-based form, tax covenants, if any, are contained in Section 12). Users may specify additional or different agreements (or make deletions) in the Schedule. See Section III(K) of this Guide for a discussion of tax covenants.

2. *Furnish Information.* The parties must specify in the Schedule or in a Confirmation any information or documents which are required to be delivered pursuant to Section 4(a). Parties may wish to include requirements for financial statements or legal opinions. Delivery of credit support documents such as letters of credit or guarantees could also be included where delivery is to occur after the execution of the agreement. Any such document should be identified as a "Credit Support Document" for purposes of the cross-references in the Representations, Events of Default and other sections, if appropriate. Note that Section 4(a)(i) of the Multi-currency form refers to tax documents and 4(a)(ii) refers to other information. Section 4(a) of the Code-based form is intended to refer only to non-tax information. Delivery of tax documents is addressed in Section 12 of that form.

F. Section 5—Events of Default and Termination Events

1. *General.* Section 5 contains the Events of Default and Termination Events. Users may specify additional or different Events of Default and Termination Events (or make deletions) in the Schedule. Users should note that the term "Specified Entity" is used in several Events of Default and Termination Events as noted below. Its meaning (which may vary depending on the usage) must be specified in the Schedule in each case where the parties intend the term to be applicable.

2. *Applicability of Events of Default and Termination Events.* All the Events of Default and Termination Events apply to both parties (unless otherwise specified in the Schedule), except as follows:

(i) *Credit Support Default.* This Event of Default refers to a default under any applicable Credit Support Document. It applies only to a party if a Credit Support Document is provided by or on behalf of that party and is identified in the Schedule.

5

(ii) *Cross-Default and Credit Event Upon Merger.* These apply to a party only if so specified in the Schedule. These provisions were structured as "opt-in" provisions because they concern credit issues where there is variation in market practice among swap participants. In addition, the "opt-in" mechanism is expected to be useful to parties who wish to make the provisions applicable to only one party or in only some swap agreements.

3. *Certain Specific Events of Default.*

(i) *Failure to Pay.* This Event of Default refers to a failure to pay any amount under the agreement.

(ii) *Breach of Covenant.* This Event of Default refers to a failure to comply with any covenant other than any payment obligation, any tax-related covenant or the obligation to give notice of a Termination Event.

(iii) *Credit Support Default.* As noted above, this Event of Default is only applicable with respect to a specified Credit Support Document. In addition, if the Credit Support Document constitutes an obligation of an entity other than a party to the agreement (such as a third party guarantee), users must specify such entity as a "Specified Entity" in the Schedule for purposes of this Event of Default.

(iv) *Misrepresentation.* This Event of Default includes a breach of any representation (other than a tax representation) made in the agreement or in a Credit Support Document by the party or any applicable Specified Entity.

(v) *Default Under Specified Swaps.* Users should note that this Event of Default is triggered by an event of default which results in the designation or occurrence of an early termination date under another agreement. The parties must define "Specified Entity" in the Schedule for purposes of this Event of Default if they intend it to cover such entities. Users should also note that the term "Specified Swap" is defined in each form to refer to other rate swaps and currency exchange transactions between the parties and their applicable Specified Entities. Users can define Specified Swap and Specified Entity so as to broaden or narrow this Event of Default as they wish.

(vi) *Cross-Default.* As noted above, this Event of Default only applies to a party if so specified in the Schedule. In addition, users must specify a "Threshold Amount" in the Schedule and may vary the definition of Specified Indebtedness contained in each form. Users must also indicate in the Schedule the Specified Entities, if any, to which this Event of Default is to apply. This Event of Default is triggered by any of the following three events, in each case in respect of a Threshold Amount of Specified Indebtedness:

(1) an event of default under the other indebtedness that has resulted in the indebtedness becoming due prior to maturity, e.g., the debt has been accelerated;

(2) an event of default under the other indebtedness that permits the holders to declare the indebtedness due prior to maturity; or

(3) a failure to pay the indebtedness at maturity (which cannot, by definition, lead to acceleration prior to maturity).

Users who wish to delete the trigger referred to in clause (2) can do so by deleting the words ", or becoming capable at such time of being declared," in clause (1) of Section 5(a) (vi).

(vii) *Bankruptcy.* The drafters of the forms recognize that swap participants are located in and organized under the laws of different countries around the world. Accordingly, the Bankruptcy Event of Default has been drafted with the intention that it be broad enough to be triggered by applicable proceedings or events (described in the forms in a general way) under whatever bankruptcy or insolvency law pertains to a particular party. However, where such a party is organized in a jurisdiction other than the United States or the United Kingdom, users may, in certain cases, wish to modify this provision to refer to specific provisions of applicable laws. In addition, users must indicate in the Schedule the Specified Entities, if any, to which this Event of Default is to apply.

4. *Certain Specific Termination Events.*

(i) *Illegality.* The definition of Illegality excludes any event which results from a breach by a party of the agreement in Section 4(b) to maintain authorizations. (See Section 14 of the Code-based form and Section 5(b) (i) of the Multi-currency form.) In addition, if an event which constitutes an Illegality also gives rise to or constitutes an Event of Default (for example, a new law makes it illegal to make a payment, and thereby results in a payment default), it is treated as an Illegality. (See Section 5(c) (ii) of the Code-based form and Section 5(c) of the Multi-currency form.)

(ii) *Tax Event.* The Tax Event Termination Event is triggered by the existence, or the substantial likelihood of the existence, of a requirement that a party pay "additional amounts" under the tax gross-up provisions. Both parts of the provision refer to a party being required to pay an additional amount on "the next succeeding" payment date. This reference is intended to provide that a Termination Event will not occur until the latest practicable time. (See Section 5(b) (ii).)

5. *Events of Default and Termination Events Related to Mergers and Similar Transactions.* Mergers, amalgamations, consolidations and transfers of all or substantially all assets are addressed in three provisions, one of which is optional, in each form. In each provision, only those mergers in which a party to the agreement merges into a third party (and therefore ceases to exist) are included, not those in which a third party merges into a party to the agreement. (All such mergers and other transactions are referred to in this Guide as "Mergers" and the party engaging in the transaction is referred to as the "Merging Party".)

(i) *Merger Without Assumption.* An Event of Default exists if any Merger occurs and (i) the obligations under the agreement are not assumed or (ii) any credit support previously provided is no longer available. This Event of Default is defined as a "Merger Without Assumption". The Merging Party is the Defaulting Party. Users should note that there is no requirement in connection with a Merger Without Assumption that the new entity be incorporated or organized in the same country as the Merging Party.

7

(ii) *Tax Event Upon Merger.* If a Merger occurs that (i) does not constitute a Merger Without Assumption but (ii) results in a requirement to withhold or deduct for taxes, then a Termination Event defined as a "Tax Event Upon Merger" exists. In such an event, only the party burdened by the tax—that is, a party who is required to gross up, or a party who receives a payment from which an amount has been deducted or withheld without a gross up—is entitled to designate an Early Termination Date. In either case, the Merging Party is the Affected Party. As in the case of a Tax Event, this Termination Event arises only after a party would be so burdened on the next payment date.

(iii) *Credit Event Upon Merger.* If a Merger occurs that (i) does not constitute a Merger Without Assumption but (ii) results in a new entity whose creditworthiness is materially weaker than that of the original party as a result of the Merger, then a Termination Event defined as a "Credit Event Upon Merger" exists, but only if the parties have specified in the Schedule that Credit Event Upon Merger applies to the Merging Party. In that case, the Merging Party is the Affected Party and the non-Merging Party is entitled to designate an Early Termination Date.

G. Section 6—Early Termination

1. *How to Terminate.*

(i) *Events of Default.* The non-defaulting party has the right to designate an Early Termination Date in the case of an Event of Default. (See Section 6(a) and, with respect to the Code-based form, Section 11.1 of the Code.) In the case of a Bankruptcy Event of Default, early termination occurs automatically. In all other cases, notice is required as set forth in Section 6(a).

(ii) *Termination Events.* The party who is entitled to designate an Early Termination Date varies in the case of each Termination Event. (See Section 6(b)(iv) and, with respect to the Code-based form, Section 11.1 of the Code.) The right to designate an Early Termination Date is conditioned upon compliance with any applicable provisions requiring a party with respect to whom the Termination Event has occurred to try to transfer the affected swaps to eliminate the Termination Event. Such an obligation is included in most cases on the assumption that it is preferable to continue swaps where possible. (In those cases, the other party has a right but not an obligation to transfer.) Notice requirements are also specified in Section 6(b)(iv).

2. *Effect of Termination.* All swaps are terminated if an Early Termination Date is designated as the result of an Event of Default or a Credit Event Upon Merger. Only the swaps affected by the Termination Event are terminated if an Early Termination Date is designated as the result of any other Termination Event. (See the definitions of "Affected Transactions" and "Terminated Transactions" in Section 14.)

The notice designating (or the deemed occurrence of) an Early Termination Date terminates each party's obligations to make periodic payments under the Terminated Transactions. However, as discussed below, the amounts that would have been due on payment dates occurring after the effectiveness of such notice but prior to the Early Termination Date (as well as any amounts that did not become payable because of the failure to satisfy all conditions precedent) are included in the definition of Unpaid Amounts and are thereby included in the calculation of the lump-sum payment due as a result of the early termination. (See Section 6(c).)

3. *Calculation of Termination Payments.* The lump-sum amount payable upon early termination consists of the sum of (i) amounts which became due but were not paid prior to the Early Termination Date, (ii) amounts which would have been due prior to the Early Termination Date if all conditions to payment (such as the absence of any Event of Default) had been satisfied or if the Early Termination Date had not been designated and (iii) amounts representing the future values of the terminated swaps. The amounts referred to in clauses (i) and (ii) are included in the definition of Unpaid Amounts and the future value of a swap is determined by a Market Quotation (or, if Market Quotation cannot be determined, Loss, as defined for purposes of the forms as described below).

These amounts are added together as follows (see Section 6(e)):

(i) *Event of Default.* In the case of an Event of Default, the Market Quotations (or Losses) for all swaps, whether positive or negative, are added together. The net amount, whether positive or negative, is then added to the Unpaid Amounts due to the non-Defaulting Party. The Unpaid Amounts due to the Defaulting Party are then subtracted from this total. The net amount, if positive, is paid by the Defaulting Party. If the net amount is negative, no payment is made.

This method gives the Defaulting Party the benefit of the future value of any swap where the Market Quotation (or Loss) runs in its favor (i.e., is negative). Such value is offset against any Market Quotations in favor of the non-Defaulting Party and the Unpaid Amounts due to the non-Defaulting Party (i.e., positive amounts). (To accomplish this result, the Code-based form uses Agreement Value—Limited Two Way Payments, calculated on the basis of Aggregation, but the concept is modified to recognize any negative Aggregate Market Quotation (or Loss) in the overall calculation.) However, in no circumstances is a non-Defaulting Party required to pay a Defaulting Party.

(ii) *Termination Event.* In the case of a Termination Event, lump-sum termination amounts are computed in the same fashion with the following modifications:

(1) payment is made on a "two-way basis"—the absolute value of the overall sum (whether such sum is positive or negative) is paid to the appropriate party. (In the Code-based form, the use of "Agreement Value—Limited Two Way Payments", which is defined in the Code, gives a positive amount owed to a particular party (which party depends on whether the Aggregate Market Quotation is positive or negative), and this amount is then netted against the Unpaid Amounts.); and

(2) where there are two Affected Parties, an average of the Market Quotations determined by both parties is computed.

4. *Loss as Back-up Measure.* Loss, which is a general indemnification provision, is used as the measure of damages with respect to the future value of a swap in the event that a Market Quotation cannot be determined. The proviso included in Section 6(e)(i)(3) of the Code-based form states that (1) a negative Loss is given effect in the case of an Event of Default and (2) only the Loss of the non-Affected Party is used in the case of a Termination Event with one Affected Party (as contrasted with computing an average of the Loss

of each party). The result should be the same in the absence of this proviso under the definition of Aggregate Market Quotation in the Code, but the proviso was added to avoid misinterpretation and to make clear that the two forms are the same in their application of Loss as the back-up measure. If parties using the Code-based form wish to use "Formula" as a back-up measure, this should be specified in the Schedule.

5. *Alternative Method of Calculating Damages.* A different method used by some participants to calculate damages in the case of an Event of Default is to provide that the Defaulting Party (1) is not entitled to the benefit, as a credit against Unpaid Amounts, of the sum of the Market Quotations if such sum is less than zero, but (2) is entitled to be paid the amount, if any, by which any net Unpaid Amounts due to it exceed the sum (if positive) of the Market Quotations. The forms can be revised to calculate damages in this manner as follows:

  (i) *Code-based Form:*

    (1) delete Section 6(e)(i)(1);

    (2) in Section 6(e)(i)(2), delete the words "if an Early Termination Date occurs as a result of a Termination Event", and add after the words "under clause (i)" the phrase "(or, where there is a Defaulting Party, due to the non-Defaulting Party)"; and

    (3) in Section 6(e)(i)(3), delete the "s" on "clauses", the words "(1) and (2)" and part (A) of the proviso.

  (ii) *Multi-currency Form:*

    (1) delete Section 6(e)(i)(1);

    (2) delete the words "(2) if there is an Affected Party", in Section 6(e)(i)(2); and

    (3) revise Section 6(e)(iii) by deleting the reference to "Section 6(e)(i)(2)" and substituting "Section 6(e)(i)".

The changes to either form can also be made by restating the appropriate provisions in the Schedule. To facilitate revision of the Multi-currency form in the manner outlined above, a proviso has been added to the definition of Settlement Amount in Section 14. The proviso requires that a Settlement Amount expressed as a negative number be disregarded in determining amounts payable to a Defaulting Party under Section 6(e). This proviso, which eliminates any benefit of a negative Market Quotation (or Loss), only has substantive effect if users amend the form to provide for a payment to a Defaulting Party.

6. *Currency of Termination Payment in Multi-currency Form.* The Multi-currency form provides that the payment due on early termination will be made in the "Termination Currency". This must be specified in the Schedule. If such currency is not available, the Termination Currency is the U.S. Dollar. In calculating damages, this form provides that all Market Quotations and Unpaid Amounts are converted to a "Termination Currency Equivalent" on the basis of an exchange rate determined by a foreign exchange agent and in accordance with the form.

7. *Bankruptcy Adjustment.* Section 6(e) (iv) provides that the amount due on early termination will be adjusted in the circumstance where an Early Termination Date is deemed to have occurred as a result of a Bankruptcy Event of Default on a date prior to a payment date on which a payment was nevertheless made (for instance, where the payer was unaware of the Bankruptcy Event of Default and the deemed termination). In the absence of an adjustment, the calculation of Market Quotation could be deemed to include the period for which such payment was made, resulting in double counting.

8. *Default Interest.* See Section III(N) (2) of this Guide for a discussion of default interest.

H. Section 7—Transfer

Section 7 contains a general prohibition on transfer of rights and obligations under the agreement without prior consent. Some market participants routinely provide exceptions to this restriction in certain circumstances. Any exceptions to the transfer restriction should be set forth in the Schedule.

I. Section 10—Multibranch Provision

Section 10 was included to facilitate use of the forms by institutions such as banks that operate through branches in several locales and may wish to use a single master agreement for all such swaps. If a party intends to make and receive payments under different swaps through different branches or offices, it should be specified in the Schedule as a Multibranch Party, and the addresses of all such branches and offices should be listed. The relevant branch or office for a particular swap transaction should be specified in the Confirmation. If the parties specify that "Net Payments—Corresponding Payment Dates" applies, payments under different swaps will be netted only where such swaps are between the *same* offices of the parties. The parties may wish to consider whether different tax representations or covenants are needed with respect to payments by or to different branches or offices.

J. Notices

Addresses and telex numbers for notices must be specified in the Schedule. All notices must be in writing. (See Section 12 of the Multi-currency form and Article 14 of the Code.)

K. Tax Matters

1. *Gross Up.* Generally, payments are required to be made without any withholding or deduction for "Taxes". However, if a party making a payment is legally required to withhold Taxes from the payment, both forms provide that the party making such withholding is required to gross up the amount of the payment for any amount it withholds on account of "Indemnifiable Taxes". However, a party is released from its gross up obligation with respect to Indemnifiable Taxes that result from a breach of a tax-related representation or covenant made by the other party (except a breach of a tax-related representation made by a party in its capacity as a payee that results from a "Change in Tax Law"). (See Section 2(d) of the Multi-currency form and Section 19.1 of the Code.)

2. *Tax Representations.* The parties must specify in the Schedule all applicable tax representations. Representations specified in the Schedule for the purposes of Section 3 (f) of the Multi-currency form correspond to the Payee Tax Representations set forth in Section 19.2 of the Code. Parties may specify in the Schedule which, if any, of these representations are applicable or set forth other representations as "Payee Tax Representations". These representations are repeated continuously. It should be noted that the Payee Tax Representations set forth as representation (a) in the Schedule of the Multi-currency form and in Section 19.2 (b) of the Code are representations as to the *party's* eligibility for treaty benefits. Neither of these representations addresses the qualification of the *payments* for treaty benefits; instead, representations to this effect are set forth as representation (b) in the Schedule of the Multi-currency form and in Sections 19.2 (c) and 19.2 (d) of the Code.

In addition, both forms contain a representation that can be specified to establish that a party is a "recognized bank" in the United Kingdom (in which case special U.K. withholding tax treatment may apply to payments made or received by it). See Section 12 (c) of the Code-based form and Section 3 (f) and the Schedule of the Multi-currency form. This representation is also made continuously.

The representation specified for the purposes of Section 3 (e) of the Multi-currency form corresponds to the Withholding Tax Representation set forth in Section 19.3 of the Code (as modified by Section 12 (a) of the Code-based form). This representation is made on each Trade Date.

For Multibranch Parties, certain tax representations may apply only to certain offices, in which case it may be necessary to attach additional sheets to the Schedule with the appropriate representations for each office. A breach of a tax-related representation does not give rise to an Event of Default but may eliminate the other party's obligation to gross up as noted in Section III (K) (1) above.

3. *Tax Covenants.* The parties agree to give notice of breaches of tax representations (Section 12 (a) of the Code-based form and Section 4 (d) of the Multi-currency form). In the Multi-currency form, the parties must specify in the Schedule any tax forms to be provided (a covenant to deliver any such form is contained in Section 4 (a) (i) of that form). In the Code-based form, the parties must specify in the Schedule whether any of the Code covenants, or the additional covenant set forth in Section 12 (d) of the form, concerning tax forms will apply. The Tax Covenant set forth in Section 12 (d) states that a party agrees to provide U.S. tax forms at the time required by the recent United States Department of the Treasury announcement on dollar-denominated interest rate swaps. Users may specify additional or different tax agreements (or make deletions) in the Schedule. (The Code-based form incorporates an obligation to give notice of breach of a tax covenant; the absence of this requirement in the Multi-currency form, however, will not result in any substantive difference between the forms where the only tax covenants relate to the provision of tax documents, because a breach of such a covenant will be apparent.) A breach of a tax-related covenant does not give rise to an Event of Default.

L. Credit Support Document

The parties should identify in the Schedule any Credit Support Document (such as a guarantee, security agreement or letter of credit) and the party whose obligations are supported. References are made to the Credit Support Document in appropriate Representations, Agreements, Events of Default and certain other sections.

M. Governing Law and Jurisdiction; Service of Process

1. *General.* The provisions of the Code-based form comparable to those in Section 13 of the Multi-currency form may be found in Sections 13.1, 13.2, 18.2 and 20.3 of the Code in addition to Section 13 of the Code-based form.

2. *Governing Law in Multi-currency Form.* When using the Multi-currency form, parties must specify in the Schedule whether New York or English law will govern. Section 13(b) of the Multi-currency form provides that the parties submit to jurisdiction of the English courts if English law applies and in New York if New York law applies. The submission to jurisdiction in New York is non-exclusive. The submission to jurisdiction of the English courts is exclusive so far as courts of Contracting States of the European Economic Community are concerned and non-exclusive as regards other courts. This is to accommodate the provisions of the Civil Jurisdiction and Judgments Act 1982, which has recently been brought into force.

3. *Waiver of Immunity.* The waiver of immunity in Section 13(d) of the Multi-currency form includes language required for purposes of English law that makes such waiver slightly broader than that in Section 18.2 of the Code.

4. *Service of Process.* If the parties wish to provide for an agent for service of process, such agent or agents should be specified in the Schedule.

N. Definitions

1. *Business Day.* The definition of Business Day in the Multi-currency form differs from that in the Code-based form in light of currency-related concerns. (See Section 14 of the Multi-currency form and Section 1.6 of the Code.) The definition in the Multi-currency form generally refers to days when foreign exchange markets and commercial banks are open in the places specified by the parties. Section 1.3 of the Currency Definitions sets forth presumptions with respect to Business Days which apply if a Confirmation does not otherwise specify Business Days. Under these presumptions Business Days are days on which commercial banks and foreign exchange markets settle payments in the same currency as the payment obligation of a party that is payable on or calculated by reference to that date in specified cities that are financial centers for that currency, except that (i) in the case of a payment obligation that is payable in the U.S. dollar, London is specified in addition to New York if (A) that obligation is calculated by reference to LIBOR or (B) the payment obligations of the other party to the swap transaction are payable in the U.S. dollar and are calculated by reference to LIBOR (see Section 1.3(a)(xii) of the Currency Definitions) and (ii) in the case of a payment obligation that is payable in the European Currency Unit ("ECU"), Business Days are determined by reference to the ECU non-settlement days established by the ECU Banking Association. ECU non-settlement days will be displayed on the page designated as page "ISDE" on

13

the Reuter Monitor Money Rates Service. They also are designated as ECU Bank Holidays on a calendar published by the ECU Banking Association.

As the presumptions in most cases relate to the currency in which a payment obligation is payable, payment dates may not coincide exactly in a swap transaction that relies on the presumptions and involves two currencies. (See Section III (O) (3) of this Guide.) If the swap transaction is related to an underlying source of funding or debt obligation, the parties should refer to that source of funding or debt obligation to determine the Business Days that are appropriate for the swap transaction if they want the payment obligations under the swap transaction to coincide exactly with the payment obligations under the source of funding or debt obligation.

The definition of Business Day in the Code-based form refers to days when commercial banks are open in New York City or in another city specified by the parties, which city may be specified in the Schedule or in a Confirmation. Section 1.2 of the Currency Definitions provides a definition of "Banking Day" which refers to days when commercial banks (including foreign exchange markets) are open in a specified city or cities.

The presumptions in the Code and in the Currency Definitions provide for the same adjustments to payment dates in a U.S. Dollar interest rate swap.

2. *Default Rate and Interest on Unpaid Amounts and Termination Payments.*

(i) *Default Rate.* The Default Rate in the Code-based form is equal to the rate determined in accordance with the Federal Funds Floating Rate Option plus the Default Spread. The Default Spread must be specified in the Schedule. In the Multi-currency form the rate is equal to the payee's cost of funding rate plus 1%, since no published index exists covering all possible currencies. Under both forms, interest is calculated on the basis of daily compounding. (See Sections 2 (e) and 14 of the Multi-currency form and Section 14 of the Code-based form and Section 10.3 of the Code.)

(ii) *Interest on Unpaid Amounts.* See Section III (G) (3) of this Guide for a general discussion of the definition of Unpaid Amounts. The interest rate applied to Unpaid Amounts as set forth in that definition is equal to the Default Rate when such amounts are due by a Defaulting Party. A lower rate is used for amounts due by a non-Defaulting Party or in connection with a Termination Event. The Multi-currency form creates two different lower rates in those cases. The rate is equal to the cost of funds to the non-Defaulting Party in the case of an Event of Default and to an average of the cost of funds to each party in the case of a Termination Event. (An average of rates is not used in the case of amounts due by a non-Defaulting Party so that such party is not obligated to obtain a rate from the Defaulting Party in order to make its calculations.) Interest is calculated on the basis of daily compounding. (See Section 14.)

(iii) *Interest on Termination Payments.* In addition to the interest on Unpaid Amounts described above, interest is calculated on termination payments under two provisions (in each case on the basis of daily compounding). Sections 6 (d) of the Code-based form and 6 (d) (ii) of the Multi-currency form provide that interest will accrue on a termination payment from the Early Termination Date to the relevant due date. The due date in the case of an Event of Default is the day that notice of the amount payable is effective and in the case of a Termination Event is the second Business Day after the day that notice of the amount payable is effective. During such period, interest accrues at the Default Rate in the case of an Event of Default and at the Default Rate minus the Default Spread (in the case of the Code-based form) or the Default Rate minus 1% (in the case of the Multi-currency form) in the case of a Termination Event. This interest is calculated on the basis of daily compounding. If the termination payment is not paid on the relevant due date, interest will accrue at the Default Rate under Section 2 (e) of the Multi-currency form and Section 10.3 of the Code.

3. *Specified Entity.* As noted earlier (see Section III (F) of this Guide), the term Specified Entity is used in relation to the following terms:

(i) "Credit Support Document" (and, in relation to a specified Credit Support Document, in Credit Support Default, Misrepresentation and Illegality);

(ii) Default Under Specified Swaps;

(iii) Cross-Default; and

(iv) Bankruptcy.

Users must specify in the Schedule the meaning of Specified Entity for each term (if applicable). This definition can be the same or may vary depending on the usage. Users can, if they wish, state that "Specified Entity" will mean "Affiliate". This term is defined in Section 14 of the Multi-currency form and Section 17.2 of the Code (and may be amended by the parties as they wish).

4. *Other Definitions.* See Section III (F) (3) (iv) of this Guide regarding the definition of Specified Swaps and Section III (F) (3) (v) regarding the definitions of Specified Indebtedness and Threshold Amount.

O. Confirmations

Exhibit I to the Code-based form sets forth a form of Confirmation for use with that agreement, and Exhibit I to the Currency Definitions sets forth a form of Confirmation for use with the Multi-currency form. These Exhibits are intended to be guides. The parties should prepare actual letter or telex Confirmations by retyping these forms, with such changes and additions as are necessary.

1. *General.* The provisions in each Confirmation for specifying payment terms are similar. The Multi-currency form Confirmation includes certain provisions ("Notional Amount") which would only be applicable if the swap transaction involves a single currency and certain provisions ("Initial Exchange", "Final Exchange", "Fixed Rate Payer Currency Amount", "Floating Rate Payer Currency Amount" and "Account for payments in [second currency]") which would only be applicable if the swap transaction involves two currencies. In addition, the Currency Definitions (which are incorporated into the Multi-currency form Confirmation) include certain terms the meaning of which may vary depending upon the currency in which the related payment obligations are payable, unless the parties specify otherwise. The Currency Definitions also set forth provisions relating to payments in European Currency Units.

Each Confirmation is designed for transactions involving one Fixed Rate

15

Payer and one Floating Rate Payer. If the transaction involves two Floating Rate Payers, the Fixed Amounts section should be deleted, and two Floating Amounts sections should be set forth. To distinguish each party's Floating Amount obligations, a party's name should be added in front of "Floating Amounts" and "Floating Rate" and in lieu of "Floating Rate Payer" in each such section.

2. *Specifying Payment Dates and Period End Dates.* Section 2 of each Confirmation sets forth a term for specifying "Fixed Rate Payment Dates" and "Floating Rate Payment Dates" and lists conventions contained in the Code and the Currency Definitions for adjusting those days should a Payment Date occur on a day which is not a good business day. The parties may need to modify these terms and choices, or use the bracketed language that refers to Period End Dates, depending on the terms of the particular transaction. The following examples illustrate some of these options:

(i) *If Payment Dates coincide with Period End Dates:* The parties should specify Payment Dates and delete the bracketed references to Period End Dates.

(ii) *If Payment Dates are to occur a fixed number of days before or after the Period End Dates:* The parties should specify Period End Dates instead of Payment Dates. The parties should also specify that "Early Payment" or "Delayed Payment" applies and the applicable number of days by which Payment Dates will precede or follow Period End Dates. Note, however, that "Delayed Payment" in the Code presumes that Payment Dates will occur five New York Banking Days after the Period End Dates; this presumption must be overridden in a Confirmation under the Code-based form if another interval is desired.

(iii) *If Payment Dates are to occur on certain fixed dates and Period End Dates are to occur on other fixed dates:* Period End Dates and Payment Dates should be specified separately.

Note that in all of these cases the parties should consider what adjustments, if any, are to be made to Payment Dates or Period End Dates occurring on days which are not Business Days. The Code and the Currency Definitions set forth presumptions as to what conventions apply in certain circumstances, and the parties must specify the appropriate convention to overrule these presumptions.

3. *Business Days.* The Multi-currency form Confirmation has specific provisions for specifying Business Days according to the currency of the related payment obligation. These provisions need not be included in the Confirmation if the parties want the presumptions of Section 1.3 of the Currency Definitions to determine Business Days for purposes of the swap transaction. The parties should be aware that if the presumptions apply to a swap transaction involving two currencies, the payment obligations of both parties to the swap transaction may not fall on the same dates. If the parties want their payment obligations to fall on the same dates, they should specify the cities or days applicable to the swap transaction in the Confirmation. Parties also can specify additional cities or days or particular cities for currencies not covered by the presumptions. If the parties want to change the presumptions of Section 1.3 by adding cities or days, they should specify all the cities and days that are to apply in the Confirmation to payment obligations in that currency or for the swap transaction. (See also Section III (N) (1) of this Guide.)

16

The Code-based form Confirmation contains no specific provision to specify Business Days. The Code presumes that Business Day will mean New York Banking Day, unless the parties specify otherwise. The parties may, of course, specify an alternative meaning in the Schedule or in a Confirmation. Note that Period End Dates, Payment Dates and the conventions for adjusting these dates in the Code refer to New York Banking Days and, where appropriate, London Banking Days, not to Business Days.

4. *Specifying Accounts and Offices.* The Multi-currency form Confirmation has specific provisions for specifying accounts for payments. When using the Code-based form of Confirmation, the parties should also specify the accounts in the Confirmation if such information is not included in the Schedule. The Multi-currency form Confirmation also includes a provision to specify the Offices through which payments are to be made and received where a party is acting as a Multibranch Party. When using the Code-based form of Confirmation, this information should also be included if applicable.

5. *Other Provisions.* The parties should add such other provisions to the Confirmation to modify or supplement their agreement with respect to the particular swap transaction as they see fit.

6. *Confirmations Where Agreement Is Not Executed.* Although the Exhibits are designed to be used for Confirmations where the parties have already entered into an Interest Rate Swap Agreement or Interest Rate and Currency Exchange Agreement, the forms may also be used, with some revisions, where the parties have not entered into such an agreement at the time they wish to confirm a transaction but anticipate doing so. The following changes may be made:

(i) Include the following paragraph in lieu of the paragraph in Section 1 of each Confirmation:

"This Confirmation evidences a complete binding agreement between you and us as to the terms of the [Rate] Swap Transaction to which this Confirmation relates. In addition, upon the execution by you and us of an [Interest Rate Swap Agreement/Interest Rate and Currency Exchange Agreement] (the "Agreement"), in the form published by the International Swap Dealers Association, Inc. [("ISDA")], with such modifications as you and we shall in good faith agree, this Confirmation will supplement, form a part of, and be subject to the Agreement. All provisions contained or incorporated by reference in such Agreement upon its execution shall govern this Confirmation except as expressly modified below."

If intending to use the Code-based form, also include the following in this paragraph:

"This Confirmation is subject to and incorporates the Code of Standard Wording, Assumptions and Provisions for Swaps, 1986 Edition, as published by ISDA. In the event of any inconsistency between the Code and this Confirmation, this Confirmation will prevail."

(ii) Include a paragraph stating each party's obligations to make payments. This paragraph would set forth the essential provisions contained in Section 2 of each form. The following are examples:

(1) For inclusion in a Confirmation under the Code-based form:

"Each party will make each payment specified in this Confirmation

17

as being payable by it by transfer of the relevant amount in freely transferable funds to the account of the other party specified below. The Fixed Amount or Floating Amount applicable to a Payment Date will be the Fixed Amount or Floating Amount calculated with reference to the Calculation Period ending on, but excluding, the Period End Date (or in case of the Final Calculation Period, the Termination Date) that coincides with, or corresponds to, that Payment Date. The obligations of the parties under this Confirmation will be calculated and payable on the basis of Net Payments."

(2) For inclusion in a Confirmation under the Multi-currency form:

"Each party will make each payment specified in this Confirmation as being payable by it, not later than the due date for value on that date in the place of the account specified below, in freely transferable funds and in the manner customary for payments in the required currency. If on any date amounts would otherwise be payable in the same currency by each party to the other, then, on such date, each party's obligation to make payment of any such amount will be automatically satisfied and discharged and, if the aggregate amount that would otherwise have been payable by one party exceeds the aggregate amount that would otherwise have been payable by the other party, replaced by an obligation upon the party by whom the larger aggregate amount would have been payable to pay to the other party the excess of the larger aggregate amount over the smaller aggregate amount."

(iv) In the Multi-currency form, insert a paragraph specifying the governing law for the Confirmation.

(v) Although it is not necessary to include any other provisions in the Confirmation in order to have a binding agreement, the parties may wish to consider including other provisions that would otherwise be in the basic agreement where such provisions are important to the business terms of the transaction (e.g., events of default, representations and agreements). Certain provisions, such as the obligation to pay without withholding for taxes, would be included in the Code-based form Confirmation because the Code is incorporated into it. Parties using the Multi-currency form Confirmation may wish to consider specifying such provisions.

1987 Interest Rate and Currency Exchange Definitions

INTERNATIONAL SWAP DEALERS ASSOCIATION, INC.

INTRODUCTION

The 1987 Interest Rate and Currency Exchange Definitions are intended for use in letter agreements and telexes that document individual swap transactions governed by the "Interest Rate and Currency Exchange Agreement" published by the International Swap Dealers Association, Inc. ("ISDA"). A sample form of letter agreement and telex is attached as Exhibit I to these definitions and provisions.

ISDA does not assume any liability for the non-availability or miscalculation of, or any error or omission in, any of the rates referred to in these definitions and provisions.

ISDA appreciates the contribution of Cravath, Swaine & Moore to these definitions and provisions.

TABLE OF CONTENTS

ARTICLE 5

FIXED AMOUNTS

ARTICLE 6

FLOATING AMOUNTS

ARTICLE 7

CALCULATION OF RATES FOR CERTAIN FLOATING RATE OPTIONS

ARTICLE 8

ROUNDING

ARTICLE 9

PAYMENTS

1987 INTEREST RATE AND CURRENCY EXCHANGE DEFINITIONS

Any or all of the following definitions and provisions may be incorporated into a document by wording in the document indicating that, or the extent to which, the document is subject to the 1987 Interest Rate and Currency Exchange Definitions (as published by the International Swap Dealers Association, Inc.). All definitions and provisions so incorporated in a document will be applicable to that document unless otherwise provided in that document, and all terms defined in these definitions and provisions and used in any definition or provision that is incorporated by reference in a document will have the respective meanings set forth in these definitions and provisions unless otherwise provided in that document. Any term used in a document will, when combined with the name of a party, have meaning in respect of the named party only.

ARTICLE 1

CERTAIN GENERAL DEFINITIONS

Section 1.1. Swap Transaction. "Swap Transaction" means a rate exchange or swap transaction, including transactions involving a single currency or two or more currencies.

Section 1.2. Banking Day. "Banking Day" means, in respect of any city, any day on which commercial banks are open for business (including dealings in foreign exchange and foreign currency deposits) in that city.

Section 1.3. Business Day. "Business Day" means, in respect of an Initial Exchange Date, a Final Exchange Date, a Payment Date, a Period End Date, a Reset Date or a Valuation Date, a day on which commercial banks and foreign exchange markets settle payments in the place(s) and on the days specified for that purpose in the document exchanged between the parties confirming the Swap Transaction and, if place(s) and days are not so specified, a day (a) on which commercial banks and foreign exchange markets settle payments in the same currency as the payment obligation that is payable on or calculated by reference to that date in (i) Sydney, if the currency is the Australian Dollar, (ii) Brussels, if the currency is the Belgian Franc, (iii) Toronto, if the currency is the Canadian Dollar, (iv) Frankfurt, if the currency is the Deutsche Mark, (v) Paris, if the currency is the French Franc, (vi) Hong Kong, if the currency is the Hong Kong Dollar, (vii) Milan, if the currency is the Italian Lire, (viii) Brussels and Luxembourg, if the currency is the Luxembourg Franc, (ix) Wellington, if the currency is the New Zealand Dollar, (x) London, if the currency is Sterling, (xi) Zurich, if the currency is the Swiss Franc, (xii) New York and London, if the currency is the U.S. Dollar and either (A) the payment obligation is calculated by reference to any "LIBOR" Floating Rate Option or (B) the payment obligations of the other party to the Swap Transaction are payable in the U.S. Dollar and are calculated by reference to any "LIBOR" Floating Rate Option, (xiii) New York, if the currency is the U.S. Dollar and neither clause (xii)(A) nor clause (xii) (B) above is applicable, and (xiv) Tokyo, if the currency is the Yen; and (b) that is an ECU Settlement Day, if the payment obligation that is payable on or calculated by reference to that date is to be made in the European Currency Unit.

Section 1.4. Currencies.

(a) **Australian Dollar.** "Australian Dollar", "A$" and "AUD" each means the lawful currency of Australia.

(b) **Belgian Franc.** "Belgian Franc", "Bfr" and "BEF" each means the lawful currency of the Kingdom of Belgium, including the Commercial Belgian Franc and the Financial Belgian Franc.

 (i) "Commercial Belgian Franc", "Commercial Bfr" and "Commercial BEF" each means the Belgian Franc that is used for transactions in foreign currencies that are required by the Belgian-Luxembourg Exchange Institute to be settled on the regulated exchange market of the Belgian-Luxembourg Economic Union.

 (ii) "Financial Belgian Franc", "Financial Bfr" and "Financial BEF" each means the Belgian Franc that is used for transactions in foreign currencies that may be settled on the exchange market of the Belgian-Luxembourg Economic Union without restriction.

(c) **Canadian Dollar.** "Canadian Dollar", "C$" and "CAD" each means the lawful currency of Canada.

(d) **Deutsche Mark.** "Deutsche Mark", "DM" and "DEM" each means the lawful currency of the Federal Republic of Germany.

(e) **Dutch Guilder.** "Dutch Guilder", "DFl" and "NLG" each means the lawful currency of The Kingdom of The Netherlands.

(f) **European Currency Unit.** "European Currency Unit", "ECU" and "XEU" each means a currency, one unit of which is equal in value to the European Currency Unit that is used in the European Monetary System, or, in the event that the European Currency Unit is no longer used in the European Monetary System, a currency, the value of which is determined as provided in Article 9 of these definitions and provisions.

(g) **French Franc.** "French Franc", "Ffr" and "FRF" each means the lawful currency of the Republic of France.

(h) **Hong Kong Dollar.** "Hong Kong Dollar", "HK$" and "HKD" each means the lawful currency of Hong Kong.

(i) **Italian Lire.** "Italian Lire", "Lire" and "ITL" each means the lawful currency of the Republic of Italy.

(j) **Luxembourg Franc.** "Luxembourg Franc", "Lfr" and "LUF" each means the lawful currency of the Grand Duchy of Luxembourg, including the Commercial Luxembourg Franc and the Financial Luxembourg Franc.

 (i) "Commercial Luxembourg Franc", "Commercial Lfr" and "Commercial LUF" each means the Luxembourg Franc that is used for transactions in foreign currencies that are required by the Belgian-Luxembourg Exchange Institute to be settled on the regulated exchange market of the Belgian-Luxembourg Economic Union.

2

(ii) "Financial Luxembourg Franc", "Financial Lfr" and "Financial LUF" each means the Luxembourg Franc that is used for transactions in foreign currencies that may be settled on the exchange market of the Belgian-Luxembourg Economic Union without restriction.

(k) **New Zealand Dollar.** "New Zealand Dollar", "NZ$" and "NZD" each means the lawful currency of New Zealand.

(l) **Sterling.** "Sterling", "£" and "GBP" each means the lawful currency of the United Kingdom.

(m) **Swiss Franc.** "Swiss Franc", "Sfr" and "CHF" each means the lawful currency of Switzerland.

(n) **U.S. Dollar.** "U.S. Dollar", "Dollar", "U.S.$", "$" and "USD" each means the lawful currency of the United States of America.

(o) **Yen.** "Yen", "¥" and "JPY" each means the lawful currency of Japan.

Section 1.5. ECU Settlement Day. "ECU Settlement Day" means any day that (a) is not either (i) a Saturday or a Sunday or (ii) a day which appears as an ECU Non-Settlement Day on the display designated as page "ISDE" on the Reuter Monitor Money Rates Service (or a day so designated by the ECU Banking Association, if ECU Non-Settlement Days do not appear on that page) and, if ECU Non-Settlement Days do not appear on that page (and are not so designated), a day on which payments in the European Currency Unit cannot be settled in the international interbank market and (b) is a day on which payments in the European Currency Unit can be settled by commercial banks and in foreign exchange markets in the place in which the relevant account for payment is located.

ARTICLE 2

PARTIES

Section 2.1. Fixed Rate Payer. "Fixed Rate Payer" means, in respect of a Swap Transaction, a party obligated to make payments from time to time during the Term of the Swap Transaction of amounts calculated by reference to a fixed per annum rate.

Section 2.2. Floating Rate Payer. "Floating Rate Payer" means, in respect of a Swap Transaction, a party obligated to make payments from time to time during the Term of the Swap Transaction of amounts calculated by reference to a floating per annum rate.

ARTICLE 3

TERM

Section 3.1. Term. "Term" means the period commencing on the Effective Date of a Swap Transaction and ending on the Termination Date of the Swap Transaction.

Section 3.2. Effective Date. "Effective Date" means the date specified as such for a Swap Transaction, which date is the first day of the Term of the Swap Transaction.

Section 3.3. Termination Date. "Termination Date" means the date specified as such for a Swap Transaction, which date is the last day of the Term of the Swap Transaction.

Section 3.4. Initial Exchange Date. "Initial Exchange Date" means, in respect of a Swap Transaction and a party, the date specified as such or, if a date is not so specified and an Initial Exchange Amount is specified, the Effective Date, except that an adjustment will be made if the Initial Exchange Date for a party would otherwise fall on a day that is not a Business Day, so that the Initial Exchange Date for that party will be the first following day that is a Business Day.

Section 3.5. Final Exchange Date. "Final Exchange Date" means, in respect of a Swap Transaction and a party, the date specified as such or, if a date is not so specified and a Final Exchange Amount is specified, the Termination Date, except that an adjustment will be made if the Final Exchange Date for a party would otherwise fall on a day that is not a Business Day, so that the Final Exchange Date for that party will be the first following day that is a Business Day.

Section 3.6. Trade Date. "Trade Date" means, in respect of a Swap Transaction, the date on which the parties enter into the Swap Transaction.

ARTICLE 4

CERTAIN DEFINITIONS RELATING TO PAYMENTS

Section 4.1. Initial Exchange Amount. "Initial Exchange Amount" means, in respect of a Swap Transaction and a party, an amount that is specified as such for that party and, subject to any applicable condition precedent, is payable by that party on the Initial Exchange Date.

Section 4.2. Final Exchange Amount. "Final Exchange Amount" means, in respect of a Swap Transaction and a party, an amount that is specified as such for that party and, subject to any applicable condition precedent, is payable by that party on the Final Exchange Date.

Section 4.3. Fixed Amount. "Fixed Amount" means, in respect of a Swap Transaction and a Fixed Rate Payer, an amount that, subject to any applicable condition precedent, is payable by that Fixed Rate Payer on an applicable Payment Date and determined by reference to a Calculation Period as provided in Article 5 of these definitions and provisions.

Section 4.4. Floating Amount. "Floating Amount" means, in respect of a Swap Transaction and a Floating Rate Payer, an amount that, subject to any applicable condition precedent, is payable by that Floating Rate Payer on an applicable Payment Date and determined by reference to a Floating Rate Option and a Calculation Period as provided in Article 6 of these definitions and provisions.

Section 4.5. Currency Amount. "Currency Amount" means, in respect of a party and any Calculation Period for a Swap Transaction involving more than one currency, the amount specified as such for the Swap Transaction or that party.

Section 4.6. Notional Amount. "Notional Amount" means, in respect of a party and any Calculation Period for a Swap Transaction involving one currency, the amount specified as such for the Swap Transaction.

Section 4.7. Calculation Amount. "Calculation Amount" means, in respect of a Swap Transaction and a party, the Notional Amount or the applicable Currency Amount, as the case may be.

Section 4.8. FRN Convention. "FRN Convention" means, with respect to either Payment Dates or Period End Dates for a Swap Transaction and a party, that the Payment Dates or Period End Dates of that party will be each day during the Term of the Swap Transaction that numerically corresponds to the preceding applicable Payment Date or Period End Date, as the case may be, of that party in the calendar month that is the specified number of months after the month in which the preceding applicable Payment Date or Period End Date occurred (or, in the case of the first applicable Payment Date or Period End Date, the day that numerically corresponds to the Effective Date in the calendar month that is the specified number of months after the month in which the Effective Date occurred), except that (a) if there is not any such numerically corresponding day in the calendar month in which a Payment Date or Period End Date, as the case may be, of that party should occur, then the Payment Date or Period End Date will be the last day that is a Business Day in that month, (b) if a Payment Date or Period End Date, as the case may be, of that party would otherwise fall on a day that is not a Business Day, then the Payment Date or Period End Date will be the first following day that is a Business Day unless that day falls in the next calendar month, in which case the Payment Date or Period End Date will be the first preceding day that is a Business Day, and (c) if the preceding applicable Payment Date or Period End Date, as the case may be, of that party occurred on the last day in a calendar month that was a Business Day, then all subsequent applicable Payment Dates or Period End Dates, as the case may be, of that party prior to the Termination Date will be the last day that is a Business Day in the month that is the specified number of months after the month in which the preceding applicable Payment Date or Period End Date occurred. "Eurodollar Convention" has the same meaning as FRN Convention.

Section 4.9. Payment Date. "Payment Date" means, in respect of a Swap Transaction and a party,

(a) if "Delayed Payment" or "Early Payment" is not specified for the Swap Transaction or that party and Payment Dates are specified or otherwise predetermined for the Swap Transaction or that party, each day during the Term of the Swap Transaction so specified or predetermined and the Termination Date;

(b) if "Delayed Payment" or "Early Payment" is not specified for the Swap Transaction or that party and the parties specify that Payment Dates for the Swap Transaction or that party will occur in accordance with the FRN Convention at a specified interval of calendar months, each day during the

5

Term of the Swap Transaction at the specified interval, determined in accordance with the FRN Convention, and the Termination Date;

(c) if "Delayed Payment" and a period of days are specified for the Swap Transaction or that party and Period End Dates are established for the Swap Transaction or that party, each day that is the specified number of days after an applicable Period End Date or after the Termination Date; or

(d) if "Early Payment" and a period of days are specified for the Swap Transaction or that party and Period End Dates are established for the Swap Transaction or that party, each day that is the specified number of days before an applicable Period End Date or before the Termination Date;

except that, in the case of subsections (a), (c) and (d) above, an adjustment will be made if any Payment Date of a party would otherwise fall on a day that is not a Business Day, so that

(e) if (i) the "Following Business Day" convention is specified for the Swap Transaction or that party or (ii) an applicable convention is not so specified, the Payment Date will be the first following day that is a Business Day;

(f) if the "Modified Following Business Day" convention is specified for the Swap Transaction or that party, the Payment Date will be the first following day that is a Business Day unless that day falls in the next calendar month, in which case the Payment Date will be the first preceding day that is a Business Day; or

(g) if the "Preceding Business Day" convention is specified for the Swap Transaction or that party, the Payment Date will be the first preceding day that is a Business Day.

Section 4.10. Period End Date. "Period End Date" means, in respect of a Swap Transaction and a party,

(a) if Period End Dates are not established for the Swap Transaction or that party, each Payment Date of that party during the Term of the Swap Transaction;

(b) if Period End Dates are specified or otherwise predetermined for the Swap Transaction or that party, each day during the Term so specified or predetermined; or

(c) if it is specified for the Swap Transaction or that party that Period End Dates will occur in accordance with the FRN Convention and an interval of calendar months is specified, and if "Delayed Payment" or "Early Payment" is specified for the Swap Transaction or that party, each day during the Term at the specified interval, determined in accordance with the FRN Convention;

except that, in the case of subsection (b) above, an adjustment may be made if any Period End Date of a party would otherwise fall on a day that is not a Business Day, so that

(d) if "No Adjustment of Period End Dates" is specified for the Swap Transaction or that party, an adjustment will not be made, notwithstanding that the Period End Date occurs on a day that is not a Business Day;

(e) if (i) the "Following Business Day" convention is specified for the Swap Transaction or that party or (ii) an applicable convention is not so specified, the Period End Date will be the first following day that is a Business Day;

(f) if the "Modified Following Business Day" convention is specified for the Swap Transaction or that party, the Period End Date will be the first following day that is a Business Day unless that day falls in the next calendar month, in which case the Period End Date will be the first preceding day that is a Business Day; or

(g) if the "Preceding Business Day" convention is specified for the Swap Transaction or that party, the Period End Date will be the first preceding day that is a Business Day.

Section 4.11. Calculation Period. "Calculation Period" means, in respect of a Swap Transaction and a party, each period from, and including, one Period End Date of that party to, but excluding, the next following applicable Period End Date during the Term of the Swap Transaction, except that (a) the initial Calculation Period for the party will commence on, and include, the Effective Date, and (b) the final Calculation Period for the party will end on, but exclude, the Termination Date.

Section 4.12. Calculation Agent. "Calculation Agent" means the party to a Swap Transaction (or a third party) designated as such for the Swap Transaction and responsible for (a) calculating the applicable Floating Rate, if any, for each Calculation Period or Compounding Period, (b) calculating any Floating Amount payable for each Calculation Period, (c) calculating any Fixed Amount payable for each Calculation Period, (d) calculating a Currency Amount by reference to a Currency Amount in another currency on or prior to the Effective Date of the Swap Transaction, (e) giving notice to the parties to the Swap Transaction on the Calculation Date for each Calculation Period, specifying (i) the date for payment for such Calculation Period, (ii) the party or parties required to make the payment or payments then due, (iii) the amount or amounts of the payment or payments then due and (iv) reasonable details as to how the amount or amounts were determined and (f) if, after notice is given, there is a change in the number of days in the relevant Calculation Period and the amount or amounts of the payment or payments due for that period, promptly giving the parties to the Swap Transaction notice of those changes, with reasonable details as to how those changes were determined. Whenever the Calculation Agent is required to select (i) banks or dealers for the purpose of calculating a Floating Rate or a Market Exchange Rate, (ii) any exchange rate or (iii) a Selected Currency, the Calculation Agent will make the selection in good faith after consultation with the other party (or the parties, if the Calculation Agent is a third party), if practicable, for the purpose of obtaining a representative rate that will reasonably reflect conditions prevailing at the time in the relevant market or designating a freely convertible currency, as the case may be.

7

Section 4.13. Calculation Date. "Calculation Date" means, in respect of any Calculation Period, the earliest day on which it is practicable to provide the notice that the Calculation Agent is required to give for that Calculation Period, and in no event later than the close of business on the Business Day next preceding the Payment Date for that Calculation Period.

ARTICLE 5

FIXED AMOUNTS

Section 5.1. Calculation of a Fixed Amount. The Fixed Amount payable by a party on each applicable Payment Date for any Calculation Period will be

(a) if an amount is specified for the Swap Transaction as the Fixed Amount payable by that party for that Calculation Period, such amount; or

(b) if an amount is not specified for the Swap Transaction as the Fixed Amount payable by that party for that Calculation Period, an amount calculated on a formula basis for that Calculation Period as follows:

$$\text{Fixed Amount} = \text{Calculation Amount} \times \text{Fixed Rate} \times \text{Fixed Rate Day Count Fraction}$$

Section 5.2. Certain Definitions Relating to Fixed Amounts. For purposes of the calculation of a Fixed Amount payable by a party:

(a) "Fixed Rate" means the per annum rate specified as such for the Swap Transaction or that party, expressed as a decimal.

(b) "Fixed Rate Day Count Fraction" means

(i) if "Actual/365" is specified for the Swap Transaction or that party as the applicable Fixed Rate Day Count Fraction, the actual number of days in the Calculation Period in respect of which payment is being made divided by 365 (or, if any portion of that Calculation Period falls in a leap year, the sum of (A) the actual number of days in that portion of the Calculation Period falling in a leap year divided by 366 and (B) the actual number of days in that portion of the Calculation Period falling in a non-leap year divided by 365);

(ii) if "Actual/365(Fixed)" is specified for the Swap Transaction or that party as the applicable Fixed Rate Day Count Fraction, the actual number of days in the Calculation Period in respect of which payment is being made divided by 365;

(iii) if "Actual/360" is specified for the Swap Transaction or that party as the applicable Fixed Rate Day Count Fraction, the actual number of days in the Calculation Period in respect of which payment is being made divided by 360; or

8

(iv) if "30/360" or "360/360" is specified for the Swap Transaction or that party as the applicable Fixed Rate Day Count Fraction, the number of days in the Calculation Period in respect of which payment is being made (calculated on the basis of a year of 360 days with 12 30-day months) divided by 360.

ARTICLE 6

FLOATING AMOUNTS

Section 6.1. Calculation of a Floating Amount. The Floating Amount payable by a party on each applicable Payment Date for any Calculation Period will be

(a) if Compounding is specified for the Swap Transaction or that party, an amount equal to the sum of the Compounding Period Amounts for each of the Compounding Periods in that Calculation Period; or

(b) if Compounding is not specified for the Swap Transaction or that party, an amount calculated on a formula basis in respect of that Calculation Period as follows:

$$\text{Floating Amount} = \text{Calculation Amount} \times \left(\text{Floating Rate} \pm \text{Spread}\right) \times \text{Floating Rate Day Count Fraction}$$

Section 6.2. Calculation of a Compounding Period Amount. The Compounding Period Amount for any Compounding Period will be an amount calculated on a formula basis in respect of that Compounding Period as follows:

$$\text{Compounding Period Amount} = \text{Adjusted Calculation Amount} \times \left(\text{Floating Rate} \pm \text{Spread}\right) \times \text{Floating Rate Day Count Fraction}$$

Section 6.3. Certain Definitions Relating to Floating Amounts. For purposes of the calculation of a Floating Amount payable by a party:

(a) "Floating Rate" means, for any Calculation Period or Compounding Period, a per annum rate, expressed as a decimal, equal to

(i) if a per annum rate is specified for the Swap Transaction or that party to be the Floating Rate applicable to that Calculation Period or Compounding Period, the Floating Rate so specified;

(ii) if only one Reset Date is established for the Swap Transaction or that party during (or with respect to) that Calculation Period or Compounding Period, the Relevant Rate for that Reset Date;

(iii) if more than one Reset Date is established for the Swap Transaction or that party during (or with respect to) that Calculation Period or Compounding Period and the "Unweighted Average Rate" method of calculation is specified, the arithmetic mean of the Relevant Rates for each of these Reset Dates;

9

(iv) if more than one Reset Date is established for the Swap Transaction or that party during (or with respect to) that Calculation Period or Compounding Period and the "Weighted Average Rate" method of calculation is specified, the arithmetic mean of the Relevant Rates in effect for each day in that Calculation Period or Compounding Period, calculated by multiplying each Relevant Rate by the number of days such Relevant Rate is in effect, determining the sum of such products and dividing such sum by the number of days in the Calculation Period or Compounding Period; or

(v) if more than one Reset Date is established for the Swap Transaction or that party during (or with respect to) that Calculation Period or Compounding Period and neither the "Unweighted Average Rate" nor the "Weighted Average Rate" method of calculation is specified, a Floating Rate determined as if "Unweighted Averate Rate" had been specified as the applicable method of calculation.

(b) "Reset Date" means each day specified as such (or determined pursuant to a method specified for such purpose) for the Swap Transaction or that party, except that an adjustment will be made if any Reset Date of a party would fall on a day that is not a Business Day, so that (i) if the payment obligations calculated by reference to that Reset Date are to be made in Sterling or the Hong Kong Dollar, the Reset Date will be the first following day that is a Business Day unless that day falls in the next calendar month, in which case the Reset Date will be the first preceding day that is a Business Day, (ii) if the payment obligations calculated by reference to that Reset Date are to be made in the Canadian Dollar, the Reset Date will be the first following day that is a Business Day, and (iii) if the payment obligations calculated by reference to that Reset Date are to be made in any other currency, the Reset Date will be the first preceding day that is a Business Day.

(c) "Relevant Rate" means (subject to the effect of any applicable Rate Cut-off Date), for any day, a per annum rate, expressed as a decimal, equal to

(i) if such day is a Reset Date, the rate determined with respect to that day for the specified Floating Rate Option as provided in Article 7 of these definitions and provisions; or

(ii) if such day is not a Reset Date, the Relevant Rate determined pursuant to clause (i) above for the next preceding Reset Date.

(d) "Rate Cut-off Date" means each day specified as such (or determined pursuant to a method specified for such purpose) for the Swap Transaction or that party. The Relevant Rate for each Reset Date in the period from, and including, a Rate Cut-off Date to, but excluding, the next applicable Period End Date (or, in the case of the last Calculation Period, the Termination Date) will (solely for purposes of calculating the Floating Amount payable on the next applicable Payment Date) be deemed to be the Relevant Rate in effect on that Rate Cut-off Date.

(e) "Spread" means the per annum rate, if any, specified as such for the Swap Transaction or the party (expressed as a decimal). For purposes of determining a Floating Amount or a Compounding Period Amount, if positive the Spread will be added to the Floating Rate and if negative the Spread will be subtracted from the Floating Rate.

(f) "Floating Rate Day Count Fraction" means, in respect of any Calculation Period or Compounding Period, (i) if any "USD-TBILL" Floating Rate Option is specified as the applicable Floating Rate Option, the actual number of days in that Calculation Period or Compounding Period divided by 365 (or, if any portion of that Calculation Period or Compounding Period falls in a leap year, the sum of (A) the actual number of days in that portion of the Calculation Period or Compounding Period falling in a leap year divided by 366 and (B) the actual number of days in that portion of the Calculation Period or Compounding Period falling in a nonleap year divided by 365), (ii) if any "GBP-LIBOR", "HKD-HIBOR", "CAD-BA" or "CAD-TBILL" Floating Rate Option is specified as the applicable Floating Rate Option, the actual number of days in that Calculation Period or Compounding Period divided by 365, and (iii) in all other cases, the actual number of days in that Calculation Period or Compounding Period divided by 360.

Section 6.4. Certain Additional Definitions Relating to Compounding. For purposes of the calculation of a Floating Amount where "Compounding" is specified:

(a) "Compounding Period" means, in respect of a Calculation Period, each period from, and including, one Compounding Date to, but excluding, the next following applicable Compounding Date during that Calculation Period, except that (i) each initial Compounding Period for a Swap Transaction will commence on, and include, the Effective Date and (ii) each final Compounding Period for a Swap Transaction will end on, but exclude, the Termination Date.

(b) "Compounding Date" means each day during the Term of a Swap Transaction specified as such (or determined pursuant to a method specified for such purpose) for the Swap Transaction or a party, except that, if the Period End Date for that Calculation Period is subject to adjustment in accordance with Section 4.10 hereof, each applicable Compounding Date in that Calculation Period will be subject to adjustment in the same manner as the Period End Date.

(c) "Adjusted Calculation Amount" means (i) in respect of the first Compounding Period in any Calculation Period, the Calculation Amount for that Calculation Period and (ii) in respect of each succeeding Compounding Period in that Calculation Period, an amount equal to the sum of the Calculation Amount for that Calculation Period and the Compounding Period Amounts for each of the previous Compounding Periods in that Calculation Period.

ARTICLE 7

CALCULATION OF RATES FOR CERTAIN FLOATING RATE OPTIONS

Section 7.1. Floating Rate Options. For purposes of determining a Relevant Rate:

(a) *Australian Dollar.*

(i) "AUD-BBR-ISDC" means that the rate for a Reset Date will be the rate for Australian Dollar bills of exchange for a period of the Designated Maturity which appears on the Reuters Screen ISDC Page as of 10:00 a.m., Sydney time, on that Reset Date. If such rate does not appear on the Reuters Screen ISDC Page, the rate for that Reset Date will be determined as if the parties had specified "AUD-BBR-Reference Banks" as the applicable Floating Rate Option.

(ii) "AUD-BBR-Reference Banks" means that the rate for a Reset Date will be the average of the mean bid and offered rates quoted by each of the Reference Banks for Australian Dollar bills of exchange for a period of the Designated Maturiy for settlement on that Reset Date and in a Representative Amount at approximately 10:00 a.m., Sydney time, on that Reset Date. The Calculation Agent will request the principal Sydney office of each of the Reference Banks to provide a quotation of its rates.

(iii) "AUD-LIBOR-BBA" means that the rate for a Reset Date will be the rate for deposits in Australian Dollars for a period of the Designated Maturity which appears on the Telerate Page 3740 as of 11:00 a.m., London time, on the day that is two London Banking Days preceding that Reset Date. If such rate does not appear on the Telerate Page 3740, the rate for that Reset Date will be determined as if the parties had specified "AUD-LIBOR-Reference Banks" as the applicable Floating Rate Option.

(iv) "AUD-LIBOR-Reference Banks" means that the rate for a Reset Date will be determined on the basis of the rates at which deposits in Australian Dollars are offered by the Reference Banks at approximately 11:00 a.m., London time, on the day that is two London Banking Days preceding that Reset Date to prime banks in the London interbank market for a period of the Designated Maturity commencing on that Reset Date and in a Representative Amount. The Calculation Agent will request the principal London office of each of the Reference Banks to provide a quotation of its rate. If at least two quotations are provided, the rate for that Reset Date will be the arithmetic mean of the quotations. If fewer than two quotations are provided as requested, the rate for that Reset Date will be the arithmetic mean of the rates quoted by major banks in Sydney, selected by the Calculation Agent, at approximately 11:00 a.m., Sydney time, on that Reset Date for loans in Australian Dollars to leading European banks for a period of the Designated Maturity commencing on that Reset Date and in a Representative Amount.

(b) *Belgian Franc.*

(i) "BEF-BIBOR-ISDB" means that the rate for a Reset Date will be the rate for deposits in Belgian Francs for a period of the Designated Maturity which appears on the Reuters Screen ISDB Page as of 11:00 a.m., Brussels time, on the day that is two Brussels Banking Days preceding that Reset Date. If such rate does not appear on the Reuters Screen ISDB Page, the rate for that Reset Date will be determined as if the parties had specified "BEF-BIBOR-Reference Banks" as the applicable Floating Rate Option.

(ii) "BEF-BIBOR-Reference Banks" means that the rate for a Reset Date will be determined on the basis of the rates at which deposits in Financial Belgian Francs are offered by the Reference Banks at approximately 11:00 a.m., Brussels time, on the day that is two Brussels Banking Days preceding that Reset Date to prime banks in the Brussels interbank market for a period of the Designated Maturity commencing on that Reset Date and in a Representative Amount. The Calculation Agent will request the principal Brussels office of each of the Reference Banks to provide a quotation of its rate. If at least two quotations are provided, the rate for that Reset Date will be the arithmetic mean of the quotations. If fewer than two quotations are provided as requested, the rate for that Reset Date will be the arithmetic mean of the rates quoted by major banks in Brussels, selected by the Calculation Agent, at approximately 11:00 a.m., Brussels time, on that Reset Date for loans in Financial Belgian Francs to leading European banks for a period of the Designated Maturity commencing on that Reset Date and in a Representative Amount.

(iii) "COMBEF-BIBOR-Reference Banks" means that the rate for a Reset Date will be determined on the basis of the rates at which deposits in Commercial Belgian Francs are offered by the Reference Banks at approximately 11:00 a.m., Brussels time, on the day that is two Brussels Banking Days preceding that Reset Date to prime banks in the Brussels interbank market for a period of the Designated Maturity commencing on that Reset Date and in a Representative Amount. The Calculation Agent will request the principal Brussels office of each of the Reference Banks to provide a quotation of its rate. If at least two quotations are provided, the rate for that Reset Date will be the arithmetic mean of the quotations. If fewer than two quotations are provided as requested, the rate for that Reset Date will be the arithmetic mean of the rates quoted by major banks in Brussels, selected by the Calculation Agent, at approximately 11:00 a.m., Brussels time, on that Reset Date for loans in Commercial Belgian Francs to leading European banks for a period of the Designated Maturity commencing on that Reset Date and in a Representative Amount.

(c) *Canadian Dollar.*

(i) "CAD-BA-ISDD" means that the rate for a Reset Date will be the rate for Canadian Dollar bankers acceptances for a period of the Designated Maturity which appears on the Reuters Screen ISDD Page as of 10:00 a.m., Toronto time, on that Reset Date. If such rate does not appear on the Reuters Screen ISDD Page, the rate for that Reset Date will be determined as if the parties had specified "CAD-BA-Reference Banks" as the applicable Floating Rate Option.

(ii) "CAD-BA-Reference Banks" means that the rate for a Reset Date will be determined on the basis of the arithmetic mean of the bid rates of the Reference Banks for Canadian Dollar bankers acceptances for a period of the Designated Maturity for settlement on that Reset Date and in a Representative Amount accepted by the Reference Banks as of 10:00 a.m., Toronto time, on that Reset Date. The Calculation Agent will request the principal Toronto office of each of the Reference Banks to provide a quotation of its rate.

(iii) "CAD-TBILL-ISDD" means that the rate for a Reset Date will be the rate for Government of Canada Treasury bills for a period of the Designated Maturity which appears on the Reuters Screen ISDD Page as of 10:00 a.m., Toronto time, on that Reset Date. If such rate does not appear on the Reuters Screen ISDD Page, the rate for that Reset Date will be determined as if the parties had specified "CAD-TBILL-Reference Banks" as the applicable Floating Rate Option.

(iv) "CAD-TBILL-Reference Banks" means that the rate for a Reset Date will be determined on the basis of the arithmetic mean of the secondary market bid rates of the Reference Banks as of 10:00 a.m., Toronto time, on that Reset Date for the issue of current Government of Canada Treasury bills with a remaining maturity closest to the Designated Maturity. The Calculation Agent will request the principal Toronto office of each of the Reference Banks to provide a quotation of its rate.

(d) *Deutsche Mark.*

(i) "DEM-LIBOR-ISDA" means that the rate for a Reset Date will be the rate for deposits in Deutsche Marks for a period of the Designated Maturity which appears on the Reuters Screen ISDA Page as of 11:00 a.m., London time, on the day that is two London Banking Days preceding that Reset Date. If such rate does not appear on the Reuters Screen ISDA Page, the rate for that Reset Date will be determined as if the parties had specified "DEM-LIBOR-Reference Banks" as the applicable Floating Rate Option.

(ii) "DEM-LIBOR-BBA" means that the rate for a Reset Date will be the rate for deposits in Deutsche Marks for a period of the Designated Maturity which appears on the Telerate Page 3750 as of 11:00 a.m., London time, on the day that is two London Banking Days preceding that Reset Date. If such rate does not appear on the Telerate Page 3750, the rate for that Reset Date will be determined as if the parties had specified "DEM-LIBOR-Reference Banks" as the applicable Floating Rate Option.

(iii) "DEM-LIBOR-Reference Banks" means that the rate for a Reset Date will be determined on the basis of the rates at which deposits in Deutsche Marks are offered by the Reference Banks at approximately 11:00 a.m., London time, on the day that is two London Banking Days preceding that Reset Date to prime banks in the London interbank market for a period of the Designated Maturity commencing on that Reset Date and in a Representative Amount. The Calculation Agent will request the principal London office of each of the Reference Banks to provide a quotation of its rate. If at least two quotations are provided, the rate for that Reset Date will be the arithmetic mean of the quotations. If fewer than two quotations are provided as requested, the rate for that Reset Date will be the arithmetic mean of the rates quoted by major banks in Frankfurt, selected by the Calculation Agent, at approximately 11:00 a.m., Frankfurt time, on that Reset Date for loans in Deutsche Marks to leading European banks for a period of the Designated Maturity commencing on that Reset Date and in a Representative Amount.

(iv) "DEM-FIBOR-ISDB" means that the rate for a Reset Date will be the rate for deposits in Deutsche Marks for a period of the Designated Maturity which appears on the Reuters Screen ISDB Page as of 12:00 noon, Frankfurt time, on that Reset Date. If such rate does not appear on the Reuters Screen ISDB Page, the rate for that Reset Date will be determined as if the parties had specified "DEM-FIBOR-Reference Banks" as the applicable Floating Rate Option.

(v) "DEM-FIBOR-Reference Banks" means that the rate for a Reset Date will be determined on the basis of the rates at which deposits in Deutsche Marks are offered by the Reference Banks at approximately 12:00 noon, Frankfurt time, on that Reset Date to prime banks in the Frankfurt interbank market for a period of the Designated Maturity commencing on that Reset Date and in a Representative Amount. The Calculation Agent will request the principal Frankfurt office of each of the Reference Banks to provide a quotation of its rate. If at least two quotations are provided, the rate for that Reset Date will be the arithmetic mean of the quotations. If fewer than two quotations are provided as requested, the rate for that Reset Date will be the arithmetic mean of the rates quoted by major banks in Frankfurt, selected by the Calculation Agent, at approximately 12:00 noon, Frankfurt time, on that Reset Date for loans in Deutsche Marks to leading European banks for a period of the Designated Maturity commencing on that Reset Date and in a Representative Amount.

(e) *Dutch Guilder.*

(i) "NLG-AIBOR-ISDB" means that the rate for a Reset Date will be the rate for deposits in Dutch Guilders for a period of the Designated Maturity which appears on the Reuters Screen ISDB Page as of 11:00 a.m., Amsterdam time, on the day that is two Amsterdam Banking Days preceding that Reset Date. If such rate does not appear on the Reuters Screen ISDB Page, the rate for that Reset Date will be determined as if the parties had specified "NLG-AIBOR-Reference Banks" as the applicable Floating Rate Option.

(ii) "NLG-AIBOR-Reference Banks" means that the rate for a Reset Date will be determined on the basis of the rates at which deposits in Dutch Guilders are offered by the Reference Banks at approximately 11:00 a.m., Amsterdam time, on the day that is two Amsterdam Banking Days preceding that Reset Date to prime banks in the Amsterdam interbank market for a period of the Designated Maturity commencing on that Reset Date and in a Representative Amount. The Calculation Agent will request the principal Amsterdam office of each of the Reference Banks to provide a quotation of its rate. If at least two quotations are provided, the rate for that Reset Date will be the arithmetic mean of the quotations. If fewer than two quotations are provided as requested, the rate for that Reset Date will be the arithmetic mean of the rates quoted by major banks in Amsterdam, selected by the Calculation Agent, at approximately 11:00 a.m., Amsterdam time, on that Reset Date for loans in Dutch Guilders to leading European banks for a period of the Designated Maturity commencing on that Reset Date and in a Representative Amount.

(f) *European Currency Unit.*

(i)   "XEU-LIBOR-ISDA" means that the rate for a Reset Date will be the rate for deposits in European Currency Units for a period of the Designated Maturity which appears on the Reuters Screen ISDA Page as of 11:00 a.m., London time, on the day that is two London Banking Days preceding that Reset Date. If such rate does not appear on the Reuters Screen ISDA Page, the rate for that Reset Date will be determined as if the parties had specified "XEU-LIBOR-Reference Banks" as the applicable Floating Rate Option.

(ii) "XEU-LIBOR-BBA" means that the rate for a Reset Date will be the rate for deposits in European Currency Units for a period of the Designated Maturity which appears on the Telerate Page 3750 as of 11:00 a.m., London time, on the day that is two London Banking Days preceding that Reset Date. If such rate does not appear on the Telerate Page 3750, the rate for that Reset Date will be determined as if the parties had specified "XEU-LIBOR-Reference Banks" as the applicable Floating Rate Option.

(iii) "XEU-LIBOR-Reference Banks" means that the rate for a Reset Date will be determined on the basis of the rates at which deposits in European Currency Units are offered by the Reference Banks at approximately 11:00 a.m., London time, on the day that is two London Banking Days preceding that Reset Date to prime banks in the London interbank market for a period of the Designated Maturity commencing on that Reset Date and in a Representative Amount. The Calculation Agent will request the principal London office of each of the Reference Banks to provide a quotation of its rate. If at least two quotations are provided, the rate for that Reset Date will be the arithmetic mean of the quotations. If fewer than two quotations are provided as requested, the rate for that Reset Date will be the arithmetic mean of the rates quoted by major banks in Luxembourg, selected by the Calculation Agent, at approximately 11:00 a.m., Luxembourg time, on that Reset Date for loans in European Currency Units to leading European banks for a period of the Designated Maturity commencing on that Reset Date and in a Representative Amount.

(iv) "XEU-PIBOR-ISDB" means that the rate for a Reset Date will be the rate for deposits in European Currency Units for a period of the Designated Maturity which appears on the Reuters Screen ISDB Page as of 11:00 a.m., Paris time, on the day that is two Paris Banking Days preceding that Reset Date. If such rate does not appear on the Reuters Screen ISDB Page, the rate for that Reset Date will be determined as if the parties had specified "XEU-PIBOR-Reference Banks" as the applicable Floating Rate Option.

(v) "XEU-PIBOR-AFB" means that the rate for a Reset Date will be the rate for deposits in European Currency Units for a period of the Designated Maturity which appears on the Telerate Page 20041 as of 11:00 a.m., Paris time, on the day that is two Paris Banking Days preceding that Reset Date. If such rate does not appear on the Telerate Page 20041, the rate for that Reset Date will be determined as if the parties had specified "XEU-PIBOR-Reference Banks" as the applicable Floating Rate Option.

(vi) "XEU-PIBOR-Reference Banks" means that the rate for a Reset Date will be determined on the basis of the rates at which deposits in European Currency Units are offered by the Reference Banks at approximately 11:00 a.m., Paris time, on the day that is two Paris Banking Days preceding that Reset Date to prime banks in the Paris interbank market for a period of the Designated Maturity commencing on that Reset Date and in a Representative Amount. The Calculation Agent will request the principal Paris office of each of the Reference Banks to provide a quotation of its rate. If at least two quotations are provided, the rate for that Reset Date will be the arithmetic mean of the quotations. If fewer than two quotations are provided as requested, the rate for that Reset Date will be the arithmetic mean of the rates quoted by major banks in Paris, selected by the Calculation Agent, at approximately 11:00 a.m., Paris time, on that Reset Date for loans in European Currency Units to leading European banks for a period of the Designated Maturity commencing on that Reset Date and in a Representative Amount.

(g) *French Franc.*

(i) "FRF-PIBOR-ISDB" means that the rate for a Reset Date will be the rate for deposits in French Francs for a period of the Designated Maturity which appears on the Reuters Screen ISDB Page as of 11:00 a.m., Paris time, on the day that is one Paris Banking Day preceding that Reset Date. If such rate does not appear on the Reuters Screen ISDB Page, the rate for that Reset Date will be determined as if the parties had specified "FRF-PIBOR-Reference Banks" as the applicable Floating Rate Option.

(ii) "FRF-PIBOR-AFB" means that the rate for a Reset Date will be the rate for deposits in French Francs for a period of the Designated Maturity which appears on the Telerate Page 20041 as of 11:00 a.m., Paris time, on the day that is one Paris Banking Day preceding that Reset Date. If such rate does not appear on the Telerate Page 20041, the rate for that

Reset Date will be determined as if the parties had specified "FRF-PIBOR-Reference Banks" as the applicable Floating Rate Option.

(iii) "FRF-PIBOR-Reference Banks" means that the rate for a Reset Date will be determined on the basis of the rates at which deposits in French Francs are offered by the Reference Banks at approximately 11:00 a.m., Paris time, on the day that is one Paris Banking Day preceding that Reset Date to prime banks in the Paris interbank market for a period of the Designated Maturity commencing on that Reset Date and in a Representative Amount. The Calculation Agent will request the principal Paris office of each of the Reference Banks to provide a quotation of its rate. If at least two quotations are provided, the rate for that Reset Date will be the arithmetic mean of the quotations. If fewer that two quotations are provided as requested, the rate for that Reset Date will be the arithmetic mean of the rates quoted by major banks in Paris, selected by the Calculation Agent, at approximately 11:00 a.m., Paris time, on that Reset Date for loans in French Francs to leading European banks for a period of the Designated Maturity commencing on that Reset Date and in a Representative Amount.

(h) *Hong Kong Dollar.*

(i) "HKD-HIBOR-ISDC" means that the rate for a Reset Date will be the rate for deposits in Hong Kong Dollars for a period of the Designated Maturity which appears on the Reuters Screen ISDC Page as of 11:00 a.m., Hong Kong time, on the Reset Date. If such rate does not appear on the Reuters Screen ISDC Page, the rate for that Reset Date will be determined as if the parties had specified "HKD-HIBOR-Reference Banks" as the applicable Floating Rate Option.

(ii) "HKD-HIBOR-HKAB" means that the rate for a Reset Date will be the rate for deposits in Hong Kong Dollars for a period of the Designated Maturity which appears on the Telerate Page 9898 as of 11:00 a.m., Hong Kong time, on the Reset Date. If such rate does not appear on the Telerate Page 9898, the rate for that Reset Date will be determined as if the parties had specified "HKD-HIBOR-Reference Banks" as the applicable Floating Rate Option.

(iii) "HKD-HIBOR-Reference Banks" means that the rate for a Reset Date will be determined on the basis of the rates at which deposits in Hong Kong Dollars are offered by the Reference Banks at approximately 11:00 a.m., Hong Kong time, on the Reset Date to prime banks in the Hong Kong interbank market for a period of the Designated Maturity commencing on that Reset Date and in a Representative Amount. The Calculation Agent will request the principal Hong Kong office of each of the Reference Banks to provide a quotation of its rate. If at least two quotations are provided, the rate for that Reset Date will be the arithmetic mean of the quotations. If fewer than two quotations are provided as requested, the rate for that Reset Date will be the arithmetic mean of the rates quoted by major banks in Hong Kong, selected by the Calculation Agent, at approximately 11:00 a.m., Hong Kong time, on that Reset Date for loans in Hong Kong Dollars to leading European banks for a period of the Designated Maturity commencing on that Reset Date and in a Representative Amount.

(i) *Italian Lire.*

(i) "ITL-LIBOR-Reference Banks" means that the rate for a Reset Date will be determined on the basis of the rates at which deposits in Italian Lire are offered by the Reference Banks at approximately 11:00 a.m., London time, on the day that is two London Banking Days preceding that Reset Date to prime banks in the London interbank market for a period of the Designated Maturity commencing on that Reset Date and in a Representative Amount. The Calculation Agent will request the principal London office of each of the Reference Banks to provide a quotation of its rate. If at least two such quotations are provided, the rate for that Reset Date will be the arithmetic mean of the quotations. If fewer than two quotations are provided as requested, the rate for that Reset Date will be the arithmetic mean of the rates quoted by major banks in Rome, selected by the Calculation Agent, at approximately 11:00 a.m., Rome time, on that Reset Date for loans in Italian Lire to leading European banks for a period of the Designated Maturity commencing on that Reset Date and in a Representative Amount.

(j) *Luxembourg Franc.*

(i) "LUF-LUXIBOR-ISDB" means that the rate for a Reset Date will be the rate for deposits in Luxembourg Francs for a period of the Designated Maturity which appears on the Reuters Screen ISDB Page as of 11:00 a.m., Luxembourg time, on the day that is two Luxembourg Banking Days preceding that Reset Date. If such rate does not appear on the Reuters Screen ISDB Page, the rate for that Reset Date will be determined as if the parties had specified "LUF-LUXIBOR-Reference Banks" as the applicable Floating Rate Option.

(ii) "LUF-LUXIBOR-Reference Banks" means that the rate for a Reset Date will be determined on the basis of the rates at which deposits in Financial Luxembourg Francs are offered by the Reference Banks at approximately 11:00 a.m., Luxembourg time, on the day that is two Luxembourg Banking Days preceding that Reset Date to prime banks in the Luxembourg interbank market for a period of the Designated Maturity commencing on that Reset Date and in a Representative Amount. The Calculation Agent will request the principal Luxembourg office of each of the Reference Banks to provide a quotation of its rate. If at least two quotations are provided, the rate for that Reset Date will be the arithmetic mean of the quotations. If fewer than two quotations are provided as requested, the rate for that Reset Date will be the arithmetic mean of the rates quoted by major banks in Luxembourg, selected by the Calculation Agent, at approximately 11:00 a.m., Luxembourg time, on that Reset Date for loans in Financial Luxembourg Francs to leading European banks for a period of the Designated Maturity commencing on that Reset Date and in a Representative Amount.

(iii) "COMLUF-LUXIBOR-Reference Banks" means that the rate for a Reset Date will be determined on the basis of the rates at which deposits in Commercial Luxembourg Francs are offered by the Reference Banks at approximately 11:00 a.m., Luxembourg time, on the day that is two Luxembourg Banking Days preceding that Reset Date to prime banks in the Luxembourg interbank market for a period of the Designated Maturity commencing on that Reset Date and in a Representative Amount. The Calculation Agent will request the principal Luxembourg office of each of the Reference Banks to provide a quotation of its rate. If at least two quotations are provided, the rate for that Reset Date will be the arithmetic mean of the quotations. If fewer than two quotations are provided as requested, the rate for that Reset Date will be the arithmetic mean of the rates quoted by major banks in Luxembourg, selected by the Calculation Agent, at approximately 11:00 a.m., Luxembourg time, on that Reset Date for loans in Commercial Luxembourg Francs to leading European banks for a period of the Designated Maturity commencing on that Reset Date and in a Representative Amount.

(k) *New Zealand Dollar.*

(i) "NZD-BBR-ISDC" means that the rate for a Reset Date will be the rate for New Zealand Dollar bills of exchange for a period of the Designated Maturity which appears on the Reuters Screen ISDC Page as of 11:00 a.m., Wellington time, on that Reset Date. If such rate does not appear on the Reuters Screen ISDC Page, the rate for that Reset Date will be determined as if the parties had specified "NZD-BBR-Reference Banks" as the applicable Floating Rate Option.

(ii) "NZD-BBR-Telerate" means that the rate for a Reset Date will be the fixed mid rate for New Zealand Dollar bills of exchange for a period of the Designated Maturity which appears on the Telerate Page 2484 as of 11:00 a.m., Wellington time, on that Reset Date. If such rate does not appear on the Telerate Page 2484, the Reset Date will be determined as if the parties had specified "NZD-BBR-Reference Banks" as the applicable Floating Rate Option.

(iii) "NZD-BBR-Reference Banks" means that the rate for a Reset Date will be determined on the basis of the average of the mean bid and offered rates of each of the Reference Banks for New Zealand Dollar bills of exchange for a period of the Designated Maturity for settlement on that Reset Date and in a Representative Amount at approximately 11:00 a.m., Wellington time, on that Reset Date. The Calculation Agent will request the principal Wellington office of each of the Reference Banks to provide a quotation of its rates.

(l) *Sterling.*

(i) "GBP-LIBOR-ISDA" means that the rate for a Reset Date will be the rate for deposits in Sterling for a period of the Designated Maturity which appears on the Reuters Screen ISDA Page as of 11:00 a.m., London time, on that Reset Date. If such rate does not appear on the Reuters Screen ISDA Page, the rate for that Reset Date will be determined as if the parties had specified "GBP-LIBOR-Reference Banks" as the applicable Floating Rate Option.

(ii) "GBP-LIBOR-BBA" means that the rate for a Reset Date will be the rate for deposits in Sterling for a period of the Designated Maturity which appears on the Telerate Page 3750 as of 11:00 a.m., London time, on that Reset Date. If such rate does not appear on the Telerate Page 3750, the rate for that Reset Date will be determined as if the parties had specified "GBP-LIBOR-Reference Banks" as the applicable Floating Rate Option.

(iii) "GBP-LIBOR-Reference Banks" means that the rate for a Reset Date will be determined on the basis of the rates at which deposits in Sterling are offered by the Reference Banks at approximately 11:00 a.m., London time, on that Reset Date to prime banks in the London interbank market for a period of the Designated Maturity commencing on that Reset Date and in a Representative Amount. The Calculation Agent will request the principal London office of each of the Reference Banks to provide a quotation of its rate. If at least two quotations are provided, the rate for that Reset Date will be the arithmetic mean of the quotations. If fewer than two quotations are provided as requested, the rate for that Reset Date will be the arithmetic mean of the rates quoted by major banks in London, selected by the Calculation Agent, at approximately 11:00 a.m., London time, on that Reset Date for loans in Sterling to leading European banks for a period of the Designated Maturity commencing on that Reset Date and in a Representative Amount.

(m) *Swiss Franc.*

(i) "CHF-LIBOR-ISDA" means that the rate for a Reset Date will be the rate for deposits in Swiss Francs for a period of the Designated Maturity which appears on the Reuters Screen ISDA Page as of 11:00 a.m., London time, on the day that is two London Banking Days preceding that Reset Date. If such rate does not appear on the Reuters Screen ISDA Page, the rate for that Reset Date will be determined as if the parties had specified "CHF-LIBOR-Reference Banks" as the applicable Floating Rate Option.

(ii) "CHF-LIBOR-BBA" means that the rate for a Reset Date will be the rate for deposits in Swiss Francs for a period of the Designated Maturity which appears on the Telerate Page 3750 as of 11:00 a.m., London time, on the day that is two London Banking Days preceding that Reset Date. If such rate does not appear on the Telerate Page 3750, the rate for that Reset Date will be determined as if the parties had specified "CHF-LIBOR-Reference Banks" as the applicable Floating Rate Option.

(iii) "CHF-LIBOR-Reference Banks" means that the rate for a Reset Date will be determined on the basis of the rates at which deposits in Swiss Francs are offered by the Reference Banks at approximately 11:00 a.m., London time, on the day that is two London Banking Days preceding that Reset Date to prime banks in the London interbank market for a period of the Designated Maturity commencing on that Reset Date and in a

Representative Amount. The Calculation Agent will request the principal London office of each of the Reference Banks to provide a quotation of its rate. If at least two quotations are provided, the rate for that Reset Date will be the arithmetic mean of the quotations. If fewer than two quotations are provided as requested, the rate for that Reset Date will be the arithmetic mean of the rates quoted by major banks in Zurich, selected by the Calculation Agent, at approximately 11:00 a.m., Zurich time, on that Reset Date for loans in Swiss Francs to leading European banks for a period of the Designated Maturity commencing on that Reset Date and in a Representative Amount.

(n) *U.S. Dollar.*

(i) "USD-LIBOR-ISDA" means that the rate for a Reset Date will be the rate for deposits in U.S. Dollars for a period of the Designated Maturity which appears on the Reuters Screen ISDA Page as of 11:00 a.m., London time, on the day that is two London Banking Days preceding that Reset Date. If such rate does not appear on the Reuters Screen ISDA Page, the rate for that Reset Date will be determined as if the parties had specified "USD-LIBOR-Reference Banks" as the applicable Floating Rate Option.

(ii) "USD-LIBOR-BBA" means that the rate for a Reset Date will be the rate for deposits in U.S. Dollars for a period of the Designated Maturity which appears on the Telerate Page 3750 as of 11:00 a.m., London time, on the day that is two London Banking Days preceding that Reset Date. If such rate does not appear on the Telerate Page 3750, the rate for that Reset Date will be determined as if the parties had specified "USD-LIBOR-Reference Banks" as the applicable Floating Rate Option.

(iii) "USD-LIBOR-LIBO" means that the rate in respect of a Reset Date will be determined on the basis of the offered rates for deposits in U.S. Dollars for a period of the Designated Maturity which appear on the Reuters Screen LIBO Page as of 11:00 a.m., London time, on the day that is two London Banking Days preceding that Reset Date. If at least two rates appear on the Reuters Screen LIBO Page, the rate for that Reset Date will be the arithmetic mean of such rates. If fewer than two rates appear, the rate for that Reset Date will be determined as if the parties had specified "USD-LIBOR-Reference Banks" as the applicable Floating Rate Option.

(iv) "USD-LIBOR-Reference Banks" means that the rate for a Reset Date will be determined on the basis of the rates at which deposits in U.S. Dollars are offered by the Reference Banks at approximately 11:00 a.m., London time, on the day that is two London Banking Days preceding that Reset Date to prime banks in the London interbank market for a period of the Designated Maturity commencing on that Reset Date and in a Representative Amount. The Calculation Agent will request the principal London office of each of the Reference Banks to provide a quotation of its rate. If at least two such quotations are provided, the rate for that Reset Date will be the arithmetic mean of the quotations. If fewer than two quotations are provided as requested, the rate for that Reset Date will be the arithmetic mean of the rates quoted by major banks in New York City, selected by the Calculation Agent, at approximately 11:00 a.m., New York City time, on that Reset Date for loans in U.S. Dollars to leading European banks for a period of the Designated Maturity commencing on that Reset Date and in a Representative Amount.

(v) "USD-Prime-H.15" means that the rate for a Reset Date will be the rate set forth in H.15(519) for that day opposite the caption "Bank Prime Loan". If on the Calculation Date for a Calculation Period such rate for a Reset Date in that Calculation Period is not yet published in H.15(519), the rate for that Reset Date will be the arithmetic mean of the rates of interest publicly announced by each bank that appears on the Reuters Screen NYMF Page as such bank's prime rate or base lending rate as in effect for that Reset Date as quoted on the Reuters Screen NYMF Page on that Reset Date or, if fewer than four rates appear on the Reuters Screen NYMF Page for that Reset Date, the rate determined as if the parties had specified "USD-Prime-Reference Banks" as the applicable Floating Rate Option.

(vi) "USD-Prime-Reference Banks" means that the rate for a Reset Date will be the arithmetic mean of the rates of interest publicly announced by each Reference Bank as its U.S. Dollar prime rate or base lending rate as in effect for that day. Each change in the prime rate or base lending rate of any bank so announced by such bank will be effective as of the effective date of the announcement or, if no effective date is specified, as of the date of the announcement.

(vii) "USD-TBILL-H.15" means that the rate for a Reset Date on which United States Treasury bills are auctioned will be the rate set forth in H.15(519) for that day opposite the Designated Maturity under the caption "U.S. Government Securities/Treasury Bills/Auction Average (Investment)". If on the Calculation Date for a Calculation Period United States Treasury bills of the Designated Maturity have been auctioned on a Reset Date during that Calculation Period but such rate for such Reset Date is not yet published in H.15(519), the rate for that Reset Date will be the Bond Equivalent Yield of the auction average rate for these Treasury bills as announced by the United States Department of the Treasury. If United States Treasury bills of the Designated Maturity are not auctioned during any period of seven consecutive calendar days ending on and including any Friday and a Reset Date would have occurred if such Treasury bills had been auctioned during that seven-day period, a Reset Date will be deemed to have occurred on the day during that seven-day period on which such Treasury bills would have been auctioned in accordance with the usual practices of the United States Department of the Treasury, and the rate for that Reset Date will be determined as if the parties had specified "USD-TBILL-Secondary Market" as the applicable Floating Rate Option (unless it is indicated for the Swap Transaction that weeks in which United States Treasury bills of the Designated Maturity are not auctioned will be ignored, in which case there will not be any Reset Date during that seven-day period).

(viii) "USD-TBILL-Secondary Market" means that the rate for a Reset Date will be the Bond Equivalent Yield of the rate set forth in H.15(519) for that day opposite the Designated Maturity under the caption "U.S. Government Securities/Treasury Bills/Secondary Market". If on the Calculation Date for a Calculation Period such rate for a Reset Date in that Calculation Period is not yet published in H.15(519), the rate for that Reset Date will be the Bond Equivalent Yield of the arithmetic mean of the secondary market bid rates of the Reference Dealers as of approximately 3:30 p.m., New York City time, on that day for the issue of United States Treasury bills with a remaining maturity closest to the Designated Maturity.

(ix) "USD-CD-H.15" means that the rate for a Reset Date will be the rate set forth in H.15(519) for that day opposite the Designated Maturity under the caption "CDs (Secondary Market)". If on the Calculation Date for a Calculation Period such rate for a Reset Date in that Calculation Period is not yet published in H.15(519), the rate for that Reset Date will be the rate set forth in Composite 3:30 P.M. Quotations for U.S. Government Securities for that day for the Designated Maturity under the caption "Certificates of Deposit". If on the Calculation Date for a Calculation Period the appropriate rate for a Reset Date in that Calculation Period is not yet published in either H.15(519) or Composite 3:30 P.M. Quotations for U.S. Government Securities, the rate for that Reset Date will be determined as if the parties had specified "USD-CD-Reference Dealers" as the applicable Floating Rate Option.

(x) "USD-CD-Reference Dealers" means that the rate for a Reset Date will be the arithmetic mean of the secondary market offered rates of the Reference Dealers as of 10:00 a.m., New York City time, on that day for negotiable U.S. Dollar certificates of deposit of major United States money market banks with a remaining maturity closest to the Designated Maturity and in a Representative Amount.

(xi) "USD-CP-H.15" means that the rate for a Reset Date will be the Money Market Yield of the rate set forth in H.15(519) for that day opposite the Designated Maturity under the caption "Commercial Paper". If on the Calculation Date for a Calculation Period such rate for a Reset Date in that Calculation Period is not yet published in H.15(519), the rate for that Reset Date will be the Money Market Yield of the rate set forth in Composite 3:30 P.M. Quotations for U.S. Government Securities for that day in respect of the Designated Maturity under the caption "Commercial Paper" (with a Designated Maturity of one month or three months being deemed to be equivalent to a Designated Maturity of 30 days or 90 days, respectively). If on the Calculation Date for a Calculation Period the appropriate rate for a Reset Date in that Calculation Period is not yet published in either H.15(519) or Composite 3:30 P.M. Quotations for U.S. Government Securities, the rate for that Reset Date will be determined as if the parties had specified "USD-CP-Reference Dealers" as the applicable Floating Rate Option.

(xii) "USD-CP-ISDD" means that the rate for a Reset Date will be the Money Market Yield of the rate for U.S. Dollar commercial paper for a period of the Designated Maturity which appears on the Reuters Screen

ISDD Page as of 4:00 p.m., New York City time, on that Reset Date. If on the Calculation Date for a Calculation Period the appropriate rate for a Reset Date in that Calculation Period does not appear on the Reuters Screen ISDD Page, the rate for that Reset Date will be determined as if the parties had specified "USD-CP-Reference Dealers" as the applicable Floating Rate Option.

(xiii) "USD-CP-Reference Dealers" means that the rate for a Reset Date will be the Money Market Yield of the arithmetic mean of the offered rates of the Reference Dealers as of 11:00 a.m., New York City time, on that day for U.S. Dollar commercial paper of the Designated Maturity placed for industrial issuers whose bond rating is "Aa" or the equivalent from a nationally recognized rating agency.

(xiv) "USD-Federal Funds-H.15" means that the rate for a Reset Date will be the rate set forth in H.15(519) for that day opposite the caption "Federal Funds (Effective)". If on the Calculation Date for a Calculation Period such rate for a Reset Date in that Calculation Period is not yet published in H.15(519), the rate for that Reset Date will be the rate set forth in Composite 3:30 P.M. Quotations for U.S. Government Securities for that day under the caption "Federal Funds/Effective Rate". If on the Calculation Date for a Calculation Period the appropriate rate for a Reset Date in that Calculation Period is not yet published in either H.15(519) or Composite 3:30 P.M. Quotations for U.S. Government Securities, the rate for that Reset Date will be determined as if the parties had specified "USD-Federal Funds-Reference Dealers" as the applicable Floating Rate Option.

(xv) "USD-Federal Funds-Reference Dealers" means that the rate for a Reset Date will be the arithmetic mean of the rates for the last transaction in overnight U.S. Dollar Federal funds arranged by each Reference Dealer prior to 9:00 a.m., New York City time, on that day.

(xvi) "USD-BA-H.15" means that the rate for a Reset Date will be the Money Market Yield of the rate set forth in H.15(519) for that day opposite the Designated Maturity under the caption "Bankers Acceptances (Top Rated)". If on the Calculation Date for a Calculation Period such rate for a Reset Date in that Calculation Period is not yet published in H.15(519), the rate for that Reset Date will be determined as if the parties had specified "USD-BA-Reference Dealers" as the applicable Floating Rate Option.

(xvii) "USD-BA-Reference Dealers" means that the rate for a Reset Date will be the Money Market Yield of the arithmetic mean of the offered rates of the Reference Dealers as of the close of business in New York City on that day for top-rated U.S. Dollar bankers acceptances of the Designated Maturity and in a Representative Amount.

(xviii) "USD-TIBOR-ISDC" means that the rate for a Reset Date will be the rate for deposits in U.S. Dollars for a period of the Designated Maturity which appears on the Reuters Screen ISDC Page as of 11:00 a.m.,Tokyo time, on the day that is two Tokyo Banking Days preceding that Reset Date. If such rate does not appear on the Reuters Screen ISDCPage, the rate for that Reset Date will be determined as if the parties had specified "USD-TIBOR-Reference Banks" as the applicable Floating Rate Option.

(xix) "USD-TIBOR-Reference Banks" means that the rate for a Reset Date will be determined on the basis of the rates at which deposits in U.S. Dollars are offered by the Reference Banks at approximately 11:00 a.m., Tokyo time, on the day that is two Tokyo Banking Days preceding that Reset Date to prime banks in the Tokyo interbank market for a period of the Designated Maturity commencing on that Reset Date and in a Representative Amount. The Calculation Agent will request the principal Tokyo office of each of the Reference Banks to provide a quotation of its rate. If at least two such quotations are provided, the rate for that Reset Date will be the arithmetic mean of the quotations. If fewer than two quotations are provided as requested, the rate for that Reset Date will be the arithmetic mean of the rates quoted by major banks in New York City, selected by the Calculation Agent, at approximately 11:00 a.m., New York City time, on that Reset Date for loans in U.S. Dollars to leading European banks for a period of the Designated Maturity commencing on that Reset Date and in a Representative Amount.

(o) *Yen.*

(i) "JPY-LIBOR-ISDA" means that the rate for a Reset Date will be the rate for deposits in Yen for a period of the Designated Maturity which appears on the Reuters Screen ISDA Page as of 11:00 a.m., London time, on the day that is two London Banking Days preceding that Reset Date. If such rate does not appear on the Reuters Screen ISDA Page, the rate for that Reset Date will be determined as if the parties had specified "JPY-LIBOR-Reference Banks" as the applicable Floating Rate Option.

(ii) "JPY-LIBOR-BBA" means that the rate for a Reset Date will be the rate for deposits in Yen for a period of the Designated Maturity which appears on the Telerate Page 3750 as of 11:00 a.m., London time, on the day that is two London Banking Days preceding that Reset Date. If such rate does not appear on the Telerate Page 3750, the rate for that Reset Date will be determined as if the parties had specified "JPY-LIBOR-Reference Banks" as the applicable Floating Rate Option.

(iii) "JPY-LIBOR-Reference Banks" means that the rate for a Reset Date will be determined on the basis of the rates at which deposits in Yen are offered by the Reference Banks at approximately 11:00 a.m., London time, on the day that is two London Banking Days preceding that Reset Date to prime banks in the London interbank market for a period of the Designated Maturity commencing on that Reset Date and in a Representative Amount. The Calculation Agent will request the principal London office of each of the Reference Banks to provide a quotation of its rate. If at least two quotations are provided, the rate for that Reset Date will be the arithmetic mean of the quotations. If fewer than two quotations are provided as requested, the rate for that Reset Date will be the arithmetic mean of the rates quoted by major banks in Tokyo, selected by the Calculation Agent, at approximately 11:00 a.m., Tokyo time, on that Reset Date for loans in Yen to leading European banks for a period of the Designated Maturity commencing on that Reset Date and in a Representative Amount.

Section 7.2. Certain Published and Displayed Sources.

(a) "H.15(519)" means the weekly statistical release designated as such, or any successor publication, published by the Board of Governors of the Federal Reserve System.

(b) "Composite 3:30 P.M. Quotations for U.S. Government Securities" means the daily statistical release designated as such, or any successor publication, published by the Federal Reserve Bank of New York.

(c) "Reuters Screen ISDA Page" means the display designated as page "ISDA" on the Reuter Monitor Money Rates Service (or such other page as may replace the ISDA Page on that service for the purpose of displaying London interbank offered rates for Deutsche Mark, European Currency Unit, Sterling, Swiss Franc, U.S. Dollar or Yen deposits).

(d) "Reuters Screen ISDB Page" means the display designated as page "ISDB" on the Reuter Monitor Money Rates Service (or such other page as may replace the ISDB Page on that service for the purpose of displaying Brussels interbank offered rates for Belgian Franc deposits, Frankfurt interbank offered rates for Deutsche Mark deposits, Amsterdam interbank offered rates for Dutch Guilder deposits, Paris interbank offered rates for European Currency Unit and French Franc deposits or Luxembourg interbank offered rates for Luxembourg Franc deposits).

(e) "Reuters Screen ISDC Page" means the display designated as "ISDC" on the Reuter Monitor Money Rates Service (or such other page as may replace the ISDC Page on that service for the purpose of displaying Australian Dollar bank bill rates, Hong Kong interbank offered rates for Hong Kong Dollar deposits, New Zealand Dollar bank bill rates or Tokyo interbank offered rates for U.S. Dollar deposits).

(f) "Reuters Screen ISDD Page" means the display designated as "ISDD"on the Reuter Monitor Money Rates Service (or such other page as may replace the ISDD Page on that service for the purpose of displaying Canadian Dollar bankers acceptance rates, Government of Canada Treasury bill rates and U.S. Dollar commercial paper rates).

(g) "Reuters Screen LIBO Page" means the display designated as page "LIBO" on the Reuter Monitor Money Rates Service (or such other page as may replace the LIBO Page on that service for the purpose of displaying London interbank offered rates of major banks for U.S. Dollar deposits).

(h) "Reuters Screen NYMF Page" means the display designated as page "NYMF" on the Reuter Monitor Money Rates Service (or such other page as may replace the NYMF Page on that service for the purpose of displaying U.S. Dollar prime rates or base lending rates of major United States banks).

(i) "Telerate Page 2484" means the display designated as "Page 2484" on the Telerate Service (or such other page as may replace Page 2484 on that service for the purpose of displaying New Zealand Dollar bank bill settlement rates).

(j) "Telerate Page 3740" means the display designated as "Page 3740" on the Telerate Service (or such other page as may replace Page 3740 on that service or such other service as may be nominated by the British Bankers' Association as the information vendor for the purpose of displaying British Bankers' Association Interest Settlement Rates for Australian Dollar deposits).

(k) "Telerate Page 3750" means the display designated as "Page 3750" on the Telerate Service (or such other page as may replace Page 3750 on that service or such other service as may be nominated by the British Bankers' Association as the information vendor for the purpose of displaying British Bankers' Association Interest Settlement Rates for Deutsche Mark, U.S. Dollar, European Currency Unit, Sterling, Swiss Franc or Yen deposits).

(l) "Telerate Page 9898" means the display designated as "Page 9898" on the Telerate Service (or such other page as may replace Page 9898 on that service or such other service as may be nominated by the Hong Kong Association of Banks as the information vendor for the purpose of displaying Hong Kong Association of Banks Interest Settlement Rates for Hong Kong Dollar deposits).

(m) "Telerate Page 20041" means the display designated as "Page 20041" on the Telerate Service (or such page as may replace Page 20041 on that service or such other service as may be nominated by the Association Francaise des Banques as the information vendor for the purpose of displaying Paris interbank offered rates for European Currency Unit or French Franc deposits).

Section 7.3. Certain General Definitions Relating to Floating Rate Options.

(a) "Representative Amount" means, for purposes of any Floating Rate Option for which a Representative Amount is relevant, an amount that is representative for a single transaction in the relevant market at the relevant time.

(b) "Designated Maturity" means the period of time specified as such for a Swap Transaction or a party.

(c) "Reference Banks" means (i) for purposes of the "AUD-BBR" Floating Rate Option, four major banks in the Australian money market, (ii) for purposes of any "BIBOR" Floating Rate Option, four major banks in the Brussels interbank market, (iii) for purposes of the "CAD-BA" and "CAD-TBILL" Floating Rate Options, four major Canadian Schedule A chartered banks, (iv) for purposes of any "LIBOR" Floating Rate Option, four major banks in the London interbank market, (v) for purposes of the "DEM-FIBOR" Floating Rate Option, four major banks in the Frankfurt interbank market, (vi) for purposes of the "NLG-AIBOR" Floating Rate Option, four major banks in the Amsterdam interbank market, (vii) for purposes of any "PIBOR" Floating Rate Option, four major banks in the Paris interbank market, (viii) for purposes of the "HKD-HIBOR" Floating Rate Option, four major banks in the Hong Kong interbank market, (ix) for purposes of any "LUXIBOR" Floating Rate Option, four major banks in the Luxembourg interbank market, (x) for purposes of the "NZD-BBR" Floating Rate Option, four major banks in the New Zealand money market, (xi) for purposes of the "USD-TIBOR" Floating Rate Option, four major banks in the Tokyo interbank market and (xii) for purposes of the "USD-Prime" Floating Rate Option, three major banks in New York City, in each case selected by the Calculation Agent or specified for the Swap Transaction.

(d) "Reference Dealers" means (i) for purposes of the "USD-TBILL" Floating Rate Option, three primary United States Government securities dealers in New York City, (ii) for purposes of the "USD-CD" Floating Rate Option, three leading nonbank dealers in negotiable U.S. Dollar certificates of deposit in New York City, (iii) for purposes of the "USD-CP" Floating Rate Option, three leading dealers of U.S. Dollar commercial paper in New York City, (iv) for purposes of the "USD-Federal Funds" Floating Rate Option, three leading brokers of U.S. Dollar Federal funds transactions in New York City and (v) for purposes of the "USD-BA" Floating Rate Option, three leading dealers of U.S. Dollar bankers acceptances in New York City, in each case selected by the Calculation Agent or specified for the Swap Transaction.

(e) "Bond Equivalent Yield" means, in respect of any security with a maturity of six months or less, the rate for which is quoted on a bank discount basis, a yield (expressed as a percentage) calculated in accordance with the following formula:

$$\text{Bond Equivalent Yield} = \frac{D \times N}{360 - (D \times M)} \times 100$$

where "D" refers to the per annum rate for the security, quoted on a bank discount basis and expressed as a decimal; "N" refers to 365 or 366, as the case may be, and "M" refers to, if the Designated Maturity approximately corresponds to the length of the Calculation Period for which the Bond Equivalent Yield is being calculated, the actual number of days in that Calculation Period and, otherwise, the actual number of days in the period from, and including, the applicable Reset Date to, but excluding, the day that numerically corresponds to that Reset Date (or, if there is not any such numerically corresponding day, the last day) in the calendar month that is the number of months corresponding to the Designated Maturity after the month in which that Reset Date occurred.

(f) "Money Market Yield" means, in respect of any security with a maturity of six months or less, the rate for which is quoted on a a bank discount basis, a yield (expressed as a percentage) calculated in accordance with the following formula:

$$\text{Money Market Yield} = \frac{D \times 360}{360 - (D \times M)} \times 100$$

where "D" refers to the per annum rate for a security, quoted on a bank discount basis and expressed as a decimal; and "M" refers to, if the Designated Maturity approximately corresponds to the length of the Calculation Period for which the Money Market Yield is being calculated, the actual number of days in that Calculation Period and, otherwise, the actual number of days in the period from, and including, the applicable Reset Date to, but excluding, the day that numerically corresponds to that Reset Date (or, if there is not any such numerically corresponding day, the last day) in the calendar month that is the number of months corresponding to the Designated Maturity after the month in which that Reset Date occurred.

Section 7.4 Corrections to Published and Displayed Rates. For purposes of determining the Relevant Rate for any day

(a) in any case where the Relevant Rate for a day is based on information obtained from the Reuter Monitor Money Rates Service or the Associated Press-Dow Jones Telerate Service, that Relevant Rate will be subject to the corrections, if any, to that information subsequently displayed by that source within one hour of the time when such rate is first displayed by such source;

(b) in any case where the Relevant Rate for a day is based on information obtained from H.15(519) or Composite 3:30 P.M. Quotations for U.S. Government Securities, that Relevant Rate will be subject to the corrections, if any, to that information subsequently published by that source within 30 days of that day;

(c) in any case where the Relevant Rate for a day is based on information obtained from Composite 3:30 P.M. Quotations for U.S. Government Securities, that Relevant Rate will be subject to correction based upon the applicable rate, if any, subsequently published in H.15(519) within 30 days of that day; and

(d) in the event that a Fixed Rate Payer or Floating Rate Payer for any Swap Transaction notifies the other party to the Swap Transaction of any correction referred to in subsections (a), (b) or (c) above no later than 15 days after the expiration of the one-hour or 30-day period referred to in such subsection, an appropriate amount will be payable as a result of such correction (whether such correction is made or such notice is given before or after the Termination Date of the Swap Transaction), together with interest on that amount at a rate per annum equal to the cost (without proof or evidence of any actual cost) to the relevant party (as certified by it) of funding that amount for the period from, and including, the day on which, based on such correction, a payment in the incorrect amount was first made to, but excluding, the day of payment of the refund or payment resulting from such correction.

ARTICLE 8

ROUNDING

All percentages resulting from any calculations referred to in these definitions and provisions will be rounded upwards, if necessary, to the next higher one hundred-thousandth of a percentage point (e.g., 9.876541% (or .09876541) being rounded to 9.87655% (or .0987655)), all U.S. Dollar amounts used in or resulting from such calculations will be rounded to the nearest cent (with one half cent being rounded up), and all amounts denominated in any other currency used in or resulting from such calculations will be rounded upwards to the next higher two decimal places in such currency.

ARTICLE 9

PAYMENTS

Section 9.1. Relating Payments to Calculation Periods. Unless otherwise provided for a Swap Transaction or a party, the Fixed Amount or Floating Amount applicable to a Payment Date will be the Fixed Amount or Floating Amount calculated with reference to the Calculation Period ending on, but excluding, the Period End Date that is (or is closest in time to) that Payment Date or, in the case of the final Calculation Period, ending on, but excluding, the Termination Date.

Section 9.2. Payments in European Currency Units After ECU Conversion Date. After the ECU Conversion Date, any obligation to make a payment in European Currency Units will be deemed to be an obligation to make a payment in the Selected Currency in the Equivalent Amount.

Section 9.3. Certain Definitions Relating to ECU Payments.

(a) "ECU Conversion Date" means the last day on which the European Currency Unit is used in the European Monetary System.

(b) "Selected Currency" means a currency selected by the Calculation Agent from among the Component Currencies and the U.S. Dollar in the event that the European Currency Unit is no longer used in the European Monetary System.

(c) "Component Currency", means any currency that, on the ECU Conversion Date, is a component currency of the European Currency Unit used in the European Monetary System.

(d) "Equivalent Amount" means, in respect of a Selected Currency, an amount determined by the Calculation Agent by adding the results obtained by converting the Component Amount of each Component Currency into U.S. Dollars at the Market Exchange Rate for converting that Component Currency into U.S. Dollars and then converting the sum of those U.S. Dollar amounts (unless the Selected Currency is the U.S. Dollar) into the Selected Currency at the Market Exchange Rate for converting U.S. Dollars into the Selected Currency.

(e) "Component Amount" means, in respect of a Component Currency, the number of units (including decimals) of that currency represented in one European Currency Unit on (i) the Valuation Date, if the European Currency Unit was used for the settlement of transactions by public institutions of or within the European Community on that date and (ii) if the European Currency Unit was not used for the settlement of transactions by public institutions of or

31

within the European Community on the Valuation Date, the last day on which the European Currency Unit was so used or the ECU Conversion Date, whichever is later.

(f) "Market Exchange Rate" means, in respect of any Component Currency, the arithmetic mean of the spot offered rates for that currency for cable transfers quoted at approximately 2:30 p.m., Luxembourg time, on the Valuation Date by three leading foreign exchange dealers, selected by the Calculation Agent, in (i) Brussels, if the currency is the Belgian Franc, (ii) Frankfurt, if the currency is the Deutsche Mark, (iii) Amsterdam, if the currency is the Dutch Guilder, (iv) Paris, if the currency is the French Franc, (v) Milan, if the currency is the Italian Lire, (vi) Luxembourg, if the currency is the Luxembourg Franc, (vii) London, if the currency is Sterling or the U.S. Dollar, and (viii) such other place as the Calculation Agent may select, if the currency is any other currency. In the event that quotations are not available for a currency as of the Valuation Date from any of the banks selected by the Calculation Agent for this purpose because foreign exchange markets are closed in the country of issue of the currency or for any other reason, the most recent direct quotations for that currency obtained by, or on behalf of, the Calculation Agent shall be used in computing the Equivalent Amount of the Selected Currency on the Valuation Date if those rates were prevailing in the country of issue not more than two Business Days before the Valuation Date. If the only rates available for such purpose are as of a date more than two Business Days before the Valuation Date, the Calculation Agent shall convert the Component Amount into U.S. Dollars or that amount into the Selected Currency on the basis of cross rates derived from the arithmetic mean or the spot offered quotations for such currencies prevailing at approximately 2:30 p.m., Luxembourg time, on the Valuation Date, as obtained by the Calculation Agent from one or more major banks, in a country other than the country of issue of such currency. For the purpose of determining a Market Exchange Rate, quotations should be obtained from the market in which a non-resident issuer of securities denominated in that currency would purchase that currency in order to make payments for the securities.

(g) "Valuation Date" means, in respect of any payments deemed to be payable in a Selected Currency, the day that is four Luxembourg Banking Days preceding the applicable Payment Date, Initial Exchange Date or Final Exchange Date.

EXHIBIT I

Sample Form of Letter Agreement or Telex

Heading for Letter

[Letterhead of Party A]

[Date]

Swap Transaction

[Name and Address of Party B]

Heading for Telex

Date:

To: [Name and Telex Number of Party B]

From: [Party A]

Re: Swap Transaction

Dear   :

The purpose of this [letter agreement/telex] is to set forth the terms and conditions of the Swap Transaction entered into between us on the Trade Date specified below (the "Swap Transaction"). This [letter agreement/telex] constitutes a "Confirmation" as referred to in the Interest Rate and Currency Exchange Agreement specified below.

The definitions and provisions contained in the 1987 Interest Rate and Currency Exchange Definitions (as published by the International Swap Dealers Association, Inc.) are incorporated into this Confirmation. In the event of any inconsistency between those definitions and provisions and this Confirmation, this Confirmation will govern.

1. This Confirmation supplements, forms part of, and is subject to, the Interest Rate and Currency Exchange Agreement dated as of [date] (the "Agreement") between you and us. All provisions contained in the Agreement govern this Confirmation except as expressly modified below.

2. The terms of the particular Swap Transaction to which this Confirmation relates are as follows:–

[Notional Amount:]

Trade Date:

Effective Date:

Termination Date:

Fixed Amounts:

    Fixed Rate Payer: [Party A/B]

    [Fixed Rate Payer Currency Amount:]

    Fixed Rate Payer Payment Dates [or   , subject to adjustment in
    Period End Dates, if Delayed Payment accordance with the [Following/
    or Early Payment   Modified Following/ Preceding]
    applies]:   Business Day convention

    Fixed Amount [or Fixed Rate and
    Fixed Rate Day Count Fraction]:

Floating Amounts:

    Floating Rate Payer: [Party B/A]

    [Floating Rate Payer Currency
    Amount:]

    Floating Rate Payer Payment Dates [or   , subject to adjustment in
    Period End Dates, if Delayed Payment accordance with the [Following/
    or Early Payment   Modified Following/ Preceding]
    applies]:   Business Day convention

    [Floating Rate for initial
    Calculation Period:]

    Floating Rate Option:

    Designated Maturity:

    Spread: [Plus/Minus   %] [None]

    Reset Dates:

    [Rate Cut-off Dates:]

    [Method of Averaging: Unweighted/Weighted Average
                           Rate]

    Compounding: [Applicable/Inapplicable]

    [Compounding Dates:]

[Initial Exchange:

    Initial Exchange Date:

    Fixed Rate Payer Initial Exchange Amount:

    Floating Rate Payer Initial Exchange Amount:

Final Exchange:

    Final Exchange Date:

    Fixed Rate Payer Final Exchange Amount:

    Floating Rate Payer Final Exchange Amount:]

[Business Days for [first currency]:
Business Days for [second currency]:]
Calculation Agent:

[3.   agrees to provide the following Credit Support Document [or agrees to provide the following in accordance with [specify Credit Support Document]:]

4. Account Details

Payments to Fixed Rate Payer:
    Account for payments in [first currency]:
    Account for payments in [second currency]:
Payments to Floating Rate Payer:
    Account for payments in [first currency]:
    Account for payments in [second currency]:

[5. Offices
(a) The Office of Fixed Rate Payer for the Swap Transaction is   ; and
(b) The Office of Floating Rate Payer for the Swap Transaction is   .]
[6. Broker/Arranger:]

Closing for Letter Agreement

    Please confirm that the foregoing correctly sets forth the terms of our agreement by executing the copy of this Confirmation enclosed for that purpose and returning it to us.

                                            Yours sincerely,
                                            [Party A]
                                            By: _____
                                                  Name:
                                                  Title:

Confirmed as of the date first written:
[Party B]
By: _____
      Name:
      Title:

Closing for Telex

    Please confirm that the foregoing correctly sets forth the terms of our agreement by a return telex to [Party A] substantially to the following effect:–
"Re:
    We acknowledge receipt of your telex dated [   ] with respect to the above-referenced Swap Transaction between [Party A] and [Party B] with an Effective Date of [   ] and a Termination Date of [   ] and confirm that such telex correctly sets forth the terms of our agreement relating to the Swap Transaction described therein. Very truly yours, [Party B], by [specify name and title of authorized officer]."

                                            Yours sincerely,
                                            [Party A]
                                            By: _____
                                                  Name:
                                                  Title:

INDEX OF TERMS

International Swap Dealers Association, Inc.

May 1989 Addendum to Schedule to
Interest Rate and Currency Exchange Agreement

Interest Rate Caps, Collars and Floors

(1) As used in this Agreement or in a Confirmation, (i) "Rate Protection Transaction" will mean any Swap Transaction that is identified in the related Confirmation as a Rate Protection Transaction, Rate Cap Transaction, Rate Floor Transaction or Rate Collar Transaction and (ii) "Specified Swap" means, notwithstanding Section 14 of this Agreement but subject to Part 1 of this Schedule, any rate swap, rate cap, rate floor, rate collar, currency exchange transaction, forward rate agreement, or other exchange or rate protection transaction, or any combination of such transactions or agreements or any option with respect to any such transaction now existing or hereafter entered into between one party to this Agreement (or any applicable Specified Entity) and the other party to this Agreement (or any applicable Specified Entity).

(2) Notwithstanding anything to the contrary in this Agreement or in any Interest Rate and Currency Exchange Definitions published by the International Swap Dealers Association, Inc. and incorporated in any Confirmation, the following provisions will apply with respect to a Rate Protection Transaction:

(a) the Floating Rate applicable to any Calculation Period will be (i) with respect to a Floating Rate Payer for which a Cap Rate is specified, the excess, if any, of the Floating Rate calculated as provided in this Agreement (without reference to this paragraph 2(a)) over the Cap Rate and (ii) with respect to a Floating Rate Payer for which a Floor Rate is specified, the excess, if any, of the Floor Rate over the Floating Rate calculated as provided in this Agreement (without reference to this paragraph 2(a));

(b) "Cap Rate" means, in respect of any Calculation Period, the per annum rate specified as such for that Calculation Period; and

(c) "Floor Rate" means, in respect of any Calculation Period, the per annum rate specified as such for that Calculation Period.

(3) For purposes of the determination of a Market Quotation for a Terminated Transaction in respect of which a party ("X") had, immediately prior to the designation or occurrence of the relevant Early Termination Date, no future payment obligations, whether absolute or contingent, under Section 2(a)(i) of this Agreement with respect to the Terminated Transaction, (i) the quotations obtained from Reference Market-makers shall be such as to preserve the economic equivalent of the payment obligations of the party ("Y") that had, immediately prior to the designation or occurrence of the relevant Early Termination Date, future payment obligations, whether absolute or contingent, under Section 2(a)(i) of this Agreement with respect to the Terminated Transaction and (ii) if X is making the determination such amounts shall be expressed as positive amounts and if Y is making the determination such amounts shall be expressed as negative amounts.

(4) Notwithstanding the terms of Sections 5 and 6 of this Agreement, if at any time and so long as one of the parties to this Agreement ("X") shall have satisfied in full all its payment obligations under Section 2(a)(i) of this Agreement and shall at the time have no future payment obligations, whether absolute or contingent, under such Section, then unless the other party ("Y") is required pursuant to appropriate proceedings to return to X or otherwise returns to X upon demand of X any portion of any such payment, (a) the occurence of an event described in Section 5(a) of this Agreement with respect to X or any Specified Entity of X shall not constitute an Event of Default or a Potential Event of Default with respect to X as the Defaulting Party and (b) Y shall be entitled to designate an Early Termination Date pursuant to Section 6 of this Agreement only as a result of the occurrence of a Termination Event set forth in (i) either Section 5(b)(i) or 5(b)(ii) of this Agreement with respect to Y as the Affected Party or (ii) Section 5(b)(iii) of this Agreement with respect to Y as the Burdened Party.

International Swap Dealers Association, Inc.

May 1989 Addendum to Schedule to
Interest Rate Swap Agreement

Interest Rate Caps, Collars and Floors

(1) As used in this Agreement or in a Confirmation, (i) "Rate Protection Transaction" will mean any Rate Swap Transaction that is identified in the related Confirmation as a Rate Protection Transaction, Rate Cap Transaction, Rate Floor Transaction or Rate Collar Transaction and (ii) "Specified Swap" means, notwithstanding Section 14 of this Agreement but subject to Section 1(c) of this Schedule, any rate swap, rate cap, rate floor, rate collar, currency exchange transaction, forward rate agreement, or other exchange or rate protection transaction, or any combination of such transactions or agreements or any option with respect to any such transaction now existing or hereafter entered into between one party to this Agreement (or any applicable Specified Entity) and the other party to this Agreement (or any applicable Specified Entity).

(2) Notwithstanding anything to the contrary in this Agreement, the following provisions will apply with respect to a Rate Protection Transaction:

(a) the Floating Rate applicable to any Calculation Period will be (i) with respect to a Floating Rate Payor for which a Cap Rate is specified, the excess, if any, of the Floating Rate calculated as provided in this Agreement (without reference to this paragraph 2(a)) over the Cap Rate and (ii) with respect to a Floating Rate Payor for which a Floor Rate is specified, the excess, if any, of the Floor Rate over the Floating Rate calculated as provided in this Agreement (without reference to this paragraph 2(a));

(b) "Cap Rate" means, in respect of any Calculation Period, the per annum rate specified as such for that Calculation Period; and

(c) "Floor Rate" means, in respect of any Calculation Period, the per annum rate specified as such for that Calculation Period.

(3) For purposes of the determination of a Market Quotation for a Terminated Transaction in respect of which a party ("X") had, immediately prior to the designation or occurrence of the relevant Early Termination Date, no future payment obligations, whether absolute or contingent, under Section 2(a) of this Agreement with respect to the Terminated Transaction, (i) the quotations obtained from Reference Market-makers shall be such as to preserve the economic equivalent of the payment obligations of the party ("Y") that had, immediately prior to the designation or occurrence of the relevant Early Termination Date, future payment obligations, whether absolute or contingent, under Section 2(a) of this Agreement with respect to the Terminated Transaction and (ii) if X is making the determination such amounts shall be expressed as positive amounts and if Y is making the determination such amounts shall be expressed as negative amounts.

(4) Notwithstanding the terms of Sections 5 and 6 of this Agreement and Section 11.6 of the Code, if at any time and so long as one of the parties to this Agreement ("X") shall have satisfied in full all its payment obligations under Section 2(a) of this Agreement and shall at the time have no future payment obligations, whether absolute or contingent, under such Section, then unless the other party ("Y") is required pursuant to appropriate proceedings to return to X or otherwise returns to X upon demand of X any portion of any such payment, (a) the occurrence of an event described in Section 5(a) of this Agreement with respect to X or any Specified Entity of X shall not constitute an Event of Default or a Potential Event of Default with respect to X as the Defaulting Party and (b) Y shall be entitled to designate an Early Termination Date pursuant to Section 6 of this Agreement only as a result of the occurrence of a Termination Event set forth in (i) either Section 5(b)(i) or 5(b)(ii) of this Agreement with respect to Y as the Affected Party or (ii) Section 5(b)(iii) of this Agreement with respect to Y as the Burdened Party.

COMMENTARY

May 1989 Addenda to ISDA Schedules
for
Interest Rate Caps, Collars and Floors

The International Swap Dealers Association, Inc. ("ISDA") has published two addenda—one each for the Interest Rate Swap Agreement and the Interest Rate and Currency Exchange Agreement—designed to enable swap counterparties to include caps, collars and floors and similar products under such Agreements. The Addenda reflect the input and suggestions of many of ISDA's members after open Documentation Committee meetings held in London, New York and Paris.

USE OF ADDENDA

Before the provisions are analyzed in detail, a word on their suggested use is warranted. Some swap counterparties with existing master swap agreements may simply amend them by adding the appropriate Addendum, so that all caps, collars and floors between the parties are included with swaps under a single master agreement and will, subject to the provisions in the Addendum, be treated uniformly under the agreement. Other counterparties may prefer to separate the documentation of caps, collars and floors from the documentation of swaps. The Documentation Committee considered preparing a separate master agreement for caps, collars and floors, but decided this was not necessary because the appropriate Addendum could be attached to an existing ISDA form and used exclusively for caps, collars and floors. Parties that prefer separate documentation would thus have two master agreements with the same counterparty—one for swaps and one for caps, collars and floors.

Participants should consult their own legal advisors to determine which approach is appropriate for them. In making such determination, participants should read the discussion of the Optional Paragraph below.

ANALYSIS OF ADDENDA

1. *Paragraph 1.* This provision adds definitions which are used elsewhere in the Addenda or may be used by participants in confirmations relating to caps, collars and floors. To implement the definition of "Rate Protection Transaction", the parties should add a line item in their confirmations, preferably toward the beginning, to the following effect:

"[Type of Transaction: Rate Protection/Cap/Collar/Floor Transaction]"

The expanded definition of "Specified Swaps" anticipates the parties' probable intent that performance under an ISDA agreement is conditioned on each party's continuing performance under *all* similar transactions between the parties, and not simply rate swap and currency exchange transactions.

2. *Paragraph 2.* This provision redefines certain terms contained in the 1987 Interest Rate and Currency Exchange Definitions (the "Definitions") and the Code of Standard Wording, Assumptions and Provisions for Swaps, 1986 Edition (the "Code"). In so doing it uses capitalized terms which are defined in the Definitions and the Code.

Paragraph 2(a) overrides the standard definition of "Floating Rate" when applied to caps, collars and floors (as well as any other transactions for which a Cap Rate or a Floor Rate is specified). Under paragraph 2(a) the Floating Rate becomes either (i) if a Cap Rate is specified, the excess of the rate determined under the applicable Floating Rate Option (*e.g.*, LIBOR) over the specified Cap Rate or (ii) if a Floor Rate is specified, the excess of the specified Floor Rate over the rate determined under such Floating Rate Option.

Paragraphs 2(b) and 2(c) provide defined terms for the specified rate at which a party buys a cap, collar or floor. These terms are used most significantly in the Floating Rate definition referred to above. It is anticipated that parties would add one or more line items to their swap confirmations, perhaps in proximity to the Floating Rate Option item, as follows:

[Cap Rate:]   [%]
[Floor Rate:]   [%]

3. *Paragraph 3.* This provision is intended to clarify the application of the definition of Market Quotation to fully paid caps and floors. In the standard definition, the quoting market maker is requested to give quotes for a transaction which would have the effect of preserving for the parties the economic equivalent of the payment obligations of both parties under the Terminated Transaction from and after the Early Termination Date to the originally scheduled Termination Date. Paragraph 3 of the Addenda simply recognizes that with a fully paid cap or floor, only one of the parties has any remaining payment obligations. Thus, it is more accurate with respect to such transactions to specify that the quotes obtained should reflect the preservation of the economic equivalent of the payment obligations of the one party still obligated to make payments.

The remainder of this provision recognizes that upon early termination a fully paid transaction can never have a negative value to the buyer because the buyer has no further payment obligations thereunder. It will cost the buyer some amount to replace a terminated cap or floor. Conversely, upon early termination a fully paid transaction will always have a negative value to a seller because the seller has potential future payment obligations. The seller will receive some amount to replace a terminated cap or floor.

4. *Paragraph 4.* It is anticipated that some parties may conduct business in such a way that from time to time one will consistently be only a purchaser of caps or floors from the other. This may be the case because one or both parties do not as a rule enter into swap transactions, because the creditworthiness of one party is such that the other would not accept the risk associated with purchasing a cap or floor from the first party or because of other reasons. If two parties do conduct such a "one-way" business, the consistent buyer might argue, not unreasonably, that it would be inappropriate for the consistent seller to designate an Early Termination Date with respect to such transactions, at least so long as the buyer has satisfied in full all its payment obligations, because the seller does not have any exposure to the credit of the buyer. On the other hand, the occurrence of certain of the Termination Events may adversely affect the seller in that it may become unduly burdensome if, for example, the seller must gross up payments as a result of a Change in Tax Law. Similarly, a change in law making it illegal for the seller to perform should enable it to designate an Early Termination Date. In such event, the buyer is not disadvantaged because the ISDA agreements call for two-way payments, thus permitting the buyer to receive the market value of all the transactions subject to the termination notice.

To give effect to the foregoing points, Paragraph 4 specifies that so long as a party ("X") has satisfied in full its basic payment obligations (and the other party is not obligated to or does not return such payments), then (a) neither an Event of Default nor a Potential Event of Default can occur with respect to X as Defaulting Party and (b) the other party ("Y") shall only be entitled to designate an Early Termination Date as a result of certain specified Termination Events.

Some parties in the position of the consistent seller may feel justified in expanding the list of events entitling it to designate an Early Termination Date to include, for example, Default under Specified Swaps (Section 5(a)(v)) or Cross Default (Section 5(a)(vi)). In such a situation, Y may be disadvantaged if it must continue to perform the caps and floors it sold under an ISDA agreement even though X has failed to perform under other agreements between the same parties.

As an alternative or in addition to the foregoing, parties may wish to consider the desirability of including contractual "set-off" provisions to cover other transactions between them not included under the ISDA agreement.

OPTIONAL PARAGRAPH

Parties which use, or are contemplating the use of, limited two-way payments (paragraph 6(e)(i) of the ISDA agreements) may wish to include in the appropriate Addendum the following provision:

"(5) For purposes of calculating payments due in respect of an Early Termination Date (including any payments under Section 6(d) and any Unpaid Amounts), an Event of Default specified in Section 5(a)(vii) of this Agreement (Bankruptcy) shall be treated as if it were a Termination Event with the Defaulting Party as the Affected Party (and for such purposes the proviso to the definition of "Settlement Amount" shall be deemed to be of no force and effect.)*. Such Event of Default treated as a Termination Event shall take precedence over any other Event of Default which is existing at the time of the designation or deemed occurrence of such Early Termination Date."

This optional provision reflects the views of a number of ISDA members that it is inappropriate to use the limited two-way payments provision contained in the standard form Agreements—at least in the case of a bankruptcy of a party—if an ISDA agreement covers caps and floors, as well as swaps. These members believe this optional provision should be included because it produces a result that would be the likely outcome if the trustee or receiver in a bankruptcy or insolvency case were to challenge the early termination payment provisions on the grounds that fully paid-for caps and floors are assets of the debtor, the value of which cannot be denied to the debtor. In addition, this optional provision is supported by those members who believe that bankruptcy should in all cases (swaps as well as caps and floors) be treated as a Termination Event rather than as an Event of Default.

At the same time, however, other ISDA members believe that this optional provision should not be included because they believe that limited two-way payments is a valid approach for an ISDA agreement that covers caps and floors, as well as swaps, and that bankruptcy should remain an Event of Default. These members believe that a court would uphold such contractual provisions, particularly when agreed to by two sophisticated, commercial parties.

Other ISDA members believe that other approaches are appropriate when an ISDA agreement covers caps and floors. As noted above, Participants are urged to consult with their legal advisors to determine which approach is appropriate for them.

---

* This parenthetical clause need only be included in the Addendum relating to the Interest Rate and Currency Exchange Agreement.

International Swap Dealers Association, Inc.

COMMENTARY

July 1990 Addenda to ISDA Schedules
for
Options

The International Swap Dealers Association, Inc. ("ISDA"), has published two addenda—one each for the Interest Rate Swap Agreement and the Interest Rate and Currency Exchange Agreement (the "ISDA Agreements")—designed to facilitate documentation of Options by swap counterparties under the ISDA Agreements. ISDA has also published sample forms of a letter agreement or telex (a "Confirmation") that may be used in conjunction with each of the Addenda for confirming an Option. The Addenda and sample forms of Confirmation reflect the input and suggestions of many of ISDA's members after open Documentation Committee meetings held in London, New York and Montreal.

The Addenda and sample forms of Confirmation represent only one possible approach to documenting Options. Other methods are currently being used by swap market participants. Each participant may elect to use approaches other than the Addenda and sample forms of Confirmation that are the subject of this Commentary.

ANALYSIS OF ADDENDA

1. *Terms Defined in the Addenda.* Paragraph 1 defines terms that are used elsewhere in the Addenda. "Option" is defined broadly to mean any Swap Transaction that is identified as an Option and provides for the grant of certain rights with respect to an "Underlying Swap Transaction" or a "Related Swap Transaction". An "Underlying Swap Transaction" will either become effective (in the case of "Physical Settlement") upon exercise of the right granted by the Option or will serve as the basis for the calculation of the amount payable, if any, upon exercise (in the case of "Cash Settlement"). The term "Related Swap Transaction" refers to a Swap Transaction that may already be effective where the right granted by the Option is, rather than to enter into or cash settle an Underlying Swap Transaction, to change one or more terms of the Related Swap Transaction.

2. *Terms Defined in the Confirmation.* Paragraph 2 identifies the capitalized terms used in the Addenda that may be defined in or pursuant to the related Confirmation or elsewhere in the ISDA Agreement.

3. *Specified Swap Definition.* In addition to the supplemental definitions contained in the Addenda, participants that have not amended their ISDA Agreements to include the applicable May 1989 Addendum to the ISDA Agreement Schedule for Interest Rate Caps, Collars and Floors published by ISDA may wish to expand the definition of Specified Swap they otherwise use in their ISDA Agreements to include a specific reference to options.

4. *Payment of Option Premium.* Paragraph 3(a) requires the Buyer to pay any Option Premium to the Seller on the Option Premium Payment Date or Dates specified in or pursuant to the Confirmation.

5. *Grant of the Option.* Paragraph 3(b) sets forth the grant of the right that is specified to be applicable to the Option. As new types of options are developed, similar "self-executing" language may be included by participants in the Schedule to their ISDA Agreements or in their Confirmations.* As used in the Addenda, "Physical Settlement" means that, upon exercise, the Underlying Swap Transaction will become effective; "Cash Settlement" means that, upon exercise, rather than becoming effective the Underlying Swap Transaction will be cash settled by the Seller paying the Cash Settlement Amount, if any, on the Cash Settlement Payment Date; and "Optional Termination" means that, upon exercise, the date specified as the Optional Termination Date will become the Termination Date and, if applicable, the Final Exchange Date for the Related Swap Transaction. This paragraph also provides that an Underlying Swap Transaction will not become effective unless Physical Settlement applies and the right has been exercised.

When Cash Settlement applies, it is anticipated that parties will define the method for determining the Cash Settlement Amount in respect of the Underlying Swap Transaction in the Schedule to their ISDA Agreement or in their Confirmations.

When Optional Termination applies, it is anticipated that parties either will specify a date certain or the means for the determination of the Optional Termination Date in the Confirmation (*e.g.*, the first date that is both a Fixed Rate Payer and Floating Rate Payer Period End Date coinciding with or following the date that the Notice of Exercise is effective) or will specify that the Optional Termination Date is an Exercise Term and, if necessary, the means by which the Optional Termination Date will be determined.

6. *Procedure for Exercise.* Paragraph 3(c) sets forth the procedure for exercising the rights granted by the Option. The Addenda do not place any conditions on the Buyer's ability to exercise the rights granted by an Option.

Depending on the circumstances, parties may wish to specify, for a particular Option or for all Options entered into with a particular counterparty, that the Buyer's ability to exercise the rights granted by an Option is subject to the satisfaction of certain conditions. For instance, parties may wish to specify that the Buyer's ability to exercise the rights granted by an Option is subject to the condition that no Event of Default shall have occurred and be continuing in respect of the Buyer as the Defaulting Party. Parties may decide that such a condition is appropriate for Options to which Physical Settlement is specified to be applicable because the exercise of the Option would result in the Underlying Swap Transaction becoming effective. It should be noted that, if no condition is included and the Buyer is allowed to exercise the Option, the non-Defaulting Party would not be required to make any payments under the Underlying Swap Transaction to the Defaulting Party because of the condition in Section 2 of each of the ISDA Agreements, and the non-Defaulting Party could terminate all Swap Transactions to which it and the Defaulting Party are parties.

As an alternative to specifying conditions to exercise, parties may wish to consider specifying that, in certain circumstances (*e.g.*, where an Event of Default has occurred and is continuing in

---

* For instance, a right to cause a partial termination could be granted in the Confirmation as follows: "On the terms set forth in this Confirmation, Seller grants to Buyer pursuant to this Option the right to cause the Notional Amount to be reduced [by/to   ] in respect of each Calculation Period commencing on or after the date that the Notice of Exercise is effective."

respect of the Buyer as the Defaulting Party), the Option could be exercised only on the basis of Cash Settlement. This would recognize that the Option has value to the Buyer, but fix the amount of that value at the time the Option otherwise would have been exercised.

The Buyer may exercise the rights granted by the Option only by giving irrevocable Notice of Exercise (which may be delivered orally) to the Seller. The Notice of Exercise must become effective during the Option Exercise Period specified in or pursuant to the Confirmation and must include any Exercise Terms set forth in the Confirmation. The time at which a notice becomes effective is determined pursuant to Section 12 of the Interest Rate and Currency Exchange Agreement or Section 14.2 of the Code of Swaps, 1986 Edition, and paragraph 3(e) of each Addendum.

7. *Automatic Exercise.* The Addenda do not include provisions for automatic exercise of the rights granted by an Option. Automatic exercise may be particularly useful for Options to which Cash Settlement is specified to be applicable to avoid any loss of value to the Buyer due to inadvertence. Parties desiring to include such provisions should include them in the Schedule to their ISDA Agreements or in their Confirmations.

8. *Written Confirmation of Notice of Exercise.* Paragraph 3(d) permits the Seller to require the Buyer to deliver an executed written or telex confirmation of any Notice of Exercise given by the Buyer. The Buyer will be obligated to deliver such an executed written or telex confirmation if "Written Confirmation" is specified to be applicable in the Confirmation. Delivery of an executed writing or telex is intended, among other things, to address any concern that, depending on the maturity and other terms of the Swap Transaction, applicable laws relating to the enforceability of oral contracts might require such documentation.

9. *Effectiveness of Oral Notices and Communications.* Paragraph 3(e) specifies when notices and communications permitted to be given orally will be effective.

10. *Market Quotation.* Paragraph 4 is intended to clarify the application of the definition of Market Quotation to an Option. So long as any right granted by the Option is or may become exercisable, the Option will have, in most cases, some value to the Buyer. Parties desiring that certain conditions be fulfilled before giving the Buyer credit for the Option in determining the Market Quotation should modify this provision accordingly.

11. *Fully Paid Transactions.* It is anticipated that some parties may conduct business in such a way that from time to time one will consistently be only a purchaser of fully paid transactions (*e.g.*, cash-settled options, caps and floors) from the other. This may be the case because one or both parties do not as a rule enter into conventional swap transactions, because the creditworthiness of one party is such that the other would not accept the risk associated with purchasing a cash-settled option, cap or floor from the first party or because of other reasons. If two parties do conduct such a "one-way" business, the consistent buyer might argue that it would be inappropriate for the consistent seller to designate an Early Termination Date with respect to such transactions, at least so long as the buyer has satisfied in full all its payment obligations, because the seller does not have any exposure to the credit of the buyer. On the other hand, the occurrence of certain of the Termination Events may adversely affect the seller in that it may become unduly burdensome if, for example, the seller must gross up payments as a result of a Change in Tax Law. Similarly, a change in law making it illegal for the seller to perform should enable it to designate an Early Termination Date. In the case of the designation of an Early Termination Date due to the Tax Event and Illegality Termination Events, the buyer would not

3

be disadvantaged because the ISDA Agreements call for two way payments, thus permitting the buyer to receive the market value of all the Terminated Transactions.*

To give effect to the foregoing concerns, Paragraph 5 specifies that so long as a party ("X") has satisfied in full its basic payment obligations, whether absolute or contingent (and the other party ("Y") is not obligated to or does not return such payments), then (a) neither an Event of Default nor a Potential Event of Default can occur with respect to X as the Defaulting Party and (b) Y shall be entitled to designate an Early Termination Date only as a result of certain specified Termination Events. The contingent payment obligations referred to in Paragraph 5 include payments in respect of an Underlying Swap Transaction which may become effective upon exercise of the right granted by the related Option.

Some parties in the position of Y, the consistent seller, may feel justified in expanding the list of events entitling it to designate an Early Termination Date to include, for example, Default under Specified Swaps (Section 5(a)(v)) or Cross Default (Section 5(a)(vi)). In such a situation, Y may be disadvantaged if it must continue to perform a fully paid transaction when X has failed to perform under other agreements between the same parties.

Since the same provision is also contained in the May 1989 Addendum to the ISDA Agreement Schedule for Interest Rate Caps, Collars and Floors, a party should omit this provision if it is already included or incorporated in the ISDA Agreement.

TERMINATION PROVISIONS

Participants using the ISDA Agreements use a variety of methods to determine termination payments following the occurrence of an Event of Default, particularly when an ISDA Agreement covers fully paid transactions such as cash-settled options, caps and floors, as well as conventional swaps. These methods include limited two way payments, which is provided for in the ISDA Agreements, as well as full two way payments for one or more Events of Default or the two pool approach.

ANALYSIS OF CONFIRMATION

1. *Introductory Paragraphs and Section 1.* These provisions conform to the standard paragraphs from the existing ISDA form of Confirmation.

Participants that enter into Options prior to amending their ISDA Agreements to include the provisions of the appropriate Addendum may include in their Confirmations the following paragraph:

If the Agreement has not been executed by you and us or if the Agreement has been executed by you and us but does not include paragraphs 1, 2 and 3 of the July 1990 Addendum to Schedule to Interest Rate [Swap] [and Currency Exchange] Agreement—Options, as published by the International Swap Dealers Association, Inc. (the "July 1990 Addendum"),

---

* Some parties, however, may feel that mid-market pricing of the Terminated Transactions in such cases is appropriate and, therefore, the calculation of payments pursuant to Section 6(e) of the ISDA Agreements in respect of the Tax Event and Illegality Termination Events should be performed as if there were two Affected Parties. In such cases, both parties may be permitted to determine the Market Quotations or the parties may provide that the non-Affected Party will determine the Market Quotations that the Affected Party would otherwise be entitled to determine.

then until the Agreement has been executed by you and us and includes therein or as an amendment thereto paragraphs 1, 2 and 3 of the July 1990 Addendum, with such modifications as you and we shall in good faith agree, the definitions and provisions of paragraphs 1, 2 and 3 of the July 1990 Addendum are incorporated herein. In the event of any inconsistency between those definitions and provisions and this Confirmation, this Confirmation will prevail.

2. *Section 2.* Section 2 contains the provisions relating to an Option, including the line items applicable to Cash Settlement, Optional Termination and the Procedure for Exercise of an Option. The appropriate portions of this section may be completed for each different right granted by the Option. An Option may provide that either "Physical Settlement" or "Cash Settlement" is permitted, in which case, parties may also provide in the Confirmation that only one of these alternative rights may be exercised and that, upon exercise, the other right granted by the Option is terminated.

3. *Section 3.* Section 3 sets forth certain terms of the Underlying or Related Swap Transaction. This Section conforms to Section 2 from the existing ISDA form of Confirmation, appropriately modified for potential caps, collars and floors.

4. *Sections 4 Through 7.* These provisions set forth the other terms of the Underlying Swap Transaction or the Related Swap Transaction.

OPTIONAL PROVISIONS

1. *Floating Rate for an Initial Calculation Period.* For an Option to which Physical Settlement applies, if the date of exercise may occur after the date on which the relevant Floating Rate ordinarily would be determined, the Seller may not adequately be able to hedge the Underlying Swap Transaction. Parties that are concerned with this potential problem may include in their Confirmations a provision along the following lines, which causes the date on which a "LIBOR"-based Floating Rate is determined to coincide with the date (if prior to the Effective Date) that the Notice of Exercise is effective:

( ) Notwithstanding anything to the contrary in this Confirmation, the Relevant Rate for any Reset Date occurring prior to the second London Banking Day following the date that Notice of Exercise with respect to the Option is effective shall be determined as if the Reset Date were such second London Banking Day.

2. *Floating Rate for a Final Calculation Period.* For an Option to which Optional Termination applies, if the Optional Termination Date is not required to coincide with a Period End Date, the parties may consider providing for determination of the Floating Rate for the Floating Rate Payer Calculation Period ending on but excluding the Optional Termination Date based on linear interpolation between Floating Rates of the Designated Maturities falling closest to the Optional Termination Date as measured from the immediately preceding Period End Date.

International Swap Dealers Association, Inc.

July 1990 Addendum to Schedule to
Interest Rate and Currency Exchange Agreement

Options

(1) As used in this Agreement or in any Confirmation, "Option" means any Swap Transaction that is identified in the related Confirmation as an Option and provides for the grant by Seller to Buyer of (i) the right to cause an underlying Swap Transaction, the terms of which are identified in that Confirmation (an "Underlying Swap Transaction"), to become effective, (ii) the right to cause Seller to pay Buyer pursuant to Section 2(a)(i) of this Agreement the Cash Settlement Amount, if any, in respect of the Underlying Swap Transaction on the Cash Settlement Payment Date, (iii) the right to cause the Optional Termination Date to become the Termination Date and, if so specified in the related Confirmation, the Final Exchange Date of the related Swap Transaction that is identified in that Confirmation (a "Related Swap Transaction") or (iv) any other right or rights specified in the related Confirmation. An Option may provide for the grant of one or more of the foregoing rights, all of which can be identified in a single Confirmation.

(2) The following capitalized terms, if used in relation to an Option, have the respective meanings specified in or pursuant to the related Confirmation (or elsewhere in this Agreement): "Buyer", "Seller", "Option Premium", "Option Premium Payment Date", "Cash Settlement Payment Date", "Cash Settlement Amount", "Optional Termination Date", "Exercise Terms" and "Option Exercise Period".

(3) The following provisions will apply with respect to an Option:

(a) Buyer will pay Seller pursuant to Section 2(a)(i) of this Agreement the Option Premium, if any, on the Option Premium Payment Date or Dates.

(b) On the terms set forth in this Agreement (including the related Confirmation), Seller grants to Buyer pursuant to the Option, (i) if "Physical Settlement" is specified to be applicable to the Option, the right to cause the Underlying Swap Transaction to become effective, (ii) if "Cash Settlement" is specified to be applicable to the Option, the right to cause Seller to pay Buyer pursuant to Section 2(a)(i) of this Agreement the Cash Settlement Amount, if any, in respect of the Underlying Swap Transaction on the Cash Settlement Payment Date or (iii) if "Optional Termination" is specified to be applicable to the Option, the right to cause the Optional Termination Date to become the Termination Date and, if so specified in the related Confirmation, the Final Exchange Date of the Related Swap Transaction. The Underlying Swap Transaction, if any, shall not become effective unless (i) "Physical Settlement" is specified to be applicable to the Option and (ii) the right to cause that Underlying Swap Transaction to become effective has been exercised.

(c) Buyer may exercise the right or rights granted pursuant to the Option only by delivering irrevocable notice (a "Notice of Exercise") to Seller (which, notwithstanding any other provision of this Agreement, may be delivered orally (including by telephone)). The Notice of Exercise must become effective during the Option Exercise Period and must include the Exercise Terms, if any.

(d)   Buyer will, if "Written Confirmation" is specified to be applicable to the Option or upon demand from Seller (which, notwithstanding any other provision of this Agreement, may be delivered orally (including by telephone)), (i) execute a written confirmation confirming the substance of the Notice of Exercise and deliver the same to Seller or (ii) issue a telex to Seller setting forth the substance of the Notice of Exercise. Buyer shall cause such executed written confirmation or telex to be received by Seller within one Local Banking Day following the date that the Notice of Exercise or Seller's demand, as the case may be, becomes effective. If not received within such time, Buyer will be deemed to have satisfied its obligations under the immediately preceding sentence at the time that such executed written confirmation or telex becomes effective.

(e)   Any notice or communication given, and permitted to be given, orally (including by telephone) in connection with the Option will be effective when actually received by the recipient.

(4)   For purposes of the determination of a Market Quotation for a Terminated Transaction that is identified as an Option, the quotations obtained from Reference Market-makers shall take into account, as of the relevant Early Termination Date, the economic equivalent of the right or rights granted pursuant to that Option which are or may become exercisable.

(5)   Notwithstanding the terms of Sections 5 and 6 of this Agreement, if at any time and so long as one of the parties to this Agreement ("X") shall have satisfied in full all its payment obligations under Section 2(a)(i) of this Agreement and shall at the time have no future payment obligations, whether absolute or contingent, under such Section, then unless the other party ("Y") is required pursuant to appropriate proceedings to return to X or otherwise returns to X upon demand of X any portion of any such payment, (a) the occurrence of an event described in Section 5(a) of this Agreement with respect to X or any Specified Entity of X shall not constitute an Event of Default or a Potential Event of Default with respect to X as the Defaulting Party and (b) Y shall be entitled to designate an Early Termination Date pursuant to Section 6 of this Agreement only as a result of the occurrence of a Termination Event set forth in (i) either Section 5(b)(i) or 5(b)(ii) of this Agreement with respect to Y as the Affected Party or (ii) Section 5(b)(iii) of this Agreement with respect to Y as the Burdened Party.

2

International Swap Dealers Association, Inc.

July 1990 Addendum to Schedule to
Interest Rate Swap Agreement

Options

(1) As used in this Agreement or in any Confirmation, "Option" means any Rate Swap Transaction that is identified in the related Confirmation as an Option and provides for the grant by Seller to Buyer of (i) the right to cause an underlying Rate Swap Transaction, the terms of which are identified in that Confirmation (an "Underlying Rate Swap Transaction"), to become effective, (ii) the right to cause Seller to pay Buyer pursuant to Section 2(a) of this Agreement the Cash Settlement Amount, if any, in respect of the Underlying Rate Swap Transaction on the Cash Settlement Payment Date, (iii) the right to cause the Optional Termination Date to become the Termination Date of the related Rate Swap Transaction that is identified in that Confirmation (a "Related Rate Swap Transaction") or (iv) any other right or rights specified in the related Confirmation. An Option may provide for the grant of one or more of the foregoing rights, all of which can be identified in a single Confirmation.

(2) The following capitalized terms, if used in relation to an Option, have the respective meanings specified in or pursuant to the related Confirmation (or elsewhere in this Agreement): "Buyer", "Seller", "Option Premium", "Option Premium Payment Date", "Cash Settlement Payment Date", "Cash Settlement Amount", "Optional Termination Date", "Exercise Terms" and "Option Exercise Period".

(3) The following provisions will apply with respect to an Option:

(a) Buyer will pay Seller pursuant to Section 2(a) of this Agreement the Option Premium, if any, on the Option Premium Payment Date or Dates.

(b) On the terms set forth in this Agreement (including the related Confirmation), Seller grants to Buyer pursuant to the Option, (i) if "Physical Settlement" is specified to be applicable to the Option, the right to cause the Underlying Rate Swap Transaction to become effective, (ii) if "Cash Settlement" is specified to be applicable to the Option, the right to cause Seller to pay Buyer pursuant to Section 2(a) of this Agreement the Cash Settlement Amount, if any, in respect of the Underlying Rate Swap Transaction on the Cash Settlement Payment Date or (iii) if "Optional Termination" is specified to be applicable to the Option, the right to cause the Optional Termination Date to become the Termination Date of the Related Rate Swap Transaction. The Underlying Rate Swap Transaction, if any, shall not become effective unless (i) "Physical Settlement" is specified to be applicable to the Option and (ii) the right to cause that Underlying Rate Swap Transaction to become effective has been exercised.

(c) Buyer may exercise the right or rights granted pursuant to the Option only by delivering irrevocable notice (a "Notice of Exercise") to Seller (which, notwithstanding any other provision of this Agreement or the Code, may be delivered orally (including by telephone)). The Notice of Exercise must become effective during the Option Exercise Period and must include the Exercise Terms, if any.

(d)   Buyer will, if "Written Confirmation" is specified to be applicable to the Option or upon demand from Seller (which, notwithstanding any other provision of this Agreement or the Code, may be delivered orally (including by telephone)), (i) execute a written confirmation confirming the substance of the Notice of Exercise and deliver the same to Seller or (ii) issue a telex to Seller setting forth the substance of the Notice of Exercise. Buyer shall cause such executed written confirmation or telex to be received by Seller within one Local Banking Day following the date that the Notice of Exercise or Seller's demand, as the case may be, becomes effective. If not received within such time, Buyer will be deemed to have satisfied its obligations under the immediately preceding sentence at the time that such executed written confirmation or telex becomes effective.

(e)   Any notice or communication given, and permitted to be given, orally (including by telephone) in connection with the Option will be effective when actually received by the recipient.

(4)   For purposes of the determination of a Market Quotation for a Terminated Transaction that is identified as an Option, the quotations obtained from Reference Market-makers shall take into account, as of the relevant Early Termination Date, the economic equivalent of the right or rights granted pursuant to that Option which are or may become exercisable.

(5)   Notwithstanding the terms of Sections 5 and 6 of this Agreement and Section 11.6 of the Code, if at any time and so long as one of the parties to this Agreement ("X") shall have satisfied in full all its payment obligations under Section 2(a) of this Agreement and shall at the time have no future payment obligations, whether absolute or contingent, under such Section, then unless the other party ("Y") is required pursuant to appropriate proceedings to return to X or otherwise returns to X upon demand of X any portion of any such payment, (a) the occurrence of an event described in Section 5(a) of this Agreement with respect to X or any Specified Entity of X shall not constitute an Event of Default or Potential Event of Default with respect to X as the Defaulting Party and (b) Y shall be entitled to designate an Early Termination Date pursuant to Section 6 of this Agreement only as a result of the occurrence of a Termination Event set forth in (i) either Section 5(b)(i) or 5(b)(ii) of this Agreement with respect to Y as the Affected Party or (ii) Section 5(b)(iii) of this Agreement with respect to Y as the Burdened Party. For purposes of this Agreement, "Potential Event of Default" means an event that with the giving of notice or lapse of time (or both) would become an Event of Default.

2

Sample Form of Letter Agreement or Telex
for a Swap Transaction that is
Identified as an Option

Heading for Letter

[Letterhead of Party A]

[Date]

Swap Transaction

[Name and Address of Party B]

Heading for Telex

Telex

Date:

To: [Name and Telex Number of Party B]

From: [Party A]

Re: Swap Transaction

Dear   :

The purpose of this [letter agreement/telex] is to confirm the terms and conditions of the Swap Transaction entered into between us on the Trade Date specified below (the "Swap Transaction"). This [letter agreement/telex] constitutes a "Confirmation" as referred to in the Interest Rate and Currency Exchange Agreement specified below.

The definitions and provisions contained in the 1987 Interest Rate and Currency Exchange Definitions (as published by the International Swap Dealers Association, Inc.) are incorporated into this Confirmation. In the event of any inconsistency between those definitions and provisions and this Confirmation, this Confirmation will govern.

1. This Confirmation supplements, forms part of, and is subject to, the Interest Rate and Currency Exchange Agreement dated as of [date], as amended and supplemented from time to time (the "Agreement"), between you and us. All provisions contained in the Agreement govern this Confirmation except as expressly modified below.

2. The particular Swap Transaction to which this Confirmation relates is an Option, the terms of which are as follows:

Seller:	[Party A/B]
Buyer:	[Party B/A]
[Option Premium:]	[$] [payable in [ ] [equal] installments on each Option Premium Payment Date] [as follows:]
[Option Premium Payment Date[s]:]	[Specify date or dates]
Expiration Date:	[ ] [(or if such day is not a [ ] Business Day, the next preceding/following [ ] Business Day)]
[Physical Settlement:	Applicable]

[Cash Settlement Provisions:]

    [Cash Settlement: Applicable]

    [Cash Settlement Payment Date:]   [The [first] [   ] Business Day next
                                               following the [Expiration Date] [earlier of
                                               (i) the Expiration Date and (ii) the day on
                                               which the Notice of Exercise is effective]]

    [Cash Settlement Amount:]   [Specify means for determination]

[Optional Termination Provisions:]

    [Optional Termination: Applicable]

    [Optional Termination Date:]   [Specify date or means for determination,
                                               including whether date specified must be
                                               prior to the specified Termination Date]

Procedure for Exercise:

    Exercise Terms: [Terms Buyer is required to specify] [None]

    Option Exercise Period: [Specify times and dates during which
                                               Option is exercisable (*e.g.*, between
                                               9:00 a.m. and 5:00 p.m., [specify place for
                                               exercise] time, on the Expiration Date)]

    [Written Confirmation: Applicable]

3. The particular terms of the [Underlying/Related] Swap Transaction to which the Option relates are as follows:

    [Transaction type: (*i.e.*, rate protection/cap/floor/collar
                                               transaction)]

    [Notional Amount:]   [$]

    Trade Date:

    Effective Date:

    Termination Date:

    Fixed Amounts:

        Fixed Rate Payer: [Party A/B]

        [Fixed Rate Payer Currency Amount:]

        Fixed Rate Payer Payment Dates [or   , subject to adjustment
        Period End Dates, if Delayed Payment   in accordance with the [Following/Modified
        or Early Payment applies]:   Following/Preceding] Business Day
                                               convention

        Fixed Amount [or Fixed Rate and
        Fixed Rate Day Count Fraction]:

    Floating Amounts:

        Floating Rate Payer: [Party B/A]

[Floating Rate Payer Currency
Amount:]

Floating Rate Payer Payment Dates   , subject to adjustment in
[or Period End Dates, if Delayed   accordance with the [Following/Modified
Payment or Early Payment applies]:   Following/Preceding] Business Day
                                           convention

[Cap Rate/Floor Rate:]   [%]

[Floating Rate for initial Calculation
Period:]

Floating Rate Option:

Designated Maturity:

Spread: [Plus/Minus   %] [None]

[Floating Rate Day Count Fraction:]

Reset Dates:

[Rate Cut-off Dates:]

[Method of Averaging:]   [Unweighted/Weighted Average Rate]

Compounding: [Applicable/Inapplicable]

[Compounding Dates:]

[Initial Exchange:

   Initial Exchange
   Date:

   Fixed Rate Payer Initial
   Exchange Amount:

   Floating Rate Payer Initial
   Exchange Amount:]

[Final Exchange:

   Final Exchange
   Date:

   Fixed Rate Payer Final
   Exchange Amount:

   Floating Rate Payer
   Final Exchange Amount:]

[Business Days for [first currency]:

[Business Days for [second currency]:

Calculation Agent:

[4.   agrees to provide the following Credit Support Document [or agrees to provide the
following in accordance with [specify Credit Support Document]:]

[5.] Account Details

Payments to Fixed Rate Payer:

   Account for payments in [first currency]:

   Account for payments in [second currency]:

3

Payments to Floating Rate Payer:

    Account for payments in [first currency]:

    Account for payments in [second currency]:

[6. Offices

(a) The Office of Fixed Rate Payer for the Swap Transaction is   ; and

(b) The Office of Floating Rate Payer for the Swap Transaction is   .]

[7. Broker/Arranger:]

Closing for Letter

    Please confirm that the foregoing correctly sets forth the terms of our agreement by executing the copy of this Confirmation enclosed for that purpose and returning it to us.

                                    Yours sincerely,

                                    [PARTY A]

                                    By:_____

                                          Name:
                                          Title:

Confirmed as of the
date first above written:

[PARTY B]

By:_____
    Name:
    Title:

Closing for Telex

    Please confirm that the foregoing correctly sets forth the terms of our agreement by a return telex to [Party A] substantially to the following effect:

    "Re:

    We acknowledge receipt of your telex dated [   ] with respect to the above-referenced Swap Transaction between [Party A] and [Party B] which is an Option with an Expiration Date of [   ] and confirm that such telex correctly sets forth the terms of our agreement relating to the Swap Transaction described therein. Very truly yours, [Party B], by [specify name and title of authorized officer]."

                                      Yours sincerely,

                                    [PARTY A]

                                    By: _____
                                        Name:
                                          Title:

Sample Form of Letter Agreement or Telex
for a Rate Swap Transaction that is
Identified as an Option

Heading for Letter

[Letterhead of Party A]

[Date]

Rate Swap Transaction

[Name and Address of Party B]

Heading for Telex

Telex

Date:

To: [Name and Telex Number of Party B]

From: [Party A]

Re: Rate Swap Transaction

Dear   :

The purpose of this [letter agreement/telex] is to confirm the terms and conditions of the Rate Swap Transaction entered into between us on the Trade Date specified below (the "Rate Swap Transaction"). This [letter agreement/telex] constitutes a "Confirmation" as referred to in the Rate Swap Agreement specified below.

1. This Confirmation supplements, forms part of, and is subject to, the Interest Rate Swap Agreement dated as of [date], as amended and supplemented from time to time (the "Rate Swap Agreement"), between you and us. All provisions contained or incorporated by reference in the Rate Swap Agreement shall govern this Confirmation except as expressly modified below.

2. The particular Rate Swap Transaction to which this Confirmation relates is an Option, the terms of which are as follows:

Seller:	[Party A/B]
Buyer:	[Party B/A]
[Option Premium:]	[$] [payable in [ ] [equal] installments on each Option Premium Payment Date] [as follows:]
[Option Premium Payment Date[s]:]	[Specify date or dates]
Expiration Date:	[ ] [(or if such day is not a [ ] Banking Day, the next preceding/following [ ] Banking Day)]
[Physical Settlement:	Applicable]
[Cash Settlement Provisions:]	
[Cash Settlement:	Applicable]

[Cash Settlement Payment Date:]	[The [first] [ ] Banking Day next following the [Expiration Date] [earlier of (i) the Expiration Date and (ii) the day on which the Notice of Exercise is effective]]
[Cash Settlement Amount:]	[Specify means for determination]

[Optional Termination Provisions:]

[Optional Termination:	Applicable]
[Optional Termination Date:]	[Specify date or means for determination, including whether date specified must be prior to the specified Termination Date]

Procedure for Exercise:

Exercise Terms:	[Terms Buyer is required to specify] [None]
Option Exercise Period:	[Specify times and dates during which Option is exercisable (*e.g.*, between 9:00 a.m. and 5:00 p.m., [specify place for exercise] time, on the Expiration Date)]
[Written Confirmation:	Applicable]

3. The particular terms of the [Underlying/Related] Rate Swap Transaction to which the Option relates are as follows:

[Transaction type:	(*i.e.*, rate protection/cap/floor/collar transaction)]
Notional Amount:	[$]
Trade Date:	
Effective Date:	
Termination Date:	

Fixed Amounts:

Fixed Rate Payor:	[Party A/B]
Fixed Rate Payor Payment Dates [or Period End Dates, if Delayed Payment or Early Payment applies]:	, subject to adjustment in accordance with the [Following/Modified Following/Preceding] Banking Day convention
Fixed Amount [or Fixed Rate and Fixed Rate Day Count Fraction]:	

Floating Amounts:

Floating Rate Payor:	[Party B/A]
Floating Rate Payor Payment Dates [or Period End Dates, if Delayed Payment or Early Payment applies]:	, subject to adjustment in accordance with the [Following/Modified Following/Preceding] Banking Day convention
[Cap Rate/Floor Rate:]	[%]

2

[Floating Rate for initial
Calculation Period:]

Floating Rate Option:

Designated Maturity:

Spread: [Plus/Minus   %] [None]

[Floating Rate Day Count Fraction:]

Reset Dates:

[Rate Cut-off Dates:]

[Method of Averaging:]   [Unweighted/Weighted Average Rate]

Compounding: [Applicable/Inapplicable]

[Compounding Dates:]

Calculation Agent:

[4.   agrees to provide the following Credit Support Document [or agrees to provide the following in accordance with [specify Credit Support Document]:]

[5.] Account Details

Account for payments to Fixed Rate Payor:

Account for payments to Floating Rate Payor:

[6. Offices

(a) The Office of Fixed Rate Payor for the Rate Swap Transaction is   ; and

(b) The Office of Floating Rate Payor for the Rate Swap Transaction is   .]

[7. Broker/Arranger:]

Closing for Letter

Please confirm that the foregoing correctly sets forth the terms of our agreement by executing the copy of this Confirmation enclosed for that purpose and returning it to us.

Very truly yours,

[PARTY A]

By:_____
        Name:
        Title:

Accepted and confirmed as of
the date first above written:

[PARTY B]

By:_____
      Name:
      Title:

3

Closing for Telex

Please confirm that the foregoing correctly sets forth the terms of our agreement by a return telex to [Party A] substantially to the following effect:

"Re:

We acknowledge receipt of your telex dated [   ] with respect to the above-referenced Rate Swap Transaction between [Party A] and [Party B] which is an Option with an Expiration Date of [   ] and confirm that such telex correctly sets forth the terms of our agreement relating to the Rate Swap Transaction described therein. Very truly yours, [Party B], by [specify name and title of authorized officer]."

Very truly yours,

[PARTY A]

By: _____

      Name:

      Title:

International Swap Dealers Association, Inc.

INTEREST RATE
SWAP AGREEMENT

Dated as of.............................

....   **and**   ....

have entered and/or anticipate entering into one or more transactions (each a "Rate Swap Transaction"). The parties agree that each Rate Swap Transaction will be governed by the terms and conditions set forth in this document (which includes the schedule (the "Schedule")) and in the documents (each a "Confirmation") exchanged between the parties confirming such Rate Swap Transactions. Each Confirmation constitutes a supplement to and forms part of this document and will be read and construed as one with this document, so that this document and all the Confirmations constitute a single agreement between the parties (collectively referred to as this "Agreement"). The parties acknowledge that all Rate Swap Transactions are entered into in reliance on the fact that this document and all Confirmations will form a single agreement between the parties, it being understood that the parties would not otherwise enter into any Rate Swap Transactions.

Accordingly, the parties agree as follows:

1.   Interpretation; Code of SWAPS

(a)   *Definitions.* The terms defined in Section 14 and in the Schedule will have the meanings therein specified for the purpose of this Agreement.

(b)   *Code of SWAPS.* This Agreement and each Rate Swap Transaction are subject to the Code of Standard Wording, Assumptions and Provisions for Swaps, 1986 Edition (as published by the International Swap Dealers Association, Inc.) (the "Code"), and will be governed in all relevant respects by the provisions set forth in the Code, without regard to any amendments to the Code subsequent to the date hereof. The provisions of the Code are incorporated by reference in, and shall be deemed to be a part of, this document and each Confirmation, as if set forth in full in this document or in that Confirmation. This Agreement constitutes a Rate Swap Agreement as that term is used in the Code.

(c)   *Inconsistency.* In the event of any inconsistency between the provisions of this document and the Code, this document will prevail. In the event of any inconsistency between the provisions of any Confirmation and this document, such Confirmation will prevail for the purpose of the relevant Rate Swap Transaction.

2.   Payments

(a)   *Obligations and Conditions.* Subject to the payment basis specified below and the other terms and conditions set forth or incorporated by reference in this Agreement (including without limitation Article 10 of the Code) or in a Confirmation, with respect to each Rate Swap Transaction, each party will make each payment specified in that Confirmation as being payable by it by transfer of the relevant amount in freely transferable funds to the account of the other party specified for that Rate Swap Transaction. Unless otherwise provided in a Confirmation, the Fixed Amount or Floating Amount applicable to a Payment Date will be the Fixed Amount or Floating Amount calculated with reference to the Calculation Period ending on, but excluding, the Period End Date (or in the case of the Final Calculation Period, the Termination Date) that coincides with, or corresponds to, that Payment Date.

(b) *Change of Account.* Either party may change its account to another account in the country originally specified, by giving notice to the other party at least five days prior to a Payment Date for which such change applies.

(c) *Netting.* The obligations of the parties under this Section 2 will be calculated and payable on the basis of Net Payments. The parties may, if so specified in the Schedule or otherwise, apply Net Payments—Corresponding Payment Dates to their respective obligations under this Section 2 with effect from the date so specified; *provided that*, in such case, Net Payments—Corresponding Payment Dates will apply separately to each Office through which a party makes and receives payments as set forth in Section 10.

3. Representations

The representations of the parties (other than those relating to tax matters, if any) are specified below and will be deemed to be repeated at the times set forth in Section 15.1 of the Code:

(a) Basic Representations;

(b) Absence of Certain Events, which in the case of an event or condition that has occurred, is continuing;

(c) Absence of Litigation; and

(d) Accuracy of Specified Information.

4. Agreements

The agreements of the parties (other than Tax Covenants, if any) are specified below:

(a) Each party agrees to deliver to the other party any documents specified in the Schedule or a Confirmation as soon as practicable or by the date specified in the Schedule or such Confirmation;

(b) Each party agrees to Maintain Authorizations and Comply with Laws, but in the case of Section 16.1(f)(i) of the Code only to the extent that each party agrees to use all reasonable efforts; and

(c) Each party agrees to pay any stamp, registration, documentation or similar tax ("Stamp Tax") levied or imposed upon it or in respect of its execution or performance of this Agreement by a jurisdiction in which it is incorporated, organized, managed and controlled, or considered to have its seat, or in which a branch or office through which it is acting for the purpose of this Agreement is located ("Stamp Tax Jurisdiction") and will indemnify the other party against any Stamp Tax levied or imposed upon the other party or in respect of the other party's execution or performance of this Agreement by any such Stamp Tax Jurisdiction which is not also a Stamp Tax Jurisdiction with respect to the other party.

5. Events of Default and Termination Events

The Events of Default and Termination Events with respect to each party are specified below. The occurrence of any Event of Default or Termination Event with respect to a Specified Entity of a party will constitute an Event of Default or Termination Event with respect to such party.

(a) *Events of Default.*

(i)   Failure To Pay following a Cure Period of three Business Days After Notice;

(ii) Breach of Covenant following a Cure Period of thirty days After Notice;

(iii) Credit Support Default which in the case of Section 11.7(b)(i) of the Code is continuing after any applicable grace period has elapsed;

(iv) Misrepresentation;

(v)   Default Under Specified Swaps;

(vi) If Cross-Default is specified in the Schedule as applying to the party, such term will mean: (1) the occurrence or existence of an event or condition in respect of such party or any applicable Specified Entity under one or more agreements or instruments relating to Specified Indebtedness of such party or any such Specified Entity in an aggregate amount of not less than the Threshold Amount (as specified in the Schedule) which has resulted in such Specified Indebtedness becoming, or becoming capable at such time of being declared, due and payable under such agreements or instruments before it would otherwise have been due and payable; or (2) the failure by such party or any such Specified Entity to make one or more payments at maturity in an aggregate amount of not less than the Threshold Amount under such agreements or instruments (after giving effect to any applicable grace period);

(vii) Bankruptcy, which will mean the occurrence of any of the following events with respect to a party or any applicable Specified Entity:

such party or any such Specified Entity (1) is dissolved; (2) becomes insolvent or fails or is unable or admits in writing its inability generally to pay its debts as they become due; (3) makes a general assignment, arrangement or composition with or for the benefit of its creditors; (4) institutes or has instituted against it a proceeding seeking a judgment of insolvency or bankruptcy or any other relief under any bankruptcy or insolvency law or other similar law affecting creditors' rights, or a petition is presented for the winding-up or liquidation of the party or any such Specified Entity, and, in the case of any such proceeding or petition instituted or presented against it, such proceeding or petition (A) results in a judgment of insolvency or bankruptcy or the entry of an order for relief or the making of an order for the winding-up or liquidation of the party or such Specified Entity or (B) is not dismissed, discharged, stayed or restrained in each case within 30 days of the institution or presentation thereof; (5) has a resolution passed for its winding-up or liquidation; (6) seeks or becomes subject to the appointment of an administrator, receiver, trustee, custodian or other similar official for it or for all or substantially all its assets (regardless of how brief such appointment may be, or whether any obligations are promptly assumed by another entity or whether any other event described in this clause (6) has occurred and is continuing); (7) any event occurs with respect to the party or any such Specified Entity which, under the applicable laws of any jurisdiction, has an analogous effect to any of the events specified in clauses (1) to (6) (inclusive); or (8) takes any action in furtherance of, or indicating its consent to, approval of, or acquiescence in, any of the foregoing acts;

other than in the case of clause (1) or (5) or, to the extent it relates to those clauses, clause (8), for the purpose of a consolidation, amalgamation or merger which would not constitute a Merger Without Assumption; or

(viii) Merger Without Assumption, which will mean that a party consolidates or amalgamates with, or merges into, or transfers all or substantially all its assets to, another entity and, at the time of such consolidation, amalgamation, merger or transfer:

(1) the resulting, surviving or transferee entity fails to assume all the obligations of such party under this Agreement by operation of law or pursuant to an agreement reasonably satisfactory to the other party to this Agreement; or

(2) the benefits of any Credit Support Document relating to this Agreement fail to extend (without the consent of the other party) to the performance by such resulting, surviving or transferee entity of its obligations under this Agreement.

(b) *Termination Events.*

(i) Illegality;

(ii) Tax Event, which will mean either:

(1) the party (which will be the Affected Party) will be required on the next succeeding Payment Date to pay to the other party an additional amount in respect of an Indemnifiable Tax under Section 19.1(b) of the Code (except in respect of default interest) as a result of a Change in Tax Law; or

(2) there is a substantial likelihood that the party (which will be the Affected Party) will be required on the next succeeding Payment Date to pay to the other party an additional amount in respect of an Indemnifiable Tax under Section 19.1(b) of the Code (except in respect of default interest) and such substantial likelihood results from an action taken by a taxing authority, or brought in a court of competent jurisdiction, on or after the Trade Date of such Rate Swap Transaction (regardless of whether such action was taken or brought with respect to a party to this Agreement);

(iii) Tax Event Upon Merger, which will mean the party (the "Burdened Party") on the next succeeding Payment Date will either (1) be required to pay to the other party an additional amount in respect of an Indemnifiable Tax under Section 19.1(b) of the Code (except in respect of default interest) or (2) receive a payment from which an amount has been deducted or withheld for or on account of any Indemnifiable Tax in respect of which the other party is not required to pay an additional amount, in either case as a result of a party consolidating or amalgamating with, or merging into, or transferring all or substantially all its assets to, another entity (which will be the Affected Party) where such action does not constitute a Merger Without Assumption; or

(iv) If Credit Event Upon Merger is specified in the Schedule as applying to the party, such term will mean that such party ("X") consolidates or amalgamates with, or merges into, or transfers all or substantially all its assets to, another entity and such action does not constitute a Merger Without Assumption but the creditworthiness of the resulting, surviving or transferee entity (which will be the Affected Party) is materially weaker than that of X immediately prior to such action.

(c) Other provisions with respect to Events of Default and Termination Events are as follows:

(i) Limited Early Termination will apply to all Termination Events other than Credit Event Upon Merger.

(ii) If an event or circumstance which would otherwise constitute or give rise to an Event of Default also constitutes an Illegality, it will be treated as an Illegality and will not constitute an Event of Default.

6. Early Termination

(a) *Right to Terminate Following Event of Default.* A party entitled to designate an Early Termination Date in respect of an Event of Default may do so by giving notice to the other party of the Early Termination Date not more than 20 days prior to the date so designated (which date may not be earlier than the date such notice is effective); *provided, however,* that Immediate Early Termination will apply with respect to an Event of Default under Section 5(a)(vii) and, in the case of an Event of Default under clause (4) thereof, the Early Termination Date shall be deemed to have occurred as of the time immediately preceding the institution of the relevant proceeding or the presentation of the relevant petition.

(b) *Right to Terminate Following Termination Event.*

(i) *Notice.* Upon the occurrence of a Termination Event, an Affected Party will, promptly upon becoming aware of the same, notify the other party thereof, specifying the nature of such Termination Event and the Affected Transactions relating thereto. The Affected Party will also give such other information to the other party with regard to such Termination Event as the other party may reasonably require.

(ii) *Transfer to Avoid Termination Event.* Notwithstanding Section 18.3 of the Code, if either an Illegality under Section 11.8(a)(i) of the Code or a Tax Event occurs and there is only one Affected Party, or if a Tax Event Upon Merger occurs and the Affected Party is the Burdened Party, the Affected Party will as a condition to its right to designate an Early Termination Date use all reasonable efforts (which will not require such party to incur a loss, excluding immaterial, incidental expenses) to transfer within 20 days after the Affected Party gives notice under Section 6(b)(i) all its rights and obligations under this Agreement in respect of the Affected Transactions to another of its offices, branches or Affiliates so that such Termination Event ceases to exist.

If the Affected Party is not able to make such a transfer it will give notice to the other party to that effect within such 20 day period, whereupon the other party may effect such a transfer within 30 days after the notice is given under Section 6(b)(i).

Any such transfer by a party under this Section 6(b)(ii) will be subject to and conditional upon the prior written consent of the other party, which consent will not be withheld if such other party's policies in effect at such time would permit it to enter into swap transactions with the transferee on the terms proposed.

(iii) *Two Affected Parties.* If an Illegality under Section 11.8(a)(i) of the Code or a Tax Event occurs and there are two Affected Parties, each party will use all reasonable efforts to reach agreement within 30 days after notice thereof is given under Section 6(b)(i) on action that would cause such Termination Event to cease to exist.

(iv)   *Right to Terminate.* Notwithstanding Section 11.6 of the Code, if:

(1) a transfer under Section 6(b)(ii) or an agreement under Section 6(b)(iii), as the case may be, has not been effected with respect to all Affected Transactions within 30 days after an Affected Party gives notice under Section 6(b)(i); or

(2) an Illegality under Section 11.8(a)(ii) of the Code or a Credit Event Upon Merger occurs, or a Tax Event Upon Merger occurs and the Burdened Party is not the Affected Party,

either party in the case of an Illegality, the Burdened Party in the case of a Tax Event Upon Merger, any Affected Party in the case of a Tax Event, or the party which is not the Affected Party in the case of a Credit Event Upon Merger, will be the party entitled to designate an Early Termination Date. Such party may designate an Early Termination Date in respect of all Affected Transactions by giving notice not more than 20 days prior to the date so designated (which date may not be earlier than the date such notice is effective).

(c)   *Effect of Designation.* Upon the effectiveness of notice designating an Early Termination Date (or the deemed occurrence of an Early Termination Date), the obligations of the parties to make any further payments under Section 2 in respect of the Terminated Transactions will terminate, but without prejudice to the other provisions of this Agreement.

(d)   *Calculations.* The amount calculated as being payable under Section 6(e) will be due on the day that notice of the amount payable is effective (in the case of an Early Termination Date which is designated or deemed to occur as a result of an Event of Default) and not later than the day which is two Business Days after the day on which notice of the amount payable is effective (in the case of an Early Termination Date which is designated as a result of a Termination Event). Such notice shall specify the account for payment.

Such amount will be paid together with (to the extent permitted under applicable law) interest thereon from (and including) the relevant Early Termination Date to (but excluding) the relevant due date, calculated as follows:

(i)   if notice is given designating an Early Termination Date or if an Early Termination Date is deemed to occur, in either case as a result of an Event of Default, at the Default Rate; or

(ii)   if notice is given designating an Early Termination Date as a result of a Termination Event, at the Default Rate minus the Default Spread.

Such interest will be computed on the basis of Compounding using daily Compounding Dates, as if the rate specified were a Floating Rate, such period were a Calculation Period and the amount due were a Notional Amount.

(e)   *Payments on Early Termination.*

(i)   *Amount Payable.* The amount payable in respect of an Early Termination Date will be calculated as follows:

(1) If there is a Defaulting Party, the Defaulting Party will pay to the other party the excess, if a positive number, of (A) the sum of (i) the amount determined in accordance with Agreement Value—Limited Two Way Payments, calculated on the basis of Aggregation (or, if the Aggregate Market Quotation calculated in determining such amount is less than zero, the amount by which such Aggregate Market Quotation is less than zero, expressed as a negative number) and (ii) the Unpaid Amounts due to the other party over (B) the Unpaid Amounts due to the Defaulting Party; and

(2) if an Early Termination Date occurs as a result of a Termination Event, the payment to be made will be the amount equal to (A) the sum of (i) the amount determined in accordance with Agreement Value—Limited Two Way Payments, calculated on the basis of Aggregation and (ii) the Unpaid Amounts due to the party ("X") entitled to receive a payment under clause (i) minus (B) the Unpaid Amounts due to the other party ("Y"). If the resulting amount is a positive number, Y will pay such amount to X. If the resulting amount is negative, X will pay the absolute value of such amount to Y; and

(3) for purposes of the foregoing clauses (1) and (2), if Market Quotation is not, or cannot be, determined with respect to a Rate Swap Transaction, the alternative measure of damages with respect to such Rate Swap Transaction will be Indemnification—Limited Two Way Payments; *provided that,* (A) in the case of clause (1)(A)(i) above, the amount, if any, by which Loss is less than zero will be given effect and (B) in the case of a Termination Event

where there is only one Affected Party, Indemnification—Limited Two Way Payments will be computed without regard to the Loss of the Affected Party.

(ii) *Adjustment for Bankruptcy.* In circumstances where an Early Termination Date is deemed to occur as a result of Immediate Early Termination, the amount determined under Section 6(e)(i) will be subject to such adjustments as are appropriate and permitted by law to reflect any payments made by one party to the other under this Agreement (and retained by such other party) during the period from the relevant Early Termination Date to the date for payment determined under Section 6(d).

(iii) *Pre-Estimate of Loss.* The parties agree that the amounts recoverable under this Section 6(e) are a reasonable pre-estimate of loss and not a penalty. Such amounts are payable for the loss of bargain and the loss of protection against future risks and except as otherwise provided in this Agreement neither party will be entitled to recover any additional damages as a consequence of such losses.

7. Transfer

Subject to Section 6(b) and to any exception provided in the Schedule, neither this Agreement nor any interest or obligation in or under this Agreement may be transferred by either party without the prior written consent of the other party (other than pursuant to a consolidation or amalgamation with, or merger into, or transfer of all or substantially all its assets to, another entity) and any purported transfer without such consent will be void.

8. Contractual Currency

All payments under this Agreement will be made in Dollars. In connection with a demand for payment of any additional amount under Section 18.1 of the Code, it will be sufficient for a party to demonstrate that it would have suffered a loss had an actual exchange or purchase been made.

9. Miscellaneous

(a) *Entire Agreement.* This Agreement constitutes the entire agreement and understanding of the parties with respect to its subject matter and supersedes all oral communications and prior writings with respect thereto.

(b) *Amendments.* No amendment, modification or waiver in respect of this Agreement will be effective unless in writing and executed by each of the parties or confirmed by an exchange of telexes.

(c) *Survival of Obligations.* Except as provided in Section 6(c), the obligations of the parties under this Agreement will survive the termination of any Rate Swap Transaction.

(d) *Remedies Cumulative.* Except as provided in this Agreement, the rights, powers, remedies and privileges provided in this Agreement are cumulative and not exclusive of any rights, powers, remedies and privileges provided by law.

(e) *Confirmations.* A Confirmation may be executed in counterparts or created by an exchange of telexes, substantially in the form of the letter or telex attached hereto as Exhibit I (or in such other form as the parties may agree), which in either case will be sufficient for all purposes to evidence a binding supplement to this Agreement. Any such counterpart or telex will specify that it constitutes a Confirmation.

10. Multibranch Parties

If a party is specified as a Multibranch Party in the Schedule, such Multibranch Party may make and receive payments under any Rate Swap Transaction through any of its branches or offices listed in the Schedule (each an "Office"). The Office through which it so makes and receives payments for the purpose of any Rate Swap Transaction will be specified in the relevant Confirmation and any change of Office for such purpose requires the prior written consent of the other party. Each Multibranch Party represents to the other party that, notwithstanding the place of payment, the obligations of each Office are for all purposes under this Agreement the obligations of such Multibranch Party. This representation will be deemed to be repeated by such Multibranch Party on each Trade Date.

11. Credit Support Document

If a Credit Support Document is specified with respect to a party in the Schedule, the obligations of such party under this Agreement and in respect of each Rate Swap Transaction will be secured or guaranteed in accordance with the provisions of that Credit Support Document.

12. Tax Matters

(a) *Representations and Covenants.* The parties make the following Tax Covenant: Give Notice of Breach of Payee Tax Representation or Tax Covenant. In addition, the parties make the Payee Tax Representations, the Withholding Tax Representation and the Tax Covenants specified in the Schedule. In addition, at all times during the Term of any Rate Swap Transaction, each party makes to the other party, and to any Specified Entity of the other party, the representations specified in the Schedule as "Payor Tax Representations". Unless otherwise specified (i) all Payee Tax Representations, Payor Tax Representations, the Withholding Tax Representation and all Tax Covenants made by a party will apply to each Office of the party and (ii) all Payee Tax Representations will be subject to the occurrence of a Change in Tax Law.

(b) *Exempt From Withholding.* If used for purposes of specifying the Withholding Tax Representation of a party in the Schedule, "Exempt from Withholding" will have the meaning set forth in the Code; *provided that,* such representation will apply to the jurisdiction from or through which a payment is made, as well as the jurisdictions specified in Section 19.3 of the Code.

(c) *Recognized Bank.* If used for purposes of specifying Payee Tax Representations or Payor Tax Representations of a party in the Schedule, "Recognized Bank" means the party represents that it is a bank recognized by the United Kingdom Inland Revenue as carrying on a bona fide banking business in the United Kingdom, is entering into this Agreement in the ordinary course of such business and will bring into account payments made and received under this Agreement in computing its income for United Kingdom tax purposes.

(d) *Provide U.S. Tax Forms if Required.* If used for purposes of specifying Tax Covenants of a party in the Schedule, "Provide U.S. Tax Forms if Required" means that the party agrees to complete, accurately and in a manner reasonably satisfactory to the other party, and to execute and deliver to the other party, a United States Internal Revenue Service Form 4224, or any successor form, in respect of any payments received or to be received by that party in connection with this Agreement that are effectively connected or otherwise attributable to its conduct of a trade or business in the United States (i) before the first payment date on which any such payment is or may be so connected or attributable, (ii) promptly upon reasonable demand by the other party, and (iii) promptly upon learning that any such form previously provided has become obsolete or incorrect.

13. Service of Process

Each party irrevocably appoints the party specified in the Schedule, if any, as its agent for service of process. If for any reason a party's agent for service of process is unable to act as such, such party will promptly notify the other party and within 30 days appoint a substitute agent for service of process acceptable to the other party. The parties irrevocably consent to service of process given in accordance with the notice provisions of Article 14 of the Code and this Agreement. Nothing in this Section will affect the right of either party to serve process in any other manner permitted by law.

14. Definitions

As used in this Agreement:

"Affected Transactions" means (a) with respect to any Termination Event to which Limited Early Termination applies under Section 5(c)(i) of this Agreement, all Rate Swap Transactions affected by the occurrence of such Termination Event and (b) with respect to any other Termination Event, all Rate Swap Transactions.

"Default Rate" means a rate per annum determined in accordance with the Federal Funds Floating Rate Option plus the Default Spread, using daily Reset Dates. For purposes of Section 10.3 of the Code, the Default Rate will be applied on the basis of Compounding as if the overdue amount were a Notional Amount and using daily Compounding Dates, and interest will accrue and be payable before as well as after judgment.

"Default Spread" will have the meaning specified in the Schedule.

"Illegality" will have the meaning set forth in Section 11.8 of the Code; *provided that*, if an event that would otherwise constitute an Illegality results from a breach by the party of its obligations under Section 16.1(f)(i) of the Code, such event will not be deemed to be an Illegality.

"Indemnifiable Tax" will have the meaning set forth in the Code; *provided that*, (a) references to the recipient of a payment shall be considered also to refer to a person related to the recipient and (b) the last clause of the definition of "Indemnifiable Tax" in Section 19.5(d) of the Code shall be considered to refer to a Credit Support Document as well as a Rate Swap Agreement.

"law" means, with respect to tax matters, any treaty, law, rule or regulation, as modified by the practice of any relevant governmental revenue authority.

"Specified Entity" will have the meaning set forth in the Schedule.

"Specified Indebtedness" means any obligation (whether present or future, contingent or otherwise, as principal or surety or otherwise) in respect of borrowed money.

"Specified Swap" means any rate swap or currency exchange transaction now existing or hereafter entered into between one party to this Agreement (or any applicable Specified Entity) and the other party to this Agreement (or any applicable Specified Entity).

"Terminated Transactions" means (a) with respect to any Early Termination Date occurring as a result of a Termination Event, all Affected Transactions and (b) with respect to any Early Termination Date occurring as a result of an Event of Default, all Rate Swap Transactions, which in either case are in effect as of the time immediately preceding the effectiveness of the notice designating such Early Termination Date (or, in the case of Immediate Early Termination, in effect as of the time immediately preceding such Early Termination Date).

"Unpaid Amounts" owing to any party means, with respect to any Early Termination Date, the aggregate of the amounts that became due and payable (or that would have become due and payable but for Section 10.2 of the Code or the designation or occurrence of such Early Termination Date) to such party under Section 2 in respect of all Terminated Transactions by reference to all Calculation Periods ended on or prior to such Early Termination Date and which remain unpaid as at such Early Termination Date, together with (to the extent permitted under applicable law and in lieu of any interest calculated under Section 10.3 of the Code) interest thereon from (and including) the date such amount became due and payable or would have become due and payable to (but excluding) such Early Termination Date, calculated as follows:

(a) in the case of amounts that became so due and payable by a Defaulting Party, at the Default Rate; and

(b) in the case of all other such amounts, at the Default Rate minus the Default Spread.

Such interest will be computed on the basis of Compounding using daily Compounding Dates, as if the rate specified were a Floating Rate, such period were a Calculation Period and the amount due were a Notional Amount.

IN WITNESS WHEREOF the parties have executed this document as of the date specified on the first page of this document.

. . . .
                (Name of party)   (Name of party)

By: . . . .   By: . . . .

Name: Name:

Title: Title:

EXHIBIT I

Heading for Letter

[Letterhead of Party]

[Date]

Rate Swap Transaction

[Name and Address of Party]

Heading for Telex

Telex

Date:

To: [Name and Address of Party]

From: [Name of Party]

Subject: Rate Swap Transaction

Dear

    The purpose of this [letter agreement/telex] is to set forth the terms and conditions of the Rate Swap Transaction entered into between us on the Trade Date referred to below. This [letter/telex] constitutes a "Confirmation" as referred to in the Rate Swap Agreement specified below.

    1. This Confirmation supplements, forms a part of, and is subject to, the Interest Rate Swap Agreement dated as of [date] (the "Rate Swap Agreement") between you and us. All provisions contained or incorporated by reference in the Rate Swap Agreement shall govern this Confirmation except as expressly modified below.

    2. The terms of the particular Rate Swap Transaction to which this Confirmation relates are as follows:

Notional Amount: $

Trade Date:

Effective Date:

Termination Date:

Fixed Amounts:

       Fixed Rate Payor: [name of party]

       Fixed Rate Payor Payment Dates   [   ], subject to adjustment
       [or Period End Dates, if Delayed   in accordance with the [Following/Modified
       Payment or Early Payment applies]:   Following/Preceding] Banking Day convention

       Fixed Amount [or Fixed Rate and Fixed
       Rate Day Count Fraction]:

Floating Amounts:

       Floating Rate Payor: [name of party]

       Floating Rate Payor Payment Dates   [   ], subject to adjustment
       [or Period End Dates, if Delayed   in accordance with the [Following/Modified
       Payment or Early Payment applies]:   Following/Preceding] Banking Day convention

Floating Rate for initial Calculation Period:

Floating Rate Option:

Designated Maturity:

Spread: [plus/minus]   %

Floating Rate Day Count Fraction:

Reset Dates:

[Rate Cut-off Dates:]

[Method of Averaging:]   [Unweighted Average Rate/ Weighted
                                         Average Rate]

Compounding: Applicable/Inapplicable

[Compounding Dates:]

[Calculation Date:]

Other provisions:

[3.   agrees to provide the following Credit Support Document [or agrees to provide the following in accordance with [specify Credit Support Document]:]

Closing for Letter

Please confirm that the foregoing correctly sets forth the terms of our agreement by executing the copy of this Confirmation enclosed for that purpose and returning it to us.

Very truly yours,

By: _____
     Name:
     Title:

Accepted and confirmed as
of the date first written:

By: _____
     Name:
     Title:

Closing for Telex

Please confirm that the foregoing correctly sets forth the terms of our agreement by a return telex to [name of party] substantially to the following effect:

"We acknowledge receipt of your telex dated   with respect to a Rate Swap Transaction between [name of party] and [name of party] with a Notional Amount of   and a Termination Date of   and confirm that such telex correctly sets forth the terms of our agreement relating to the Rate Swap Transaction described therein. Very truly yours, [name of party], by (specify name and title of authorized officer)."

Very truly yours,

By: _____
     Name:
     Title:

SCHEDULE

to the

Interest Rate Swap Agreement

dated as of . . . .

between. . . . . and . . . .
            ("Party A")   ("Party B")

1.   **Definitions**

(a)   *"Default Spread"* means . . . .

(b)   *"Specified Entity"* means in relation to Party A for the purpose of:

      Section 5(a)(iii) and (iv) and 5(b)(i),. . . . .

      Section 5(a)(v),. . . . .

      Section 5(a)(vi), ...

      Section 5(a)(vii),. . . . .

      and in relation to Party B for the purpose of:

      Section 5(a)(iii) and (iv) and 5(b)(i),. . . . .

      Section 5(a)(v),. . . . .

      Section 5(a)(vi), ...

      Section 5(a)(vii),. . . . .

(c)   *"Specified Swap"* will have the meaning specified in Section 14 unless another meaning is specified
      here: . . . .

      . . . .

2.   **Payments**

(a)   The Calculation Agent will be. . . . .

(b)   If indicated here, Net Payments—Corresponding Payment Dates will apply with effect from the date
      of this Agreement: _____

3.   **Representations**

      "Accuracy of Specified Information" in respect of a party will apply to the information which is

      required to be delivered by it under Section 4 of this Schedule, unless otherwise specified below . . . . . .

      . . . .

4.   **Agreements**

      For the purpose of Section 4(a), the documents to be delivered (other than tax forms) are:

Party required to deliver document	Document	Date by which to be delivered
. . . .	. . . .	. . . .
. . . .	. . . .	. . . .
. . . .	. . . .	. . . .

ISDA 1987

5. Events of Default

(a) The *"Cross-Default"* provisions of Section 5(a)(vi) will/will not* apply to Party A
will/will not* apply to Party B

If such provisions apply:

"Specified Indebtedness" will have the meaning specified in Section 14 unless another meaning is

specified here ....

....

"Threshold Amount" means ....

....

(b) The *"Credit Event Upon Merger"* provisions of Section 5(b)(iv) will/will not* apply to Party A
will/will not* apply to Party B

6. Transfer

Exceptions to the Transfer provisions of Section 7, if any, are ....

....

7. Addresses for Notices

Address for notices or communications to Party A:

Address: ....

Attention: ....

Telex No.: .... Answerback: ....

(For all purposes/only with respect to Rate Swap Transactions through that Office*.)

Address for notices or communications to Party B:

Address: ....

Attention: ....

Telex No.: .... Answerback: ....

(For all purposes/only with respect to Rate Swap Transactions through that Office*.)

8. Specification of Multibranch Party

Party A is/is not* a Multibranch Party and, if so, may act through the following Offices: ....

....

Party B is/is not* a Multibranch Party and, if so, may act through the following Offices: ....

....

* Delete as applicable

9. **Specification of Credit Support Document**

10. **Tax Matters**

    (a) Party A: (b) Party B:

        (i) *Payee Tax Representations*   (i) *Payee Tax Representations*

            ____ Eligible for Treaty Benefits*   ____ Eligible for Treaty Benefits*
            ____ Ordinary Business Use   ____ Ordinary Business Use
            ____ Qualify as Business Profits   ____ Qualify as Business Profits
            ____ Effectively Connected   ____ Effectively Connected
            ____ Recognized Bank   ____ Recognized Bank
            ____ Other (specify)   ____ Other (specify)

        (ii) *Payor Tax Representations*   (ii) *Payor Tax Representations*

            ____ Recognized Bank   ____ Recognized Bank
            ____ Other (specify)   ____ Other (specify)

        (iii) *Withholding Tax Representation*   (iii) *Withholding Tax Representation*

            ____ Exempt from Withholding   ____ Exempt from Withholding

        (iv) *Additional Tax Covenants*   (iv) *Additional Tax Covenants*

            ____ Provide Form 1001   ____ Provide Form 1001
             ____ Provide Form 4224   ____ Provide Form 4224
            ____ Provide Tax Forms   ____ Provide Tax Forms
            ____ Provide U.S. Tax Forms if Required   ____ Provide U.S. Tax Forms if Required
           ____ Other (specify)   ____ Other (specify)

               *"*Specified Treaty*" means . . . .

. . . .

11. **Agent for Service of Process**

Party A appoints as its agent for service of process . . . .

. . . .

Party B appoints as its agent for service of process . . . .

. . . .

12. **Other Provisions**

International Swap Dealers Association, Inc.

INTEREST RATE
AND
CURRENCY EXCHANGE AGREEMENT

Dated as of...

.... and ....

have entered and/or anticipate entering into one or more transactions (each a "Swap Transaction"). The parties agree that each Swap Transaction will be governed by the terms and conditions set forth in this document (which includes the schedule (the "Schedule")) and in the documents (each a "Confirmation") exchanged between the parties confirming such Swap Transactions. Each Confirmation constitutes a supplement to and forms part of this document and will be read and construed as one with this document, so that this document and all the Confirmations constitute a single agreement between the parties (collectively referred to as this "Agreement"). The parties acknowledge that all Swap Transactions are entered into in reliance on the fact that this document and all Confirmations will form a single agreement between the parties, it being understood that the parties would not otherwise enter into any Swap Transactions.

Accordingly, the parties agree as follows:-

1. Interpretation

(a) *Definitions.* The terms defined in Section 14 and in the Schedule will have the meanings therein specified for the purpose of this Agreement.

(b) *Inconsistency.* In the event of any inconsistency between the provisions of any Confirmation and this document, such Confirmation will prevail for the purpose of the relevant Swap Transaction.

2. Payments

(a) *Obligations and Conditions.*

(i) Each party will make each payment specified in each Confirmation as being payable by it.

(ii) Payments under this Agreement will be made not later than the due date for value on that date in the place of the account specified in the relevant Confirmation or otherwise pursuant to this Agreement, in freely transferable funds and in the manner customary for payments in the required currency.

(iii) Each obligation of each party to pay any amount due under Section 2(a)(i) is subject to (1) the condition precedent that no Event of Default or Potential Event of Default with respect to the other party has occurred and is continuing and (2) each other applicable condition precedent specified in this Agreement.

(b) *Change of Account.* Either party may change its account by giving notice to the other party at least five days prior to the due date for payment for which such change applies.

(c)   *Netting.* If on any date amounts would otherwise be payable:–

    (i)   in the same currency; and

    (ii) in respect of the same Swap Transaction,

by each party to the other, then, on such date, each party's obligation to make payment of any such amount will be automatically satisfied and discharged and, if the aggregate amount that would otherwise have been payable by one party exceeds the aggregate amount that would otherwise have been payable by the other party, replaced by an obligation upon the party by whom the larger aggregate amount would have been payable to pay to the other party the excess of the larger aggregate amount over the smaller aggregate amount.

If the parties specify "Net Payments — Corresponding Payment Dates" in a Confirmation or otherwise in this Agreement, sub-paragraph (ii) above will cease to apply to all Swap Transactions with effect from the date so specified (so that a net amount will be determined in respect of all amounts due on the same date in the same currency, regardless of whether such amounts are payable in respect of the same Swap Transaction); *provided that,* in such case, this Section 2(c) will apply separately to each Office through which a party makes and receives payments as set forth in Section 10.

(d)   *Deduction or Withholding for Tax.*

    (i)   *Gross-Up.* All payments under this Agreement will be made without any deduction or withholding for or on account of any Tax unless such deduction or withholding is required by any applicable law, as modified by the practice of any relevant governmental revenue authority, then in effect. If a party is so required to deduct or withhold, then that party ("X") will:–

        (1)   promptly notify the other party ("Y") of such requirement;

        (2)   pay to the relevant authorities the full amount required to be deducted or withheld (including the full amount required to be deducted or withheld from any additional amount paid by X to Y under this Section 2(d)) promptly upon the earlier of determining that such deduction or withholding is required or receiving notice that such amount has been assessed against Y;

        (3)   promptly forward to Y an official receipt (or a certified copy), or other documentation reasonably acceptable to Y, evidencing such payment to such authorities; and

        (4)   if such Tax is an Indemnifiable Tax, pay to Y, in addition to the payment to which Y is otherwise entitled under this Agreement, such additional amount as is necessary to ensure that the net amount actually received by Y (free and clear of Indemnifiable Taxes, whether assessed against X or Y) will equal the full amount Y would have received had no such deduction or withholding been required. However, X will not be required to pay any additional amount to Y to the extent that it would not be required to be paid but for:–

            (A)   the failure by Y to comply with or perform any agreement contained in Section 4(a)(i) or 4(d); or

            (B)   the failure of a representation made by Y pursuant to Section 3(f) to be accurate and true unless such failure would not have occurred but for a Change in Tax Law.

    (ii) *Liability.* If:–

        (1)   X is required by any applicable law, as modified by the practice of any relevant governmental revenue authority, to make any deduction or withholding in respect of which X would not be required to pay an additional amount to Y under Section 2(d)(i)(4);

        (2)   X does not so deduct or withhold; and

        (3)   a liability resulting from such Tax is assessed directly against X,

then, except to the extent Y has satisfied or then satisfies the liability resulting from such Tax, Y will promptly pay to X the amount of such liability (including any related liability for interest, but including any related liability for penalties only if Y has failed to comply with or perform any agreement contained in Section 4(a)(i) or (d)).

(e)   *Default Interest.* A party that defaults in the payment of any amount due will, to the extent permitted by law, be required to pay interest (before as well as after judgment) on such amount to the other party on demand in the same currency as the overdue amount, for the period from (and including) the original due date for payment to (but excluding) the date of actual payment, at the Default Rate. Such interest will be calculated on the basis of daily compounding and the actual number of days elapsed.

3. Representations

Each party represents to the other party (which representations will be deemed to be repeated by each party on each date on which a Swap Transaction is entered into and, in the case of the representations in Section 3(f), at all times until the termination of this Agreement) that:–

(a)   *Basic Representations.*
        (i)   *Status.* It is duly organised and validly existing under the laws of the jurisdiction of its organisation or incorporation and, if relevant under such laws, in good standing;

        (ii)   *Powers.* It has the power to execute and deliver this Agreement and any other documentation relating to this Agreement that it is required by this Agreement to deliver and to perform its obligations under this Agreement and any obligations it has under any Credit Support Document to which it is a party and has taken all necessary action to authorise such execution, delivery and performance;

        (iii)   *No Violation or Conflict.* Such execution, delivery and performance do not violate or conflict with any law applicable to it, any provision of its constitutional documents, any order or judgment of any court or other agency of government applicable to it or any of its assets or any contractual restriction binding on or affecting it or any of its assets;

        (iv)   *Consents.* All governmental and other consents that are required to have been obtained by it with respect to this Agreement or any Credit Support Document to which it is a party have been obtained and are in full force and effect and all conditions of any such consents have been complied with; and

        (v)   *Obligations Binding.* Its obligations under this Agreement and any Credit Support Document to which it is a party constitute its legal, valid and binding obligations, enforceable in accordance with their respective terms (subject to applicable bankruptcy, reorganisation, insolvency, moratorium or similar laws affecting creditors' rights generally and subject, as to enforceability, to equitable principles of general application (regardless of whether enforcement is sought in a proceeding in equity or at law)).

(b)   *Absence of Certain Events.* No Event of Default or Potential Event of Default or, to its knowledge, Termination Event with respect to it has occurred and is continuing and no such event or circumstance would occur as a result of its entering into or performing its obligations under this Agreement or any Credit Support Document to which it is a party.

(c)   *Absence of Litigation.* There is not pending or, to its knowledge, threatened against it or any of its Affiliates any action, suit or proceeding at law or in equity or before any court, tribunal, governmental body, agency or official or any arbitrator that purports to draw into question, or is likely to affect, the legality, validity or enforceability against it of this Agreement or any Credit Support Document to which it is a party or its ability to perform its obligations under this Agreement or such Credit Support Document.

(d)   *Accuracy of Specified Information.* All applicable information that is furnished in writing by or on behalf of it to the other party and is identified for the purpose of this Section 3(d) in paragraph 2 of Part 3 of the Schedule is, as of the date of the information, true, accurate and complete in every material respect.

(e)   *Payer Tax Representation.* Each representation specified in Part 2 of the Schedule as being made by it for the purpose of this Section 3(e) is accurate and true.

(f)   *Payee Tax Representations.* Each representation specified in Part 2 of the Schedule as being made by it for the purpose of this Section 3(f) is accurate and true.

4. Agreements

Each party agrees with the other that, so long as it has or may have any obligation under this Agreement or under any Credit Support Document to which it is a party:–

(a) *Furnish Specified Information.* It will deliver to the other party:–

(i) any forms, documents or certificates relating to taxation specified in Part 3 of the Schedule or any Confirmation; and

(ii) any other documents specified in Part 3 of the Schedule or any Confirmation,

by the date specified in Part 3 of the Schedule or such Confirmation or, if none is specified, as soon as practicable.

(b) *Maintain Authorisations.* It will use all reasonable efforts to maintain in full force and effect all consents of any governmental or other authority that are required to be obtained by it with respect to this Agreement or any Credit Support Document to which it is a party and will use all reasonable efforts to obtain any that may become necessary in the future.

(c) *Comply with Laws.* It will comply in all material respects with all applicable laws and orders to which it may be subject if failure so to comply would materially impair its ability to perform its obligations under this Agreement or any Credit Support Document to which it is a party.

(d) *Tax Agreement.* It will give notice of any failure of a representation made by it under Section 3(f) to be accurate and true promptly upon learning of such failure.

(e) *Payment of Stamp Tax.* It will pay any Stamp Tax levied or imposed upon it or in respect of its execution or performance of this Agreement by a jurisdiction in which it is incorporated, organised, managed and controlled, or considered to have its seat, or in which a branch or office through which it is acting for the purpose of this Agreement is located ("Stamp Tax Jurisdiction") and will indemnify the other party against any Stamp Tax levied or imposed upon the other party or in respect of the other party's execution or performance of this Agreement by any such Stamp Tax Jurisdiction which is not also a Stamp Tax Jurisdiction with respect to the other party.

5. Events of Default and Termination Events

(a) *Events of Default.* The occurrence at any time with respect to a party or, if applicable, any Specified Entity of such party, of any of the following events constitutes an event of default (an "Event of Default") with respect to such party:–

(i) *Failure to Pay.* Failure by the party to pay, when due, any amount required to be paid by it under this Agreement if such failure is not remedied on or before the third Business Day after notice of such failure to pay is given to the party;

(ii) *Breach of Agreement.* Failure by the party to comply with or perform any agreement or obligation (other than an obligation to pay any amount required to be paid by it under this Agreement or to give notice of a Termination Event or any agreement or obligation under Section 4(a)(i) or 4(d)) to be complied with or performed by the party in accordance with this Agreement if such failure is not remedied on or before the thirtieth day after notice of such failure is given to the party;

(iii) *Credit Support Default.*

(1) Failure by the party or any applicable Specified Entity to comply with or perform any agreement or obligation to be complied with or performed by the party or such Specified Entity in accordance with any Credit Support Document if such failure is continuing after any applicable grace period has elapsed;

(2) the expiration or termination of such Credit Support Document, or the ceasing of such Credit Support Document to be in full force and effect, prior to the final Scheduled Payment Date of each Swap Transaction to which such Credit Support Document relates without the written consent of the other party; or

(3) the party or such Specified Entity repudiates, or challenges the validity of, such Credit Support Document;

(iv) *Misrepresentation.* A representation (other than a representation under Section 3(e) or (f)) made or repeated or deemed to have been made or repeated by the party or any applicable Specified Entity in this Agreement or any Credit Support Document relating to this Agreement proves to have been incorrect or misleading in any material respect when made or repeated or deemed to have been made or repeated;

(v) *Default under Specified Swaps.* The occurrence of an event of default in respect of the party or any applicable Specified Entity under a Specified Swap which, following the giving of any applicable notice or the lapse of any applicable grace period, has resulted in the designation or occurrence of an early termination date in respect of such Specified Swap;

(vi) *Cross Default.* If "Cross Default" is specified in Part 1 of the Schedule as applying to the party, (1) the occurrence or existence of an event or condition in respect of such party or any applicable Specified Entity under one or more agreements or instruments relating to Specified Indebtedness of such party or any such Specified Entity in an aggregate amount of not less than the Threshold Amount (as specified in Part 1 of the Schedule) which has resulted in such Specified Indebtedness becoming, or becoming capable at such time of being declared, due and payable under such agreements or instruments, before it would otherwise have been due and payable or (2) the failure by such party or any such Specified Entity to make one or more payments at maturity in an aggregate amount of not less than the Threshold Amount under such agreements or instruments (after giving effect to any applicable grace period);

(vii) *Bankruptcy.* The party or any applicable Specified Entity:–

(1) is dissolved; (2) becomes insolvent or fails or is unable or admits in writing its inability generally to pay its debts as they become due; (3) makes a general assignment, arrangement or composition with or for the benefit of its creditors; (4) institutes or has instituted against it a proceeding seeking a judgment of insolvency or bankruptcy or any other relief under any bankruptcy or insolvency law or other similar law affecting creditors' rights, or a petition is presented for the winding-up or liquidation of the party or any such Specified Entity, and, in the case of any such proceeding or petition instituted or presented against it, such proceeding or petition (A) results in a judgment of insolvency or bankruptcy or the entry of an order for relief or the making of an order for the winding-up or liquidation of the party or such Specified Entity or (B) is not dismissed, discharged, stayed or restrained in each case within 30 days of the institution or presentation thereof; (5) has a resolution passed for its winding-up or liquidation; (6) seeks or becomes subject to the appointment of an administrator, receiver, trustee, custodian or other similar official for it or for all or substantially all its assets (regardless of how brief such appointment may be, or whether any obligations are promptly assumed by another entity or whether any other event described in this clause (6) has occurred and is continuing); (7) any event occurs with respect to the party or any such Specified Entity which, under the applicable laws of any jurisdiction, has an analogous effect to any of the events specified in clauses (1) to (6) (inclusive); or (8) takes any action in furtherance of, or indicating its consent to, approval of, or acquiescence in, any of the foregoing acts;

other than in the case of clause (1) or (5) or, to the extent it relates to those clauses, clause (8), for the purpose of a consolidation, amalgamation or merger which would not constitute an event described in (viii) below; or

(viii) *Merger Without Assumption.* The party consolidates or amalgamates with, or merges into, or transfers all or substantially all its assets to, another entity and, at the time of such consolidation, amalgamation, merger or transfer:–

(1) the resulting, surviving or transferee entity fails to assume all the obligations of such party under this Agreement by operation of law or pursuant to an agreement reasonably satisfactory to the other party to this Agreement; or

(2) the benefits of any Credit Support Document relating to this Agreement fail to extend (without the consent of the other party) to the performance by such resulting, surviving or transferee entity of its obligations under this Agreement.

(b) *Termination Events.* The occurrence at any time with respect to a party or, if applicable, any Specified Entity of such party of any event specified below constitutes an Illegality if the event is specified in (i) below, a Tax Event if the event is specified in (ii) below, a Tax Event Upon Merger if the event is specified in (iii) below or a Credit Event Upon Merger if the event is specified in (iv) below:–

(i) *Illegality.* Due to the adoption of, or any change in, any applicable law after the date on which such Swap Transaction is entered into, or due to the promulgation of, or any change in, the interpretation by any court, tribunal or regulatory authority with competent jurisdiction of any applicable law after such date, it becomes unlawful (other than as a result of a breach by the party of Section 4(b)) for such party (which will be the Affected Party):–

(1)   to perform any absolute or contingent obligation to make a payment or to receive a payment in respect of such Swap Transaction or to comply with any other material provision of this Agreement relating to such Swap Transaction; or

(2)   to perform, or for any applicable Specified Entity to perform, any contingent or other obligation which the party (or such Specified Entity) has under any Credit Support Document relating to such Swap Transaction;

(ii)   *Tax Event.*

(1)   The party (which will be the Affected Party) will be required on the next succeeding Scheduled Payment Date to pay to the other party an additional amount in respect of an Indemnifiable Tax under Section 2(d)(i)(4) (except in respect of interest under Section 2 (e)) as a result of a Change in Tax Law; or

(2)   there is a substantial likelihood that the party (which will be the Affected Party) will be required on the next succeeding Scheduled Payment Date to pay to the other party an additional amount in respect of an Indemnifiable Tax under Section 2(d)(i)(4) (except in respect of interest under Section 2(e)) and such substantial likelihood results from an action taken by a taxing authority, or brought in a court of competent jurisdiction, on or after the date on which such Swap Transaction was entered into (regardless of whether such action was taken or brought with respect to a party to this Agreement);

(iii)   *Tax Event Upon Merger.* The party (the "Burdened Party") on the next succeeding Scheduled Payment Date will either (1) be required to pay an additional amount in respect of an Indemnifiable Tax under Section 2(d)(i)(4) (except in respect of interest under Section 2(e)) or (2) receive a payment from which an amount has been deducted or withheld for or on account of any Indemnifiable Tax in respect of which the other party is not required to pay an additional amount, in either case as a result of a party consolidating or amalgamating with, or merging into, or transferring all or substantially all its assets to, another entity (which will be the Affected Party) where such action does not constitute an event described in Section 5(a)(viii); or

(iv)   *Credit Event Upon Merger.* If "Credit Event Upon Merger" is specified in Part 1 of the Schedule as applying to the party, such party ("X") consolidates or amalgamates with, or merges into, or transfers all or substantially all its assets to, another entity and such action does not constitute an event described in Section 5(a)(viii) but the creditworthiness of the resulting, surviving or transferee entity (which will be the Affected Party) is materially weaker than that of X immediately prior to such action.

(c)   *Event of Default and Illegality.* If an event or circumstance which would otherwise constitute or give rise to an Event of Default also constitutes an Illegality, it will be treated as an Illegality and will not constitute an Event of Default.

6.   Early Termination

(a)   *Right to Terminate Following Event of Default.* If at any time an Event of Default with respect to a party (the "Defaulting Party") has occurred and is then continuing, the other party may, by not more than 20 days notice to the Defaulting Party specifying the relevant Event of Default, designate a day not earlier than the day such notice is effective as an Early Termination Date in respect of all outstanding Swap Transactions. However, an Early Termination Date will be deemed to have occurred in respect of all Swap Transactions immediately upon the occurrence of any Event of Default specified in Section 5(a)(vii)(1), (2), (3), (5), (6), (7) or (8) and as of the time immediately preceding the institution of the relevant proceeding or the presentation of the relevant petition upon the occurrence of any Event of Default specified in Section 5(a)(vii)(4).

(b)   *Right to Terminate Following Termination Event.*

(i)   *Notice.* Upon the occurrence of a Termination Event, an Affected Party will, promptly upon becoming aware of the same, notify the other party thereof, specifying the nature of such Termination Event and the Affected Transactions relating thereto. The Affected Party will also give such other information to the other party with regard to such Termination Event as the other party may reasonably require.

(ii)   *Transfer to Avoid Termination Event.* If either an Illegality under Section 5(b)(i)(1) or a Tax Event occurs and there is only one Affected Party, or if a Tax Event Upon Merger occurs and the Burdened Party is the Affected Party, the Affected Party will as a condition to its right to designate an Early Termination Date under Section 6(b)(iv) use all reasonable efforts (which will not require such party to incur a loss, excluding immaterial, incidental expenses) to transfer within 20 days after it gives notice under Section 6(b)(i) all its rights and obligations under this Agreement in respect of the Affected Transactions to another of its offices, branches or Affiliates so that such Termination Event ceases to exist.

If the Affected Party is not able to make such a transfer it will give notice to the other party to that effect within such 20 day period, whereupon the other party may effect such a transfer within 30 days after the notice is given under Section 6(b)(i).

Any such transfer by a party under this Section 6(b)(ii) will be subject to and conditional upon the prior written consent of the other party, which consent will not be withheld if such other party's policies in effect at such time would permit it to enter into swap transactions with the transferee on the terms proposed.

(iii) *Two Affected Parties.* If an Illegality under Section 5(b)(i)(1) or a Tax Event occurs and there are two Affected Parties, each party will use all reasonable efforts to reach agreement within 30 days after notice thereof is given under Section 6(b)(i) on action that would cause such Termination Event to cease to exist.

(iv) *Right to Terminate.* If:–

(1) a transfer under Section 6(b)(ii) or an agreement under Section 6(b)(iii), as the case may be, has not been effected with respect to all Affected Transactions within 30 days after an Affected Party gives notice under Section 6(b)(i); or

(2) an Illegality under Section 5(b)(i)(2) or a Credit Event Upon Merger occurs, or a Tax Event Upon Merger occurs and the Burdened Party is not the Affected Party,

either party in the case of an Illegality, the Burdened Party in the case of a Tax Event Upon Merger, any Affected Party in the case of a Tax Event, or the party which is not the Affected Party in the case of a Credit Event Upon Merger, may, by not more than 20 days notice to the other party and provided that the relevant Termination Event is then continuing, designate a day not earlier than the day such notice is effective as an Early Termination Date in respect of all Affected Transactions.

(c) *Effect of Designation.*

(i) If notice designating an Early Termination Date is given under Section 6(a) or (b), the Early Termination Date will occur on the date so designated, whether or not the relevant Event of Default or Termination Event is continuing on the relevant Early Termination Date.

(ii) Upon the effectiveness of notice designating an Early Termination Date (or the deemed occurrence of an Early Termination Date), the obligations of the parties to make any further payments under Section 2(a)(i) in respect of the Terminated Transactions will terminate, but without prejudice to the other provisions of this Agreement.

(d) *Calculations.*

(i) *Statement.* Following the occurrence of an Early Termination Date, each party will make the calculations (including calculation of applicable interest rates) on its part contemplated by Section 6(e) and will provide to the other party a statement (1) showing, in reasonable detail, such calculations (including all relevant quotations) and (2) giving details of the relevant account to which any payment due to it under Section 6(e) is to be made. In the absence of written confirmation of a quotation obtained in determining a Market Quotation from the source providing such quotation, the records of the party obtaining such quotation will be conclusive evidence of the existence and accuracy of such quotation.

(ii) *Due Date.* The amount calculated as being payable under Section 6(e) will be due on the day that notice of the amount payable is effective (in the case of an Early Termination Date which is designated or deemed to occur as a result of an Event of Default) and not later than the day which is two Business Days after the day on which notice of the amount payable is effective (in the case of an Early Termination Date which is designated as a result of a Termination Event). Such amount will be paid together with (to the extent permitted under applicable law) interest thereon in the Termination Currency from (and including) the relevant Early Termination Date to (but excluding) the relevant due date, calculated as follows:–

(1) if notice is given designating an Early Termination Date or if an Early Termination Date is deemed to occur, in either case as a result of an Event of Default, at the Default Rate; or

(2) if notice is given designating an Early Termination Date as a result of a Termination Event, at the Default Rate minus 1% per annum.

Such interest will be calculated on the basis of daily compounding and the actual number of days elapsed.

(e) *Payments on Early Termination.*

(i) *Defaulting Party or One Affected Party.* If notice is given designating an Early Termination Date or if an Early Termination Date is deemed to occur and there is a Defaulting Party or only one Affected Party, the other party will determine the Settlement Amount in respect of the Terminated Transactions and:–

(1) if there is a Defaulting Party, the Defaulting Party will pay to the other party the excess, if a positive number, of (A) the sum of such Settlement Amount and the Termination Currency Equivalent of the Unpaid Amounts owing to the other party over (B) the Termination Currency Equivalent of the Unpaid Amounts owing to the Defaulting Party; and

(2) if there is an Affected Party, the payment to be made will be equal to (A) the sum of such Settlement Amount and the Termination Currency Equivalent of the Unpaid Amounts owing to the party determining the Settlement Amount ("X") less (B) the Termination Currency Equivalent of the Unpaid Amounts owing to the party not determining the Settlement Amount ("Y").

(ii) *Two Affected Parties.* If notice is given of an Early Termination Date and there are two Affected Parties, each party will determine a Settlement Amount in respect of the Terminated Transactions and the payment to be made will be equal to (1) the sum of (A) one-half of the difference between the Settlement Amount of the party with the higher Settlement Amount ("X") and the Settlement Amount of the party with the lower Settlement Amount ("Y") and (B) the Termination Currency Equivalent of the Unpaid Amounts owing to X less (2) the Termination Currency Equivalent of the Unpaid Amounts owing to Y.

(iii) *Party Owing.* If the amount calculated under Section 6(e)(i)(2) or (ii) is a positive number, Y will pay such amount to X; if such amount is a negative number, X will pay the absolute value of such amount to Y.

(iv) *Adjustment for Bankruptcy.* In circumstances where an Early Termination Date is deemed to occur, the amount determined under Section 6(e)(i) will be subject to such adjustments as are appropriate and permitted by law to reflect any payments made by one party to the other under this Agreement (and retained by such other party) during the period from the relevant Early Termination Date to the date for payment determined under Section 6(d)(ii).

(v) *Pre-Estimate of Loss.* The parties agree that the amounts recoverable under this Section 6(e) are a reasonable pre-estimate of loss and not a penalty. Such amounts are payable for the loss of bargain and the loss of protection against future risks and except as otherwise provided in this Agreement neither party will be entitled to recover any additional damages as a consequence of such losses.

7. Transfer

Subject to Section 6(b) and to any exception provided in the Schedule, neither this Agreement nor any interest or obligation in or under this Agreement may be transferred by either party without the prior written consent of the other party (other than pursuant to a consolidation or amalgamation with, or merger into, or transfer of all or substantially all its assets to, another entity) and any purported transfer without such consent will be void.

8. Contractual Currency

(a) *Payment in the Contractual Currency.* Each payment under this Agreement will be made in the relevant currency specified in this Agreement for that payment (the "Contractual Currency"). To the extent permitted by applicable law, any obligation to make payments under this Agreement in the Contractual Currency will not be discharged or satisfied by any tender in any currency other than the Contractual Currency, except to the extent such tender results in the actual receipt by the party to which payment is owed, acting in a reasonable manner and in good faith in converting the currency so tendered into the Contractual Currency, of the full amount in the Contractual Currency of all amounts due in respect of this Agreement. If for any reason the amount in the Contractual Currency so received falls short of the amount in the Contractual Currency due in respect of this Agreement, the party required to make the payment will, to the extent permitted by applicable law, immediately pay such additional amount in the Contractual Currency as may be necessary to compensate for the shortfall. If for any reason the amount in the Contractual Currency so received exceeds the amount in the Contractual Currency due in respect of this Agreement, the party receiving the payment will refund promptly the amount of such excess.

(b)   *Judgments.* To the extent permitted by applicable law, if any judgment or order expressed in a currency other than the Contractual Currency is rendered (i) for the payment of any amount owing in respect of this Agreement, (ii) for the payment of any amount relating to any early termination in respect of this Agreement or (iii) in respect of a judgment or order of another court for the payment of any amount described in (i) or (ii) above, the party seeking recovery, after recovery in full of the aggregate amount to which such party is entitled pursuant to the judgment or order, will be entitled to receive immediately from the other party the amount of any shortfall of the Contractual Currency received by such party as a consequence of sums paid in such other currency and will refund promptly to the other party any excess of the Contractual Currency received by such party as a consequence of sums paid in such other currency if such shortfall or such excess arises or results from any variation between the rate of exchange at which the Contractual Currency is converted into the currency of the judgment or order for the purposes of such judgment or order and the rate of exchange at which such party is able, acting in a reasonable manner and in good faith in converting the currency received into the Contractual Currency, to purchase the Contractual Currency with the amount of the currency of the judgment or order actually received by such party. The term ''rate of exchange'' includes, without limitation, any premiums and costs of exchange payable in connection with the purchase of or conversion into the Contractual Currency.

(c)   *Separate Indemnities.* To the extent permitted by applicable law, these indemnities constitute separate and independent obligations from the other obligations in this Agreement, will be enforceable as separate and independent causes of action, will apply notwithstanding any indulgence granted by the party to which any payment is owed and will not be affected by judgment being obtained or claim or proof being made for any other sums due in respect of this Agreement.

(d)   *Evidence of Loss.* For the purpose of this Section 8, it will be sufficient for a party to demonstrate that it would have suffered a loss had an actual exchange or purchase been made.

9.   Miscellaneous

(a)   *Entire Agreement.* This Agreement constitutes the entire agreement and understanding of the parties with respect to its subject matter and supersedes all oral communication and prior writings with respect thereto.

(b)   *Amendments.* No amendment, modification or waiver in respect of this Agreement will be effective unless in writing and executed by each of the parties or confirmed by an exchange of telexes.

(c)   *Survival of Obligations.* Except as provided in Section 6(c)(ii), the obligations of the parties under this Agreement will survive the termination of any Swap Transaction.

(d)   *Remedies Cumulative.* Except as provided in this Agreement, the rights, powers, remedies and privileges provided in this Agreement are cumulative and not exclusive of any rights, powers, remedies and privileges provided by law.

(e)   *Counterparts and Confirmations.*
     (i)   This Agreement may be executed in counterparts, each of which will be deemed an original.
     (ii)   A Confirmation may be executed in counterparts or be created by an exchange of telexes, which in either case will be sufficient for all purposes to evidence a binding supplement to this Agreement. Any such counterpart or telex will specify that it constitutes a Confirmation.

(f)   *No Waiver of Rights.* A failure or delay in exercising any right, power or privilege in respect of this Agreement will not be presumed to operate as a waiver, and a single or partial exercise of any right, power or privilege will not be presumed to preclude any subsequent or further exercise of that right, power or privilege or the exercise of any other right, power or privilege.

(g)   *Headings.* The headings used in this Agreement are for convenience of reference only and are not to affect the construction of or to be taken into consideration in interpreting this Agreement.

10. Multibranch Parties

If a party is specified as a Multibranch Party in Part 4 of the Schedule, such Multibranch Party may make and receive payments under any Swap Transaction through any of its branches or offices listed in the Schedule (each an "Office"). The Office through which it so makes and receives payments for the purpose of any Swap Transaction will be specified in the relevant Confirmation and any change of Office for such purpose requires the prior written consent of the other party. Each Multibranch Party represents to the other party that, notwithstanding the place of payment, the obligations of each Office are for all purposes under this Agreement the obligations of such Multibranch Party. This representation will be deemed to be repeated by such Multibranch Party on each date on which a Swap Transaction is entered into.

11. Expenses

A Defaulting Party will, on demand, indemnify and hold harmless the other party for and against all reasonable out-of-pocket expenses, including legal fees and Stamp Tax, incurred by such other party by reason of the enforcement and protection of its rights under this Agreement or by reason of the early termination of any Swap Transaction, including, but not limited to, costs of collection.

12. Notices

(a)   *Effectiveness.* Any notice or communication in respect of this Agreement will be sufficiently given to a party if in writing and delivered in person, sent by certified or registered mail (airmail, if overseas) or the equivalent (with return receipt requested) or by overnight courier or given by telex (with answerback received) at the address or telex number specified in Part 4 of the Schedule. A notice or communication will be effective:–

(i)   if delivered by hand or sent by overnight courier, on the day it is delivered (or if that day is not a day on which commercial banks are open for business in the city specified in the address for notice provided by the recipient (a "Local Banking Day"), or if delivered after the close of business on a Local Banking Day, on the first following day that is a Local Banking Day);

(ii)   if sent by telex, on the day the recipient's answerback is received (or if that day is not a Local Banking Day, or if after the close of business on a Local Banking Day, on the first following day that is a Local Banking Day); or

(iii)   if sent by certified or registered mail (airmail, if overseas) or the equivalent (return receipt requested), three Local Banking Days after despatch if the recipient's address for notice is in the same country as the place of despatch and otherwise seven Local Banking Days after despatch.

(b)   *Change of Addresses.* Either party may by notice to the other change the address or telex number at which notices or communications are to be given to it.

13. Governing Law and Jurisdiction

(a)   *Governing Law.* This Agreement will be governed by and construed in accordance with the law specified in Part 4 of the Schedule.

(b)   *Jurisdiction.* With respect to any suit, action or proceedings relating to this Agreement ("Proceedings"), each party irrevocably:–

(i)   submits to the jurisdiction of the English courts, if this Agreement is expressed to be governed by English law, or to the non-exclusive jurisdiction of the courts of the State of New York and the United States District Court located in the Borough of Manhattan in New York City, if this Agreement is expressed to be governed by the laws of the State of New York; and

(ii)   waives any objection which it may have at any time to the laying of venue of any Proceedings brought in any such court, waives any claim that such Proceedings have been brought in an inconvenient forum and further waives the right to object, with respect to such Proceedings, that such court does not have jurisdiction over such party.

Nothing in this Agreement precludes either party from bringing Proceedings in any other jurisdiction (outside, if this Agreement is expressed to be governed by English law, the Contracting States, as defined in Section 1(3) of the Civil Jurisdiction and Judgments Act 1982 or any modification, extension or re-enactment thereof for the time being in force) nor will the bringing of Proceedings in any one or more jurisdictions preclude the bringing of Proceedings in any other jurisdiction.

(c)   *Service of Process.* Each party irrevocably appoints the Process Agent (if any) specified opposite its name in Part 4 of the Schedule to receive, for it and on its behalf, service of process in any Proceedings. If for any reason any party's Process Agent is unable to act as such, such party will promptly notify the other party and within 30 days appoint a substitute process agent acceptable to the other party. The parties irrevocably consent to service of process given in the manner provided for notices in Section 12. Nothing in this Agreement will affect the right of either party to serve process in any other manner permitted by law.

(d)   *Waiver of Immunities.* Each party irrevocably waives, to the fullest extent permitted by applicable law, with respect to itself and its revenues and assets (irrespective of their use or intended use), all immunity on the grounds of sovereignty or other similiar grounds from (i) suit, (ii) jurisdiction of any court, (iii) relief by way of injunction, order for specific performance or for recovery of property, (iv) attachment of its assets (whether before or after judgment) and (v) execution or enforcement of any judgment to which it or its revenues or assets might otherwise be entitled in any Proceedings in the courts of any jurisdiction and irrevocably agrees, to the extent permitted by applicable law, that it will not claim any such immunity in any Proceedings.

14.   Definitions

As used in this Agreement:–

"Affected Party" has the meaning specified in Section 5(b).

"Affected Transactions" means (a) with respect to any Termination Event consisting of an Illegality, Tax Event or Tax Event Upon Merger, all Swap Transactions affected by the occurrence of such Termination Event and (b) with respect to any other Termination Event, all Swap Transactions.

"Affiliate" means, subject to Part 4 of the Schedule, in relation to any person, any entity controlled, directly or indirectly, by the person, any entity that controls, directly or indirectly, the person or any entity under common control with the person. For this purpose, "control" of any entity or person means ownership of a majority of the voting power of the entity or person.

"Burdened Party" has the meaning specified in Section 5(b).

"Business Day" means (a) in relation to any payment due under Section 2(a)(i), a day on which commercial banks and foreign exchange markets are open for business in the place(s) specified in the relevant Confirmation and (b) in relation to any other payment, a day on which commercial banks and foreign exchange markets are open for business in the place where the relevant account is located and, if different, in the principal financial centre of the currency of such payment.

"Change in Tax Law" means the enactment, promulgation, execution or ratification of, or any change in or amendment to, any law (or in the application or official interpretation of any law) that occurs on or after the date on which the relevant Swap Transaction is entered into.

"consent" includes a consent, approval, action, authorisation, exemption, notice, filing, registration or exchange control consent.

"Credit Event Upon Merger" has the meaning specified in Section 5(b).

"Credit Support Document" means any agreement or instrument which is specified as such in this Agreement.

"Default Rate" means a rate per annum equal to the cost (without proof or evidence of any actual cost) to the relevant payee (as certified by it) of funding the relevant amount plus 1% per annum.

"Defaulting Party" has the meaning specified in Section 6(a).

"Early Termination Date" means the date specified as such in a notice given under Section 6(a) or 6(b)(iv).

"Event of Default" has the meaning specified in Section 5(a).

"Illegality" has the meaning specified in Section 5(b).

"Indemnifiable Tax" means any Tax other than a Tax that would not be imposed in respect of a payment under this Agreement but for a present or former connection between the jurisdiction of the government or taxation authority imposing such Tax and the recipient of such payment or a person related to such recipient (including, without limitation, a connection arising from such recipient or related person being or having been a citizen or resident of such jurisdiction, or being or having been organised, present or engaged in a trade or business in such jurisdiction, or having or having had a permanent establishment or fixed place of business in such jurisdiction, but excluding a connection arising solely from such recipient or related person having executed, delivered, performed its obligations or received a payment

under, or enforced, this Agreement or a Credit Support Document).

"law" includes any treaty, law, rule or regulation (as modified, in the case of tax matters, by the practice of any relevant governmental revenue authority) and *"lawful"* and *"unlawful"* will be construed accordingly.

"Loss" means, with respect to a Terminated Transaction and a party, an amount equal to the total amount (expressed as a positive amount) required, as determined as of the relevant Early Termination Date (or, if an Early Termination Date is deemed to occur, as of a time as soon thereafter as practicable) by the party in good faith, to compensate it for any losses and costs (including loss of bargain and costs of funding but excluding legal fees and other out-of-pocket expenses) that it may incur as a result of the early termination of the obligations of the parties in respect of such Terminated Transaction. If a party determines that it would gain or benefit from such early termination, such party's Loss will be an amount (expressed as a negative amount) equal to the amount of the gain or benefit as determined by such party.

"Market Quotation" means, with respect to a Terminated Transaction and a party to such Terminated Transaction making the determination, an amount (which may be negative) determined on the basis of quotations from Reference Market-makers for the amount that would be or would have been payable on the relevant Early Termination Date, either by the party to the Terminated Transaction making the determination (to be expressed as a positive amount) or to such party (to be expressed as a negative amount), in consideration of an agreement between such party and the quoting Reference Market-maker and subject to such documentation as they may in good faith agree, with the relevant Early Termination Date as the date of commencement of such agreement (or, if later, the date specified as the effective date of such Terminated Transaction in the relevant Confirmation), that would have the effect of preserving for such party the economic equivalent of the payment obligations of the parties under Section 2(a)(i) in respect of such Terminated Transaction that would, but for the occurrence of the relevant Early Termination Date, fall due after such Early Termination Date (excluding any Unpaid Amounts in respect of such Terminated Transaction but including, without limitation, any amounts that would, but for the occurrence of the relevant Early Termination Date, have been payable (assuming each applicable condition precedent had been satisfied) after such Early Termination Date by reference to any period in which such Early Termination Date occurs). The party making the determination (or its agent) will request each Reference Market-maker to provide its quotation to the extent practicable as of the same time (without regard to different time zones) on the relevant Early Termination Date (or, if an Early Termination Date is deemed to occur, as of a time as soon thereafter as practicable). The time as of which such quotations are to be obtained will, if only one party is obliged to make a determination under Section 6(e), be selected in good faith by that party and otherwise will be agreed by the parties. If more than three such quotations are provided, the Market Quotation will be the arithmetic mean of the Termination Currency Equivalent of the quotations, without regard to the quotations having the highest and lowest values. If exactly three such quotations are provided, the Market Quotation will be the quotation remaining after disregarding the quotations having the highest and lowest values. If fewer than three quotations are provided, it will be deemed that the Market Quotation in respect of such Terminated Transaction cannot be determined.

"Office" has the meaning specified in Section 10.

"Potential Event of Default" means any event which, with the giving of notice or the lapse of time or both, would constitute an Event of Default.

"Reference Market-makers" means four leading dealers in the relevant swap market selected by the party determining a Market Quotation in good faith (a) from among dealers of the highest credit standing which satisfy all the criteria that such party applies generally at the time in deciding whether to offer or to make an extension of credit and (b) to the extent practicable, from among such dealers having an office in the same city.

"Relevant Jurisdiction" means, with respect to a party, the jurisdictions (a) in which the party is incorporated, organised, managed and controlled or considered to have its seat, (b) where a branch or office through which the party is acting for purposes of this Agreement is located, (c) in which the party executes this Agreement and (d) in relation to any payment, from or through which such payment is made.

"Scheduled Payment Date" means a date on which a payment is due under Section 2(a)(i) with respect to a Swap Transaction.

"Settlement Amount" means, with respect to a party and any Early Termination Date, the sum of:–

(a)   the Termination Currency Equivalent of the Market Quotations (whether positive or negative) for each Terminated Transaction for which a Market Quotation is determined; and

(b)   for each Terminated Transaction for which a Market Quotation is not, or cannot be, determined, the Termination Currency Equivalent of such party's Loss (whether positive or negative);

provided that if the parties agree that an amount may be payable under Section 6(e) to a Defaulting Party by the other party, no account shall be taken of a Settlement Amount expressed as a negative number.

"Specified Entity" has the meaning specified in Part 1 of the Schedule.

"Specified Indebtedness" means, subject to Part 1 of the Schedule, any obligation (whether present or future, contingent or otherwise, as principal or surety or otherwise) in respect of borrowed money.

"Specified Swap" means, subject to Part 1 of the Schedule, any rate swap or currency exchange transaction now existing or hereafter entered into between one party to this Agreement (or any applicable Specified Entity) and the other party to this Agreement (or any applicable Specified Entity).

"Stamp Tax" means any stamp, registration, documentation or similar tax.

"Tax" means any present or future tax, levy, impost, duty, charge, assessment or fee of any nature (including interest, penalties and additions thereto) that is imposed by any government or other taxing authority in respect of any payment under this Agreement other than a stamp, registration, documentation or similar tax.

"Tax Event" has the meaning specified in Section 5(b).

"Tax Event Upon Merger" has the meaning specified in Section 5(b).

"Terminated Transactions" means (a) with respect to any Early Termination Date occurring as a result of a Termination Event, all Affected Transactions and (b) with respect to any Early Termination Date occurring as a result of an Event of Default, all Swap Transactions, which in either case are in effect as of the time immediately preceding the effectiveness of the notice designating such Early Termination Date (or, in the case of an Event of Default specified in Section 5(a)(vii), in effect as of the time immediately preceding such Early Termination Date).

"Termination Currency" has the meaning specified in Part 1 of the Schedule.

"Termination Currency Equivalent" means, in respect of any amount denominated in the Termination Currency, such Termination Currency amount and, in respect of any amount denominated in a currency other than the Termination Currency (the "Other Currency"), the amount in the Termination Currency determined by the party making the relevant determination as being required to purchase such amount of such Other Currency as at the relevant Early Termination Date with the Termination Currency at the rate equal to the spot exchange rate of the foreign exchange agent (selected as provided below) for the purchase of such Other Currency with the Termination Currency at or about 11.00 a.m. (in the city in which such foreign exchange agent is located) on such date as would be customary for the determination of such a rate for the purchase of such Other Currency for value the relevant Early Termination Date. The foreign exchange agent will, if only one party is obliged to make a determination under Section 6(e), be selected in good faith by that party and otherwise will be agreed by the parties.

"Termination Event" means an Illegality, a Tax Event, a Tax Event Upon Merger or a Credit Event Upon Merger.

"Unpaid Amounts" owing to any party means, with respect to any Early Termination Date, the aggregate of the amounts that became due and payable (or that would have become due and payable but for Section 2(a)(iii) or the designation or occurrence of such Early Termination Date) to such party under Section 2(a)(i) in respect of all Terminated Transactions by reference to all periods ended on or prior to such Early Termination Date and which remain unpaid as at such Early Termination Date, together with (to the extent permitted under applicable law and in lieu of any interest calculated under Section 2(e)) interest thereon, in the currency of such amounts, from (and including) the date such amounts became due and payable or would have become due and payable to (but excluding) such Early Termination Date, calculated as follows:–

(a)   in the case of notice of an Early Termination Date given as a result of an Event of Default:–

(i) interest on such amounts due and payable by a Defaulting Party will be calculated at the Default Rate; and

(ii) interest on such amounts due and payable by the other party will be calculated at a rate per annum equal to the cost to such other party (as certified by it) if it were to fund such amounts (without proof or evidence of any actual cost); and

(b) in the case of notice of an Early Termination Date given as a result of a Termination Event, interest on such amounts due and payable by either party will be calculated at a rate per annum equal to the arithmetic mean of the cost (without proof or evidence of any actual cost) to each party (as certified by such party and regardless of whether due and payable by such party) if it were to fund or of funding such amounts.

Such amounts of interest will be calculated on the basis of daily compounding and the actual number of days elapsed.

IN WITNESS WHEREOF the parties have executed this document as of the date specified on the first page of this document.

....
(Name of party)   (Name of party)

By: ....   By: ....

Name: Name:

Title: Title:

SCHEDULE
to the
Interest Rate and Currency Exchange Agreement

dated as of ....

between .... and ....
                 ("Party A")   ("Party B")

Part 1
Termination Provisions

In this Agreement:–

(1)   *"Specified Entity"* means in relation to Party A for the purpose of:–

      Section 5(a)(iii) and (iv) and Section 5(b)(i), ...

      Section 5(a)(v), ...

      Section 5(a)(vi), ...

      Section 5(a)(vii), ...

                       in relation to Party B for the purpose of:–

      Section 5(a)(iii) and (iv) and Section 5(b)(i), ...

      Section 5(a)(v), ...

      Section 5(a)(vi), ...

      Section 5(a)(vii), ...

(2)   *"Specified Swap"* will have the meaning specified in Section 14 unless another meaning is specified here...

....

....

(3)   The *"Cross Default"* provisions of Section 5(a)(vi) will/will not* apply to Party **A**
                                                will/will not* apply to Party **B**

If such provisions apply:–

"Specified Indebtedness" will have the meaning specified in Section 14 unless another meaning is specified here ....

....

"Threshold Amount" means ....

....

(4)   *"Termination Currency"* means .... , if such currency is specified and freely available, and otherwise United States Dollars.

(5)   The *"Credit Event Upon Merger"* provisions of Section 5(b)(iv) will/will not* apply to Party **A**
                                                will/will not* apply to Party **B**

*Delete as applicable   15   ISDA 1987

Part 2

Tax Representations

Representations of Party A

(1) *Payer Tax Representation.* For the purpose of Section 3(e), Party A will/will not* make the following representation:–

It is not required by any applicable law, as modified by the practice of any relevant governmental revenue authority, of any Relevant Jurisdiction to make any deduction or withholding for or on account of any Tax from any payment (other than interest under Section 2 (e)) to be made by it to the other party under this Agreement. In making this representation, it may rely on:–

(i) the accuracy of any representation made by the other party pursuant to Section 3(f);

(ii) the satisfaction of the agreement of the other party contained in Section 4(a)(i) and the accuracy and effectiveness of any document provided by the other party pursuant to Section 4(a)(i); and

(iii) the satisfaction of the agreement of the other party contained in Section 4(d).

(2) *Payee Tax Representations.* For the purpose of Section 3(f), Party A makes the representation(s) specified below:–

(a) The following representation will/will not* apply:–

It is fully eligible for the benefits of the "Business Profits" or "Industrial and Commercial Profits" provision, as the case may be, the "Interest" provision or the "Other Income" provision (if any) of the Specified Treaty with respect to any payment described in such provisions and received or to be received by it in connection with this Agreement and no such payment is attributable to a trade or business carried on by it through a permanent establishment in the Specified Jurisdiction.

If such representation applies, then:–

"Specified Treaty" means ....

"Specified Jurisdiction" means ....

(b) The following representation will/will not* apply:–

Each payment received or to be received by it in connection with this Agreement relates to the regular business operations of the party (and not to an investment of the party).

(c) The following representation will/will not* apply:–

Each payment received or to be received by it in connection with this Agreement will be effectively connected with its conduct of a trade or business in the Specified Jurisdiction.

If such representation applies, then *"Specified Jurisdiction"* means ....

(d) The following representation will/will not* apply:–

It is a bank recognised by the United Kingdom Inland Revenue as carrying on a bona fide banking business in the United Kingdom, is entering into this Agreement in the ordinary course of such business and will bring into account payments made and received under this Agreement in computing its income for United Kingdom tax purposes.

(e) Other representations:– ....

....

....

....

N.B. The above representations may need modification if either party is a Multibranch Party

*Delete as applicable　　　　　　　　16　　　　　　　　　　ISDA 1987

Representations of Party B

(1) *Payer Tax Representation.* For the purpose of Section 3(e), Party B will/will not* make the following representation:–

It is not required by any applicable law, as modified by the practice of any relevant governmental revenue authority, of any Relevant Jurisdiction to make any deduction or withholding for or on account of any Tax from any payment (other than interest under Section 2 (e)) to be made by it to the other party under this Agreement. In making this representation, it may rely on:–

(i)   the accuracy of any representation made by the other party pursuant to Section 3(f);

(ii) the satisfaction of the agreement of the other party contained in Section 4(a)(i) and the accuracy and effectiveness of any document provided by the other party pursuant to Section 4(a)(i); and

(iii) the satisfaction of the agreement of the other party contained in Section 4(d).

(2) *Payee Tax Representations.* For the purpose of Section 3(f), Party B makes the representation(s) specified below:–

(a)   The following representation will/will not* apply:–

It is fully eligible for the benefits of the "Business Profits" or "Industrial and Commercial Profits" provision, as the case may be, the "Interest" provision or the "Other Income" provision (if any) of the Specified Treaty with respect to any payment described in such provisions and received or to be received by it in connection with this Agreement and no such payment is attributable to a trade or business carried on by it through a permanent establishment in the Specified Jurisdiction.

If such representation applies, then:–

"Specified Treaty" means ....

"Specified Jurisdiction" means ....

(b)   The following representation will/will not* apply:–

Each payment received or to be received by it in connection with this Agreement relates to the regular business operations of the party (and not to an investment of the party).

(c)   The following representation will/will not* apply:–

Each payment received or to be received by it in connection with this Agreement will be effectively connected with its conduct of a trade or business in the Specified Jurisdiction.

If such representation applies, then *"Specified Jurisdiction"* means ....

(d)   The following representation will/will not* apply:–

It is a bank recognised by the United Kingdom Inland Revenue as carrying on a bona fide banking business in the United Kingdom, is entering into this Agreement in the ordinary course of such business and will bring into account payments made and received under this Agreement in computing its income for United Kingdom tax purposes.

(e)   Other representations:– ....

....

....

....

N.B. The above representations may need modification if either party is a Multibranch Party.

Part 3
Documents to be delivered

For the purpose of Section 4(a):–

(1) Tax forms, documents or certificates to be delivered are:–

Party required to deliver document	Form/Document/ Certificate	Date by which to be delivered
....	....	....
....	....	....
.....................,.	....	....
....	....	....
....	....	....

(2) Other documents to be delivered are:–

Party required to deliver document	Form/Document/ Certificate	Date by which to be delivered	Covered by Section 3(d) Representation
....	....	....	Yes/No*
....	....	....	Yes/No*
....	....	....	Yes/No*
....	....	....	Yes/No*
....	....	....	Yes/No*

Part 4
Miscellaneous

(1) *Governing Law*. This Agreement will be governed by and construed in accordance with English law/the laws of the State of New York without reference to choice of law doctrine*.

(2) *Process Agent*. For the purpose of Section 13(c):–

Party A appoints as its Process Agent ....

....

....

Party B appoints as its Process Agent ....

....

....

(3) *"Affiliate"* will have the meaning specified in Section 14 unless another meaning is specified here

....

....

* Delete as applicable   18   ISDA 1987

(4) *Multibranch Party.* For the purpose of Section 10:–

Party A is/is not* a Multibranch Party and, if so, may act through the following Offices:–

....

....

Party B is/is not* a Multibranch Party and, if so, may act through the following Offices:–

....

....

(5) *Addresses for Notices.* For the purpose of Section 12(a):–

Address for notices or communications to Party A:–

Address: ....

Attention: ....

Telex No: .... Answerback: ....

(For all purposes/only with respect to Swap Transactions through that Office*.)

Address for notices or communications to Party B:–

Address: ....

Attention: ....

Telex No: .... Answerback: ....

(For all purposes/only with respect to Swap Transactions through that Office*.)

(6) *Credit Support Document.* Details of any Credit Support Document:–

....

....

....

....

(7) *Netting of Payments.* If indicated here, "Net Payments – Corresponding Payment Dates" will

apply for the purpose of Section 2(c) with effect from the date of this Agreement:–_____**

Index